An Introduction to Healthcare Informatics

An Introduction to Healthcare Informatics
Building Data-Driven Tools

Peter Mccaffrey

ELSEVIER

ACADEMIC PRESS
An imprint of Elsevier

Academic Press
125 London Wall, London EC2Y 5AS, United Kingdom
525 B Street, Suite 1650, San Diego, CA 92101, United States
50 Hampshire Street, 5th Floor, Cambridge, MA 02139, United States
The Boulevard, Langford Lane, Kidlington, Oxford OX5 1GB, United Kingdom

Notices

Knowledge and best practice in this field are constantly changing. As new research and experience broaden our understanding,
changes in research methods, professional practices, or medical treatment may become necessary.

Practitioners and researchers must always rely on their own experience and knowledge in evaluating and using any
information, methods, compounds, or experiments described herein. In using such information or methods they should be
mindful of their own safety and the safety of others, including parties for whom they have a professional responsibility.

To the fullest extent of the law, neither the Publisher nor the authors, contributors, or editors, assume any liability for any injury
and/or damage to persons or property as a matter of products liability, negligence or otherwise, or from any use or operation of
any methods, products, instructions, or ideas contained in the material herein.

Library of Congress Cataloging-in-Publication Data
A catalog record for this book is available from the Library of Congress

British Library Cataloguing-in-Publication Data
A catalogue record for this book is available from the British Library

ISBN: 978-0-12-814915-7

For information on all Academic Press publications
visit our website at https://www.elsevier.com/books-and-journals

Publisher: Masucci, Stacy
Acquisitions Editor: Teixeira, Rafael E.
Editorial Project Manager: Fernandez, Billie Jean
Production Project Manager: Raviraj, Selvaraj
Cover designer: Hitchen, Miles

Typeset by SPi Global, India

To my wife, Kaytlin

To my wonderful children, Briar and Huxley

Contents

Author's biography...xiii
Foreword..xv

SECTION 1 STORING AND ACCESSING DATA..................................1

Chapter 1: The healthcare IT landscape..3
1.1   How we got here and the growth of healthcare IT......................................3
1.2   The role of informatics...5
1.3   Common architectural aspects of healthcare IT..6
1.4   Device and application levels..7
1.5   Communication level...9
1.6   Process level...9
1.7   Common organizational aspects of healthcare IT......................................11
1.8   Physician and nurse informaticists...12
1.9   Regulatory aspects of healthcare IT...13
1.10   Challenges and opportunities..13
1.11   Conclusion..14
References...15

Chapter 2: Relational databases...17
2.1   A brief history of SQL and relational databases...17
2.2   Overview of the relational model...18
2.3   Differences between the relational model and SQL.....................................20
2.4   Primary and foreign keys...21
2.5   ACID and transactions with data...24
2.6   Normalization...26
2.7   Conclusion..28
References...29

Chapter 3: SQL...31
3.1   Getting started with SQL...31
3.2   Structure of SQL databases...31
3.3   Basic SQL: SELECT, FROM, WHERE, and ORDER BY statements............33
3.4   Basic SQL: GROUP BY and general aggregate functions............................36

3.5 Intermediate SQL: Joins...38
3.6 Advanced SQL: Window functions...40
3.7 SQL concept: Indexes...41
3.8 SQL concept: Schemas...42
3.9 Advanced SQL: SubQueries...42
3.10 Conclusion..43

Chapter 4: Example project 1: Querying data with SQL......................*45*
4.1 Introduction and project background..45
4.2 Viewing tables...46
4.3 Querying tables...53
    4.3.1 Average number of visits per day per location......................54
    4.3.2 Average patient age and patient sex per location..................56
    4.3.3 Average number of patient visits per provider.....................57
    4.3.4 Counts of diagnosis codes and average age per clinic location........58
4.4 Conclusion..59

Chapter 5: Nonrelational databases...*61*
5.1 Early nonrelational models..61
5.2 The rise of modern nonrelational models..64
5.3 Key-value stores..65
5.4 Document stores..66
5.5 Column stores...68
    5.5.1 Traditional column stores..68
    5.5.2 Wide column stores..69
5.6 Graph databases..71
5.7 Conclusion..72
Reference...73

Chapter 6: M/MUMPS...*75*
6.1 A brief history and context..75
6.2 The M language...76
6.3 General concepts regarding arrays and MUMPS..............................78
6.4 Arrays and MUMPS..81
6.5 MUMPS, globals, and data infrastructure.......................................85
6.6 Conclusion..87
References...88

SECTION 2 UNDERSTANDING HEALTHCARE DATA...................*89*

Chapter 7: How to approach healthcare data questions..........................*91*
7.1 Introduction..91
7.2 Healthcare as a CAS..91
7.3 Drivers of fallacy: Chance and bias...95

7.4 Missingness..96
7.5 Selecting tractable areas for intervention......................................99
7.6 Data and trust..100
7.7 Conclusion...101

Chapter 8: Clinical and administrative workflows: Encounters, laboratory testing, clinical notes, and billing..103
8.1 Introduction..103
8.2 Encounters, patients, and episodes of care....................................103
8.3 Laboratory testing, imaging, and medication administration........106
8.4 Clinical notes and documentation..109
8.5 Billing..111
8.6 Conclusion...112

Chapter 9: HL-7, clinical documentation architecture, and FHIR.........113
9.1 Introduction..113
9.2 HL7 and HL7v2...113
9.3 RIM, HL7v3, and clinical documentation architecture...................116
9.4 FHIR..123
9.5 DICOM..125
9.6 Vendor standards...125
9.7 Cloud services..126
9.8 Conclusion...126
References..127

Chapter 10: Ontologies, terminology mappings, and code sets.............129
10.1 Introduction..129
10.2 Diagnostic ontologies: ICD and ICD-CM..129
10.3 Procedure ontologies: ICD-PCS, CPT, and HCPCS.......................132
10.4 General ontologies: SNOMED, SNOMED-CT..................................135
10.5 Other specific ontologies: LOINC and NDC...................................138
10.6 Summative ontologies: DRG..139
10.7 Conclusion...141
References..141

SECTION 3 ANALYZING DATA..143

Chapter 11: A selective introduction to Python and key concepts.........145
11.1 Python: What and why...145
11.2 A note on Python 2 and 3...146
11.3 General structure of the language...146
11.4 Type system..147
11.5 Control flow..148
11.6 Functions..149

11.7 Objects..149
11.8 Basic data structures...151
    11.8.1 Lists...152
    11.8.2 Sets..154
    11.8.3 Tuples...155
    11.8.4 Dictionaries...155
    11.8.5 List and dictionary comprehensions...156
11.9 Conclusion..157
Reference..157

Chapter 12: Packages, interactive computing, and analytical documents...............159
12.1 Introduction..159
12.2 Packages and package management...159
12.3 Key packages..163
12.4 Jupyter..169
12.5 Analytical documents and interactive computing..171
12.6 Conclusion..174

Chapter 13: Assessing data quality, attributes, and structure.............................175
13.1 Introduction..175
13.2 Importing, cleaning, and assessing data..175
13.3 Tidying data..186
13.4 Handling missing values...188
13.5 Conclusion..189

**Chapter 14: Introduction to machine learning: Regression, classification,
and important concepts...191**
14.1 The aim of machine learning..191
14.2 Regression..192
14.3 Functions as hypotheses...194
14.4 Error and cost...198
14.5 Optimization...201
14.6 Classification..205
14.7 Additional considerations: Normalization, regularization, and
    generalizability..209
14.8 Conclusion..210

**Chapter 15: Introduction to machine learning: Support vector machines,
tree-based models, clustering, and explainability.......................................211**
15.1 Introduction..211
15.2 Support vector machines...211
15.3 Decision trees..219
15.4 Clustering..221
15.5 Model explainability..223
15.6 Conclusion..225

Chapter 16: Computational phenotyping and clinical natural language processing...227
16.1 Introduction...227
16.2 Manual review and general review considerations...............................227
16.3 Computational phenotyping: General considerations...........................230
16.4 Supervised methods..233
16.5 Unsupervised methods..235
16.6 Natural language processing..236
16.7 Conclusion..242

Chapter 17: Example project 2: Assessing and modeling data.....................243
17.1 Introduction and project background...243
17.2 Data collection..243
17.3 Data assessment and preparation..245
17.4 Model creation..246
    17.4.1 Logistic regression..247
    17.4.2 Decision tree...254
    17.4.3 Support vector machine...256
17.5 Exporting and persisting models...257
17.6 Conclusion..259

Chapter 18: Introduction to deep learning and artificial intelligence.....................261
18.1 Introduction..261
18.2 What exactly is deep learning..261
18.3 Feed forward networks...262
18.4 Training and backpropagation...269
18.5 Local versus global minima..270
18.6 Convolutional networks..272
18.7 Adversarial examples and local minima...274
18.8 Recurrent networks..275
18.9 Autoencoders and generative adversarial networks............................275
18.10 Conclusion..276
Reference...276

SECTION 4 DESIGNING DATA APPLICATIONS.....................277

Chapter 19: Analysis best practices.....................279
19.1 Introduction..279
19.2 Workflow..279
19.3 Documentation..284
19.4 Data governance..287
19.5 Conclusion..289

Chapter 20: Overview of big data tools: Hadoop, Spark, and Kafka.....................291
20.1 Introduction..291
20.2 Hadoop...292

Contents

20.3 Spark..299
20.4 Kafka...304
20.5 Conclusion...305

Chapter 21: Cloud technologies...307

21.1 Introduction...307
21.2 Data storage...307
21.3 Compute..310
21.4 Machine learning and analysis services...314
21.5 Conclusion...316

Index...317

Author's biography

Peter McCaffrey, MD, is a physician informaticist who currently serves as both Co-Founder and Chief Technology Officer at VastBiome, a computational drug discovery company investigating novel cancer therapies, as well as Director of Pathology Informatics and Director of Laboratory Information Systems at The University of Texas Medical Branch. Dr. McCaffrey attended medical school at The John Hopkins University School of Medicine and completed his Residency and Chief Residency in Clinical Pathology and Laboratory Medicine at Harvard Medical School and Massachusetts General Hospital. In addition to his current roles, Dr. McCaffrey has also previously served as Co-Founder and Chief Technology Officer of Hadera Technologies, where he led the development of several production healthcare applications focusing on streaming data analysis and predictive analytics as well as Founder and CEO of Accetia where his team focused on building cloud platforms for the analysis of next-generation sequencing data. Dr. McCaffrey has worked with hospitals in Massachusetts, Texas, California, and overseas in project areas ranging from application development to analytics, application architecture, and IT project management.

Foreword

To say that healthcare is rapidly evolving is an understatement. At the time of this writing, there are several disruptive forces presently changing the nature of this field not to mention several even more impactful ones preparing to do so. Whether it be the potential for artificial intelligence to triage medical images or even render diagnoses from them, the ability to predict hospital complications days in advance, the ability to unify patient data across the continuum of care, or even the ability to know how many patients present to an emergency department on a daily basis, locating data and utilizing them to solve problems is fast becoming a core competency for the healthcare workforce. This would, of course, not be the first time that healthcare has witnessed the growth and development of new forms of professional value as it intersects with a technological domain. For example, my own field of pathology was created through the integration of microscopy into medical science and the formalization of microscopic imaging as a diagnostic tool and then further evolved through the advent of genomics and molecular testing.

At present, healthcare is finding data more easily available and its analytical uses more realistic and enticing. This is further supported by growth in parallel sectors producing ever newer and more powerful database technologies, large-scale data processing frameworks, analytics tools, and artificial intelligence applications. Amidst all of this, we see the concept of the healthcare data scientists and informaticists becoming more and more tangible as these skills move from the domain of research and recreational interest to that of primary role and central focus. This book, therefore, aims to outline the skills and concepts upon which these roles are—and will be—built and to unite both technical and healthcare subjects into one cohesive core. The following 21 chapters are at times applied and at times theoretical, but they all focus on enabling readers to understand how to collect and analyze data in the healthcare setting. Equally important, this book aims to match its general curricular elements with advice and best practice grounded in my experience building data-driven tools in hospitals. Lastly, Chapters 4 and 17 contain projects that solidify database, programming, and analysis concepts by walking through their application to healthcare problems.

If anything, it is my hope that this book serves merely as the beginning of a career-long commitment to continued learning and skill building in the pursuit of ever more useful, efficient, and insightful analysis and a deeper understanding of hospitals, healthcare systems, and patient care. These are exceptionally exciting times to be in the healthcare field as there are so many opportunities to innovate and improve through the use of healthcare's growing data footprint. By deciding to read this book, you have already taken a first step toward this exciting future. As you progress through the chapters that follow, I encourage you to think about how each concept and skill can enable you to solve problems currently facing you and your institution and to crystallize those concepts through experimentation by applying them to those projects and problems of your own.

Storing and accessing data

CHAPTER 1

The healthcare IT landscape

1.1 How we got here and the growth of healthcare IT

As a member of the modern healthcare workforce, technology seems like an inextricable part of the clinical experience. For many, interacting with the myriad components of healthcare technology can represent an onerous aspect of clinical work and the blame for such burdensome interactions is commonly placed on IT departments and hospital management as being woefully out of touch with providers on the front lines. While this certainly bears some truth, there is much more to the story of how healthcare IT has evolved. In this section, we will discuss the developmental history of modern healthcare IT with the goal of understanding of the dynamics that have shaped its current incarnation.

Without reaching back too far in the history of healthcare, it can be said that much of the deep history of medical practice (mainly that preceding the late 19th century) was without a central organizing force.[1] Professional and intellectual societies certainly offered a central space for aggregating and sharing knowledge of diagnostic and treatment practices, and yet healthcare remained largely a cottage industry of individual practitioners. Clinical luminaries such as Dr. William Osler certainly improved upon this state of personalized, artisanal medicine by leading in the development of more consistent and robust training processes in the form of the clinical residency, the routine use of laboratory testing, and the establishment of routine clinical rounds but, still, the professional implementation of healthcare was situated mainly in the small clinic and placed within the hands of the expert individual.[2]

The advent of modern health insurance, however, represented a deeply transformative force in healthcare. Although there had been insurance products focused on disability and coverage for accidents, it was not until the 1920s that hospitals began offering payment plans through which patients could cover medical expenses themselves. These hospital-based policies quickly became aggregated into the first Blue Cross organizations in the 1930s. The second World War accelerated the growth of structured medical expense coverage as the wage freeze drove employers to create and offer employer-sponsored health benefits as a means of attracting employees.[3] This was mirrored in a Federal effort to provide such coverage benefits to those without employer-sponsored or private plans, leading to the development of Medicare in the mid-1960s.[4] Further maturation of insurance instruments brought about more complex

An Introduction to Healthcare Informatics. https://doi.org/10.1016/B978-0-12-814915-7.00001-6

processes for defining and submitting claims, such as the creation of diagnosis-related groups in the 1980s, which required more data to be provided to insurers.[5]

Healthcare systems responded to thinning profit margins and increasingly complex requirements for successful reimbursement by consolidating into large, multiinstitution integrated delivery networks. These became a popular trend in the 1990s and required hospitals to share and reconcile information not just intra- but intermurally.[6] Importantly, the 90s and 2000s brought about an increasing concern on the part of payers (largely the Centers for Medicare and Medicaid Services) that physician fee-for-service practice was susceptible to exploitation through overutilization of tests and procedures. The response was a shift toward outcomes-based payment instruments, which again heightened the demand both for more detail in claims submissions and for analytical reporting of key performance and outcomes measures such as readmission rates.[7]

The relevance of these historical punctuations and their impact on the implementation of healthcare cannot be understated. With the rapid growth and development of health insurance and the accordant rise in healthcare costs, the industry itself became financially operated by the insurance industry and, as a direct consequence, the mechanics of healthcare became increasingly parceled into claimable and billable services. Healthcare facilities, in an attempt to render billable services at scale, became powerful instruments of insurance revenue provided that they could efficiently track and execute services rendered and their resulting claims.

This historical context lends strong justification to the axiom that data are the currency of healthcare because without the ability to track and organize data in order to prove that services were justified and implemented, the entire hospital organism ceases to function. It is unsurprising, then, that some electronic systems naturally arose from this demand but perhaps equally unsurprising that, for many institutions, such systems did not. Early examples of electronic health information systems began to appear in the 1960s with Massachusetts General Hospital's creation of MUMPS, a database and early programming language for storing patient record data on mainframe systems and the subject of an entire chapter of this book, and the Regenstrief Institute's development the first electronic medical record system shortly thereafter. Although such systems provided clear benefit in the ability to store, retrieve, and organize record data, these earlier attempts were often confined to government hospitals and more tech-forward medical institutions, while mainstream physician practices and hospitals were turned off by the high cost and staffing demands required to maintain and operate these systems.

The digital transformation proceeded slowly over the concluding decades of the 20th century, but it was 2009, and the passing of the American Reinvestment & Recovery Act (ARRA) that brought unprecedentedly rapid digitization to healthcare organizations. Among the many modernization efforts included in this legislation was the Health Information Technology for Economic and Clinical Health (HITECH) Act, which introduced the concept of meaningful use, a regulated definition of the implementation and systematic engagement with electronic medical information systems.[8] Importantly, meaningful use was incentivized through payments disbursed by the Centers for Medicare & Medicaid Services—the largest healthcare payer in the United States. This combined effectively with the aforementioned evolution in health insurance to catalyze the mass transformation of healthcare from paper to digital infrastructure. This transformation has been brisk as healthcare institutions have faced financial pressure to demonstrate meaningful use through pervasive and consistent interaction with electronic information systems and to preserve revenue amid increasing demand for claim auditability, contextual information, and performance monitoring. Likewise, this has created a welcome boom for the providers of electronic health information systems, many of whom had tools based upon more antiquated technology, which were presented with a sudden need to scale through federally driven market demand.

This rapid scaling has not been without its share of serious complications, foremost of which is the security of healthcare information as it flows through complex and often adolescent technical ecosystems. Healthcare institutions are caught between an immense pressure to continue to drive revenue through successfully reimbursed claims, which requires increasing the fluidity of data collection and access, and the grave threats of financial penalty and loss of accreditation that accompany any misadventure in doing so.

1.2 The role of informatics

The trajectory of healthcare information technology and the pressures that have shaped its history and current form hopefully prove useful in understanding why healthcare information systems face the challenges of interoperation for which they are so often criticized. This historical context hopefully also sheds light on why the management of these systems is traditionally focused on risk aversion and change mitigation before technical and developmental creativity and offers some measure of explanation as to why analytics can be so often frustrated by uncooperative technology. The story of the growth and development of healthcare IT is, in essence, one of unsynchronized timing where what is ideal from a technology standpoint, what is achievable from a pragmatic standpoint, and what is imminently necessary from a regulatory compliance standpoint are almost never aligned. This is, however, the setting in which the healthcare informaticist and data engineer work and for whom understanding the many forces that shape the healthcare IT landscape is so critical.

Although this book informs the reader about the many shapes and functions of healthcare data, it also serves as a statement about the expected role of informatics and the locations in which technical creativity must be deployed. Healthcare is a challenging environment but at the time of this writing, new, formerly hypothetical advances in the form of big data, rich reporting, machine learning, and artificial intelligence are nonetheless quickly becoming vehicles for real value in adjacent fields. Granted, their origins are comparatively unencumbered by the technical debt present in so many healthcare systems, but the need to make healthcare fertile ground for their growth and impact is perhaps more real now than ever before. Thus, the goal of informatics is to understand the often suboptimal anatomy of healthcare IT and the principles of effective problem solving and analytical engineering such that those suboptimal obstacles may not simply be identified or accommodated but that they may be solved. This is a rigorous and ambitious task, but it is wholly worth the requisite effort.

The following three sections will serve as a review of the key pillars of this landscape: architectural aspects, organizational aspects, regulatory forces, and challenges and opportunities. This will serve as a foundation upon which to frame rest of this book. By the end of this chapter, you should feel comfortable understanding how data generally flow throughout a prototypical healthcare IT system and you should have an understanding of the stakeholders involved in healthcare information management and the pressures that define their roles, equipping you to align the value proposition of informatics projects along both technical and organizational axes.

1.3 Common architectural aspects of healthcare IT

Healthcare IT architectures are complex and organic. As such, they often have an admixture of automated and human components, policies, and standards. Understanding this, there are still common design patterns at the core. We focus on the operational landscape, being the set of tools and processes likely to be encountered today in currently deployed systems as these components support the core business functions of most hospitals. As a first step in breaking down the complexity of the healthcare IT organism, consider it across a few key Levels:

- The device Level, which consists of workstations, tablets, phones, telemetry, barcode readers, and all other tools that provide terminal inputs and outputs between the system and the outside world.
- The application Level, which consists of the individual programs and their respective groups of features with which users interact. These consist of items like the electronic clinical documentation or provider order entry applications.
- The communication level, which consists of the standards and networking components required to transfer data between applications. These consist of things like HL7 and DICOM, which we investigate in later chapters.
- The process level, which is more abstract but which refers to enterprise-wide services utilized by elements of the application level. This consists of things such as health information exchanges and master patient Indices.

1.4 Device and application levels

The device level is largely self-explanatory and so we can begin with a focus on the application level as that with which most users in healthcare directly interact. Most healthcare IT systems consist of several core applications, each serving specific roles. Often, the segregation of these elements is not immediately apparent to the end user and there is really no individual user who interacts with all of these application components. Nonetheless, they still exist with separate and complementary concerns. Exemplary core applications and their main purposes are as follows:

- *Computerized provider order entry (CPOE)*: This allows clinical personnel to enter medication, laboratory, and procedure orders electronically, storing and transmitting these order messages.
- *Pharmacy information system*: This exists to serve the pharmacy, allowing its users to track incoming orders, dispense ordered medications, and manage pharmacy inventory among other things.
- *Electronic prescribing (e-prescribing)*: This allows clinical personnel to enter prescriptions, storing a history of prescription orders and transmitting those orders electronically to partner pharmacies.
- *Electronic medication administration*: This tracks the timing of medication order fulfillment and may be used to record metadata such as patient discomfort or alterations to normal protocol.
- *Laboratory information system (LIS)*: This exists to record laboratory test orders after dispatch from the CPOE as well as test results upon completion. In addition, this application tracks samples, and monitors reagent inventory among other things.
- *Radiology information system (RIS)*: This exists to facilitate scheduling of radiology appointments, implementation of studies, and recording of patient imaging history.
- *Picture archive and communication system (PACS)*: This exists to archive radiology images of all types.
- *Billing and coding*: This exists to track procedure and diagnostic codes, claims, bills, and accounts receivable.
- *Clinical documentation, electronic medical record (EMR)*: This exists to facilitate writing and retrieving notes, viewing laboratory results, and viewing radiology images among other things.
- *Clinical decision support (CDS)*: Perhaps the most abstract and challenging component, this exists to provide clinical staff with diagnoses, suggestions for potential tests or procedures, warnings for errors such as medication interactions, and even current clinical evidence. CDS is most commonly implemented as a collection of alerts and pop-ups within the EMR user

experience leading many to lament the "alert fatigue" resulting from too many popups and warnings. More elegant implementations are almost universally sought but are rarely achieved. As a medical informaticist having a deep understanding of healthcare's technical and organizational infrastructure coupled with a key analytical skillset, you will hopefully be positioned to develop uniquely engaging and valuable CDS tools.

Each of these components would be an island unto itself save for one critical application known as the interface engine. Interface engines exist to efficiently and securely traffic messages between applications. In order to do this, interface engines are configured with various policies that determine where they should listen for specific messages (e.g., what port), how they should parse messages, and where those messaged should go. For example, an interface engine can be instructed to listen specifically for laboratory test result messages from the LIS and to forward those to the EMR so that physicians can view resulted laboratory tests. These rules can be as simple as forwarding messages from one application to another and as complex as listening for a specific category of messages, re-structuring the message (perhaps to accommodate sender and recipient applications, which might have different versions of software and, therefore, expect different message types), and sending the restructured message to multiple recipient applications. Interface engine serves the core duty of being a message broker between applications in the Application Level. Fig. 1.1 depicts a potential schematic for interlinked applications with an interface engine performing the critical role of message broker.

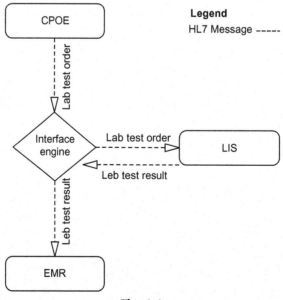

Fig. 1.1
Draft schematic showing the message flow from test order to test result with the interface engine playing the central role in message brokering.

1.5 Communication level

With this context in place, we can now consider the communication level. Each of the aforementioned applications generates and displays data and, therefore, each requires the ability to transmit data to and from other application components. The interface engine serves the role of conveying that information as a message, but it still remains a considerable design requirement to determine how such a message ought to look. Healthcare IT systems are complex assortments of specialized functional units and it is not uncommon for a single system to span different vendors, versions, and technologies across its applications. This makes it all the more critical that there be a rational and consistent definition of how data should look so that each of these applications—and the interface engine that brokers their messages—can package and unpackage pieces of information for transmission. Multiple standards exist to support this the most predominant of which is known as HL7v2 as it specifically describes the formatting of messages as sent between components of a larger healthcare record system. Chapter 9 will cover HL7v2 in detail as well as other related communications standards such as HL7v3, CDA, and FHIR, which span both the communication and process levels.

1.6 Process level

Finally, there is the process level, which refers to enterprise-level resources that serve more abstract purposes. Core examples of process-level components include:

- Master Patient Indexes (MPIs)
- Health Information Exchanges (HIEs)

MPIs exist as a registry to coordinate and associate the myriad patient identifiers, which exist within different applications. Many patient registration systems are quite fragile when it comes to permutations in patient names, addresses, and other information such that a patient whose name is John Doe, for example, could present to a hospital in which he already has a patient record but, for whatever reason, could be registered using his middle initial, John R. Doe, which would result in the creation of a new record. When this happens, a situation can easily arise wherein there are two separate patient records both of which actually refer to the same person. When one considers the added complexity of managing records and registrations across hospitals, outpatient centers, surgery centers, and other facilities, the need for a master patient identifier becomes clear. Most MPIs, therefore, are both a database, which contains a master patient identification code and all associated record identification codes, as well as an application that can scan registration data and identify records, which likely refer to the same patient.

HIEs, on the other hand, perform an analogous—albeit far broader—purpose. HIEs often work with MPIs to standardize and organize patient identification, but their focus is on aggregating comprehensive patient medical record data for the purposes of interfacility transmission and auditing with an aim to reduce repeat testing, readmissions, and medical error. HIEs often receive periodic dispatches of record data from affiliated healthcare facilities, including diagnoses, test results, imaging, prescriptions, orders, and more. HIEs also offer a more organized and central point of data transfer, which can be securely governed.

A special case of a process-level tool is a data warehouse. Where HIEs exist first and foremost to support clinical practice and may accommodate analysis, data warehouses exist for the express purposes of analytics. This distinction runs far deeper than the simple intent by which data are accessed and extends to the tools and techniques used for collecting, storing, and querying data, each of which we will discuss in depth in subsequent Chapters. Suffice it to say that many healthcare institutions have built—or are actively planning to build—an enterprise-level data warehouse along with multiple departmental and project-focused warehouses supporting a variety of data-driven applications. As a medical informaticist, you may propose solutions, which connect to an existing warehouse or you may propose a novel warehouse design altogether. Either way, this brief mention of data warehouses seeks simply to establish their place as a global organizational resource, while much of the remainder of this book will bring additional detail to warehouse design and use and their relationship to the broader concept of a "data lake."

Additional process-level tools, which are yet to mature within healthcare, are artificial intelligence, real-time analytical monitoring, or data science platforms as these are typically absent from most institutions, at least in any meaningful sense. These represent an exciting future for healthcare informatics as their eventual entry is inevitable. The concepts and tools covered in this Book serve not only to teach the practice of informatics within systems of the present but also to equip readers to lead in the development and implementation of these future tools. We previously introduced CDS as an example at the application level. While this is true of the healthcare IT landscape of the present day, it is very unlikely to remain so in the future. CDS has traditionally had a very constrained definition, which equated to simple and atomic alerts about specific items of information such as a medication interaction or a duplicate order. Going forward, CDS is poised to take a much more intuitive and nuanced role as enabling data and machine-learning technologies give it the ability to perform analysis and render advice with increasing depth. If this book contains anything that amounts to a prediction of future trends, it is that the growth and infusion of intelligence within CDS will alter the mode within which providers interact with the medical record and through which they perform patient care. Of course, this is far from the present state and one significant limiting factor is a difficulty in designing and implementing effective systems for the aggregation and analysis of data. Thus, the effective practice of data engineering and analysis in healthcare will enable CDS to realize its transformative capacity and grow from a discrete application-level entity to a ubiquitous and generalized process-level entity.

1.7 Common organizational aspects of healthcare IT

Stepping away from discrete technical components, we should discusses the organization roles within many healthcare institutions, which govern and maintain various healthcare IT systems. Understanding these stakeholders and the pressures, which shape their roles, is a critical step to identifying and articulating the value of any informatics project and, critically, any important future value can only be accessed through the execution of present projects.

Most healthcare institutions are helmed by a Board of Directors, which typically includes a President and CEO. The Board's responsibilities are usually high-level yet essential and mission-oriented and include concerns such as selection and evaluation of the CEO, approval of mergers and large investments, procurement of trust and other funding sources, and ensuring that an acceptable quality of care is delivered. More specific decisions to this effect are the responsibility of the CEO who makes more tactical decisions regarding how to accomplish these goals and manages other Chief roles in their subsidiary responsibilities.

The CEO is accompanied by several such Chiefs, each of whom owns a key organizational function. Examples include the Chief Financial Officer, Chief Medical Officer, and Chief Operations Officer and, increasingly, several IT-focused management roles, which have grown in scope and relevance over the recent years. The distinction between Chief IT roles can be subtle and generally it is only larger medical centers, which have allocated each of these responsibilities. Nonetheless, a quick review of them is useful:

- Chief Medical Informatics Officer. Most often filled by a physician with a technical background, CMIOs serve the role of understanding and communicating the "front-line" clinical needs to the IT management. CMIOs have both clinical and IT concerns such as whether current or proposed technology drives value to physicians and patients or whether and how to train clinical staff to make better use of technology.
- Chief Technology Officer. Traditionally CTOs focus on a company's own technical product. In healthcare, hospitals generally do not produce technical product as such. Instead, CTOs focus on the development and maintenance of an "IT roadmap," which frames decisions about which software products, initiatives, and technology to which to allocate time and money.
- Chief Information Officer. While similar in spirit to the CTO, CIOs focus more specifically on the governance and use of health information. CIOs make decisions such as which analytics architectures may be most appropriate or which data points from patient wearables should be collected and how. Moreover, CIOs consider scalability and security throughout these decision-making processes.
- Chief Security Officer. While all IT executives and team members consider the security implications of technological and organizational decisions, the CSO focuses squarely on this matter and manages a hospital's security team. In so doing, the CSO and her team focus on

initiatives such as inventorying all applications in the institution, monitoring applications configuration, vetting new applications, ensuring proper password usage and renewal, and establishing monitoring and protection systems for intrusive network behavior such as phishing or port scanning.

- Chief Data Officer. A more recently evolving role, the CDO is typically responsible for establishing a roadmap and architecture for how analytical data is collected, stored, and used to drive value for an organization. With an increasing trend in federation of hospitals, the role of the CDO is both more complex and more urgent. CDOs concern themselves with the establishment of data warehouses and data lakes, the governance of these repositories, and the leveraging of these data to demonstrate useful insights that impact a hospital's bottom line.

1.8 Physician and nurse informaticists

As clinical professionals in the field, physicians and nurses possess the most specific and granular understanding of the problems facing care delivery and the opportunities for improvement. The physician and nurse informaticist, therefore, are without equal in their ability to take real clinical needs, articulate their cost and the value proposition in solving them, and drive these proposed solutions up the management chain to achieve support from hospital and technical management and ultimately to benefit patients, departments, and even entire health systems.

As such many physician and nurse informaticists operate as much in the realm of technology as that of politics with a goal both to articulate the technical "how" of a solution as well as to politically rally managers and colleagues behind the "why." Many informatics initiatives focus on process exclusively. Examples of these might include anything from documenting "tips and tricks" to improve physician use of the EMR in a specific clinical setting to advocating for the introduction of a new PACS system. Many other informatics initiatives are more conventionally technical and include clinician-led development of analytical reports and dashboards while others are a hybrid to include initiatives such as advocacy for a data warehouse, which may involve direct development of analytical logic alongside gaining political support from the CDO, CIO, and CTO. This book will focus more on the second two— the purely technical and the technical/organizational hybrids—as it seeks to equip physicians, nurses, and other clinical professionals with a substantial technical breadth to conceive of and even build technical solutions to clinically relevant problems.

Regardless of which project is chosen, it will almost certainly require articulating the specific problem being solved and the value added by solving it. Moreover, it will require articulating these things to the technical management (the Chief IT roles and their departments) and doing so using the technical parlance with which they are familiar. Being able to trace a proposed technical solution from the involved applications, messages, and data sources (as described in this chapter) through the specific analytical and technical components involved in building, it will help to scope an appropriately feasible solution, estimate resource needs alongside technical and organizational impact, and explain the solution details to security and IT collaborators.

1.9 Regulatory aspects of healthcare IT

If it was not already apparent from the preceding discussion, regulation drives the state of healthcare. Regulation exists in many forms, some of which we have already introduced but we will summarize some key points here. The desire to organize the economics of healthcare has generated regulations focused on billing, which have heavily influenced the design of healthcare record systems. Moreover, the urgency of their deployment, being motivated by their benefit to patient safety, was actually made tangible by meaningful use, which resulted in a digitized healthcare landscape that was comparatively far more mature in its ability to support billing and coding than in its ability to support flexible exploration and analysis. Adding to this, the Health Insurance Portability & Accountability Act (HIPAA), which established several important regulations around protection and confidential handling of patient health information, has created a perception among many that flexible data flow and flawed security are synonymous. This is, of course, untrue but it is very likely that an informatics project will be scrutinized under a vague notion of HIPAA compliance. It is critical to mention that HIPAA compliance is real and incredibly important, but it is also quite achievable even while building technically creative and robust tools. Finally, a more recent advancement of special relevance to this book is the 21st Century Cures Act and the FDA's newly proposed framework for regulating AI in healthcare. These regulations establish a distinction between CDS tools, which are regulated medical devices and those that are not based upon whether the underlying logic of such tools are auditable by human users. In other words, the boundaries between a decision support tool and a medical device—even if that device consists solely of software—are in the transparency of the methods by which the CDS tool analyzes data and formulates conclusions. Although early, the regulatory borders starting to take root are traced at the edges of model design and transparency, which are top-level considerations for analytical projects aimed at supporting clinical workflows.

1.10 Challenges and opportunities

Finally, we address two general challenges within healthcare IT and the symmetric opportunities they present. First among these is the challenge of visibility. In many institutions, many of the discussions that would normally depend upon operational data occur in the absence of it as the collection and presentation of relevant information is too cumbersome to incorporate routinely into decision-making processes. This leaves healthcare stakeholders in a difficult position of having to prioritize quality improvement, investment, staffing, and other initiatives without a quantitative framework in which to compare potential needs. The result is that many institutions select projects based upon assumptions about their relevance or based upon what seems most feasible to accomplish. Unfortunately, while healthcare operations are full of potential projects, the Pareto principle, or "80–20 rule," would tell us that only a few of these really move the needle. Without the ability to identify the 80 from the 20 in such cases, many teams routinely deploy time and effort to resolve trivial issues while leaving significant problems unsolved. The symmetric opportunity this presents is one of systematic assessment of needs areas and selection of worthwhile projects, resulting in more effective teams and more satisfied stakeholders. This opportunity is situated well within the data engineering and analysis wheelhouse since it is impossible to describe current operations or plan future ones without effective use of data.

The second challenge is one of communication. An often-encountered practice in healthcare is the use of analytical report writers who, while very useful for reasons of efficiency and organization, often have a nonoverlapping scope of practice and knowledgebase compared to those requesting reports. This results in a workflow where abstract clinical questions, which originate from providers, are sent "over the fence" to be translated into SQL queries and charts by analysts who are nonclinical. Suboptimal results take two forms: one in which visualizations are incorrect and based on misunderstandings and one in which correct reports are produced but the number of revisions required to do so represents inordinate cost with regard to clinician and analyst time. Understanding proper analytical process and the way in which data must be transformed in order to achieve a desired result may allow for more self-service analysis or at the very least deepen this communication such that accurate reports are efficiently produced. As with improved visibility, this is a workforce multiplier across teams and projects.

1.11 Conclusion

This chapter has hopefully served to illuminate many of the common technical and political components, which comprise a healthcare organization's IT landscape and to provide a foundation of context for conceptualizing technological solutions. Going forward, the subsequent chapters will each cover important and specific technical concepts such as databases, big data tools, machine-learning techniques, and cloud design patterns in greater detail. By the end of this book, you will be able to take your keen understanding of clinical and operational problems and articulate your proposed solution with an understanding of where healthcare data originate from, how they travel, how they are stored and processed, and who is critically responsible for those aspects. Additionally, you will be able to speak confidently in terms of important and relevant technologies for aggregating and processing data at scale.

References

1. Rae A. Osler vindicated: the ghost of Flexner laid to rest. *CMAJ*. 2001;164(13):1860–1861.
2. Golden RL. William Osler at 150: an overview of a life. *JAMA*. 1999;282(23):2252–2258. https://doi.org/10.1001/jama.282.23.2252.
3. Reed LS. Private Health Insurance in the United States: An Overview; 1965. *Soc Secur Admin Bull* 1965;28:3. https://www.ssa.gov/policy/docs/ssb/v28n12/v28n12p3.pdf.
4. Rajaram R, Bilimoria KY. Medicare. *J Am Med Assoc*. 2015;314(4):420. https://doi.org/10.1001/jama.2015.8049.
5. Kahn KL, Rubenstein LV, Draper D, et al. The effects of the DRG-based prospective payment system on quality of care for hospitalized medicare patients: an introduction to the series. *J Am Med Assoc*. 1990;264(15): 1953–1955. https://doi.org/10.1001/jama.1990.03450150053030.
6. Burns LR, Pauly MV. Integrated delivery networks: a detour on the road to integrated health care? *Health Aff*. 2002;21(4):128–143. https://doi.org/10.1377/hlthaff.21.4.128.
7. Vlaanderen FP, Tanke MA, Bloem BR, et al. Design and effects of outcome-based payment models in healthcare: a systematic review. *Eur J Health Econ*. 2019;20(2):217–232. https://doi.org/10.1007/s10198-018-0989-8.
8. Jha AK. Meaningful use of electronic health records: the road ahead. *J Am Med Assoc*. 2010;304(15):1709–1710. https://doi.org/10.1001/jama.2010.1497.

CHAPTER 2

Relational databases

2.1 A brief history of SQL and relational databases

Databases have served a central role in civilization for millennia and, at its core, anything which stores information persistently is a form of database. Cave paintings, stone tablets, and papyrus are all valid examples of a database, but they each have their own critical shortcomings. The history of databases is essentially motivated by a quest to build systems, which can simultaneously meet the demands of accurately and durably storing information over long periods of while also allowing users to effectively search for information from among the stored data. The advent of computers unleashed new horizons for database technology, allowing information stored on disk to be rapidly created and accessed; however, simply having a computerized system does not automatically make data powerfully interactive. In fact, it was a parallel and powerful achievement in engineering to create a system of representing information, which would allow for much more than just targeted retrieval but also for the creation of an expressive language interrogating stored information.

Although the terms "SQL" and "relational database" are often used interchangeably, they are quite distinct entities. SQL or the "structured query language" is an implementation of the underlying relational model, which is a mathematical and logical format for how data should be represented such that they can be effectively queried. The relational model thus preceded its implementation in SQL and was the product of computer scientist and mathematician Edgar F. Codd, which he first described in 1969.[1] This model was deeply influential and the formal implementation of the relational model was led by Donald Chamberlain and Raymond Boyce at IBM who, after learning about it, set about the creation of the Structured English Query Language, at that time called SEQUEL, in the early 1970s.[2] Later in the decade, a company by the name of Relational Software Inc. (now Oracle Corporation) introduced the first commercially available implementation of SQL, which they dubbed "Oracle V2." The applications to business intelligence were clear and, by 1986, SQL had become an official and organized language implemented almost ubiquitously in data products. There are several mission critical and extremely popular modern relational database products such as PostgreSQL, MySQL, Oracle, Microsoft SQL Server, a testament to the lasting value of SQL as a way to interrogate stored information. Almost invariably, hospital data warehouses rely upon some form of relational database, typically one of the aforementioned products. SQL even persists in modern Big Data technologies such as Spark, which we discuss later in Chapter 20.

An Introduction to Healthcare Informatics. https://doi.org/10.1016/B978-0-12-814915-7.00002-8

2.2 *Overview of the relational model*

The core of the relational model is, unsurprisingly, the "relation," which is a conceptual schematic for representing information that consists of "tuples" of data and "headers" that describe the elements of those tuples. In order to unpack this, let's start with tuples: a tuple is data structure that resembles a list with the constraint that each element must be unique (and as a convention, tuples are often represented with parentheses at either end). For example, a tuple consisting of four elements describing a patient might look like this:

```
('Peter', 'McCaffrey' 30, 'Male')
```

The tuple itself is a "record" and each element in the tuple is an attribute of that record providing information about something that record described. In this example, the patient tuple is a collection of four pieces of information and because each of these pieces of information resides within the same tuple, they all apply to the same thing, in this case the same patient. The concept of a "Relation" extends this notion in some important ways. Imagine for a moment that we have the four following tuples:

```
('Peter', 'McCaffrey', 30, 'Male)
('Hydrocodone', 5, 'mg', 'BID', 'PO')
('John', 'Smith', 25, 'Male')
('Paul', 'Jones', 'MD')
```

We can understand that the information *within* each of these tuples is connected in that it describes the same thing, but how do we organize these tuples to understand how they relate to one another and how do we know exactly what sort of attributes these tuples are intended to describe? The Relation solves this problem by linking a tuple of values to a tuple of attributes known as a header. We can thus turn the aforementioned tuples into relations by providing these attributes (in bold):

```
('FirstName', 'LastName', 'Age', 'Sex')
('Peter',    'McCaffrey', 30,   'Male')

('MedicationName', 'Dose', 'Units', 'Frequency', 'Route')
('Hydrocodone',    5,      'mg',    'BID',        'PO')

('FirstName', 'LastName', 'Age', 'Sex')
('John',      'Smith',    25,    'Male')

('FirstName', 'LastName', 'IdNumber', 'State')
('Paul',      'Jones',    210214,     'MD')
```

Now two powerful things have happened. First, we can determine, for an individual tuple, what it is intended to describe; we know that 30 corresponds to Peter's age and not something else and we know that 210214 corresponds to Paul's ID Number, not his age. Second, we know that the tuples describing Peter McCaffrey and John Smith are both talking about the same attributes. The power of Relations is that we can know this sort of depth about how records describe the world and we can aggregate records that describe the same kinds of things. A Relation in the strict sense is therefore a collection of one or more tuples, which share the same collection of attributes. Quite naturally, this lends itself to a familiar understanding of a Relation as a table with the attributes describing its columns and the record tuples describing its rows.

Perhaps more importantly is that this strict organization of data under a header and the resulting assignment of unambiguous meaning to each element in a record allows for meaningful logical statements to be applied to data contained within a relation. In other words, if we lacked this strict association between data and a header, we would not be able to formulate a question such as "return all patient records where the first name is Peter" because, lacking a clear way to determine whether the element "Peter" in a given record refers to a patient's first name or something else, we would not be able to tell for which records the query statement was true or false. In relational theory, this is referred to as describing a predicate over a set of predicate variables where a "predicate" is simply a function that can be evaluated as true or false (i.e., our query) and "predicate variables" are the elements of data in the record which would determine whether a predicate evaluates to true or false. While this might seem like a simple concept in this example, this logically consistent way to constrain how data are stored and retrieved is what allows the relational model—and its implementation in SQL—to reliably construct and execute rich analytical queries over billions of rows of data.

Putting all of this together, Fig. 2.1 depicts the connection between tuples, headers, and relations. Databases often contain anywhere from tens to potentially tens of thousands (in the case of some healthcare data warehouses) of relations. Typically, a single relation describes a single type of entity such as patients or encounters and each row or tuple within that relation describes an instance of that entity such as a particular patient or a particular encounter.

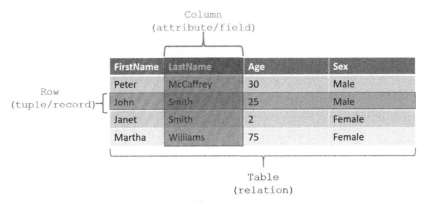

Fig. 2.1

"Patients" table as a relation with a standard tuple of attributes and multiple tuples describing specific patients as rows.

As we will discuss in the next chapter covering the mechanics of SQL, any individual table may be specified as the target of a search query and through a process known as "joining" tables, multiple tables can be elegantly combined in the process of resolving a query to retrieve data.

One last but very important point to make with regard to the relational model is that it was designed from the very beginning to support a "declarative" formulation for queries and this declarative nature is an important strength of SQL as a language. In many conventional programming languages, the author writing statements in the language is concerned not just with the inputs and outputs of her program but also with the intricate internal details of how those inputs are handled and how outputs are generated. In other words, the user of the language takes significant responsibility for the execution of her code. The relational model was designed to fulfill the goal of supporting a purely declarative query language, which stood apart from the implementation details of the queries it describes. The mathematical underpinnings of relational theory could ensure that, as long as data were represented and queried in accordance with their premises, there would be logical integrity across many different approaches to execution of that query. As you will see later when we discuss SQL, composing SQL queries really amounts to describing the query output one desires without much focus on exactly how those queries are run or optimized. Many relational database products contain complex and sometimes proprietary internal "query planner," which handle many of a query's implementation details on the user's behalf. This flexibility is one of the reasons why SQL has retained its wide popularity and grown across so many platforms and products. It's worth mentioning that the existence of a query planner does not obviate the need to write queries thoughtfully as certain questions—especially those containing complex joins—can lead to inefficient query execution. Getting around this is a task both for query writing but also for database design itself.

2.3 Differences between the relational model and SQL

Although the relational model is the underpinning of SQL, the Query Language itself—and the practices of those who create and maintain databases–often does not completely adhere to the model's restrictions. That being said, it is far more important for you as an informaticist to be familiar with SQL as a language and as an interface to retrieving data from relational databases than it is for you to be a master of the relational model. Nonetheless, understanding a few of the most important differences between the model and the language will deepen your perspective as a user.

First and foremost is the fact that, in relational theory, every value in every tuple must be such that a predicate function can determine whether it is true or false. This means no NULL values as NULL values are logically ambiguous. In reality, NULL values are rampant in databases but, strictly speaking, they violate the logical integrity of relations. This is more than an esoteric aside as there is a long-standing discussion in the field of database theory as to what to do with NULL values stemming from the fact that NULL values are often coerced to false—that is, they are assumed to be equivalent to FALSE—even though they do not have such a logical meaning. In fact, Codd himself proposed an alternative, 3-value logic system that accounts for intermediacy between true and false although this is not widely implemented.[3]

Second, there is the fact that relations are formally defined as collections of unique tuples. That is, tables that truly capture relations shouldn't have any duplicate rows and yet this is very common in practice. The motivation in relational theory was that a predicate function should evaluate uniquely for each set of variables and, thus, having duplicate rows means that there are identical collections of predicate variables for which the predicate function (again, the query) redundantly evaluates the same. Having two identical rows each describing Peter McCaffrey in the patient's table is ambiguous because, without additional information, it is unclear *why* there are two identical rows. Could this mean two visits? We have no idea unless the relation contains some other attribute like a VisitID. Strictly identical tuples are like NULLs in the sense that they mask some real information. Relational database products don't impose this restriction though, and this is a very good example of the subtle differences between the academic and mathematical concepts of relational theory and the practical decisions made when designing a product for people to use.

There are also several additional departures, which exist to make SQL more convenient to write. As such, it is most accurate to describe modern SQL databases as "pseudo-relational," although most just call them "relational." Another important semantic detail is that, while SQL is a query language almost ubiquitously used for accessing and manipulating data within a relational database, many products like Microsoft SQL Server or MySQL are referred to as "Relational Database Management Systems" (RDBMS) because they themselves are a collection of features and user interfaces for the purpose of interacting with data stored (mostly) according to the relational model.

2.4 Primary and foreign keys

Having covered the relational model and the representation of data as tuples of information according to various attributes, it's appropriate to discuss another fundamental concept in relational databases: keys. Keys accomplish two critically important tasks. They ensure that rows are unique within tables and they provide associations between rows in different tables, allowing logic to be applied across more than one type of thing. In the next chapter we will discuss the SQL language itself and, in that discussion, we will cover JOINs as a way to query using data from multiple tables. This section serves as a good foundation for that discussion as JOINing would not be possible without the associations provided by keys. Before going further, however, let's introduce an additional Encounters relation in our database:

```
('EncounterID', 'Clinic', 'Date')
(1,             'Uptown', 10/6/2018)
```

```
(2,           'Uptown',  10/6/2018)
(2,           'Downtown', 12/10/2018)
(1,           'Downtown', 3/10/2019)
```

This relation contains four records and three attributes: the ID of the encounter itself, the clinic site where the encounter occurred, and the date of the encounter. Importantly, the Encounter ID is unique for each record, providing a way to individually identify encounters even if all of the other information is identical between rows. In this example, we have two encounters on 10/6/2018 at the Uptown clinic, but we can ensure these are unique rows by giving them each a unique Encounter ID. We could to the same with our Patients relation as well, granting each Patient a unique ID:

```
('PatientID', 'FirstName', 'LastName',  'Age', 'Sex')
(1,           'Peter',     'McCaffrey', 30,    'Male')
(2,           'John',      'Smith',     25,    'Male')
```

In both cases, we have provided each relation with a "primary key," which is an attribute or a collection of attributes sufficient to uniquely identify each row. It may be the case that some tables have preexisting attributes adequate for this purpose, as with our Patients relation where we could have used just the FirstName, LastName, or Age in order to uniquely identify each row. This is risky, though, because we don't know what future data our table may end up containing and, however unlikely, it is certainly possible that we could have another 30-year-old male patient named Peter McCaffrey. Therefore, it is common practice to create an attribute designated for this purpose that uniquely identifies each row, just like a row number as we have done here. For most relational database systems, users declare an attribute to be the primary key when they initially create a relation and this declaration enforces that all values in that attribute are unique and defined for each row (that is they are not NULL anywhere). Moreover, most relational database systems optimize searching based upon the primary key, which, if you have a table with millions or even billions of rows, can become quite important.

Now let's imagine that we wish to link encounters to the Patients who had those encounters. Thanks to the Primary Keys Encounter ID and Patient ID we have the foundations to do this because we can talk about specific encounters and specific patients. The missing link, however, comes when we need to add information to the records of one relation that associates it to the record of another. One easy way to do this is to add a PatientID attribute to the Encounters relation:

```
('EncounterID', 'Clinic',   'Date',        'PatientID')
(1,             'Uptown',   10/6/2018,  1)
(2,             'Uptown',   10/6/2018,  2)
(2,             'Downtown', 12/10/2018, 1)
(1,             'Downtown', 3/10/2019,  2)
```

Now we have the ability to determine which specific Patient was present for a particular encounter. In this capacity, the PatientID attribute serves as a "Foreign Key" within the Encounters relation. It does not have to be unique for each row in that relation—that's the job of the primary key—but it must correspond to a primary key in another table for which its values are unique. Thus, foreign keys serve the complementary purpose of referencing a primary key for another, associated relation. Almost invariably, relational databases contain multiple relations that describe things for which we would want to use their data together to describe a query. In our database, we have a Patients relation and an Encounters relation and we would often want to access tuples in one relation based upon information in another relation. Therefore, since encounters belong to patients and we want to maintain organization and association between encounters in the Encounters relation and the patients to whom those Encounters refer, then we need a Foreign Key to link these relations. Having this foreign key in place lets us unambiguously resolve a single patient to whom a single encounter refers using their linked Patient IDs—this is critical for relational databases to function properly.

This concept is technically termed "referential integrity" and is one of the core requirements of a functional relational database. Strictly speaking, referential integrity means that each foreign key in a relation must refer to a real primary key in another relation; otherwise, references made by that foreign key would be invalid. If there was a PatientID referenced in the Encounters relation to which encounters were assigned but there was no corresponding Patient in the Patients relation who had that ID, then we would have broken referential integrity.

As mentioned previously, Foreign Keys need not be unique and most often they are not. The Encounters relation, for example, would likely have many encounters for each patient as patients typically have multiple appointments and so there would be several tuples for which the PatientID attribute was identical. This is totally permissible for foreign keys but inadmissible for Primary Keys as each time a PatientID appears in the Encounters relation, it denotes one of potentially countless encounters for a given patient but each time a PatientID appears in the Patients relation, it must denote one unique and individual person. Likewise, the Encounter ID of the Encounters relation can correspond to a Foreign Key in other relations such as an Orders relation, which would often list several orders for a single encounter. Relational databases typically have many relations with complex linkages to one another. Fortunately, these databases will typically have documentation often including a schematic representation of all tables and their linkages to one another via keys, known as an "entity relationship diagram." If available, it is wise to request and gain access to such a representation to aid in your ability to navigate and explore these databases. Fig. 2.2 depicts an entity relationship diagram for our example database.

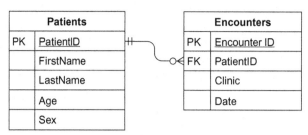

Fig. 2.2

Entity relationship diagram showing Patients and Encounters relations and their keys. Primary Keys are labeled "PK" and underlined. Foreign Keys are labeled "FK."

2.5 ACID and transactions with data

Now that we've covered the relational model and keys, which maintain the associations between relations, we need to cover another essential concept: state. As mentioned at the beginning of the chapter, databases are only valuable insofar as they preserve data with integrity. The "state" of database—that is, the particular information constituting the tuples of the relations in a database—must be preserved and consistent over time or else the database becomes a corrupted record. Relational databases aren't just records from which users read data but also records to which users write data and many mainstream relational databases universally support multiple users performing read and write operations simultaneously. This greatly enhances the value of these databases but also greatly increases the risk that the data they contain becomes inconsistent or incorrect.

Fortunately, this has been thought about extensively in the development of relational database technology and has culminated in the development of a collection of properties that form the acronym ACID and which comprise the core constraints that must exist around interactions with data in order to ensure that these interactions don't compromise the integrity of the database. Typically, these interactions are called "transactions," which begin with data in a given initial state, include one or more operations performed upon that data, and conclude with data in another state. We will cover each property briefly and then walk through some explanatory scenarios that should illustrate value of these properties. The ACID properties are as follows:

"Atomicity" means that the collections of mutations performed on the database in adding or updating information is an all-or-nothing process and that the state of the database will either remain as it was before the user performed any alterations or will be wholly converted to the state after the user performed all of their alterations. In either case, a transaction will not conclude with the state anywhere in between these two poles. To see why this is critically important, imagine a billing database that tracks claims and reimbursements. To completely record a reimbursement requires two important steps: a claim has to be declared to be reimbursed and removed from accounts receivable and money has to be added to the institution's bank account. If only one of these operations occurred, the database would be erroneous either regarding a bill as paid but not reflecting the payment in the hospital's account or in double dipping by recording the payment in the account but still marking the claim as unpaid and needing to be resubmitted to insurance. Therefore, in order for a claim to be fulfilled, it must be a single atomic mutation to both update the status of the claim and the amount of money in the account.

The remaining three ACID components are simpler to explain and can be covered more briefly. "Consistency" means that mutations made to a database must only occur in allowable ways. That is, these mutations must adhere to the constraints placed upon attributes and relations such as data types and uniqueness of primary keys must be enforced. For example, we should not be able to write a number in the FirstName attribute of the Patient's relation. "Isolation" means that the state of one transaction does not depend upon the state of another simultaneous transaction. If two users are both trying to update the value of an account and process a claim, they will each be operating within their own independent transaction. Recall that the intermediate steps of a transaction can create invalid states in the database, such as having a claim declared resolved before the payment is reflected in the account balance. Atomicity ensures that either both steps or no steps of this transaction will occur but Isolation ensures that simultaneous transactions do not see or work off of the intermediately inconsistent representations of data contained within each other's transactions. Lastly, "Durability" simply means that once a given state has been recorded for the database, data are preserved in that state unless operated upon by another transaction. After all, a database that could randomly lose or revert parts of its state would be hopelessly invalid. Many relational database products allow for multiple strategies through which to set up backups, fail overs, and redundancy in order to help improve durability.

Given all of these requirements, one might ask how database technology actually keeps transactions in order especially when working with multiple users. In reality, systems often record a log of all transactions, known as a "write-ahead log." The purpose of this log is to record each transaction and each SQL statement contained within each transaction before initiating any of those transactions against the actual database. While this delay is imperceptibly brief in practice, this serves as a sort of buffer to ensure that the state of the database at any point in time is not only valid at that moment but can also be reverted back to any previous point or recreated from its origin since every mutating operation performed on the database has been recorded in order in the log sequence.

2.6 Normalization

Before concluding, there is one last and critical aspect of relational databases that merits discussion. Heretofore, we have discussed relations, keys, and transactions through which data can be created and modified. One question a scrupulous reader may ask is why databases contain multiple tables at all and why everything isn't just one big table. In practice, you will likely find that operational systems have complex relationships between several relations each of which contains a few attributes, while data warehouses and analytical databases more often contain one or a few very large relations with many attributes. This is not by chance. Instead, there is a very specific design principle known as "normalization" that accounts for this schematic difference.

When Edgar Codd conceived of the relational model, he also put forth the concept of normalization in order to reduce the redundancy of specific records and improve the overall integrity of relational databases. Under this model, normalization proceeds in three successive forms from the first normal form through to the third normal form. In the first form, the domain of each attribute can contain only atomic values and that the values for that attribute are singular for each record. In other words, attributes cannot correspond to lists of other values. The second normal form extends this definition to include the requirements that every nonprime attribute of the relation—that is, any attribute which isn't the primary key and thus does not have to contain unique values—is dependent upon the primary key. In other words, the attribute must be determined by the primary key and, therefore, describe what the primary key identifies. If we have a patients table that contains attributes, which aren't dependent upon the PatientID and therefore, don't describe a particular patient, then normalization would remove them from the table. This is a large reason why many relational databases contain separate relations with only the attributes necessary to describe properties of that relation. Our patients relation should not contain attributes regarding the appointment date as any given patient can have many such dates. Instead, appointment date should be an attribute of an encounter relation. Lastly, third normal form stipulates that all attributes of a relation should be dependent upon the primary key and not upon each other. For example, in our patients table, we may include the date of birth or the age but to include both is to include columns, which are "transitively dependent" in that the value of one can be determined from the value of the other even without knowledge of the primary key.

These normal forms are difficult to grasp by description so we will walk through an example. First, let's add to our patients relation a phone number attribute and consider that a patient may easily have two or more phone numbers (note that the square brackets indicate a list of values):

```
('PatientID', 'First Name', 'Last Name', 'Age', 'Sex', 'PhoneNumber')
(1,           'Peter',      'McCaffrey', 30,    'Male', [1234567890, 4562223333])
```

Because Peter has two phone numbers, the "value" for the PhoneNumber attribute in that tuple is a list containing two items. In order to be in first normal form, we need to ensure that each attribute contains single values. To accomplish this, we may create an additional relation that associates phone numbers to PatientIDs like so:

```
('PhoneNumberID', 'PatientID', 'PhoneNumber')
(1,              1,            1234567890)
(2,              1,            4562223333)
```

Notice how, for this relation, the PatientID is a foreign key that refers to the associated primary key in the patients relation. Moreover, these two tuples contain the same PatientID since they belong to the same patient. Also note that we have a primary key for this relation, which we call PhoneNumberID and this does have to be unique for all tuples in this relation. As we see here, it is quite common that normalization results in data being broken out into multiple smaller relations. This is an important difference between normalized and denormalized databases where the former, often used for production applications, contains many tables with more complex relationships and the latter, often used for analytical data warehouses, contains fewer tables.

Second normal form requires that the primary key for each relation be contained within a single attribute. This is important because it ensures that all attributes in a relation serve to describe a single instance of the things the relation describes. Fortunately, we fulfill this requirement because we explicitly included PatientID, PhoneNumberID, and EncounterID attributes. Sometimes, however, this is not the case. Imagine that our patients relation looked like this:

```
('PatientID', 'FirstName', 'LastName', 'Age', 'ClinicID', 'VisitLocation')
(1,           'Peter',     'McCaffrey', 30,   1,          'Downtown')
(1,           'Peter',     'McCaffrey', 30,   2,          'Uptown')
(2,           'John',      'Smith',     25,   1,          'Downtown')
```

Here, the VisitLocation is dependent upon the ClinicID and uniquely identifying a tuple here actually requires a "composite key" created by combining both the PatientID and the ClinicID attributes. Following second normal form, we could break this apart into two relations for which the attributes depend only upon the single-attribute primary key of their respective relation.

```
('PatientID', 'FirstName', 'LastName', 'Age')
(1,           'Peter',     'McCaffrey', 30)
```

```
('ClinicID', 'Location')
(1,          'Downtown')
```

Also, since a patient may visit many clinics and have many ClinicIDs associated with him, we associate the clinic and patient tuples through the encounter relation:

```
'EncounterID', 'PatientID', 'ClinicID', 'Date')
(1,            1,           1,          10/6/2018)
```

Lastly, as the third normal form requires that all attributes be "nontransitively dependent" so we would avoid relations that might have records like this:

```
('EncounterID','PatientID','Date',      'Discharge','LengthOfStay')
(1,            1,          10/6/2018, 10/8/2018,  2)
```

To one resembling our conventional encounters table since LengthOfStay is entailed by the dates of the encounter.

One might reasonably ask what the value is in normalizing databases at all since it is seems to make things more scattered. The answer ultimately boils down yet again to preserving database integrity, especially in highly trafficked operational systems. When data are denormalized, it may be easier to browse and query for some purposes, but the tradeoff is that individual pieces of data are replicated across tuples. Consider the relation we discussed in second normal form:

```
('PatientID', 'FirstName', 'LastName', 'Age', 'ClinicID', 'VisitLocation')
(1,           'Peter',     'McCaffrey', 30,    1,          'Downtown')
(1,           'Peter',     'McCaffrey', 30,    2,          'Uptown')
(2,           'John',      'Smith',     25,    1,          'Downtown')
(2,           'John',      'Smith',     25,    1,          'Downtown')
```

We have first names, last names, ages, locations, and IDs all repeated in multiple locations. In an analytical warehouse where we intend almost exclusively to read this information, this is acceptable but in an operational application, this introduces risk. Imagine we needed to update a value such as the last name for patient ID 1, changing from "McCaffrey" to "Wilson." Managing that transaction to update the same value in several locations amid high-volume read and write operations traffic bears the risk of failure wherein the last name is updated in some places but not others and this violates database integrity. Thus, normalization, while it complicates database schema by expanding the number of relations, protects database integrity by limiting redundancy and database mutation.

2.7 Conclusion

We've discussed the relational model behind many popular databases that support SQL as well as key concepts around keys, transactions, and normalization. In the next Chapter, we will discuss SQL as a language and how to construct and interpret SQL queries. Although many try to learn SQL without insight into the relational model that underlies it, being equipped with a conceptual grasp of relations, tuples, attributes, and keys will significantly enhance your ability not just to understand but to master SQL as a language and to use if effectively. Furthermore, as we proceed throughout subsequent chapters, these concepts will add important context and bearing for understanding "nonrelational" systems.

References

1. Baxendale P, Codd EF. Information Retrieval A Relational Model of Data for Large Shared Data Banks. *Commun ACM*. 1970;13.
2. Chamberlin DD, Boyce RF. Sequel: A Structured English Query Language B. Proceedings of the ACM SIGFIDET Workshop on Data Description, Access, and Control. https://doi.org/10.1145/800296.811515.
3. Codd EF. The Relational Model for Database Management: Version 2. Addison Wesley; 1990.

CHAPTER 3

SQL

3.1 Getting started with SQL

In the previous chapter, we discussed relational theory as the motivation and defining theoretical framework behind SQL. Now, we will consider the SQL language itself and the database products that implement it. In doing this, we will walk through several example queries and discuss their respective outputs as a method of understanding the mechanics of the language. This chapter assumes you are new to SQL and so we really focus on unpacking a series of these examples. In the next chapter, we will progress to an end-to-end project, which you can read and even follow along running commands yourself. Once you have a working understanding of SQL, it is beneficial to set up your own database environment and connect to it using one of many user-friendly graphical database exploration tools. A popular example of such tools is known as DBViz and it will allow you to construct and run SQL code as well as visually explore tables in a relational database. We leave this as a more advanced exercise for you to pursue.

3.2 Structure of SQL databases

Before going into the syntax and format of SQL queries, it is beneficial to quickly review the general architecture of a relational database as applications. In the last chapter, we discussed the important difference between the relational model as a logical system and SQL as a language designed to query and manipulate data stored according to a relational model. We also discussed the fact that SQL is a declarative language whose statements describe the rules by which the database should fetch and return data but that the details regarding how to optimize and implement SQL queries themselves are largely governed by the "query planner," which is an internal component within database applications. In fact database applications contain many additional functionalities beyond just storing tabular information, including the creation of users and rules governing which tables user can access and what actions they can perform, the creation of indexes to make tables easier to search (which we will discuss later in this chapter), and the creation of schemas which determine how tables are organizes (which we will also discuss later in this chapter). For these reasons, relational database applications are commonly called "Relational Database Management Systems" (RDBMS) as they support several data manipulation and management functions. Fig. 3.1 depicts the general architecture of such an RDBMS system.

An Introduction to Healthcare Informatics. https://doi.org/10.1016/B978-0-12-814915-7.00003-X

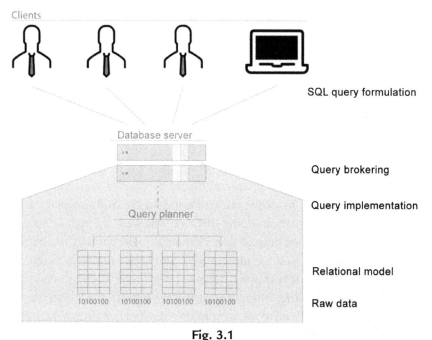

Clients

SQL query formulation

Database server

Query brokering

Query implementation

Query planner

Relational model

10100100 10100100 10100100 10100100   Raw data

Fig. 3.1

RDBMS architecture consisting of a database server that receives SQL queries from client users and applications and implements those queries on its constituent tables. These tables themselves are abstractions on underlying raw data.

An additional point to discuss is the distinction in vocabulary between the relational model and SQL as a language which, although similar, are not quite the same. In a general sense, we can assume equivalences between relations and tables, attributes and columns, and tuples and rows and it is common practice to do so. However, recall from the previous chapter that, strictly speaking, this separation in vocabulary is appropriate because, although a row and a tuple are very similar, a row has no strict limitation that all values must be unique. This is a subtle but important example of the difference between the relational model as a theoretical construct and an RDBMS as an actual product that relaxes the clean and strict rules of the relational model to provide flexibility and convenience to users. Going forward, we will keep the discussion appropriately focused on SQL and, therefore, we will be talking in terms of tables, columns, and rows. We will also frequently describe "standard" SQL as those commands, keywords, and operators, which are part of the core definition of the SQL language as maintained by the American National Standards Institute, known as "ANSI SQL." Specific database products often extend ANSI SQL to over additional powerful but vendor-specific functionality, giving rise to several different "dialects" of SQL specific to different RDBMS systems.

3.3 Basic SQL: SELECT, FROM, WHERE, and ORDER BY statements

As a simple starting point, we will begin with the SELECT statement, used to retrieve data from a target table. We will start with an example statement first and then dissect the statement and its output. Consider the following SQL query:

```
SELECT TOP 2 * FROM Patients WHERE FirstName = 'Peter',
```

which returns the output:

PatientID	FirstName	LastName	Age	Sex
1	Peter	McCaffrey	30	Male
2	Peter	Parker	22	Male

What can we assume about this query just by reading as though it was a plain English commands? The statement we just ran roughly means "Select all of the columns of the top two rows in the table called Patients for which the value of the FirstName column is Peter." The relation is the Patients table, the predicate variable is the FirstName attribute, and the predicate is the test for whether the FirstName attribute of a row in the Patients relation is equal to "Peter" and the predicate is true for the two rows returned to us. Thus, the SQL query declares certain conditions for which only rows which are TRUE under those conditions are returned.

This is the most basic and essential example of an SQL query and it uses the three most common key words in SQL, so it's a worthwhile exercise to step through the statement above a bit more carefully. This is what's generally referred to as a "SELECT statement" and such statements are expected to contain—at a minimum—the SELECT key word followed by a range of columns (or "attributes" in the relational parlance) being selected, followed by the FROM keyword followed by the table (or relation) where those columns are to be found. In this command, we used an asterisk, which is a common SQL notation indicating that we want all columns of the target table. Thus, a minimal SELECT statement could read "SELECT * FROM Patients," which would return all the information in the Patients table. However, selecting all the information from a table without any conditions is rarely useful and, thus, the most minimal SQL statement you will likely see in practice also contains an additional WHERE keyword followed by one or more conditions specified with regard to some set of columns, such as WHERE FirstName = "Peter." Suffice it to say, all filters need not be strict equivalences. Instead, values can be filtered using a range of comparison operators as listed in Table 3.1.

Standard SQL also contains several logical operators, which can be invoked with special keywords and which can be used in conjunction with the earlier comparison operators to create rich filtering conditions. For example, both the AND and OR operators are used to combine

Table 3.1 Example valid SQL comparison operators.

Operator description	Operator symbol
Not equal to	!=
Greater than	>
Less than	<
Greater than or equal to	>=
Less than or equal to	<=

multiple comparison clauses either additively or optionally. For example, if we wanted to be very specific with regard to which Peter we wanted to retrieve from the database, we could add an additional condition on the age column and require that both be true using the AND key word like so:

```
SELECT * FROM Patients WHERE FirstName = 'Peter' AND Age = 30
```

Let's take a moment to understand the relational mechanics going on here. When a SELECT statement such as this is issued, it targets a relation, here being the Patients relation, then it establishes a range of attributes along which to "project" meaning that it only considers these elements of the relation's tuples when applying filtering logic. In the case of SELECT * as we have earlier, such projection is unnecessary because we want all attributes of the Patients relation. However, we commonly want only some attributes such as only the FirstName and LastName columns. After projecting along a Relation's attributes, the filtering logic is applied to "restrict" the collection of projected tuples according to their predicate evaluation (e.g., only those for which the FirstName is "Peter"). Finally we "select" the tuples that evaluate as TRUE and return them in a new Relation containing the query results. Fig. 3.2 depicts this process graphically, color coding each step.

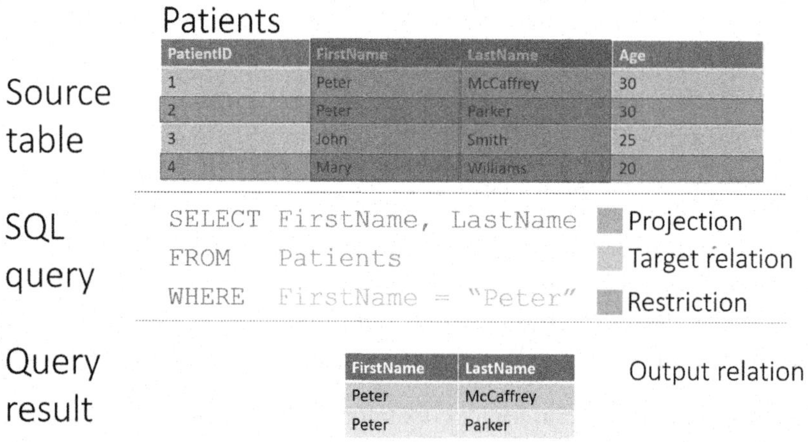

Fig. 3.2

Subcomponents of a conventional SELECT operation, including PROJECT and RESTRICT relational operations.

More specialized operators you are likely to encounter in practice include DISTINCT and COUNT, which are useful for exploring information in database tables. As the name implies, the DISTINCT key word is used to restrict a select statement to only unique values since, as we have seen, database columns can often contain many redundant values. If we were interested in knowing all of the unique first names in the FirstName column, we would employ the DISTINCT key word like so:

```
SELECT DISTINCT FirstName FROM Patients
```

which would return Peter and John because, though there are multiple rows in the table and multiple Peters and Johns, there are only really two unique first names in the FirstName column.

COUNT serves a different but often complementary purpose as it can be optionally applied to other statements to return a count of the values in a target column. If we wanted, for example, to know how many entries are in our patients table, we could use the COUNT key word like so:

```
SELECT COUNT(*) FROM Patients
```

And if we wanted to know how many unique last names were in our Patients table, we would combine COUNT and DISTINCT like so:

```
SELECT COUNT (DISTINCT LastName) FROM Patients
```

The last basic SQL key word we will introduce in this section is ORDER BY, which is used to organize the results returned from a SELECT statement. This ends up being quite a powerful convenience especially when exploring large tables. For example, if you were interested in discovering the upper and lower boundaries for the values in a column or if you were interested in ordering by a time stamp to see the most recent or the oldest entries. In our Patients table, we can sort our results in descending order of age like so:

```
SELECT * FROM Patients ORDER BY Age DESC
```

It's also possible to sort in ascending order using the ASC keyword and also to sort by multiple columns, which will nest the sorting operation by the order in which the columns were listed. Thus, if we wrote something like this:

```
SELECT * FROM Patients ORDER BY FirstName, Age DESC
```

We would have the results alphabetized by first name but, any entries that shared the same first name and were thus at the same alphabetical level would be further sorted by age.

The simple filter and select operations are universal in SQL and are the building blocks for subsequent functionality. Next, we will discuss a widely popular and essential key word in SQL: GROUP BY.

3.4 Basic SQL: GROUP BY and general aggregate functions

As we have seen, SELECT statements are powerful tools to fetch one or many rows in a table based upon conditions applied to the columns in that table. Using SELECT statements alone, we can craft many powerful queries using an assortment of evaluation operators. That being said, there is much more to the SQL language even when it comes to querying data within a single table. The GROUP BY statement is widely used and a critically important concept to understand, illustrating how SQL goes far beyond a simple retrieval language to become the rich query language its name implies.

We'll introduce the GROUP BY statement by example and then walk through its results. To begin, let's examine the structure of our Encounters table by peeking at the top two rows:

```
SELECT TOP 2 * FROM Encounters
```

And we can see that each row contains the date of a patient encounter along with the ID of each patient for whom that encounter took place:

EncounterID	Clinic	Date	PatientID
1	Uptown	10/06/2019	1
2	Uptown	12/07/2019	1

There are many rows in our Encounters table and we certainly don't want to sift through them manually but we would like to know how many encounters occur per day and so we run the following query on our Encounters table:

```
SELECT COUNT(EncounterID), MAX(Date) FROM Encounters GROUP BY Date
```

And we get this in return:

Count	Date
10	10/06/2019
8	10/07/2019
9	10/08/2019

To walk through what just happened, we need to understand the workflow of a GROUP BY operation. First, when this key word is used, there must be a column (or a group of columns) following it as those columns are used to create the groups. In this example, we used Date as the GROUP BY column, which splits the table up into groups of rows that share the same value for the Date column. These don't need to be evenly sized groups, but they must share the same Date value. Second, COUNT and MAX (termed "aggregate functions" as they are special operators intended to summarize data in a group of rows) are applied to their respective column in each group of rows. Third and last, the results of the Count and Max aggregate functions calculated for each group are put together to form the results table that gets returned as depicted in Fig. 3.3. Thus, the statement can be read as "Create a table that contains the count of EncounterIDs and the maximum Date value for each group of rows in the Encounters table that share the same Date value." This workflow is very similar to the "split-apply-combine" workflow popularized in R and Python and similar to the MapReduce workflow popularized by Hadoop, which we will discuss in subsequent chapters.

If you are a bit confused by the use of MAX(Date), this is understandable. This is a common convention used to format the table returned from the query. When we create groups of rows using the date column, it's certainly true that each group will have identical values for that column. However, it will still be the case that there are multiple identical date values in that group and so, if we wish to present a single date value for each group in our results, we have to "flatten" that list to a single value. Since all values are the same, the MAX() aggregate function will pick a single value from the each group's set of identical date values. Alternatively, the MIN() aggregate function would accomplish this same purpose when referring to the column used to partition the groups.

The SQL standard contains many powerful aggregate functions such as percentile and correlation calculations, averages, and even regression slopes. It is increasingly common in practice to separate such computations—especially more advanced ones—from data storage and instead to do them in a different environment and with different tools such as Python. Toward the end of this chapter, however, we will cover a special advanced aggregate function known as WINDOW, which is fairly common to use in SQL queries.

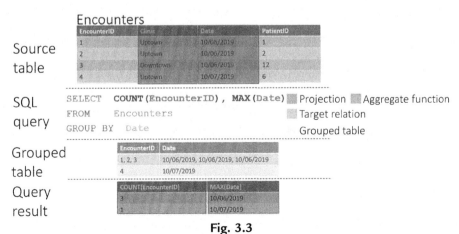

Fig. 3.3
Workflow for a SQL GROUP BY operation with aggregate functions.

3.5 Intermediate SQL: Joins

Now that we have discussed basic SELECT statements and, we can cover one more fundamental concept in SQL: Joins. Joins describe the combination of two or more tables and are used very commonly in practice to write effective queries. Joins are essential because many healthcare enterprise warehouses contain data spread across hundreds to thousands of different tables, thereby making it all but inevitable that any meaningful query will have to deal with data in several tables. Joins are the solution to that logistical challenge by allowing users to describe a query that fetches columns from separate tables while maintaining a logical integrity that keeps results from those separate tables organized.

You, as a reader, may reasonably find yourself wondering why joins are made necessary and why all databases do not consist of one large table. If so, consider the following vignette. Imagine that you are designing a medical record system and you wish to track vital signs, medications, inputs and outputs, telemetry, and several other attributes. If your database consists of one large table, then you will likely be forced into a table design wherein each row corresponds to an atomic observation and likely the most atomic observation. Thus, in this example, each cycle of the blood pressure cuff in an ICU bed would generate a new row for that patient in this table. However, being as there is only one table, all those patient's other attributes such as age, weight, room number, and insurance would also have to be duplicated on each of these new rows effectively copying the entire patient chart each time any new atomic piece of data is added to the table. Not only is this extremely inefficient from a storage perspective but, what's worse, imagine that you needed to update the patient's FirstName or LastName. Depending upon the acuity and activity involved in their chart, that patient's first and last names may exist in the table thousands of repeated times. This creates a real risk for database integrity where items of data are wantonly replicated and increases the risk of an incomplete update of a field such as this. Fig. 3.4 compares this kind of repetitive data model to a more normalized version spit across two tables, showing the reduction in redundant values this achieves.

In SQL syntax, a Join is declared by use of the JOIN key word and requires the provision of a shared column between joined tables, a purpose served by the primary and foreign keys discussed in the previous Chapter. Let's imagine that we wanted to return the first and last names of every patient who had an encounter on October 6, 2019. While ostensibly simple, this query does require data that spans both our Patients and our Encounters tables. In order to use the Date column from our Encounters table as a filter for the FirstName and Last Name values of our Patients Table, we need to JOIN these two tables on the shared key, the PatientID column, which links the two tables together like so:

```
SELECT Patients.FirstName, Patients.LastName
FROM Patients
JOIN Encounters
```

Patients

PatientID	FirstName	LastName	BloodPressure
1	John	Smith	128/78
1	John	Smith	120/60
1	John	Smith	130/82

Patients

PatientID	FirstName	LastName
1	John	Smith

BloodPressures

BloodPressureID	PatientID	BloodPressure
1	1	128/78
2	1	120/60
3	1	130/82

Fig. 3.4

Comparison of denormalized and normalized versions representing blood pressure data for patients before (top) and after (bottom) moving blood pressure recordings to their own table.

```
ON Patients.PatientID = Encounters.PatientID
WHERE Encounters.Date=10/8/2018
```

To step through the verbiage of this query, we first state which columns we want returned as well as which table we want them returned from and, at the end, the condition we want applied to filter those results. As a convention, since we are referring to more than one table, we explicitly state both the table name and the column name together with a dot separating them. This keeps it clear and organized as to which table we are referring to when we mention a column since different tables can have the same column names. In the middle of our query, we use the JOIN key word, stating the table we want to join to our Patients table (i.e., Encounters) and, using the ON key word, what columns in those joined tables we want to use to link them (i.e., PatientID). In plain English, this query would read "Select the first and last name columns from the patients table but do this only for those patients for whom their encounters in the Encounters table had a Date of 10/8/2018 and use the PatientID column in both tables to determine which Encounters apply to which Patients." This JOIN operation is depicted in Fig. 3.5. Hopefully, it is becoming clear how expressive and powerful SQL can be.

There are multiple forms of JOIN statements, which differ according to how they treat situations where the joined columns do not match cleanly. By default, when you use the JOIN key word, you are invoking an INNER JOIN, which will return only those rows where there was a matching PatientID value in the Patients and Encounters tables. Alternatively, you could specify an OUTER/FULL JOIN, which will return all rows in both tables, a LEFT JOIN, which will return all records in the first specified table (in this case Patients) along with only those records from the second table (in this case Encounters) for which the PatientID matches one in the Patients table, or a RIGHT JOIN, which is the opposite of a left join in that it will return all records in the second specified table (Encounters) while retuning only those from

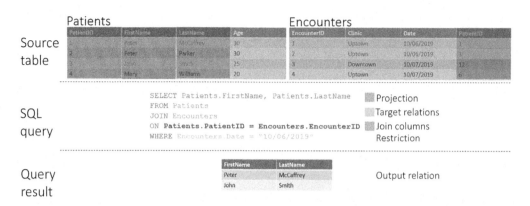

Fig. 3.5
Example SQL JOIN statement between two tables.

the first specified table (Patients) for which the PatientID matches one in the Encounters table. You are more likely to see INNER joins in practice but, for illustrative purposes, a motivation for using a LEFT JOIN, for example, would be if you wanted to return ALL patients, including those who have not yet had an encounter as those patients with no encounter would have no row in the Encounters table containing their PatientID.

3.6 Advanced SQL: Window functions

Finally, we will discuss an advanced SQL function, which you may encounter and which will prove quite useful. WINDOW functions are very similar to aggregate functions in that they apply some analytical logic to a group of rows. However, WINDOW functions do not operate within the groups established by a GROUP BY clause. Instead, WINDOW functions accept a partitioning clause, which is used to divide the table into groups of rows to which aggregate operations are applied. As an additional quirk, WINDOW functions are executed using the OVER and PARTITION BY key words. As an example, let's take a deeper look at the Encounters table:

PatientID	Date
1	10/6/2018
2	10/6/2018
3	10/8/2018
2	10/7/2018
1	11/6/2018
2	12/1/2018

Notice that PatientID 3 has one encounter, while PatientID 2 has three encounters and PatientID 1 has two encounters. Suppose we wanted to organize this table by PatientID, presenting the number of encounters and the first and last dates for each PatientID. The following WINDOW function would produce that for us:

```
SELECT PatientID, COUNT(Date), MIN(Date), MAX(Date)
OVER (PARTITION BY PatientID) CountDate
FROM Encounters
```

This would produce the following result:

PatientID	Count(Date)	MIN(Date)	MAX(Date)
1	2	10/6/2018	11/6/2018
2	3	10/6/2018	12/1/2018
3	1	10/8/2018	10/8/2018

3.7 SQL concept: Indexes

Heretofore, we've focused on the query linguistics around the SQL language partly because this is by far the most used part of a SQL knowledgebase for any informaticist but also because this is the most generalizable across specific RDBMS products. That being said, there are additional important concepts, which are very likely to come up in conversation with IT colleagues if not directly in analysis. Among these are indexes and schemas the first of which we address here.

As mentioned previously, composed SQL queries are ultimately reduced to a query plan that is often designed and optimized by internal components within a given RDBMS product. While this true, these query plans face a common bottleneck in being able to retrieve rows described in queries. For example, if we were to write a query asking for patient encounters between 7/4/2016 and 8/14/2016 at most medical centers, we're asking the database to retrieve a relative handful of rows from millions of pieces of information. A naïve algorithm may be for the database to simply iterate over every row in the Encounters table and test for whether that row's dates fall within the specified range. This is known as a "full table scan" and is prohibitively inefficient in almost every case. Instead, a more elegant approach is to make use of an index, which, as the name suggests, is an ancillary data structure that expedites the identification of relevant rows by storing precomputed mappings between rows and some relevant or "index" variable. This is very analogous to a book's index wherein the precomputed mapping is between an alphabetized list of important key words and their page number. Typically, when querying a large database, you will want to perform selection and filtration using indexed columns in order to benefit from a significant gain in efficiency and speed. Typically, indexed columns are those which are most used and useful for formulating queries relevant to business needs. If querying for encounters using a date range, for example, it is very likely that the date column will be indexed as this is a very common attributes by which to filter rows. By contrast, if performing a research query for a more esoteric purpose such as all patients who had a particular insurer, it may very well rely on an unindexed column.

3.8 SQL concept: Schemas

Schemas are an important but relatively simple concept for users of any SQL database. Schemas can be thought of as a container of database objects, which include tables but also other things such as stored procedures and triggers (these latter two which are of less relevance here). Schemas serve a very important role of partitioning what would otherwise be a massive sea of tables into separate buckets, which may, therefore, have separate access policies, table structures, and import/export schedules. This is relevant to an informaticist in two ways. The first is that, when granted access to a SQL database, you will almost always needs to identify the schema that actually contains the tables of interest and either refer to it in queries or have an administrator provide access to that particular schema if such access hasn't already been provisioned. The second is that you may be granted the ability to create tables within an individualized schema provisioned for your user, allowing you to store certain summarizations of data within the database itself. Typically, this might be seen if one were wanting to report in repeated aggregate measures such as the daily average number of samples received in a clinical lab. In this case, the raw data necessary for the averages could be queried and the averages computed daily storing only the average itself in a separate table and thereby allowing for rapid summarization of the averages themselves (such as plotting moving averages over time).

3.9 Advanced SQL: SubQueries

As a final advanced SQL concept, subqueries offer a powerful additional layer of expression. In summary, a subquery can be thought of as a query within a query. Daunting at first, this is quite straightforward and best illustrated using an example. Imagine that we wanted to know how many patients who had an encounter on a certain day also had an echocardiogram performed by the Cardiology Fellow. Writing a single join statement, while workable, leaves much up to the RDBMS' query planner and runs the risk of the query planner executing a broad search across source tables in order to map out joined columns prior to filtering by selected dates. Instead, a more efficient and often more readable approach is to think of the final query as a query among the results of more basic queries. In this example, we have on the one hand a list of medical record numbers for patients who had an encounter within our target dates and on the other hand we have a list of medical record numbers for patients who had an echocardiogram performed by the cardiology fellow. Therefore, the final results are a matter of joining between these two tables on intersecting MRNs.

The subquery allows this because it lets us define a select statement on the fly within a larger select statement like so:

```
SELECT MRN FROM
        (SELECT MRN FROM Patients
        WHERE Encounters.Date > StartDate AND Encounters.Date >
         EndDate
        JOIN Encounters
        ON MRN) AS encounters
INNER JOIN
        (SELECT MRN FROM Patients
            WHERE Procedures.Physician == "Cardiology Fellow"
        JOIN Procedures
        ON MRN) as fellowProcedures
ON encounters.MRN = fellowProcedures.MRN
```

Take a minute to let the query sink in. The parentheses allow us to describe an entire SELECT statement where we would otherwise include a reference to a table forcing the query planner to explicitly break the query up into subparts and run them in order of dependency. More specifically, as the query planner maps out the query and encounters the SELECT statements in lieu of table references, it just executes the parenthetical SELECT statements and stores the results as an intermediate variable before dropping back into the original query and finishing It as a SELECT upon the intermediate tables.

3.10 Conclusion

Throughout this chapter, we have focused mainly in the ANSI standard definition of SQL. This can be thought of as a "core" SQL definition. However, many SQL products have their own extension of this core definition referred to as "dialects" of SQL often containing unique key words and powerful functions. For Microsoft, their dialect is called "Transact SQL" or T-SQL, for Oracle it's called PL/SQL, and for PostgreSQL it's called PL/pgSQL and each contain their own special enhancements to the language. Each of these dialects still enforces the ANSI SQL standard, thus allowing you to implement the key words and queries discussed in this chapter. It's also worth noting that there is a broad spectrum of analytical practice ranging from working entirely within SQL to performing simpler SELECTs and JOINs in SQL and subsequent analyses in another environment like Python. This book certainly advocates for the latter, but this is not universal practice nor is it required in order to produce meaningful analyses. It is most important to embrace each of these concepts and find a combination of tools that minimizes the time and effort required to get answers to analytical questions.

CHAPTER 4

Example project 1: Querying data with SQL

4.1 Introduction and project background

Although it is certainly useful to read this chapter, it is even more useful to try out these queries yourself and follow along with the code examples. There are many ways one can interact with a relational database using SQL but among the simplest initial modalities is through an online SQL sandbox. We have set up a convenient environment using Katacoda, which will allow you to run SQL commands and view their output in a web browser without having to install any database systems on your local computer. In either case, this chapter will present all queries and query results necessary to collect and analyze data relevant to our problem.

Suppose that we had an executive at our hospital who is interested in profiling patients' visits at our various outpatient clinics. In actuality, this is quite a common question as understanding volume is important for determining staffing requirements, for budgeting for construction or expansion of new clinics or even for guiding contract negotiations. Consider that we have one outpatient clinic farther to the north of our other locations and consider also that this northern clinic location is actually very close to a hospital renowned or management of heart failure. Knowing this, we might decide that this northern clinic should participate in an Accountable Care Organization (ACO) run by its neighboring hospital caring for heart failure patients handling outpatient checkups for patients with frequent exacerbations. Understanding clinic load, demographics, and "case mix"—or which diagnoses a given clinic normally sees—can be of considerable strategic value.

Without getting too far ahead of ourselves, as a first step, we would discuss with our executives what information they need, being sure to address both specific information items as well as more general business and strategic questions motivating the need for those items. This latter point can be quite helpful as it often reveals information elements that would likely be useful but which were not mentioned by the requesting team. In these discussions, we can imagine that we come to the following basic requirements:

- We need to know how many visits each clinic site sees on average per day
- We need to know the distribution of patient age and sex for visits at each clinic
- We need to know how many patients each provider sees
- We need to know what diagnoses patients at various clinic sites have and the number of patients with those diagnoses

An Introduction to Healthcare Informatics. https://doi.org/10.1016/B978-0-12-814915-7.00004-1

Furthermore, we may also learn than our executives are interested in the data because they are considering expanding their physician group practice and they will come to rely on this information in understanding to which clinics providers should be assigned based upon clinic load and provider areas of clinical expertise.

With this information in hand, we can focus on the practical, step-by-step methods to address these sorts of questions as we use SQL to understand the structure of our data and run queries on it.

4.2 Viewing tables

In a real-world setting, the location and type of database—much less its underlying table structure—may not be known and so we may have to do some preliminary investigation in the form of identifying which data sources are even required to collect the information we're looking for. In this case, we know that, at the very least, we need to access patient visits and we need to be able to connect those visits to information about the visit date and time, the patient and her demographic information, the clinic location, the provider who was seen, and the clinical attributes of the patient. Fortunately for us, we can make the simplifying assumptions that this information is all contained within our enterprise data warehouse, that this warehouse is a relational database, and we have access to connect to it and run SQL queries against it. Helpful though this is, we still do not know how many tables this database has, what those tables look like, or how many of them we will need in order to collect all of our desired information. Thus, we are in the incredibly common situation of having to explore a relational database by viewing tables and their respective schemas.

In order to do this we can take advantage of the fact that Relational Database Management Systems (RDBMS) store the names and structures of their tables. Moreover, they organize these tables into larger and broader groups known as "schemas," which may include tables alongside other objects such as triggers, views, and indexes. In our following example, we have a schema called "`public`" that contains the relevant data tables for our database. Importantly, the database uses a table to keep track of which tables belong to which schemas and so we can query this table, known here as `information_schema.tables` and filter the results for only those rows there the schema is public and for only the column containing the table name like so:

```
SELECT table_name
FROM information_schema.tables
WHERE table_schema ='public';
```

Which produces the following table:

```
| table_name |

| providers |
| visits    |
| diagnoses |
| patients  |
```

If we didn't filter these results for tables belonging to the `public` schema, we would get many more tables in return, some examples of which—in the case of PostgreSQL—include `pg_policy` which records security policies for other tables controlling which users can access which table elements elsewhere in the database and `pg_collation` which contains a list of the available collations for the database. The exact function of all of these tables is not critically important but it is useful to understand the broad segregation between tables that serve such housekeeping and operational purposes for the RDBMS itself and those that are created by users for the storage of user data. In our example, the `public` schema is where external user data about patients, doctors, and visits are located and it's where we will search for tables that contain relevant information for our project. Note that we're keeping to a simplified example here in that we only have four tables. In many real-world data warehouses, we may have hundreds or even thousands of tables, necessitating the use of some sort of data catalog or data dictionary. For the time being, however, we will explore the database directly as made possible by its small size and simple structure.

Keeping in mind our target data elements we can already suspect in which tables might find them and we may conclude that the `patients` table is a great place to start. At this point, we want to understand what this table looks like, how many rows it has, and what sort of columns there are. Starting with the former use case we can utilize SQL's `Count()` function as we mentioned previously and just provide an asterisk, informing SQL to provide the count of all rows in the database:

```
SELECT Count(*)
FROM patients;
```

Which returns the following:

```
| count |

| 801   |
```

So we know there are 801 rows in this table. Note that the use of the asterisk here is a convenience akin to saying "just give me the count of all rows across all columns." We could alternatively provide a specific column name and get the count of rows in that columns. Unsurprisingly, this will also return 801; thus, using the asterisk here is beneficial both because we don't have to specify a column name but also because at this point we don't even know what the column names are within this table. To determine that, we can use the SELECT statement with FETCH FIRST, to get a look at all columns but only for a few rows:

```
SELECT *
FROM patients
FETCH FIRST 3 ROWS ONLY;
```

id	patient_id	age	sex	mrn
1	280	49	UNKNOWN	856346I
2	294	50	UNKNOWN	322136W
3	148	51	F	1592620

This is a handy way to efficiently peek at tables and get a feel for how they're put together. We can appreciate that we have five columns and we get age, sex, and medical record numbers for patients. We can also see that sex likely has three values here: F and UNKNOWN, which we can see and likely also M. We can test this theory simply by looking at the distinct values in the sex column and verify that only values of these three options are present:

```
SELECT DISTINCT(sex) FROM patients;
```

sex
UNKNOWN
F
M

We can also assume that id and patient_id may serve as keys here. For our purposes the ability to use them as such boils down to two questions: are the values unique and are they indexed? Uniqueness is important here because we want to find a column that will definitely uniquely identify each patient and something that can pair with a foreign key if we see a_ patient_id in another table. We can easily verify the uniqueness of each of these values like so:

```
SELECT
    Count(*)
FROM patients
GROUP BY patient_id
ORDER BY count DESC
FETCH FIRST 3 ROWS ONLY;
```

```
| count |

| 1     |
| 1     |
| 1     |
```

This shows us that each `patient_id` only appears once in the table as even if we're not looking at all rows, ordering the count in descending order would put the highest count value at the top. Thus, if the top count is a 1, then we know that the count of all the other counts are 1 as well. We can do this same query substituting `id` for `patient_id` also verifying that these are all unique. So it seems that both have the capability to serve as primary keys for the table. With regard to indexing, we may care about this since filtering tables by indexed columns is considerably faster than the alternative. In our case, this table only has 801 rows, so performance won't be an issue. Nonetheless, we can utilize those housekeeping tables we mentioned earlier to understand if there are any indexes on these columns. In the case of PostgreSQL, we can find this information in the `pg_indexes` table:

```
SELECT
FROM pg_indexes
WHERE tablename = 'patients';
```

tablename	indexdef
patients	CREATE UNIQUE INDEX patients_pkey ON patients using btree(id)

This output is a bit more complicated but it tells us what command the database used to create indexes for this table and we can see that there is a single binary tree (btree) index build using the `id` column and that the `patient_id` column is actually not indexed. At this point, we want to see if we find any of these id or patient_id columns in other tables as this will help us understand how we might join tables. We can investigate the `visits` table next:

```
SELECT * FROM visits FETCH FIRST 3 ROWS ONLY;
```

visit_id	patient_id	visit_date	provider_id	location
57734	280	2019-10-01	8551	Country Regional
22435	294	2019-10-02	5392	Country Regional
99589	148	2019-10-03	5392	Country Regional

Here already we realize something interesting: there is no `id` column in the `visits` table but instead there is a `patient_id` column and it consists of three-digit numbers just like we saw in the `patients` table. In this table, the `patient_id` column would be functioning as a foreign key and since a single patient could have multiple visits, we would not expect it to be unique here:

```
SELECT
    Count(*)
FROM visits
GROUP BY patient_id
ORDER BY count DESC
FETCH FIRST 3 ROWS ONLY;
```

count
4
4
4

And indeed this seems to be correct as we have some `patient_id` values appearing as much as four times in this table. This also highlights the fact that often database systems and warehouses don't totally conform to expected standard practices. For example, in our patients table, the `id` column is set as the primary key when, in actuality, it's the `patient_id` column that we'll use as such. We also noticed a `provider_id` column in our visits table and we can guess that this probably corresponds to a unique `provider_id` column in our `providers` table:

```
SELECT *
FROM providers
FETCH FIRST 3 ROWS ONLY;
```

provider_id	provider_name
8617	Pena, Robert
4724	Cutrona, Carl
5392	Merrill, Natalie

This looks to be true going both by the column names and the fact that provider_id consists of four-digit numbers in both the visits and providers tables. We can also verify the uniqueness of this column:

```
SELECT
    Count(*)
FROM providers
GROUP BY provider_id
ORDER BY count DESC
FETCH FIRST 1 ROWS ONLY;
```

count
1

Lastly, we can investigate the diagnoses table:

```
SELECT *
FROM diagnoses
FETCH FIRST 3 ROWS ONLY;
```

id	patient_id	icd_10_code
1	0	E119
2	1	J069
3	2	Z79899

Where once again we have a question regarding the uniqueness of these columns. We may suspect that a single patient could have one or many diagnoses. If that is true, what might we expect to see when we count distinct values for the id, patient_id, and icd_10_code columns?

```
SELECT
    Count(*)
FROM diagnoses
GROUP BY id
ORDER BY count DESC
FETCH FIRST 1 ROWS ONLY;
```

```
_____

| count |
_____

| 1     |
_____
```

```
SELECT
    Count(*)
FROM diagnoses
GROUP BY patient_id
ORDER BY count DESC
FETCH FIRST 1 ROWS ONLY;
```

```
_____

| count |
_____

| 4     |
_____
```

```
SELECT
    Count(*)
FROM diagnoses
GROUP BY icd_10_code
ORDER BY count DESC
FETCH FIRST 1 ROWS ONLY;
```

```
_____

| count |
_____

| 86    |
_____
```

We can see from these results that the id column is unique while patient_id and icd_10_code are repeated multiple times. This implies that there patients can occur in this table many times as can diagnoses, which is expected since a patient can have many diagnoses and a diagnosis can be true for several different people.

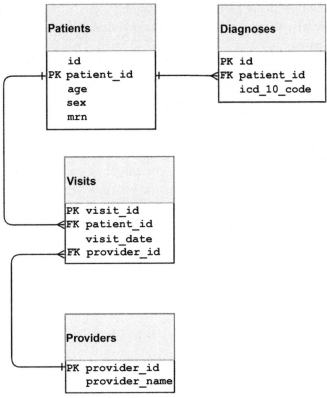

Fig. 4.1

Example entity relationship diagram derived from exploring our tables. Note that "PK" denotes Primary Key, "FK" denotes Foreign Key, a single cross arrowhead denotes one and a branched arrowhead denotes many.

Finally, after this sort of exploration, we can piece together an entity relationship diagram in our heads that looks like what we see in Fig. 4.1.

This sort of database exploration is very common practice especially in complex enterprise warehouses where there may not be single source for documenting table structure or where that structure may have evolved over time as additional data were imported into the warehouse. Fortunately for us, this exploration proved useful, allowing us to derive a theoretical structure for the underlying tables and their relationships. Now that we know where our data lives, we can move on to answering some of our analytical questions.

4.3 Querying tables

To review, we have four specific analytical questions we're seeking to answer:

- We need to know how many visits each clinic site sees on average per day
- We need to know the distribution of patient age and sex for visits at each clinic

- We need to know how many patients each provider sees
- We need to know what diagnoses patients at various clinic sites have the number of patients with those diagnoses

Starting with the first item, we know from our previous exploration that the `visit_date`, `visit_id`, and `location` are all contained within the `visits` table and this should be enough to answer this question. We know we'll want to make use of an aggregate function where we can group up our visits by the day. More specifically, we can probably already tell we'll want to count the number of those daily visits for each clinic location and then we would also like to get the average of those counts. We'll actually be grouping by two different things actually, one being the location and then, within those groups, the visit date which is already specified to the day. SQL's flexibility means that we don't have to have this query perfectly sculpted from the get-go but we can work it out in a few tries.

4.3.1 Average number of visits per day per location

For starters, we can try grouping our table by both the `location` and `visit_date`, getting the number of rows that fall within each group:

```
SELECT
    Count(*)
FROM visits
GROUP BY location, visit_date;
```

```
_____

| count |
_____

| 2     |
| 1     |
| 2     |
| ...   |
_____
```

This is going in the right direction but it's incomplete. We can tell that some clinic had two visits on a day while another had one and so forth, but we don't know what day or what clinic location to which these counts correspond. Fortunately, we can use other aggregate functions to do this and we can leverage the fact that if we're grouping by an attribute like `location`, then all of the rows in that group would—by definition—have the same value for that attribute. Thus, picking the maximum location value for that group—or the maximum `visit_date` value since we're also grouping by that—will extract the `location` or `visit_date` representing that whole group. Importantly, we can also use aliases to rename these aggregate outputs, producing a convenient table:

```
SELECT
    Count(*),
    MAX(location) as "location",
    MAX(visit_date) as "visit_date"
FROM visits
GROUP BY location, visit_date;
```

count	location	visit_date
2	Northwood	2019-11-14
1	Northwood	2019-12-19
2	Country Regional	2019-12-01
...	...	...

Finally, we can summarize this into the average number of patient visits per day per location by treating the table as a subquery and using another aggregate function to get the mean count by location:

```
SELECT
    MAX(location) as "location",
    ROUND(AVG(count), 2) as "avg_daily_visits"
    FROM (SELECT
                Count(*),
                MAX(location) as "location",
                MAX(visit_date) as "visit_date"
            FROM visits
            GROUP BY location, visit_date) as daily_visits_by_location
GROUP BY location;
```

Where here we pass our previous SQL query in place of a table name after the FROM keyword. This use of subqueries allows us to formulate an SQL query from a table that is itself the output of another SQL query. Thus, we can succinctly express our question and get a clean and direct answer from the database:

location	avg_daily_visits
Country Regional	1.82
Northwood	1.54
Central City	3.23
East Town Center	2.05

4.3.2 Average patient age and patient sex per location

In order to answer this question, we need to associate visits and their locations to information pertaining to the patients who have those visits. This will therefore require that we utilize information from both the `visits` table and the `patients` table and that we have a way to keep track of which visit belongs to which patient through use of the `patient_id` column that appears in both tables. This is a great use case for a JOIN where we will join rows of these two tables together based upon the `patient_id` column and then we will group by location and sex using aggregate functions to get the average age and count of patients.

```
SELECT
    MAX(visits.location) as "location",
    MAX(patients.sex) as "sex",
    COUNT(*),
    ROUND(AVG(patients.age), 2) as "avg_age"
FROM visits
JOIN patients
ON visits.patient_id = patients.patient_id
GROUP BY location, sex
ORDER BY location, sex;
```

location	sex	count	avg_age
Central City	F	68	37.54
Central City	M	159	40.55
Central City	UNKNOWN	70	40.39
Country Regional	F	50	43.18
Country Regional	M	75	33.75
...	...	...	...

Notice also that we sorted the results first in order of location, which is alphabetical here, and then within that ordering by sex. Already, we can see some interesting things such as the fact that the clinic at Central City has significantly more visits with male patients than with female patients and that while the mean age for male patients is higher than for female patients at Central City, it's lower than that for female patients at Country Regional. As a detail about this query, it's important to understand what we are and what we are not answering. Here we have the mean age and count-by-sex of visits per location but not of patients per location. This is what we're after and this is appropriate in this case since we're trying to describe the number and type of visits. Bear in mind, however, that we must always be clear about how data are interpreted and about caveats that arise when it is used to derive other conclusions. If we had a 45-year-old male patient who had 10 frequent visits at Central City, then this query will count that patient 10 times. Again, this is appropriate when what we're after is an understanding of the average age of a patient at any given visit, but this is not the same as calculating the average age of the patients at the Central City clinic. If we wanted that information, we would want to group by patient_id and deduplicate this patient information and, in either case, we always want to be clear about the data we produce.

4.3.3 Average number of patient visits per provider

We'll also want to use our JOINs to get at the answer to this question since we will need provider names that come from the providers table as well as visit information from the visits table and we can JOIN these tables together through the provider_id column.

```
SELECT
    MAX(providers.provider_name) as "provider_name",
    COUNT(*) as "number_of_visits"
FROM visits
JOIN providers
ON visits.provider_id = providers.provider_id
GROUP BY providers.provider_name
ORDER by number_of_visits DESC;
```

provider_name	number_of_visits
Cutrona, Carl	103
Gebhardt, Patricia	98
Pena, Robert	96
Merrill, Natalie	94
Beckstead, Johnny	79
...	...

Note here that we sorted the results in descending order so that we would have the providers with the most visits at the top. Also, we did this by using a column what wasn't in any of the original table but instead was one of the aliases we defined after the COUNT() aggregate function.

4.3.4 Counts of diagnosis codes and average age per clinic location

This last question is a bit of a special case because we have to join three tables in order to answer it. We need diagnosis codes from the `icd_10_code` column of the `diagnoses` table, we need `location` values from the `visits` table, and we need to count the unique patients by using the `mrn` column of the `patients` table.

```
SELECT
    MAX(visits.location) as "location",
    MAX(diagnoses.icd_10_code) as "icd_10_code",
    COUNT(DISTINCT(patients.mrn)) as "number_of_patients",
    COUNT(*)
FROM visits
JOIN patients
ON visits.patient_id = patients.patient_id
JOIN diagnoses
ON patients.patient_id = diagnoses.patient_id
GROUP BY visits.location, diagnoses.icd_10_code
ORDER BY location, count DESC;
```

location	icd_10_code	number_of_patients	count
Central City	Z79899	36	58
Central City	Z1231	31	55
Central City	J069	30	54
...	...	...	...
Country Regional	I10	22	44
Country Regional	Z1231	21	35

Note that here we are trying to count the number of different patients with each diagnosis code and so we `COUNT()` the number of `DISTINCT` medical record numbers (`mrn`) in each group. We would get this exact same result if we counted the number of distinct `patient_id` values as well, but it is critical that we count unique values and not just all values. Also, it is important to understand that the `count` column tallies the number of times each diagnosis code occurred at each clinic location or, in other words, it tallies the number of visits to which that diagnosis code was attached. If a patient has a chronic illness for which that diagnosis is true for the entire year in which she goes to the clinic for five different appointments, then this will count that diagnosis code five times. This is intentional for this specific question since we are trying to understand the clinical context for each visit but, again, it is critical that we understand and are clear about interpretation.

With these four questions answered, we can then share this information either by defining a VIEW in our database that others can connect to and query, or by exporting the data to a file to be imported into a dashboard or other visualization tool.

4.4 Conclusion

This chapter has hopefully demonstrated how we can use SQL to answer specific questions relevant to us. In walking through this example project, we have covered SELECT statements, aggregate functions and GROUP BY clauses as well as JOINs, which comprise the common core of SQL functionality. As with anything getting better as SQL is a function of practice but these examples should provide a strong bases for additional experimentation and enhanced understanding. You may also notice that this chapter is entitled "Part 1" and that is because we continue this example later in Chapter 17 in our discussion of Machine Learning by taking tabular data from this sort of database and building a predictive model on top of it. The connection between these chapters and project parts also highlights the analytical continuum between exploring and querying data at rest and bringing that through successive stages of analysis some of which are fairly straightforward as in this case and other which involve deeper transformation, inference, and prediction. In any case, SQL is a near-ubiquitous tool that comes up again and again throughout this book and throughout the world of informatics and it should be a key area of focus for anyone interested in developing a powerful informatics skill set.

CHAPTER 5

Nonrelational databases

5.1 Early nonrelational models

Although it is common to make a general distinction between relational and nonrelational data models, there are a few contextual highlights, which are important to understand. First, relational systems, as a category, have much tighter consistency between products and implementations as they are constrained by the formalities of relational algebra and the functional scope of SQL. As such, the term "relational database" refers to a design philosophy shared among all such products. By some contrast, "nonrelational" encompasses a far more heterogeneous class of data models, which are those that simply do not embody a strictly relational design. Conventionally, nonrelational databases are often designed to accommodate irregularly organized data or to capture certain types of relationships for which SQL and relational schemas are not optimized.

By contrast, relational databases do a lot to represent data in a format geared toward complex and idiosyncratic queries via SQL even if the tabular structure of relational databases is suboptimal in terms of speed or maintainability. A very relevant example of this is medical record data which, as we will explore further, contain many specific properties, which may make them challenging for relational representation such as missing values and a dynamic schema with an evolving scope of columns. Patient data are nonetheless very often stored in relational systems because of the powerful analytical features unlocked by doing so, but this does introduce specific design considerations around how that data are represented. Although many electronic medical record products offer a relational data warehouse through which SQL-based analyses can be performed, many of these products actually implement nonrelational databases for production work, again, because such a nonrelational model is better geared toward the requirements of medical data.

Given the breadth of the nonrelational category, it may come as no surprise that the earliest computer database systems were, in fact, nonrelational databases. We can look to the Conference/Committee on Data Systems Languages (CODASYL), formed in 1959, as a motivating force behind the first formalized computer database systems.[1] The CODASYL group was a consortium founded to establish technical standards and guide the development of programming languages, which could be used across multiple computing environments. The consortium has two important historical legacies: the development of the COBOL

An Introduction to Healthcare Informatics. https://doi.org/10.1016/B978-0-12-814915-7.00005-3

programming language (which we won't discuss in any detail) and standardizing database tools. With regard to the latter legacy, CODASYL formed the List Processing Task Force in 1965, which was later renamed to the Data Base Task Group (DBTG) in 1967. The DBTG published technical standards, which described the "network database model," which was the core design behind several early commercial database systems such as Honeywell's Integrated Data Store (IDS/2) and Cullinet's Integrated Database Management System (IDMS), which still has running implementations to this day.

In short, the network database model is an earlier example of more modern graph databases (which we will discuss later in this Chapter) in that it allows for many-to-many relationships to exist between database records. In this model, nodes correspond to pieces of data such as patients and their corresponding identifiers, while links represent relationships between these pieces of data. Fig. 5.1 depicts an example network model being used to represent two patients' medication record.

The network model was a natural fit for many complex, real-world data types as many-to-many relationships are a common feature of realistic data sets. Also important, this structure allowed for fairly efficient location and selection of disparate sets of information so long as there was a known relationship between them. Ultimately, however, the network model fell out of favor with the rise of relational systems for many of the same reasons it was valuable in the first place as its flexibility made it difficult to package into a usable product and it lacked a constrained and formalized query language like SQL. Another important limitation of the network data model was that it was particularly fragile to data *mutation*. We discussed this point briefly regarding relational databases and we described normalization as a relational technique, which helps support the resiliency and accuracy of a database when items are changed. This is a necessary consideration for any production system, or any "transactional" database, because user operations often result in modifications to existing data fields, which will introduce a new state

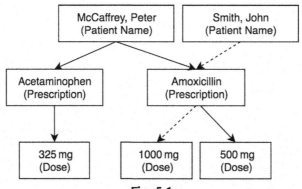

Fig. 5.1

Network data model showing two patients and their prescribed medications. Each boxed value corresponds to a "node" while each arrow corresponds to a "link."

of the database that must propagate throughout the many relationships bound to that piece of data. We discussed the example of a user on an e-commerce site changing her mailing address and the fact that limiting the number of places where that address is recorded in the database is crucial to governing such an update without corrupting the database. In the network model, this problem was amplified because, without certain conventions such as primary and foreign keys, complex relationships were bound to specific items of data. If, for example, a drug manufacturer to which many drugs had SOLD_BY relationships was changed, then these relationships would need to be remapped and this was clearly a challenge.

Another important early nonrelational database model is known as the "hierarchical" model, which was the first database model created by IBM in the 1960s for use in its early mainframe and subsequently the IBM Information Management System (IMS). In this model, records may hold a unidirectional one-to-many relationship in contrast to the many-to-many relationships allowable with the network model. As implied by the name, hierarchical databases are organized in a tree-like structure with records containing related fields of information. Each record may be linked to only one "parent" record but to potentially many "child" records. Such hierarchical models can be exceptionally performant if designed in such a way that locating information does not require searching down multiple branches and, in fact, hierarchical systems enjoy popular and well-known modern product use cases such as IMS (which is still a current IBM product), Microsoft's Windows Registry, which stores settings for programs and hardware on the Windows Operating System, and Microsoft's Active Directory, which manages permissions and access to networked resources.

Despite specific performant use cases, these databases fell out of favor for most business applications with the rise of relational systems, and this illustrates an important point about data applications, which is that performance and amenability to being queried easily are typically competing aims and that they carry different weights in different contexts. Just because a database is fast does not necessarily mean that it is superior for a given use case. Performance for analytical systems almost always boils down to how fast information can be fetched and how this speed is impacted by different combinations of items being selected. By contrast, performance for transactional systems is determined heavily by how fast specific pieces of information can be located and updated, which is generally of far lesser importance to analytical implementations. As a result many data ecosystems extract and transform data between several different models depending upon the intended use, whether transactional or analytical.

There is, of course, one critically important and especially relevant nonrelational database technology and that is M/MUMPS and its popular commercial implementation in the form of Intersystems Cachè, which is the operational database behind many of the most popular electronic medical record systems today. We don't go into great depth regarding M/MUMPS in this chapter because we have an entire chapter devoted to it. In summary, M/MUMPS models data as a multidimensional array with a hierarchical structure and is particularly well suited for representation of medical data. Moreover, the Cachè database product has the capability of supporting SQL queries over the nonrelational M/MUMPS database assuming that certain design constraints are obeyed. We dive into much greater detail in its dedicated chapter, but M/MUMPS is an absolutely critical technology to understand for medical data analysis as it is almost inevitable that some components of a medical dataset originated from a M/MUMPS environment.

5.2 The rise of modern nonrelational models

As mentioned earlier, nonrelational databases are geared more toward the demands of the data they seek to model than the need to meet specifications of a formalized query language. It is therefore of no surprise that relational database products replaced nonrelational products for many business use cases where data querying was an important consideration but nonrelational models persisted in areas where specific performance or modeling demands made them indispensable. This is same driver is responsible for the renaissance of nonrelational systems and their growth in popularity over the past 25 years not always as a replacement for relational databases but often as a necessary accomplice.

The popularization of the internet in the 1990s led to a boom in "unstructured" data. This refers to data that does not consistently follow a predefined row-column format and may not have a consistent set of attributes. Examples range from text in forum posts to user profiles to audio and video, to search histories. In fact, the vast majority of data generated is unstructured. The deluge of this type of data necessitated the creation of performant models to represent it and paved the way for a reprisal of nonrelational technology as a leading approach to high-performance data representation and operation. That being said, a few specific design considerations accompanied these more recent nonrelational tools, which focused on the mutual requirements of scalability and robustness as internet-scale performance requirements often meant that databases needed to be distributed across many separate servers. More formally, these considerations formed the components of the tripartite CAP Theorem, which states that such a high-throughput system can, at most, meet any two of three abstract aims:

- Consistency, meaning that data within the database represents one single and accurate state of information. If a value is mutated, that mutation should be propagated to all servers participating in the distributed database such that different servers should not disagree regarding the correct state of data in the database.

- Availability, meaning that a system—even one that comprises several different servers—should always be accessible and responsive to operations on its data.

- Partition Tolerance, meaning that the system should still be able to facilitate database operations even if communication between servers has been interrupted.

Strictly speaking, these are requirements applicable to any distributed system, but it was the volumetric demands of storing unstructured data from internet use cases that drove these considerations into database design. As such, there is a historical context to the colocation of nonrelational databases, sometimes referred to as "No-SQL" databases because some of them do not support the SQL query language and distributed databases. That being said, there are more modern implementations and versions of nonrelational databases that seek increasing support of SQL and, simultaneously, many modern versions of popular relational database systems support distribution across multiple servers.

This historical context may seem lengthy but it is often as important to understand why a given technology exists as it is to understand how to use it. This is especially true of these nonrelational technologies because, though you may not need to directly interact with them to query data, you will almost certainly have to understand and deal with data coming from one of these systems. In the sections that follow, we will discuss four important nonrelational database models and their modern implementations: Key-Value Stores, Document Stores, Column Stores, and Graph Databases.

5.3 Key-value stores

Key-value stores exemplify an important and pervasive design pattern in computer science. In fact, as we delve into Python in Chapter 6, we will explore a data structure known as a "dictionary," which is, in essence, a key-value store packaged into python as one of its core object types. Similarly, fundamental data structures such as associative arrays and hash tables are likewise examples of key-value stores that appear often in discussions around programming design patterns and programming language tutorials. This pervasiveness is driven largely by the sheer versatility and functionality key-value stores provide.

In a key-value store, atomic elements of data—known as "values"—are each associated with a unique label—or "key." The term "store" is appropriate here because it creates an image more like a bag of labeled items than an ordered database of complex and inter-related records. As a result, key-value stores can be highly performant over a limited scope of data manipulations typically allowing only the retrieval, creation, or mutation is single elements of data. Similarly, most key-value store implementations consider stored values as opaque pieces of information and do not store metadata or schema-related information about those values as relational databases often do. Instead, key-value stores are used as efficient back-ends to which to write and fetch atomic data elements while providing context to, grouping, and performing analytical manipulation upon those elements are left to the application interactive with the store.

Popular examples of key-value stores include Redis and Microsoft's Azure Cosmos DB and these are typically implemented as a complement to—rather than as a replacement of—other nonrelational or relational databases. A conventional example of a key-value store is as a cache, which serves the purpose of making applications more responsive by loading and saving certain commonly requested data, which can serve as a near-instantaneous response to subsequent requests for that same data. You may encounter examples of this wherein web servers cache certain webpage assets in order to make web applications seem highly responsive while reducing the volume of repetitive queries that result in database operations. This was exactly the strategy I employed when creating a laboratory analytics application for the Massachusetts General Hospital in Boston. For this application, users were able to parameterize a dashboard describing laboratory test order and fulfillment metrics with a given date range, creating a scenario where many separate users redundantly request the same date and redundantly require computation of all daily metrics for that date. In order to mitigate this, I used a key-value store to cache all report queries for a rolling month. This way, only the first user to request a given day would have to wait while the results of that query were computed by the database. By contrast, all subsequent queries for that same date would simply search a key-value store for a key corresponding to that date and return the value which was a list of precomputed metrics. This drastically decreased response times for loading dashboards and significantly improved the application's user experience. Importantly, the key-value store was not used as a primary database for laboratory data nor was it used to execute complex analytical queries upon that data. Instead, its purpose was served as an intermediary between the data and the end user and in such a context—acting as a cache—that leveraged its focused strength of performant data retrieval.

5.4 Document stores

A more interesting and robust nonrelational example is the document store. You can imagine a document store as an enhanced and much more flexible extension of a key-value store. In this model, data are represented as sets of key-value pairs, which together form a "document." Compared to key-value stores, document stores also introduce significant flexibility in what is considered a valid value. For example, a patient could be represented as a document as depicted in Fig. 5.2.

In this representation, there are certain keys such as "name" and "age," which have single corresponding values, while other keys such as "phone numbers" or "physician" have lists containing multiple phone numbers or multiple physician names. Commonly a document groups together all data describing a single entity and, while there is certainly some ambiguity as to what constitutes an "entity," a healthcare application might typically consider a patient as one entity, including demographic information describing that person, a patient's medication list as another entity, and a patient clinical note with all of its respective attributes as yet a third. While it may seem disorganized at first glance, this turns out to be an advantageous modeling strategy because a single document can group together related items that might otherwise be spread across many different tables in a relational database. It is this "schemaless" property of document stores and their allowance of different—sometimes

```
{
  "firstName" : "Peter",
  "lastName" : "McCaffrey",
  "age" : 30,
  "phoneNumbers" : [
      2129076542,
      2716284516 ],
  "physicians" : [
      "Dr. Jones",
      "Dr. Wilson" ]
}
```

Fig. 5.2

Document model representing a Patient as a collection of keys and their corresponding values. Note that values can be singleton elements of data or other more complex entities such as lists. Note that the document is enclosed in curly brackets.

arbitrary—aggregations of key-value pairs that makes them suitable for healthcare use cases. In fact, many popular Electronic Medical Record systems such as Epic and Meditech implement document store data models.

Going a step further, it is possible with a document store to have every document in the entire database be a unique combination of properties, although this isn't the common case. This is a useful observation to ponder, though, because it highlights a motivating strength of document stores. When building a relational database, as we discussed earlier, the database developer has to make several hard commitments about what data will look like and how pieces of data will relate to one another. The rigidity of these decisions about schema is what allows for efficient operation even across a wide range of idiosyncratic queries supported by the SQL language. This, however, isn't always the most important factor. Because document stores require no a priori commitments about the structure of a given document, these data objects can be stored in the form in which they are encountered and they don't have to be extensively transformed into a representation that maps onto a preexisting relational model enforced by the database. For example, when storing patient medical charts, document stores allow for each individual chart to be defined as whatever collection of data attributes are present in that chart and gracefully accommodate the fact that many charts contain nonoverlapping information. Two patients may have completely different medications, diagnoses, problem lists, lab tests, and imaging. In a relational database, there would have to be reference tables for diagnoses, problems, lab tests, etc. to which each of these items in a patient chart can have a foreign key. Although not impossible, it is a far more encumbered way to store this information, especially if the purpose of the database is to capture and retrieve individual charts.

Retrieving data from a document store is flexible but not always performant. Typically, document store databases allow for the declaration of certain document properties to serve as "document keys," which are unique identifiers that are often specifically indexed for rapid location and retrieval. Alternatively, it is possible in many document store products to query data using other groups of document attributes but this may result in slow retrieval. Modern implementations often support updating document properties in place and many even support transactions when updating multiple properties. Popular examples include Amazon's Dynamo DB and Mongo DB.

5.5 Column stores

Column stores (and Graph Databases which we will discuss shortly) are particularly important for data practitioners to understand as these models are very often used for analytical rather than operational purposes owing to their unique strengths in supporting efficient and powerful ways to interrogate data. In discussing this topic, we will break the concept of column stores into two different models: traditional column stores and wide column stores and discuss both their similarities and their differences.

5.5.1 Traditional column stores

While traditional column store databases enforce a notion of rows and columns, they depart substantially from relational databases in how they organize those columns. Column store databases perform an organizational technique called "vertical partitioning" wherein columns are stored as separate data structures. By contrast, relational databases store columns together in tables as a single data structure. To understand why this is important, imagine we had a data warehouse of insurance claims wherein each row was a single claim and columns represented claim properties such as claim amount, source facility, related procedure, and patient. Now imagine we wanted to perform a query to find all records from Central Medical Center and compute the average of the claim amounts. In a relational data warehouse, we might have this huge table indexed on a primary key column such as Claim ID to speed up location and retrieval of specific claim rows and we might even have an additional index on Claim Submission Date to facilitate quick selections based upon time windows. If we were to run our query against this table in a relational database, these indices would do little to help us and our database would have to perform what is known as a "table scan" and loop over all rows in search of claims that are from Central Medical Center. Moreover, because the table is a single data structure, the query engine will have to read over not only each row but each column in each row wasting considerable time and effort scanning through irrelevant information. This would ultimately lead to a painfully slow query. You might initially think that a reasonable solution would be to add yet another index to the source facility column. This, however, reveals a much deeper design issue. Analytical queries are, by nature, idiosyncratic and if we really want this large table to serve the needs of analytical investigation we would likely end up having to create an index on every column and, with a table like this, we could easily have 100 columns or more.

The clever innovation of column store database and vertical partitioning is that, in circumstances such as this where the query is concerned with a narrow range of columns but a very wide range of rows, the query planner can only scan over the individual columnar data structure of interest and never have to read over any unnecessary columns. As an additional optimization, column stores typically also implement "horizontal partitioning" wherein column data structures are further broken apart into chunks with a set number of rows (e.g., 8 million rows in the case of InfiniDB). This further reduces query time by allowing for parallelization of these column scans within separate chunks. Finally, because column-level data structures maintain the same offset, that is the 5th entry in one column refers to the same row as the 5th entry in any other column, they can exploit what is known as "auto indexing" using this offset. For example, when we run our query over our billion row claims table, the column store can first make the optimization of only considering relevant column data structures, source facility, and claim amount, and then, once it has calculated the offset for the rows containing our target source facility, it can efficiently subselect only the specific row chunks from the claim amount column data structures that share the same offset. This results in a profound improvement in performance and is a genius strategy for making huge data table accessible to flexible analytical queries. Popular examples of traditional column store databases include Hewlett-Packard's Vertica and Amazon Redshift.

5.5.2 Wide column stores

Wide column stores are a bit different and, when compared to traditional column stores, adopt a much more flexible organizational structure. Instead of assuming that each row has values for a given set of columns, wide column stores allow specific columns to pertain to only a subset of rows in a table and grouping-related columns into "column families," which are usually retrieved and operated upon together. New columns can be added arbitrarily to column families and each of those specific columns may only apply to a specific subgroup of rows. In this way column families are simply a secondary grouping of columns based upon those columns having similar meaning and, therefore, likely being interrogated together. This approach is particularly effective when data are sparse, that is, when records have many possible attributes but have actual values for only a few of those attributes. Sparsity is a very important problem in many data disciplines especially healthcare as a patient chart, for example, has an expansive scope of potential attributes such as all potential tests in the laboratory test menu or all potential procedures in the CPT procedure code book, but only a very small subset of these attributes actually have values for any given patient.

Wide column stores implement the concept of a "keyspace" as opposed to a formal schema. The keyspace contains all column families with each column family existing like a flexible table wherein each row is a record but rows may have different combinations of the columns that comprise the column family. Fig. 5.3 depicts what this would look like when representing a patient medical record.

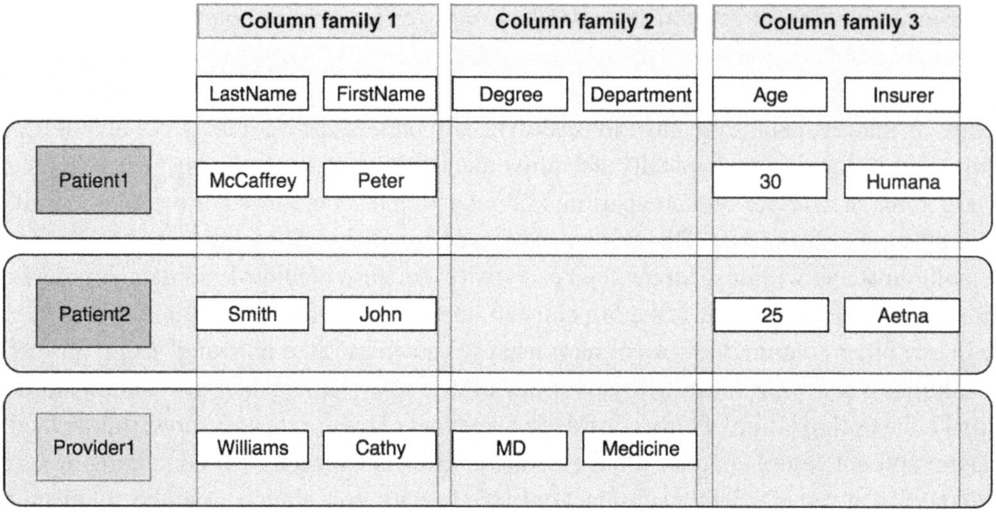

Fig. 5.3

Example wide column store depicting patients and providers. Note that patients and providers have overlapping and nonoverlapping elements in different column families.

Looking at the depiction, one of the critical distinctions of the wide column store comes into focus. In this model, columns are restricted only to single rows and are not presumed to be data dimensions that span all rows in a table. In this way, the wide column store can be seen either as a more formalized document store wherein column families contain groups of nonidentical but similarly formatted documents with a uniform document key or they can be seen as a less formal relational database wherein each row has been separated into its own single-row table but those tables have been linked together in related families.

Wide column stores, therefore, sit in an intermediate position between document stores and strictly relational databases by allowing for utter flexibility regarding the columns for which a given row has values while still storing data in key order, meaning that there is a global ordering to rows, columns, and column families in a column store table. This allows for many of the performance enhancements enjoyed by relational databases such as table indexes and efficient key-based look-ups while being able to gracefully handle sparse and semistructured data. Popular examples of wide column stores include HBase, a widely used Apache open-source project, and the underlying technology behind tools such as Microsoft's HDInsight, Google's BigTable, and Cassandra DB, which originated from Facebook.

We've discussed columns store's ability to handle sparse data as a key strength, but there are a few additional merits worth mentioning. Column store databases are very popular in Big Data applications because they handily support compression since columns only exist for rows about which they record a value. As such the database does not need to store or manipulate huge tables with many null values. For many of these same reasons, column stores are also very scalable and readily support partitioning across different servers since each row is ultimately a separate and atomic document. Another important strength of column stores is that they are adept at aggregation queries such as the SUM, AVG, and COUNT operations we discussed in the SQL chapter. This is because, even with massively large databases column stores can quickly locate the specific column to which those aggregations are applied due to the column family organizational structure and only those rows which have real values have to be operated upon in order to produce the aggregate calculation.

5.6 Graph databases

A fitting conclusion to this chapter, graph databases embody an extremely powerful, if slightly more esoteric, approach to data representation. Where the other nonrelational examples focus chiefly on flexibility in the properties of database records and allowing different pieces of data to have different attributes, graph databases focus on flexibility in relationships between records. An important disambiguation to make here is that "graph" in the sense of a graph database does not refer to a plot but, instead, to a formal mathematical construct describing relationships between objects in a group. In this concept, these objects are called "vertices" or "nodes," and represent things in the real word, and their relationships are called "edges." Fig. 5.4 depicts a graph capturing the relationship between a group of providers a group of patients in whose care they participated. Since each provider care for one patient, all patients, or any combination of patients the relationships even in a simple example can be complex.

If we were to model even this simple case with a relational database, we can already see an issue beginning to arise. We would need a provider's table, a patient's table, and a table linking providers to patients for whom they cared. Certainly, this is possible to do with a relational database, but it already seems awkward in that we have to create an entirely separate join table just for this simple case. To add further complexity, multiple providers can care for a single patient together or potentially any combination of providers can contribute to the care of any patient. Even further, if we were to consider nurses, residents, and medical students we need to

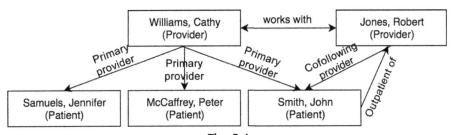

Fig. 5.4

Example graph data model representing providers and patients. Note that relationships (edges) can go in either direction and that they may have their own data type corresponding to the type of relationship they represent.

add several more join tables and we end up with a complex schema wherein every entity (attending, nurse, resident, medical student, patient) has its own table and there are lots of many-to-many tables linking these entities together. If we were then to add a new patient to this database, we would have to update the patient's table as well as each of these join tables in order to maintain integrity. This quickly becomes unacceptably cumbersome.

In a graph data structure, each of these entities would simple be a vertex with a descriptive label such as the entity's name and whether they are an attending, nurse, resident, or medical student. Then, if one of those entities participated in the care of a patient, an edge would be created. These edges have "direction" meaning that they "start from" and "go to" specific vertices. If attending Dr. John Smith cared for patient Sally Jones, then an edge would start from John Smith and go to Sally Jones. Especially powerful, if we wanted to also represent whether entities were on the same care team we could have to change nothing about our vertices. All we would have to do is introduce another edge representing membership on the same care team and use those edges to link vertices from members of the same care team.

Representing data in this way is powerful not only because it leads to a simpler schema for these many-to-many relationships but also because it allows for "traversals," which are powerful operations to select and group vertices according to their relationships. For example, if we wanted to know all of the patients that Dr. John Smith has cared for, all we would need to do is start at the John Smith vertex and select all vertices, which are connected to John Smith by a "cared-for" edge. Conversely, if we wanted to find all of the medical staff who have cared for Sally Jones, we could select all vertices connected to her vertex by a "cared-for" edge. Trivially, we could chain these two operations to very efficiently determine all medical staff who cared for the same patients that Dr. John Smith cared for.

Graph databases represent data as a graph object, allowing powerful traversals to be used on interrelated information. Many graph database products also support more complex query functions like aggregations and sorting. Where SQL is the standard query language for relational databases, the standard query interface for graph databases is known as TinkerPop, which provides the Gremlin graph traversal language. Popular examples of graph databases include Titan DB, Amazon Neptune, and Neo4j.

5.7 Conclusion

As you can see, nonrelational databases encompass a variety of important tools with different design philosophies, motivations, and strengths. Depending upon the problem being solved, each of these may be essential to building a data-driven application. In the next chapter, we will extend this discussion of nonrelational databases into M/MUMPS, a core component of many widely used healthcare applications. Armed with these nonrelational concepts, you will be able to understand the design of M/MUMPS and why it has maintained such popularity as a healthcare database.

Reference

1. Belzer J, Holzman AG, Kent A. Encyclopedia of Computer Science and Technology: Volume 5—Classical Optimization to Computer Output/Input Microform. Google Books. https://books.google.com/books?id=G6a2tSuOoq8C&pg=PA74&lpg=PA74&dq=codasyl+1959&source=bl&ots=5EzJ-FSNCm&sig=ACfU3U1Rv-ZNwFtu9OYFxlWK87gFMwkPww&hl=en&sa=X&ved=2ahUKEwj33oDd_Z3nAhUZOs0KHdRsDhEQ6AEwBXoECAoQAQ#v=onepage&q=codasyl1959&f=false. (Accessed January 24, 2020).

CHAPTER 6

M/MUMPS

6.1 A brief history and context

We have discussed at fair length relational and nonrelational databases and compared their relative strengths and weaknesses. This information, while deeply relevant and highly valuable to any work in medical informatics, only tells part of the story. Healthcare is a unique mixture of the idiosyncratic and optimal and being effective in medical informatics necessitates mutual mastery of each of these domains. This brings us to the topic of this chapter, which is a specific nonrelational database technology with surprisingly deep historical roots and a pervasive influence in healthcare: M/MUMPS.

The Massachusetts General Hospital Utility Multiprogramming System, also referred to as the "M" programming language, dates back to 1966 when Neil Pappalardo, Curt Marble, and Robert Greenes developed the language in the laboratory of Dr. Octo Barnett at the Massachusetts General Hospital in Boston.[1] Although some aspects of MUMPS may seem antiquated now, it was by many standards remarkably ahead of its time. Moreover, MUMPS was designed specifically to address the fluid and often sparse nature of patient records, a property it shares with many of the more modern nonrelational systems.[2] MUMPS was built to work on a shared mainframe and support both the development of applications as well as the persistence of their data and was quickly put into practice in hospital admissions and laboratory test reporting as part of the Hospital's new Information System. Another distinct design goal of MUMPS was portability, which, although common now, was a powerful factor in its rapid adoption by the medical community. By the 1970s, many hospitals were using MUMPS-based systems typically modified and customized based upon institution-specific needs.

The story of MUMPS' growth is one of commercialization and standardization wherein an initially very heterogeneous ecosystem incrementally converged on leading commercial distributions. To complicate this tale a bit is the fact that, being as MUMPS serves as the data persistence and transaction layer for many medical record systems, different MUMPS implementations map to different EMR products. The first notable example of this is MEDITECH, which was created in 1969 by MUMPS developer Neil Pappalardo and based upon a specific and proprietary implementation of MUMPS known as the Meditech Interpretive Information System (MIIS). This proprietary divergence from the open-source MUMPS implementation would prove to be very influential as the large community of open-source

An Introduction to Healthcare Informatics. https://doi.org/10.1016/B978-0-12-814915-7.00006-5

MUMPS users crystallized into a more formal MUMPS Users Group, which standardized the open source language by 1974. This standard MUMPS implementation was soon distributed by commercial vendors such as InterSystems, founded in Boston in 1978, which over the following 30 years would incrementally acquire other commercial MUMPS distributions to become the predominant global MUMPS product, which it remains to this day. As a particularly interesting note, InterSystems and its DBMS known as Cachè is predominately sold as an embedded component of other enterprise systems such as Epic, SunQuest, and many others. Although there are other MUMPS distributions, such as Fidelity Information Systems' GT.M, which is notable for being available under the GPL license, these have not been able to match InterSystems' market traction. Thus, the predominant manifestation of MUMPS in healthcare is as the InterSystems Cachè product serving as database system within an enterprise application such as an EMR or LIS.

In almost any case, MUMPS is not directly used to create predictive models or conduct iterative analysis, but it is used to perform operational transactions on EMR databases, to create reusable reporting interfaces to real-time operational data, and to establish data pipelines to migrate information from transactional to analytical databases. As such, it is thoroughly possible that designing, optimizing, or troubleshooting a data pipeline may require accessing or reviewing MUMPS code and/or a MUMPS-based data architecture. In the next sections, we will discuss the general MUMPS data model and we will cover some very relevant details about the MUMPS language itself. As we proceed through this chapter, you may notice a certain conflation between MUMPS as a language and MUMPS as a database. This is a partly historical convention as one of the unique features of the MUMPS language is the ability to store data in a structure known as a "global" and to save that information to disk. In so doing, MUMPS has a dual purpose as both a programming language and a database system. The nuances of globals will become clearer in subsequent sections, but we will start with the basic linguistic components. Since it is unlikely that, as a medical informaticist, you would use MUMPS as a pure language and technology, our discussion will quickly focus on globals and data storage and will cross over into some healthcare specific examples addressing how MUMPS-based systems represent medical data and how those systems function in a larger data infrastructure. As such, the goal is not necessarily to know all of MUMPS or even to create MUMPS scripts. Instead, the goal of this chapter is to leave you with a mental picture of the MUMPS global and an ability to approximate how data, which eventually exist in a reporting database or a model, originate in this most primary form.

6.2 The M language

Much like modern languages such as Python or R, MUMPS installations include an interpreter, allowing users to interactively formulate and execute MUMPS commands. We don't cover installation and set-up, instead leaving that as an optional exercise. For those interested,

MUMPS may be readily installed either as GT.M, which can be downloaded freely from Sourceforge or as InterSystems Cachè, which can be obtained as an evaluation version for personal, noncommercial use. In either case, users obtain a database application as well as a MUMPS interpreter, which may be initiated as an interactive terminal session. For the remainder of this chapter, we highlight the syntax of example MUMPS code both to make it more readable and to distinguish it from discussions of SQL, Python, or other examples.

Likely a departure from languages with which you may be familiar, all execution tasks in MUMPS are performed through explicit commands and this includes the creation and declaration of variables. Somewhat confusingly, commands in MUMPS may either be completely written out as a relevant keyword or contracted into a single character abbreviation. Commands may be followed by arguments, which are specific values either operated on by the command or used to modify how the command operates on other values. For example, to create the variable x and assign it the value 24, we would write:

```
set x=24
```

with `set` being the command to define a variable and `x=24` being the argument used by that command. In contracted form, this statement would read like so:

```
s x=24
```

Alternatively, in order to write out the variable we have created to the terminal, we would use the `write` command:

```
write x
```

Notably, standard MUMPS does not contain embedded blanks, which may lead to code which can seem inscrutable and highly compact. However, after familiarizing yourself with the language conventions and reading and writing MUMPS code, it will become easy to understand.

MUMPS is often described as supporting two basic data types, numbers and strings, but it is worth noting that, in actuality, all values are really stored as strings. This is a critical difference from other languages such as Java, which maintain a very explicit type system and which regard an integer and a text string as fundamentally different things. By contrast, the distinction between numbers and strings in MUMPS is enforced by how the values behave. In other words, a number is considered numeric because it is amenable to numeric operations such as addition and subtraction, whereas attempting to add two strings will not result in expected behavior. This may seem like an esoteric point but it serves to illustrate that, where many other languages contain inherent constraints such as a strict system of value types, MUMPS considers these the responsibility of application design. We will see this come back again shortly as we discuss globals.

When variables are created in MUMPS, they may either be defined locally or globally. By contrast, in most other programming languages, including Python, which we discuss later in the Book, all variables defined within the language are local meaning that they only exist within the runtime of the language interpreter and will cease to exist when the program that created them terminates. The only way to persist variables beyond the termination of a program in Python is to store that information in a file or external database. However, since MUMPS is a unique hybrid of a programming language and database, variables may be declared as "globals" meaning that they are saved to disk and will persist until explicitly deleted without the need for an external database system.

A potentially confusing point here concerns the meaning of local and global. In more modern programming contexts, these refer to a variable's "scope" or, in other words, whether that variable is accessible to code in different contexts. This is not the only way these words are used in the context of MUMPS wherein local and global most often refer to whether data created by a MUMPS process is written to disk and persists beyond the termination of that process. For the remainder of this chapter, our use of global and local will refer to whether a variable persists beyond termination of the program that created it.

The distinction between local and global variables is made by prepending a circumflex "^" to variable names when the intention is to save them to disk. In the previous example where we set x to 24, if we were to restart our program and issue the command write x, we would get an error saying that no variable x exists. By contrast, if we were to set the variable x as follows:

```
set ^x=24
```

Then this variable and its value would persist and be accessible even if we were to start a new MUMPS session. It should now be clear why MUMPS-based medical record systems are described to store information in "globals" as these comprise a formal database assessible to separate MUMPS sessions and programs and whose data are written to disk and stored persistently.

Much as variables may be created with the set command, they may also be specifically deleted using the kill command like so:

```
kill x
```

6.3 General concepts regarding arrays and MUMPS

With that introduction in place, we can discuss the real meat of data modeling in MUMPS: the global array and, by extension, the global multidimensional array. Our previous example created a variable, x, that contained a single value, 24. Arrays store one or more values in an accessible list. Arrays in MUMPS behave a bit differently than you might expect from other languages. First, arrays do not need to be created with specific dimensions. That is, instead of declaring an array of 3 items upfront arrays of any length can be created and arbitrarily updated to include new values. Another important detail is that arrays in MUMPS are sparse meaning that they need only contain the values explicitly assigned to them and they do not need to contain intermediate values. If an array is declared that contains 1, 3, and 7, then that array has three items not seven items. In other words, it is not necessary to declare a 2, 4, 5, or 6, but these could optionally be added to the array later.

Importantly, arrays have dimensions, which describe the size and structure of their values. This is a broader concept that ties into core data structures of many languages and even many machine learning algorithms and so we'll take our time a bit in this chapter talking about arrays as it will also drive home many critical concepts.

First, let's consider the general case where we may have an array of three items:

1,2,3

Here we have one list containing three items and, thus, its dimensions are 1 by 3. Typically, this is referred to as the "dimensionality" of the array. Often, this is represented as an array itself where each value corresponds to the size of one of its dimensions. For example, the dimensionality of above array would be 1,3. By extension, the list:

1,2,6,6,7,3,5

Has a dimensionality of 1,7. These are technically one-dimensional arrays, which are often more colloquially referred to just as arrays. You may also notice that arrays can have repeat values (as we see earlier) and that the order of items in arrays is preserved and meaningful. This is in contrast to mathematical "sets," which we will encounter later or dictionaries which we will discuss in the Python chapter as those do not preserve the order of values and they require entries to be unique. The utility afforded by preserving position in arrays is that specific items within an array can be inserted, altered, or read, based upon the position they occupy within the list. For example, we can create an array like so:

1987,1,12

Which stores a birthdate in year, month, day format and we can reliably read and write such values knowing that the first item is always the year, the second always the month, and the third is always the day. To bring the discussion of simple arrays more full circle, we can also mix and match between value types within a list and store a patient like so:

"Peter", "McCaffrey", 1987,1,12

Knowing that we can reliably read and write these identifiers consistently in first name, last name, birth year, birth month, and birth day format.

We can extend this example to address the "multidimensional" case wherein the items of an array are themselves other arrays and, in some instances, the items of those arrays are also other arrays. Consider the case where we may wish to represent multiple patients together as a group. Such a multidimensional array may build upon the simpler patient information array we just discussed and compose those into a larger collection. In this example we will use square brackets to denote the beginning and end of each array including the overall array composed of patient-specific arrays:

[["Peter","McCaffrey",1987,1,12],
["Jonathan","McCaffrey",1986,8,21],
["John","Smith",1985,7,16]]

The dimensionality of such an array would be 3,5 because there are three arrays here each of which has five items. This can be extended even further by nesting these arrays into other arrays. For example, we may wish to represent an operating room schedule as a nested array with three dimensions structured such that the first array represents operating rooms themselves within which are arrays of patients scheduled for a specific OR within which are patient-specific attributes like so:

[[["Peter","McCaffrey",1987,1,12],
["Jonathan","McCaffrey",1991,8,21],
["John","Smith",1985,7,16]],

[["BoB","WIlson",1971,4,22],
["Kyle","Bartlett",1990,8,08],
["Sam","Michaels",1965,2,11]]]

In such an example, we describe two ORs each containing three patients on the schedule. The dimensionality of this array is 2,3,5. Arrays of any dimensionality allow for "addressing" or locating specific values within them based upon the position in which arrays that value can be found. In the example, the address 1,2,3 would locate the value 1991 as it looks for the first item in the outermost array (that would be the first batch of three patients pertaining to the first OR), the second item in that array (that would be Jonathan McCaffrey) and, finally, the third item in that array (that would be the year 1991). Because arrays maintain the order in which values are stored, addresses are consistent and represent a reusable and critical interface through which to deposit and extract values from arrays of varying dimension.

These multidimensional arrays should look and seem similar to the relational database tables we discussed previously. Indeed, relational tables in a traditional RDBMS can be thought of in many cases as a multidimensional array such that a table is an array of rows each of which is an array of values corresponding to the column attributes defined for that table. Recall, however, that in the pure relational algebra underlying relational tables, rows are considered mathematical sets and thus cannot formally contain repeat values. These constraints are relaxed almost ubiquitously in the implementation of relational databases such that the behavior is more like a multidimensional array as described here. That being said, there is one last conceptual point to flesh out here. The arrays we have been discussing have a certain convenience about them because they are "dense" or "full" meaning that each position has a corresponding value. Such density is important when one seeks to maintain a structure or "schema" to the data being stored. Recall from our previous discussions that this was a core strength and design consideration of relational database systems and that, for each row, each column had to have some value, even if this value represented a blank (e.g., NULL). Recall also that nonrelational systems departed from this constraint and found favor in circumstances where data being stored contained irregularly formatted records. More free-form data models like key-value stores or document stores accommodate data that aren't truly tabular and don't have a universal number of columns or attributes for each record. MUMPS at its core behaves much more like the latter that the former, allowing for the creation of multidimensional arrays, their persistence on disk as "global" arrays, and the allowance that such arrays may be sparse (i.e., two items may be stored within one global without them having to share the same set of defined attributes).

As a practical note, MUMPS and some of its primary commercial implementations such as InterSystems Cachè have evolved to emulate both relational and nonrelational behavior. As the unconstrained multidimensional array is a low-level and incredibly flexible data structure, it can be used in a variety of ways to store very heterogeneous or entirely homogeneous items. In the latter case, logic around how records within the global are created and updated can be defined in such a way as to enforce a standard schema and, in so doing, behave just like a relational database. In the case of InterSystems Cachè, for example, this behavior extends all the way to supporting actual SQL queries upon globals as though they were relational tables. The requirement for this to work, of course, is that those globals must be created with appropriate constraints. Typically, this means that the globals are defined as classes with a strict and formal set of attributes using a proprietary language of InterSystems' design known as ObjectScript. We will touch upon this again later in this chapter but for now we will focus on the pure MUMPS multidimensional array.

6.4 Arrays and MUMPS

Finally, now that we have a useful concept of arrays, we can discuss some MUMPS-specific implementation details. Note that to many people who are either newcomers to the MUMPS language or who primarily use another technology such as relational databases, arrays in MUMPS and the way in which arrays are used to define globals as a core data structure is a turn-off. This isn't without reason. As we mentioned earlier, MUMPS is a very simple and low-level language and it lacks many higher-level safeguards or constraints present in other languages and especially other database technologies. The first oddity, which will become immediately apparent, is the way in which arrays distribute values. As will become clear, the implementation resembles a document or a set of key value pairs as described in the chapter on nonrelational databases.

Let's start by creating a simple array called "myArray" and store within it a single value as follows:

```
set ^MyArray(1)="myValue"
```

and we can write our array back to the screen (note that, in these examples, we imagine we are logged into a MUMPS session as "USER" and so all responses from MUMPS are prepended with USER>):

```
write ^MyArray(1)
USER> "myValue"
```

Let's dissect the statement. As we discussed previously, we use the set and write commands to create and read values. We also define an array with a unique name and a parenthesis. Lastly, we make our array a global by prepending the statement with a circumflex ("^"), which instructs MUMPS to save the array to disk. Another important thing to note is that, in creating this array, we actually created an expression, which defined a specific value within the parenthesis and set that value equal to the string "myValue."

This behavior is different from what we would typically see in another language such as Python and different from the simpler conceptual arrays discussed previously. In the pure sense, an array is just an ordered collection of values such as [1,2,3] and can be created as such. In Python, for example, we could make such an array like so (don't worry if the exact syntax is a bit foreign as we will cover Python in Chapter 9):

```
myArray = [1,2,3]
```

and we could print that array by referring to its name like so:

```
print(myArray)
>>> [1,2,3]
```

And we could also specifically print the second value, for example, by referring to its address like so (bear in mind that, in Python, arrays are "zero-indexed" and so the first position is considered position 0, the second position, position 1, and so on):

```
Print(myArray[1])
>>>[2]
```

MUMPS arrays are importantly different because they aren't used to store unlabeled values like this. Instead, MUMPS arrays are inherently structured to store both values and addresses explicitly. The Python array does this implicitly but the behavior is not as robust. For example, we could access the second item in our array by referring to its numerical position within the array, but this doesn't tell us what that second item represents. By contrast MUMPS arrays allow for creating addresses using both numeric and text values and they allow for using lists of those values to create long, multidimensional arrays with complex indices. Importantly, because MUMPS arrays can be sparse, we can arbitrarily insert values at any array address we choose. To bring this full circle, let's consider a Patients global, which would contain different patients with unique numerical IDs. Each of these patients can have multiple attributes captured both by their address and record information:

```
set ^Patients("CentralHospital",1)="Peter`McCaffrey`1987`1`12"
```

Here we have created a Patients array (a "global" array by virtue of being saved to disk as denoted by the prepending "^") and defined an address within that array that contains the name of a specific hospital, "CentralHospital," and a numerical patient ID, 1. Already we can see how this could be a flexible data structure as we could easily include a record from "NorthernHospital" as well like so:

```
set ^Patients("NorthernHospital",1)="Michael`Wilson`1954`8`21"
```

or a second patient from "CentralHospital":

```
set ^Patients("CentralHospital",2)="Jonathan`McCaffrey`1991`8`21"
```

or even an arbitrary 99th patient from "CentralHospital" (and without the need for defining patients 2 through 98):

```
set ^Patients("CentralHospital",99)="Elizabeth`Wells`1971`12`11"
```

Each of these addresses can be thought of as a record locator, which, in this example, contains information about a hospital and a patient number. This is arbitrary of course and there would be no strict constraints against adding additional address elements to certain records like so:

```
set ^Patients("CentralHospital","GreenWard","Bed3")="Bob`Wilson`1981`10`30"
```

Although, in practice, this cannot be totally free form without being unmanageable and so MUMPS globals are manipulated with both rhyme and reason. The important thing to be aware of is that this rhyme and reason are deliberate design decisions, which are maintained by the code that writes to, reads, and updates globals rather than being an intrinsic formality of the data structure itself. Global arrays in MUMPS can support values being arbitrarily inserted and mutated at any address and they allow for any potential collection of numerical and text values to serve as an address.

Our Patients array is additionally interesting because of the way in which we assign values to the addresses. Strictly speaking, MUMPS globals accept single numeric or text values at specific addresses; however, these values can be "delimited" meaning that they contain certain key characters reserved for the special purpose of representing divisions between specific values. In the case of our first patient, while the address (`"CentralHospital",1`) stores a single text string `"Michael'Wilson'1954'8'21"`, this string contains the tilde character ("'") used specifically and exclusively for the purpose of marking the barrier between specific values such as the first name, last name, birth year, birth month, and birth date. Thus, when a MUMPS program reads, writes, or updates a patient record from this global, it can rely on the fact that patient records are stored in this way and that, once a specific record has been found by its address, the third value within that record corresponds to the birth year and this would be baked into all mumps code interacting with this global. Routines that write data would take the first name, last name, birth year, birth month, and birth date values, insert a tilde character between them and form a single text string before writing that string to the desired address and, likewise, routines that read or mutate that information would expect to receive a text string from a given address that contains four tildes sitting at the borders between five separate values in consistent order corresponding to the first and last name and birth date.

MUMPS provides a useful command known as $piece, which suits this purpose and accepts as arguments the text string we wish to parse, the character used to demarcate different values, and the position of the value we wish to retrieve. We could take our patient text string and parse out the patient's last name (the second value demarcated by a tilde) like so:

```
write $piece("Peter'McCaffrey'1987'1'12", "'", 2)
USER> McCaffrey
```

This allows us to extend our global's functionality a bit and retrieve the last name of patient 2 at CentralHospital in a single statement like so:

```
write $piece(^Patients("CentralHospital",2), "'", 2)
```

which would also return the last name:

```
USER> McCaffrey
```

Heretofore, we've focused much of this discussion on the structure of globals and the most basic commands set, write, and $piece. Standard MUMPS also includes select higher-level operations known as routines, which are made available to the MUMPS runtime for execution. Although there are many routines that come with a given MUMPS installation, we will focus on one relevant to our purposes, which allows us to print either entire globals or sections of globals to the screen for examination. The common syntax for executing a routine is as follows:

```
Do ^%G
```

Where the `Do` command is followed by the name of a given routine starting with a percent sign. Note that routines are themselves global values (being persisted to disk) and are thus also prepended with a circumflex. When executed, this routine in particular will prompt the user for the name of a global, which may optionally include an address within that global and it will print that information to the screen. We could print out the entire ^Patients global or, more commonly, we could print out a section of that global such as all patients from CentralHospital like so:

```
Do ^%G
Global: ^Patients("CentralHospital","")
```

Where we leave the numerical id portion of the address as an empty string. This routine can prove to be quite useful for exploring the structure of globals and tracing exported data back to its original MUMPS-based form.

6.5 MUMPS, globals, and data infrastructure

In most settings, you are unlikely to manipulate MUMPS globals and, in the circumstance where working directly with globals is required, you are unlikely to do so by writing totally custom scripts in MUMPS. Instead, many MUMPS-based systems abstract away from the standard MUMPS globals and language in two different ways.

One is by using a higher-level language that extends MUMPS, such as InterSystems' ObjectScript, which is a modern object-oriented programming language. ObjectScript buries the core MUMPS logic in a more user-friendly programming interface, which even supports SQL queries atop globals. The tradeoff is some loss in the flexibility of bare globals for a gain in consistency, uniformity, and ease. SunQuest Information Systems' Laboratory is an example of such a product. Interoperation is aided by the fact that it leverages many of InterSystems' Cache's more modern features, which include SQL interactivity and the enforcement of a schema upon globals that defines a strict set of properties with strict value types. It is of course still possible to compose custom MUMPS code that interacts with these globals, but this is not typically done for analytical purposes. Instead, when products such as SunQuest Laboratory are integrated into an analytical data infrastructure, the SQL interactivity is sufficient to extract information from globals. It is nonetheless still critical to understand globals and to grasp how globals capture data as, even though such systems may support SQL interactivity, creating analytical pipelines often requires inspecting globals, understanding which globals are able to be queried and auditing the logic used when data from two globals are joined in a query. Errors in any of these will have pervasive impact upon the integrity of any resulting data at all subsequent phases of analysis.

The other way in which systems abstract away from the standard MUMPS language is through the use of many custom routines, which come packaged with a specific product and are deployed with that product's installation. Epic is likely the most significant example of this. The operational database underlying the Epic's many applications and which serves as the primary database from which clinical users read and to which clinical users write when interacting with the medical record is a MUMPS-based database called Chronicles. Importantly, when a clinical site sets up Chronicles, the deployment includes the installation of many custom MUMPS routines developed by Epic, which collectively comprise an API through which even Chronicles programmers primarily interact with the globals that make up Chronicles. These routines involve many convenience functions focused on reading, traversing, and printing information from globals. Importantly, this additional MUMPS code packaged at installation may also include custom scripts that map globals to tables and support SQL interactivity in a way similar to Intersystems' ObjectScript. In the case of Epic Chronicles, this is called KB_SQL from Knowledge-Based Systems, which allows Chronicles to bridge the gap between MUMPS globals and SQL in a vendor-independent manner and which serves as the primary interface through which data are transferred from Chronicles to Epic's Relational Data Warehouse System known as Clarity.

As a final exercise, we can consider how a SQL to MUMPS interconversion might work. Imagine our ^Patients global with five patients across two hospitals. We can print the entire global like so:

```
Do ^%G
Global: ^Patients

^Patients("CentralHospital",1)="Peter`McCaffrey`1987`1`12"
                           2)="Jonathan`McCaffrey`1991`8`21"
                           3)="Jeff`Johnson`1976`10`16"
                           99)="Elizabeth`Wells`1971`12`11"
^Patients("NorthernHospital",1)="Michael`Wilson`1954`8`21"
                           2)="Will`Johnson`1998`1`22"
```

Now if we were to execute a SQL statement to select the first name and last name of the patient from this global with id 2, our SQL command might read like so:

```
SELECT FirstName, LastName
FROM Patients
WHERE Patients.ID = 2
```

For a MUMPS implementation of this query, we can make use of the $get function, which will retrieve items in a global based upon a complete or partial address. The SQL statement could be expressed in MUMPS like so:

```
set firstName=$piece($get(^Patients("CentralHospital",1)),"`",1)
set lastName=$piece($get(^Patients("CentralHospital",1)),"`",2)
```

```
write firstName
    write lastName

    USER> Peter
    USER> McCaffrey
```

As a final exercise, we could grab the first names of all patients at Central Hospital to emulate the following SQL query:

```
SELECT FirstName
FROM Patients
WHERE Hospital="NorthernHospital"
```

This is a bit more complex of an exercise but can be accomplished in MUMPS like so:

```
for i=1:1 quit:$order(^Patients("NorthernHospital",i))="" write ^Patients
("NorthernHospital",i),!
```

Succinctly, what this code does is locate the "CentralHospital" address range within the ^Patients global and loop through each record whose address falls under "CentralHospital," extracting the second value (the patient last name) from each record. This would output the following information to the screen:

```
    USER> Michael
    USER> Will
```

6.6 Conclusion

This chapter hopefully provided a conceptual overview of the MUMPS programming language and the global array data structure. The intention of this chapter is not to equip you to develop MUMPS-based applications as doing so is unlikely to be required of you as a medical informaticist. What is important, however, is being able to trace data in a chart, underlying relational database, or even a python script back to its origins, which may very well be somewhere within one or many MUMPS globals. As such, this chapter focused mostly on how data live in globals and how users with access to a MUMPS-based healthcare database can inspect globals.

We leave out many details of the MUMPS language such as loops, conditionals, postconditionals, and indirection. For the interested reader, exploring such things is certainly a rewarding process but it likely will not be necessary for creation of data-driven applications. As you will see throughout this book, there is a broad range of technologies with which one must be familiar in order to be an effective informaticist and it is unfeasible to master all of these initially. Instead, it is better to crystallize the most important parts of each relevant technology and channel deeper research efforts into other skills such as SQL (which we have previously discussed), Python, and predictive modeling (both of which we will discuss later on).

References

1. Fitzmaurice JM, Adams K, Eisenberg JM. Three decades of research on computer applications in health care: medical informatics support at the agency for healthcare research and quality. *J Am Med Inform Assoc.* 2002; 9(2):144–160. https://doi.org/10.1197/jamia.M0867.
2. Blum BI, Orthner HF. *The MUMPS Programming Language in Implementing Healthcare Information Systems, Springer*;1989: 396–420. https://doi.org/10.1007/978-1-4612-3488-3_23.

Understanding healthcare data

CHAPTER 7

How to approach healthcare data questions

7.1 Introduction

As we have already seen, healthcare contains a varied landscape of data at rest. This information may be stored within several different enterprise applications each with its own relational database, there may additionally be MUMPS-based systems, and data stored in structured or unstructured files. Querying this information is one task the underpinnings of which were the focus of the chapters in the preceding section. Making sense of this information, however, is quite another task, one that requires understanding an assortment of topics specific to the domain of healthcare. Many of these topics will be covered in subsequent chapters within this section of the book, but it is important to provide some form of broader context for these lessons. This context is the focus of this chapter. Here we will consider the healthcare system as a whole and highlight two divergent models of understanding it: as a complex adaptive system (CAS) or as a deterministic one. Following this, we will discuss the core drivers of fallacy, which derail many analytical endeavors and about which informaticists must remain continually vigilant. Next, we will introduce some concept around missingness in data as an upstream concern. Finally, we will discuss a framework for selecting problems amenable to improvement, the use of which will help to prevent analytical effort from being deployed in futile circumstances.

7.2 Healthcare as a CAS

It is probably obvious to most that healthcare is complex but that observation is worth reiterating again here because it is still true, and perhaps truer for healthcare than for any other industry. That being said, a CAS is more than this just a system that is complicated. Many of the models for understanding healthcare operations assume a deterministic behavior. In other words, these models of thinking about healthcare consider the system and its operation as entirely—or almost entirely—predictable according to rules, which are time-invariant in both their state and their effect size. Necessarily, such models tend to consider the problem at hand in relative isolation from much of the broader context in which it resides. For example, we may be tempted to consider the rate of repeat blood draws within a particular unit as a target measure and we may therefore only consider the number of repeat events within that unit in our analysis. We may decide to deploy an intervention such as an alert within the medical record system notifying providers that they are about to place a repeat order and we may assess

An Introduction to Healthcare Informatics. https://doi.org/10.1016/B978-0-12-814915-7.00007-7

the impact of this intervention by considering the number of repeat blood draws both before and after its deployment. Tempting though this is, we must admit that this model of understanding is actually influenced by numerous factors, which are unaccounted for. In what units were these patients located both before and after that in which the number of repeat draws are tracked? If patients were coming onto the target unit from an ICU as opposed to a hospitalist floor, this may have a large impact on whether the team is likely to order repeat tests. Can we say that a decline in repeat events is purely the result of our alert intervention or is it also driven by the patient's acuity level, provider, and medical history? It turns out that we can keep unraveling these questions into more questions and yet more questions without an obvious end. The realization that this is so is a core tenet of a complexity-based understanding of healthcare.

A CAS is a system that comprises interconnected and diverse components, which have nonlinear effects on one another. To unpack this further, "complex" here means that those components are both heterogeneous and numerous, "system" means that they are highly interconnected, and "adaptive" means that the interconnected system is capable of change. The components of a CAS are independent agents such as a provider or a patient each of whom acts according to his or her own local knowledge and conditions. Importantly, the behavior of these agents is not centrally controlled. While perhaps foreign to some students of management or systems design, this concept is likely familiar to many in healthcare who have confronted examples of many biological CASs such as jungle ecosystems, immune systems, and bacterial colonies. Another important property of CASs is that connections between components often represent bidirectional influence wherein components both influence and are influenced by those to which they are connected such that is difficult to identify exactly where the chain of influence within a CAS starts or ends. Adding further to this definition is the fact that, in healthcare as with many other circumstances, components within a CAS—such as an individual doctor—are also CASs themselves inasmuch as they comprise a system of interconnected tissues, cells, beliefs, experiences, and so forth. One of the important tenets of the CAS model of thinking is that such systems are not the effect of comprehensive, detailed, top-down planning but rather the complexity is an emergent property, which arises in the backdrop of fewer and simpler initial rules. This may seem contradictory or even impossible, but this sort of emergent complexity is actually demonstrable. One of the most compelling examples of this is known as the "cellular automaton," which is a mathematical simulation wherein a grid of colored cells evolves over successive iterations according to a limited set of rules, which color each cell based upon the color of its neighboring cells. One might be tempted to assume that simple rules such as "if the cell directly above is black but the cells directly on either side are white, turn this cell black" would inevitably lead to repeated, predictable, and likewise simple patterns. However, the cellular automaton is capable of giving rise to unpredictable and highly irregular patterns as shown in Fig. 7.1.

What can we learn from cellular automata and how are CASs useful? Understand that CASs are a metaphor in the domain of complexity science and that this domain is not as mature as other

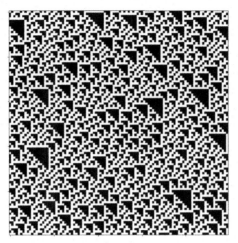

Fig. 7.1
Example automaton showing a complex, nonrepeating pattern of *black* and *white* cells surprisingly generated by a consistent set of simple initial rules.

scientific fields. Thus, the future may hold new axioms, observations, and tools for understanding CASs, which are not currently available. Nonetheless, we can extract a very important and practical lesson from them at present, which is that if we are interested in analyzing real phenomena to substantiate real and effective interventions, we should look first for evidence of core behavioral rules. Often, analytics are used simply to report on present phenomena much like describing the irregular patterns in the cellular automaton as they exist in the grid. Unfortunately, in a CAS such as healthcare, this task is both practically unfeasible to do comprehensively and, worse, it is of limited use as knowing the present state of the automaton does not equate to knowing the rules by which is arose. Given the breakdown between the state of the organization and the drivers that make it so, there is a need for analyses, which can identify and explore those drivers rather than their artifacts. Thus, the virtues of analysis in the healthcare context could be enumerated as simplicity, efficiency, and relevance.

Simplicity recognizes the fact that, as incredibly complex systems, healthcare organizations have countless phenomena to measure. Thus, the goal of analysis cannot be to describe all of the specific phenomena that happen within an organization. This might seem obvious, but it is a deceptively easy trap to fall into. Consider the simple example of a single operating room where the goal is to capture and assess data so as to ensure optimum performance and throughput of the OR facility. We could measure the time patients spend in an operation, the number of doctors in the operating room, or the number of surgical instruments used just to name a few. If we think about this problem, however, several additional questions come to mind such as which minutes of the operation are spent on which phases (preop checklist, intraoperative time, closing time, etc.), how many custodial staff are required to clean the room and prepare it for the next operation, and which blood products are required by operations. Iterating over this question again, we can think of yet more questions still which derive from the questions we just asked such as the ratio among used blood products of packed red blood cells versus fresh frozen plasma (which takes longer to prepare). The point is that we can easily become lost in an endless recursion of questions which beget more questions which beget more questions and so forth until we end up chasing a seemingly endless menu of measurements without actually organizing those measurements for some analytical purpose. This phenomenon is farcically described in Lewis Carroll's "Sylvie and Bruno Concluded," which describes the art of map making as improving upon pocket-sized maps to resemble the mapped territory in more and more detail with the ultimate achievement being a map, which resembles its territory at the scale of one to one. The punch line is that, because that map is itself the size of the entire country it depicts, it has never been unfolded. We cannot measure everything and we should not attempt to do so. Instead, like a map, we must abstract enough to distinguish important landmarks from unimportant milieu. This in the process of measuring OR throughput, we simply cannot put a number on all of the measurements we can enumerate, we have to measure some things and not others.

Efficiency extends the notion of simplicity to recognize the fact that those things we do choose should be calculable and recalculable without unnecessary complexity, cost, or time requirements. A great embodiment of efficiency in this sense of the "Pareto principle," also known as the "80/20" rule, which states that for many events roughly 80% of the effect is attributable to only 20% of the causes. In the case of the OR example, we may be interested in knowing which types of surgical cases or which surgical teams run over their scheduled intraoperative time. Moreover, we may also note that there are potentially hundreds of procedure types in our database some of which are only very rarely practiced (e.g., a hemipelvectomy, although complex, is must less common than a total knee arthroplasty). Should we really calculate and attempt to track and present the mean OR time vs predicted OR time for every one of these procedures? Likely not. Instead, we would benefit from applying the Pareto principle and looking for only those procedure types, which account for the majority of OR traffic. This makes it easier to organize and compute OR procedure reports and, even more importantly, it streamlines the discussions around the data as there are clearly core outliers and drivers on which to focus.

Finally, relevance describes the fact that what we measure must be guided by a motivating goal or problem and, thus what we consider in analysis should be that which allows us to assess and improve progress toward those overall goals. Considering again the example of OR throughput, the simplified set of measurements should be those which would identify drivers of decreased throughout and which would be amenable to some intervention aimed at improvement. For example, identifying the most commonly used intraoperative fluids (e.g., normal saline versus lactated Ringer's) would do little to describe throughput or to provide a foothold for its improvement. However, identifying the most common procedures performed is more relevant as we may be able to enhance throughput by consolidating certain case types to specific ORs. Thus, armed with the tenets of simplicity, efficiency, and relevance, we can focus the efforts of data engineering and analysis and identify targets ripe for impacting actual change.

7.3 Drivers of fallacy: Chance and bias

We have talked thus far about healthcare's complexity and we have enumerated the core virtues of analysis. Now we will shift our discussion to the drivers of fallacy, which often work to make simple, efficient, and relevant measurements incorrect. Being aware of these drivers will allow us to identify, remediate, and even prevent them, improving the trustworthiness of analytical results.

Chance can be summarized as the randomness of a given attribute. We commonly use chance to consider things like "what is the chance that I will get a two if I roll this dice?" but what we are really asking is, of all of the outcomes I would possibly expect to have from rolling a dice, how often would it be that the outcome is two? This might seem trivial, but it has some pretty serious implications. Imagine something as simple as assessing the use of imaging in an emergency department. When we consider data from our hospital, what we are actually considering is a subset—a sample—of all of the people who could have come to our hospital's emergency department and the imaging which was performed on those patients. Say, for example, that we draw a conclusion about the use of imaging such as "10% of the head CTs ordered in the Emergency Department are unnecessary" that is averaged over some bounded, 3-month time period. If we expand that time period to 18 months, however, we may see that the 3 months we had considered actually all had a higher-than-average rate of inappropriate head CTs being ordered. Upon further investigation, we may also discover that the 3-month period we had examined overlapped with the onboarding of new residents but that the monthly average rate of inappropriate head CTs both before and since that time is actually 5%. This highlights one of the incredibly challenging things about chance which is that we unavoidably work with some sample of data from the world and we must extrapolate from that sample to reason about data which we have not sampled.

Chance also plays an important role when assessing the difference in some value between two or more groups. For example, imagine we deploy new screensavers and employee education modules encouraging use of hand sanitizers and we wish to assess the rate of sanitizer use between units which received the training material and notifications and those who did not. We may turn to measures of significance such as P-values and credible intervals when trying to determine whether there is a legitimate intergroup difference. Importantly, these measures determine "statistical significance" by establishing a chance that—if there really was no difference between populations—then samples as divergent or more divergent than the observed group samples would be obtained by random chance. Thus, a P-value of 0.05, which is a commonly used threshold for significance, means that there is only a 5% chance that the two group samples would be obtained by chance alone, but it is not equivalent to saying that the observed group differences represent a real phenomenon, although it is often assumed that P-values have this meaning. Importantly, when comparing many events such as the difference in the rate of hand sanitizer use before and after deployment of an alert between all units, we increase the chance of stumbling upon "significant" P-values by chance alone, known as the false discovery rate. Thus, multiple comparisons should be corrected for the false discovery rate, conventionally resulting in "corrected" P-values or q-values.

Bias is likely a more familiar concept which simply means the data under consideration are recorded or handled in such a way that systematically alters its values. A particularly insidious example of this is known as "selection bias" wherein we define or access a patient population in a way that over- or underrepresents some patients. For example, imagine that we wish to measure the number of patients who report vaping and, although we have outpatient clinics located throughout the city, we are only unable to obtain data from any of the clinics located near our city's college campus. We can count the reports of vaping in the data we do have, but our selection excludes a highly relevant group without which our calculations are almost certainly off. Selection bias is especially important since it occurs so upstream and thus it cannot be remedied by analytical techniques; we simply lack necessary information. Another abundant form of bias is known as "information bias," which is introduced in the way in which data is recorded. Information bias is commonly encountered in diagnostic coding, where different groups may use different ICD-10 codes or more ICD-10 codes to describe similar patients, and especially in natural language processing where providers may document the same phenomena in different ways. As a result, care must be taken to understand when codes and terms are equivalent for the analytical question at hand and when documentation, coding, and other practices differ as a matter of local facility or unit practice rather than as a function of patient diagnosis.

7.4 Missingness

Of all the problems we may encounter when working with healthcare data, one of the most common and challenging is that of missing information. There are many reasons why data can be missing from analysis: certain tests may have associated LOINC codes (which we will discuss in subsequent chapters) while others do not, certain units may not respond to given questionnaire, or certain tables in a data warehouse may never have been mapped to upstream ETL processes. Moreover, many of the recorded events in healthcare occur at irregular and uneven time intervals where the recording of hematocrit, serum potassium, and blood pressure may all have different and uneven frequencies. Missingness can take several forms depending upon its cause. Data may be missing completely at random in which case we can simply ignore observations, which contain missing attributes because there is no correlation between missingness and the phenomena being analyzed. Unfortunately, data are rarely missing completely at random and instead either just "missing at random"—meaning that missing data can be inferred from what is not missing—or missing "not at random," which means that missing data are actually absent due to some reason, which we have not captured in the dataset.

Missingness is a broad topic and there are many potential techniques available for addressing missing values. Among them is "complete case analysis," which we described wherein observations with any missing values are simply ignored. Other common approaches include replacement of missing values with one of the aggregate measures of the nonmissing values such as the mean (otherwise known as "mean imputation"). Both of these approaches are problematic, however, because complete case analysis tends to ignore too much information while substitution with aggregate values tends to misrepresent the variance of the underlying data itself. More useful techniques include "sensitivity analysis," which is an empirical approach comparing related analyses where missing values are assumed to be different things. For example, if we were trying to assess the impact of a phlebotomy stewardship initiative by comparing the hematocrit values between patients in two separate units but 10 patients in each unit had missing hematocrit values, we might try our analysis once substituting the missing values with the minimum hematocrit and again substituting them with the maximum hematocrit. If a statistically significant difference in hematocrit between units is present in both analyses, then we know that our conclusions are not sensitive to missingness in our dataset.

Finally, we may handle missing values using more advances imputation techniques such as "single imputation," "stochastic imputation," or "multiple imputation." To review, the goals when performing analysis with missing data are to reduce bias, maximize the data available for computation, and preserve appropriate estimates of uncertainly about that data. In the case of single imputation, missing values are replaced after by regression to other values. We get more into the concept of regression in the next chapter but, in general, this technique can be described as follows. Imagine that we have a population of 100 patients but for 10 of them we have no recorded hematocrit value. Wishing to use hematocrit values in subsequent analyses, we attempt to populate those missing values by taking the hematocrit values we do have from the other 90 patients, estimating how those values correlate with some other nonmissing data such as patient age for those same 90 patients and then using that relationship to predict the 10 missing hematocrits using the age of those 10 patients. As shown in Fig. 7.2, this approach gives us unusually clean predicted values, which all exhibit a linear relationship to age and, since other predictive models cannot distinguish between which hematocrits were real versus imputed, it tends to overestimate the relationship between features and lead to unnaturally well-performing models, which don't hold up as well in reality.

Stochastic imputation attempts to preserve the notion of noise and variability even among predicted values by performing the regression as with single imputation but also by shifting each imputed point off of the regression line by a random amount, typically sampled from a normal distribution with zero mean and variance equal to that of the actual values as shown in Fig. 7.3.

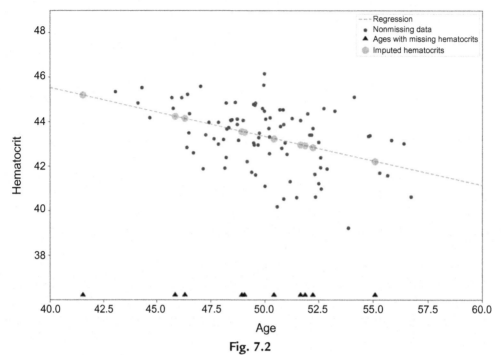

Fig. 7.2

Deterministic regression depicting imputation of 10 missing hematocrits [*in orange (light gray* in print version)] based upon a linear regression learned using the nonmissing ages and hematocrit values [*blue (gray* in print version)].

Finally, multiple imputation extends the notion of stochastic imputation where different random samples of the nonmissing data are used to perform multiple regressions and therefore multiple different predictions for the missing values. Following this, the missing value predictions for each separate regression are used in combination with the nonmissing values to calculate separate aggregate measurements for the hematocrit in this case. This results in multiple possible mean hematocrits each relying upon the substitution of missing values according to a regression performed on only a random snapshot of the nonmissing data. Finally, these multiple means are themselves averaged in order to provide a single predicted mean with an accompanying variance measure such as standard deviation capturing how variable the separate means were given separate regressions.

It is important to keep in mind that the purpose of imputing missing values is not to predict what those individual values are in reality but rather to correctly reproduce the variance within—and covariance between—values, which would exist if the data was complete. When doing imputation, it is important that the imputation model being used, such as regression in the situations we have discussed, includes the same variables as in our downstream predictive model that we wish to ultimately build. If, for example, we hope to predict a patient's serum potassium values using a model that looks at hematocrit, white blood cell count, age, and

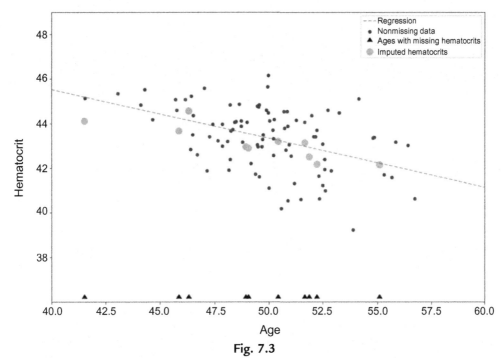

Fig. 7.3
Stochastic imputation wherein hematocrits imputed by linear regression are shifted by a random value from a normal distribution with zero mean and unit variance.

platelet count, then we should perform multiple imputation with hematocrit, white blood cell count, age, and platelet count. If, for example, we included age in our final predictive model but not in our imputation model, then every imputed hematocrit value would represent an assumption that hematocrit has zero correlation with age and, since we would use age in the final predictive model, this would make it more difficult for the model to learn relationships from the data because we have obscured them by adding several imputed values, which falsely under-represent their correlation with age.

7.5 Selecting tractable areas for intervention

Among the most challenging aspects of any healthcare data analysis project is determining whether the effort and idea is truly worth pursuing or whether it will turn out to be a waste of time. While there is way to know this with absolute certainty, the domain of implementation science has given rise to several frameworks for assessing feasibility and monitoring the effect if interventions. Although a comprehensive review of implementation science is certainly beyond the scope of this book, we will discuss framework popular for assessing potential threats and opportunities for larger organizational interventions in healthcare: the Consolidated Framework for Implementation Research (CFIR). As the name suggests, CFIR is a composite of several different frameworks consisting of five domains. First is that of the "intervention," which describes a proposed change in terms of whether that intervention is supported by external published examples or by the opinion of internal experts, whether stakeholders believe the intervention would be successful especially compared to other potential interventions under consideration, whether the intervention could be piloted before being deployed across the organization, and whether the intervention seems to entail higher costs than other options. As it relates to data engineering and analysis, interventions could be data products themselves, such as individual or unit performance reports, or they could be downstream opportunities, which require the creation and use of underlying data. In the latter case, CFIR may be useful in deciding where to deploy resources for constructing and validating data warehouses and data lakes according to whether potential downstream interventions seem tractable.

The second CFIR domain is that of the "outer setting," which considers the overarching financial, political, and economic environment surrounding an intervention. Third is the "inner setting," which considers local context in the form of organizational culture and readiness to change. Fourth are "individuals," which are the intervention stakeholders. Consideration of individuals involves understanding whether project members truly understand the planned intervention and whether they are invested in making the changes necessary to ensure its success. Finally, the fifth domain is the "implementation process," which concerns specific steps for executing a planned intervention such as engaging and training users. Each of these domains offers important upstream considerations for analytical projects and the framework as a whole is useful for because it forces a systematic assessment of potential pitfalls. As with any planning exercise, the real value comes with the discussion around the questions and their ability to encourage teams to investigate potential issues together. Although it is tempting to complete such inventories quickly by providing some answer to each question or consideration, team members—and especially team leaders—should be careful not to let this become a compulsory act.

7.6 Data and trust

In the final section of this book, we discuss the concept of data governance and we introduce the concept of data stewardship as a core component of governance frameworks. There, we focus on best practice considerations surrounding governance and provide some practical advice regarding delegating stewardship responsibilities. Here, however, we will discuss the abstract principle that motivates the data stewardship and governance more broadly. Simply put, data and analytical reports constitute claims about how the real world—the hospital or health system in the case of readers of this book—operates. If relevant, those claims will substantiate real decisions that impact patients, employees, and finances. Thus, presenting analytical information assumes a level of trust granted by the larger analytical team and the audience consuming analytical results. Demonstration that metrics are inaccurate will damage that trust after which is it is difficult to rebuild. Understanding that there is this relationship between data and trust should remain top of mind when designing and conducting analytical work.

7.7 Conclusion

This chapter marks a transition from a structural discussion about databases in the preceding section to a domain-specific discussion about methods of representing healthcare knowledge and activities. As we discuss the various complicated and sometimes unusual practices specific to healthcare data, it will become increasingly clear both how challenging it can be do achieve accurate measurement and clear analysis and how such efforts can require significant time and energy. You simply cannot measure, analyze, and impact everything that happens in a healthcare organization. Instead, you must choose what is important and what isn't, what is possible to do and what isn't and, once that selection is made, you must commit to leading the analytical team—and ultimately the broader clinical and operational teams—to make real changes based upon truthful information. This is not always easy, but it is not impossible. Armed with a healthy respect for the inevitable challenges of analytical work in healthcare and the importance of early planning, you will be well prepared to lead useful and impressive analytical projects worthy of impacting meaningful change in your organization.

Clinical and administrative workflows: Encounters, laboratory testing, clinical notes, and billing

8.1 Introduction

Up to this point, we have discussed the structure of data "in the wild" and outlined several considerations regarding how data are mechanically collected, organized, and stored. These are critical concept without which it is impossible to identify sources of data corruption, to estimate the feasibility of a potential project, or to construct and initiate a plan around a project, but these are not sufficient to make a successful medical informaticist. A theme, which we recurrently highlight throughout this book, is that of the difference between the ideal and the actual. In other words, the difference between what we assume data in a database means and what that actually represents. This was a key subject of the preceding chapter, but that discussion is extended here as we dive into specific workflows and organizational concepts that give rise to healthcare data. Even for those who work in a hospital, these processes may be mysterious as they are rarely laid out in any complete sense. Thus, the aim here is to impart an understanding of the "data-generating processes" in healthcare as these are critical to ensuring that a database, query, or resulting analysis actually represents what we hope and often assume they represent.

8.2 Encounters, patients, and episodes of care

We first begin with the core unit of patient care, the encounter. The encounter encapsulates an interaction between a patient and the medical facility and represents a variety of situations, including an outpatient visit, inpatient admission, emergency department visit, or more unusual types such as an "orders-only" encounter or an appointment as part of a research study. Understanding the type of encounter we are and are not interested in is important because they represent different levels of medical complexity and acuity and they operate under different billing rules. For example, in the United States, inpatient encounters are billed according to a pricing model based upon the patient's medical condition and overall level of complexity, while outpatient encounters are billed in an itemized fashion according to which test and procedures were performed. It is typical in a healthcare data warehouse to have a column representing the encounter type of a given patient, which either explicitly states the type of encounter or serves as a foreign key to a table, which contains that information.

Equally important is that medical record systems associate each encounter with a unique identifier, sometimes referred to as a contact serial number (CSN) or encounter ID. For any given patient, it is likely that she will have many CSNs each referring to a specific medical appointment or hospital stay. Fortunately, these CSNs are also typically associated with a relevant encounter-defining timestamp such as a visit date or admit date into the hospital. Thus, it is possible to time order encounters for a given patient. You may have noticed that we keep saying "patient" as opposed to "medical record number," (MRN) which you may rightfully assume equates to a unique patient. Unfortunately, this is not always the case. Certainly, the purpose of the MRN is to serve as a unique patient identifier within a medical record system, but the boundaries delimiting where one medical record system ends and another begins are increasingly blurred as hospitals and clinics merge into larger health systems. In practice, institutions typically use a secondary patient identifier known as an "Enterprise Master Patient ID" (EMPI) in which the various MRNs in different medical record systems belonging to a single patient are rolled up into one master label. This proves to be quite important as patients often have encounters at separate medical facilities as exemplified in the case of pregnancy and childbirth where a patient may have an outpatient visit at one clinic, a lab draw visit at another facility, an inpatient admission for labor and delivery, and a postpartum appointment at another outpatient clinic. If queries regarding this patient were restricted to a site-specific MRN, critical pieces of the clinical dataset may be absent. Thus, there is an important association between CSNs, MRNs, and EMPIs such that one EMPI represents one or more MRNs each of which may have one or more relevant CSNs. Fig. 8.1 depicts this association.

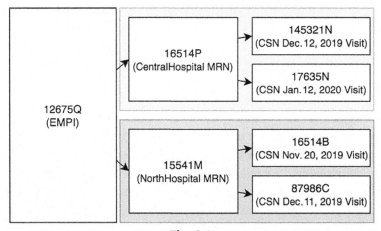

Fig. 8.1
Hierarchical association between EMPI, MRN, and CSN as shown linking encounters for the same patient at two different hospitals, CentralHospital and NorthHospital.

There is certain to be institutional variation between different medical centers, but this abstraction is a useful one and broadly applicable. There are some circumstances where certain queries or analysts prefer to use the hospital account as a means of identifying individual patients, but there are a few words of caution regarding that practice. First of all, hospital accounts—as we will discuss at greater length in the billing section of this chapter—are typically created for inpatient encounters but are often not generated for outpatient encounters. Moreover, while they are unique, they are usually assigned after patient registration and may be reassigned if, for example, a patient was erroneously registered under the wrong name or demographic information and needs to be re-registered. This is understandable because the hospital account number serves a dual purpose of identifying a patient while also linking that patient to a billing vehicle while the CSN simply exists to enumerate patient encounter and, as such, typically is not reassigned and is often automatically generated when a patient presents to the hospital or clinic and a visit is created even before they are registered.

During an inpatient hospital stay, many things happen and many different teams may collaborate in patient care. While this might seem to be one large encounter, it is not uncommon that this be structured as a group of related encounters within the medical record system. For example, we may have a patient admitted for an exacerbation of congestive heart failure during which time the physical medicine and rehabilitation (PM&R) team visits the patient, performs an evaluation, and makes plans. In such a circumstance, PM&R's assessment of the patient may qualify as an encounter, which happened during and overarching hospital encounter. Healthcare systems may do this to make it easier to track services and costs generated by teams that perform inpatient consults or which serve as common entry points from which patients are admitted to the hospital. Mechanically, this involves designating such groups as hospital outpatient departments, thereby granting them the ability to perform hospital outpatient visits. This is important to understand when trying to piece together the events of a patient encounter as a CSN for an entire inpatient stay may contain hospital outpatient visit CSNs representing times when consulting groups assess a patient during her stay. Various potential methods exist for associating these CSNs, which include marrying them to the same hospital account or date of service.

Finally, there is another useful concept known as the "episode of care," which represents a group of encounters which are typically related to the same medical problem, although the exact criteria for relating encounters are flexible. An example of an episode of care would be the visits related to pregnancy and childbirth mentioned earlier encompassing prenatal visits, inpatient delivery, and postpartum visits. The specific implementation details vary by record system but knowing what episode groupings are performed in your organization can be a powerful tool to efficiently collect relevant patient encounters. Moreover, if there is a specific interest in a clinical condition, which does not currently represent an episode of care, it may be possible to designate it as such.

8.3 Laboratory testing, imaging, and medication administration

During a patient encounter, clinicians most often place orders for various measurements such as laboratory tests and radiology imaging assessment and interventions such as medications or procedures. We will start by considering the laboratory testing workflow and then extend this concept to these other circumstances. When patient appears for a visit, an encounter and corresponding CSN are generated. Within the course of this encounter, suspected diagnoses motivate the selection of certain laboratory tests, which begin as orders. Within many record systems, there is a module known as the Computerized Provider Order Entry (CPOE) system, the purpose of which is to allow clinicians to select from among a menu of possible tests and initiate one on a particular patient in the form of an order. Orders are typically created within the context of a specific patient encounter and, as such, are associated with a given CSN representing that encounter. Moreover, each order typically has a unique order id and a collection of related timestamps representing key steps along the order-test-result workflow. When an order is first written, the initial order entry timestamp is recorded and typically appears in a table with the data warehouse along with a given order id. This is a useful timestamp to know because it is particularly relevant to certain questions such as "what was the first test ordered on this patient?" or "are separate providers placing duplicate orders for the same patient?" Equally important, the order time is a critical boundary on the overall laboratory testing lifecycle, which extends from the time an order for a test is entered to the time the result of that test reported into the patient chart. Orders also bear another important consideration. In most medical facilities—especially those with teaching programs—patient care is guided by an attending physician, the top-ranking clinician, but implemented by residents and interns operating under the attending. As such orders typically have more than one associated author: the ordering provider (typically the Resident or Intern who authored or "placed" the order) and the authorizing provider (typically the attending who approved or "signed off" on the order) and we may preferentially consider one of these more than the other depending upon the question at hand. For example, if we want to identify people who place orders for serum sodium measurements using the wrong test name we likely want to identify the resident who actually wrote the order but if we want to identify drivers of inappropriate testing, we may rather care about the attending who is often ultimately guiding the team on the diagnostic process and desired tests.

Now we can dive deeper into the laboratory testing workflow itself. When a clinician places an order, the order contains specific information regarding the desired test and level of urgency. For example, a physician places a STAT order for a basic metabolic panel. Importantly, many tests contain multiple components each of which refers to a specific itemized measurement. In the case of the basic metabolic panel, this test contains seven components: sodium, potassium, chloride, bicarbonate, blood urea nitrogen, creatinine, and glucose. Once placed, orders are transferred to the laboratory information system (LIS) typically as an HL7 message at which point it sits in a queue of unresulted tests within the laboratory. Initially thee unresulted tests refer to both the intended assay (e.g., basic metabolic panel) and the type of material on which that test is run (e.g., peripheral blood). Thus, the submission of these orders to the lab generates an unfulfilled request for the collection of a specimen upon which the test will be run. These requests are then routed to a work queue for a nurse or phlebotomist who then initiates specimen collection by printing a label typically containing the patient's identifying information as well as a unique identifier known as an accession number, which denoted each particular test-specimen combination. The printed label is then affixed to a container such as a serum separator tube or urine cup and the specimen is collected from the target patient into the container marked with the appropriate label. Finally, the labeled tubes are sent to the laboratory, which receives the specimens by joining their accession numbers with the corresponding unfulfilled test order and then running the desired testing. Finally, when test results are generated, they are filed within the medical record under the appropriate test name for the patient and the order-result loop is complete. As a side note, it is not uncommon for laboratory test results to be accompanied by explanatory test called "result comments" which may indicate abnormalities or offer interpretive guidance.

Unsurprisingly, this process generates several timestamped events: the order time, specimen collection time, received time within the laboratory, and test resulted time, including, in some cases, other even more specific events such as when the specimen label was printed or when the test result information was sent to the patient's medical record. In most contemporary cases, this process is mediated by direct messaging between electronic components of the medical record system as they are "interfaced" to exchange orders and results between one another. This aids in the process of tracking the granular timestamps of this workflow so that they can be loaded into an analytical data warehouse. In some circumstances, however, elements of this process may still be performed on paper as is the case, for example, when laboratories accept test orders through paper forms rather than computerized entry. To the extent that timestamps are electronically recorded and provided in a dataset, understanding this process makes it possible to organize the events across the timeline of test ordering, collection, and completion.

Certain unique cases may arise though. One example of this is the presence of laboratory tests, which seem to have no corresponding patient with a chart in the medical record system. This typically happens when laboratories provide testing services for outside institutions like nursing homes or urgent care centers, which are able to order tests and provide patient specimens to the lab purely for the service of testing and without the patient being tested being within the medical system. In some circumstances, these outside patients may have a placeholder medical chart or they may not depending upon specific configuration details. A second interesting edge case occurs with paradoxical timestamps such as a specimen collection timestamp, which occurs before a label-printing timestamp. Such a case could be explained by a relatively common shortcut whereby several patients are collected and then labels are printed and attached as a means of saving time. This is a frowned-upon practice because it opens up the possibility for specimen mislabeling, but it occurs nonetheless. Third, there is the case where an order lacks a corresponding result, which may be caused by the cancelation of a test and, fourth, there may be certain test results whose timestamps indicate that they were resulted and reported significantly later than other test results on the same specimen, which can be seen in the case of "add-on" tests. As with anything, tactical choices around query design are motivated by the question at hand. If, for example, we are looking to understand the average creatinine result for patients with diabetes, we would look for the result values as unresulted orders would be entirely unhelpful but if we were looking to assess which tests physicians typically think of when managing a trauma patient, we may rather consider orders even if those orders were eventually canceled at a later time. As an additional point, test orders may be canceled for categorically different reasons. For example, the ordering clinician may cancel a test because she believes it is no longer needed or, alternatively, the laboratory may cancel a test because it was delivered to the lab in the wrong tube, without appropriate labeling, or in insufficient quantity necessary to run the test. Many data warehouses will denote these reasons for cancelation both categorically (e.g., "wrong container," "missing patient id," or "quantity not sufficient") and with additional free text commentary providing additional information regarding reasons for cancelation. These may be particularly valuable for analytical questions concerning quality and consistency of blood draws or sample handling.

Imaging is similar in the sense that it follows an order-fulfillment cycle, but it bears a few important differences. First among these is the fact that imaging analyses typically require the patient to go to a specific location within the hospital. Therefore, when a clinician places an order for an imaging study, selecting from among a menu of possible imaging procedures they wish to have performed on their patient, this also typically creates an imaging appointment, which encapsulates the interaction between the patient and the radiology imaging equipment, which, in addition to running the imaging machinery itself, may also include patient premedication, performance of a biopsy, or placement of a central line. These appointments are a form of encounter and typically generate their own CSNs, which can occur amid a broader CSN representing a patient's hospital stay. As with laboratory testing, certain abnormalities may exist such as when an imaging order exists without a corresponding appointment resulting from a cancelation. This case is of particular relevance to imaging as it is fairly common to monitor the rate of executed versus canceled assessments for purposes of reducing unnecessary cost. Compared to the laboratory, radiologists have a more direct involvement in the completion of orders. Clinicians therefore typically order an imaging procedure such as a noncontrast head CT, which is transferred to the radiology information system (RIS), where it becomes a collection of specific imaging exams on a work queue to be performed by a radiology technician. These might include the specific images to be captured and machine settings to be used. Finally, when the exam is performed, it is packaged up into a study to be reviewed by a radiologist who composes an interpretation explaining the findings and clinical meaning of the images.

Lastly, we turn to the process of medication ordering and administration. As with both laboratory tests and imaging studies, the process begins with an order placed by a clinician. Placement of this order then typically results in the appearance of the medication in the medication administration record (MAR) according to the order details (e.g., give once STAT or give three times per day for 5 days' routine). Once in the MAR, the medication orders become scheduled medication administration instructions to be completed by nursing. Medication orders also appear in the pharmacy so that pharmacy personnel can prepare the requested medication. Once the time comes to actually administer a medication dose, the pharmacy then dispenses the scheduled dose to be received by nursing and administered to the patient. Note that this workflow describes the typical case for inpatients. For outpatients, there isn't an MAR and several medication doses are dispensed directly to patients instead. Each of these medication dispensing events is often recorded with a timestamp in the medical record system, including corresponding timestamps denoting when the clinical unit received the dispensed medication and when the medication was administered to the patient.

8.4 Clinical notes and documentation

Clinical notes are a treasure trove of valuable information about patients, but their interpretation warrants a few important considerations. First, clinical notes are represented often by unstructured free text, which makes them a challenging target for computational phenotyping algorithms, as we will discuss in a later chapter. As such, it is more typical that patient information be collected using more discrete attributes such as lab values, encounters, and coded problem, and diagnosis codes and that free text clinical notes be subsequently gathered from patients matched by those criteria after which they may undergo more customized analysis. Nonetheless, clinical notes are the structural backbone of the medical record and represent a time-ordered series of documents authored by all members of the medical team, including physicians, nurses, technicians, and consulting services. As with test orders, clinical notes typically have a tiered system of authorization where trainees may draft the initial note while the attending physicians sign off on the note as accurate. Moreover, in many medical record systems notes can be comprehensively grouped by encounter or divided into subgroups according to time, author, clinical service (e.g., surgery or internal medicine), or note type. The exact taxonomy of note types differs from institution to institution, but there are still meaningful general categories. For example, outpatient visits may contain one encounter with one "clinic note" written by the physician. Inpatient encounters, on the other hand, typically start with a comprehensive report of the patient's initial reported symptoms, medical history, and diagnostic findings in the form of a "history and physical" (H&P) note followed by daily progress notes written by the clinical team managing the patient and concluding with a discharge summary, which provides an overview of the patient's diagnosis, hospital course, and next steps after discharge from the hospital. When other services, such as PM&R, are asked to visit admitted patients, they may write their own consult notes filed into the patient's chart or—if following the patient over multiple days—they may write their own daily progress notes on the patient.

Among the important considerations around working with medical notes are the fact that many notes are a hybrid of manually and programmatically authored information. This is driven by a few factors one of which is convenience and efficiency of the medical staff, but another important driver is that of billing, which relies upon the notes as a key source of documentation by which to tally medications, procedures, and findings from a patient for the purpose of submitting claims to insurance. As a result, a typical medical note adheres to a certain structure known as the "SOAP" format denoting four primary sections. The first is the subjective information such as how the patient appears to be doing, what symptoms they report, and what medical conditions they have. The second is the objective information such as the most recent laboratory values, medications, and vital signs at the time the note was authored—these are typically autofilled by the medical record system—and the physical examination. The third is the assessment, which includes the possible diagnosis the patient may have, and an explanation of how the subjective and objective information supports or refutes certain diagnosis and the fourth is the plan, which includes the next steps in management and desired tests or consults along with their rationale. This can make medical notes quite long and, for any given analytical question, useful only with regard to certain parts. Lastly, the practice around clinical documentation is quite time consuming for clinicians and with increasing pressure to see more and more patients without compromising the detail of the clinical note, it is common to see elements of the note copied from previous notes. This is called "copy forwarding" and it is typically seen when a patient has many successive progress notes over a clinical stay. For each progress note, the overall clinical picture may not have significantly changed and so the patient's history, their assessment, and even their plan, may be copied from the prior day. This can become an issue when certain changes in the clinical picture are uncaptured because the prior day's assessment or plan was copy forwarded into the current day. This could happen, for example, when the clinical team begins to expect a pulmonary embolism overnight in a patient and is preoccupied with working up that condition. In such a circumstance, the note may not mention a pulmonary embolism but may have been filed at the same time as an order for a CT scan or heparin or as a consult from the pulmonary service. When selecting notes from multiple patients, it may be useful to quantity the presence and prevalence of copy-forwarding by looking for identical phrases between consecutive notes. Ultimately, however, understanding notes requires knowing the workflow of documentation and applying methodical critical thinking to the note text between progress notes, consult notes, lab values, imaging, and other sources of information.

8.5 Billing

Finally, we discuss the high-level billing workflow. We stick to a more abstract discussion here because billing or "revenue cycle management" is a large and complex entity the details of which are primarily relevant only insofar as they impact the data we collect on patients. As we will discuss in our chapter on computational phenotyping, billing data can serve as a useful angle from which to identify relevant patients but are subject to their own specific forms of fragility. The billing process generally begins with the creation of an appointment and registration of a patient, generating a CSN, and a hospital account number. This is followed by an encounter over which various things are done to and for the patient and documented in the form of notes, tests, medications, and procedures. After these services are rendered, the encounter is "coded" meaning that specific diagnostic and procedural codes are applied to the chart based upon what was documented and these codes are ultimately bundled up into a claim for remuneration to insurance. From there, claims go into accounts receivable where they await payment before being closed out. The bills generated by a given hospital encounter fall into one of two categories: professional and institutional. Professional billing refers to work done by physicians such as test interpretation, procedures, and examination, whereas institutional billing refers to work done by hospitals such as use of rooms, equipment, laboratory, and radiology testing. The distinction between physician and institutional reflects the fact that, in many healthcare institutions, physicians are actually employed by a physician group, which has contracted with the facility to perform physician services.

If anything, this illustrates the fact that billing is driven by documentation and documentation is used by billing to apply items from certain terminology mapping and code sets. In addition to partially explaining why clinical notes may have verbose sections on medications, test results, and physical examinations, these also illustrate specific dimensions on which to describe patients. These include the diagnosis-related group (DRG), which serves as a summative category of the patient's overall ailment, the current procedural terminology (CPT) codes, which denote very specific procedures performed on patients, and the International Classification of Diseases and Related Health Problems (ICD), which denote specific medical conditions, including, in some case, causes and context surrounding those conditions. The strength of these labels is that they are almost always completed for a patient encounter, but the drawback is that they are not necessary applied for the purpose of imparting meaningful medical information, rather, they are often applied in combinations designed to maximize claim amount and likelihood of reimbursement. This is not to say that they are fraudulently applied, but it is to say that patients are complex and could potentially be coded and summarized in a number of different ways and the purpose of these coding and summarization approaches is generally not to facilitate your specific analytical project. Thus, these data—as with anything—must be considered as part of an ensemble of patient information and weighed in the context of other information and of the question at hand. For example, if we are interested in assessing the rates of intraoperative bleeding as it related to patient age, DRG codes would not be entirely helpful as "bled during surgery" is not a DRG. Moreover, there may be many specific diagnoses, which would prompt surgery and give rise to relevant patients. Instead, we may tackle this problem instead by looking at the procedure codes for a variety of surgeries or ICD codes for intraoperative bleeding such as 197.42 for "intraoperative hemorrhage." Even in this case, the ICD code may be of limited help to us depending upon our question because we may still be interested in patients with bleeding even if that bleeding was not significant enough to complicate the surgical procedure. As a result, we may just stick with CPT codes to find surgical patients and then examine the operative notes documenting the surgeries for those patients, looking for mentions of the estimated blood loss and the corresponding amount.

8.6 Conclusion

In this chapter, we have focused on some of the key workflows specific to the healthcare setting. By no means a comprehensive examination, many of these workflows are common and illustrative of general strengths and weaknesses in healthcare delivery and its documentation. As such, knowing these workflows is absolutely necessary to making sense of data once collected and in being methodical about which tables and columns to consider in pursuit of a specific analysis. Hopefully, this chapter has highlighted the medical informaticist's intersectional job between quantitative and qualitative domains understanding how to gather information but also how to approach it. This knowledge of healthcare workflow is of particular use because data warehouses often contain cryptically labeled columns and tables and generally lack robust documentation regarding the intended or possible uses of their attributes.

CHAPTER 9

HL-7, clinical documentation architecture, and FHIR

9.1 Introduction

As we introduced in Chapter 1, healthcare systems often exist as a federated collection of separate, more narrowly focused modules (e.g., laboratory information systems, radiology information systems, clinical documentation systems), which constantly communicate between one another. As a result, almost all data within a healthcare system exist at some point in a transmission format. In this chapter, we will discuss common transmission formats, HL7v2 and FHIR as well as HL7v3 and the clinical document architecture, which puts forth a standard representative schema for patient medical data in support of interoperable exchange. The chapter concludes with a contextual statement about how hospitals use these standards and compares them to more newly emergent commercial products which aim to enhance data interoperability and standardization as well.

9.2 HL7 and HL7v2

The health level 7 standard was introduced in Chapter 1 as a messaging format to support standard communication between healthcare applications at the application layer of the OSI model. Here, we will dive deeper into the standard itself and how specific messages are formed according to it. We will begin our discussion with a focus on a specific messaging standard authored by HL7 known as HL7v2, which is widely prevalent to this day and is colloquially what is often meant by the term "HL7 message." First, though, let us consider a functional example of an HL7v2 message as it might convey and impact data of interest. Imagine a patient presents to the emergency department under suspicion of a heart attack and the triage nurse places an initial order for troponin laboratory testing. Already we have relied upon HL7v2 messages at several key points, including the conveyance of the patient's arrival from the registration system to the emergency department's clinical system, the movement of the patient from ED waiting to ED evaluation within the clinical system, the transmission of an order to the laboratory and several others. We may have a very practical interest in the content of these messages depending upon our analytical question. For example, if we wanted to monitor the presentation of patients to the emergency department who might be having a heart attack and we wished to do so in real time, then we may not be able

An Introduction to Healthcare Informatics. https://doi.org/10.1016/B978-0-12-814915-7.00009-0

to wait until data are transformed and loaded into a data warehouse as this typically occurs one or more days following the clinical activity. Instead, we may want to process the data immediately as they are generated meaning that we may have to work with streams of HL7v2 messages. With that in mind, we consider the structure of a prototypical message.

Continuing the example, as our patient presents to the ED, his registration results in the creation and transmission of a type of HL7v2 message known as an ADT or admit discharge transfer message. ADT messages are among the most common types of HL7v2 messages and are used to keep the various medical record components synchronized with regard to the status and location of patients.[1] ADT messages are generated in response to "trigger events" such as, in this case, patient registration but, in total, there are actually 51 different types of ADT message. Fig. 9.1 depicts what is known as an ADT A04 message for a patient John Smith in the HL7v2 format as would be triggered by patient registration.

Several things are notable about this message, but the first is that it is composed of a series of "segments," which cluster together groups of related information. Here we have five such segments, MSH, EVN, PID, PV1, and IN1. Each of these labels serves as a segment ID and the HL7v2 standard establishes a list of available segment IDs from which a message can be composed. Depending on the specific version and subversion of HL7 being used, the vocabulary of acceptable segments varies and consists of well over 100 possible types although not all IDs are required for any particular message. The four IDs used here are commonly encountered starting with the message header segment denoted by MSH. Within the MSH segment, for example, it is apparent that the segments themselves are divided into smaller pieces known as "fields," which are separated by a vertical pipe character and within which there are subfields further divided by a caret. For this reason, the HL7v2 message format is sometimes referred to as "pipe and hat" but, more specifically, this message format is known as the electronic data interchange or "EDI" and was developed in the late 1970s at a time when message size was a significant constraint for computer programs owing to disk size and bandwidth limitation. Thus, much like we saw with MUMPS, the design constraints of the

```
MSH|^~\&|NorthSystemRegistration|CentralHospital|NorthSystemED|CentralHospital|
20190812103030||ADT^A04|HL7MSG025146|P|2.3

EVN|A04|20190812103030||

PID|||257165||Smith^John^^^Mr.||19920714|M|||12 Cedar St.^^Boston^MA^02114^USA||
(123)456-7890||||||12345|123-45-6789

PV1||E|Main^745|||||^Mccaffrey^Peter|||ED|||||||||||||||||||||||||||||||||||||||||||20190812103030

IN1|1|PPO|25|ACME HEALTH INSURANCE|PO BOX 98777^^SOMEWHERE^TX^75230^|||15000321000001|ACME
SERVICES INC|19|ACME HEALTH INSURANCE|""|""||2|Smith^John^1|19920714|12 CEDAR
ST.^"""^BOSTON^MA^02114^""||||||||||||||||15243635|||||||1||M|123 WILLIAMS
RD^^WALTHAM^MA^02003|152456
```

Fig. 9.1
Example ADT message in HL7v2 format.

day demanded messages to be dense, which, in many cases, led them also to be somewhat inscrutable. Nonetheless, the general organization of an MSH segment is as follows:

```
MSH|encoding characters|sending application|sending facility|receiving
application|receiving facility|date and time of message|security|message
type|message id|processing id|version id
```

Notably, not all fields need to be populated within an HL7 message as exemplified by the places in the example where there are adjacent vertical pipes with no intervening text. To interpret our example message according to this schema, it would say that we have a message being sent from the North System Registration application located at Central Hospital to the North System ED application also located at Central Hospital being sent on 08-12-2019 at 10:30:30 with the unique message ID "HL7MSG025146" being used in Production ["P" denotes a production environment versus debugging ("D") or training ("T")] and this message adheres to the HL7v2.3 standard.

The EVN segment denotes the triggering event here being patient registration, represented by the code A04, and the event time being 08-12-2019 at 10:30:30. The following segments represent patient identification (PID), visit (PV1), and insurance (IN1) information and have many optional fields. In our example, the PID segment reads that the patient being registered is named John Smith, born 07-14-1992, is male, and has the listed home address, phone number, account number, and social security number. The PV1 segment reads that this is an emergency patient (patient class "E") being seen at the ED located at 745 Main, is being seen by Dr. Peter McCaffrey on the ED clinical team and that this encounter is happening at 08-12-2019 10:30:30. Lastly, the IN1 segment reads that this patient has a PPO insurance plan provided by ACME whose business address is in Somewhere, TX. Additionally, this message contains the patient's insurance group id (19) and the name of the insured policy holder (since this name is the patient's this indicates that the patient has his own insurance policy). Note that, within certain fields such as those representing the patient's name, the caret is used to divide first name, last name, prefix such as with "Smith^John^^Mr". Even here, there are adjacent carets with no intervening information because not all of these subfields are required. In HL7v2, the patient name field can, in fact accommodate the first name, last name, middle initial, suffix, and prefix, but here only three of these pieces of information are provided. This results in messages that can appear variably sparse and may sometimes have many repeated delimiting characters. Lastly, each segment within a message is delimited by a newline character. Some additional examples of common message types include ORU (for observations such as laboratory results) and ORM (for orders such as medications) messages.

The evolution of healthcare has complicated the HL7v2 messaging standard as it has tried to extend the scope of information that messages can contain. With a delimited formatting system such as that we see, the only feasible way to extend the standard is to add additional fields at the end of message segments, else the order of all fields will be offset and consequentially uninterpretable to the message recipient who relies upon an implicit agreement with the message sender regarding the number and order of sent fields. Thus, specific vendors and healthcare institutions who implement the HL7v2 standard would often "extend" the standard in just this way, by adding additional fields. This is largely why the HL7v2 standard has been referred to as a "nonstandard" standard because, although there is core guidance, it is often the case that any given hospital or software introduced specific idiosyncrasies in how messages are transmitted necessitating custom adaptation of the standard to each site and circumstance. The HL7v2 standard loosely accommodates this through the creation of a Z-segment, which is user-defined. However, as successive minor versions of HL7v2 (v2.3, v2.4, v2.5, and so on) have added a broad range of segment and message types, the use of the Z-segment is largely forbidden from contemporary implementations. Nonetheless, you may encounter it when looking at applications for which the message streams were implemented in the past.

The HL7v2 standard suffers from a few additional and more general obstacles. First, the standard's development was driven primarily by the needs of application interfacing and was conceived under a model of triggered notification. As such, HL7v2 does not attempt to consider the patient medical record as a whole nor does it attempt to encode context in the form of referencing additional information regarding the patient or event in question. Instead, HL7v2 messages are atomic transmissions, which push status throughout interconnected applications. This proved to be challenging for the development of a durable and robust standard because as the patient medical record grew to encompass more varied forms of information and as healthcare operations became more complex, the only way to codify these under a purely transmission-focused standard was to add more message types and segments. Consider the following scenario: suppose we develop a messaging standard at a time when all that exists are outpatient clinics and the only messages, which need to be sent, are patient registration and discharge messages between a note-taking system and a billing system. Because the messaging standard has no mappable relationship to foundational concepts such as patients, providers, and visits if we were to add a function to the workflow such as a patient transfer to a nearby hospital, we would have to create an additional message to represent that function. Moreover, the similarities between patient registration and transfer would not be apparent to the standard because there is no overarching concept of a patient encounter within which to place these related things. As a result, the standard grows in complexity and fragility over time

9.3 RIM, HL7v3, and clinical documentation architecture

Due to the fragility of HL7v2, the HL7 group took a step back with the v3 standard and developed the RIM or "reference information model." The RIM is a complex entity, but its purpose is foundational to HL7v3. The RIM is an ANSI- and ISO-approved standard, which aims to abstract the patient medical record into a consistent arrangement of related concepts, data types, and terminologies. The initial release of the RIM was the normative release 1, which contains four broad concepts at the top of its hierarchy: entities, roles, participations, and acts. The motivation behind this approach was to consider the medical record as a record of actions, which illustrate the diagnosis and care of patients. Under this conceptual model, an order is a form of action, as is the reporting of a test result, as is the creation of a diagnosis and assignment of a diagnostic label to a patient, as is the prescription and application of treatment to the patient. Thus, under the RIM, everything that happens is an act of some sort and these acts are tied to one another through Act Relationships. Participation exists to provide context for an Act such as the performer versus subject and the Roles provide depth to the participants such as physicians, patients, and even specimens. Roles may be related to one another through role links, which capture relationships such as employer-employee or consultant-primary physician. Finally, the roles are be fulfilled by entities such as people, materials, places, or devices. Consider the example of Dr. McCaffrey who may fulfill the role of a performing surgeon at North Regional Medical Center where he performs knee replacements but who also may fulfill the role of a patient at South Regional where he receives a knee replacement. Under the RIM, we can capture these relationships because we can capture the various roles and contexts in which entities relate to one another. One often perplexing aspect of the RIM is the existence of "mood" codes. Moods apply to actions by giving them certain forms of more subtle context. For example, a knee replacement may have happened, may be currently happening, may be intended to happen for a patient, or may have been requested to happen but not yet intended to actually occur. Each of these is a separate mood of the action. Thus, the RIM has, as its backbone, six main classes: entities, roles, participations, acts, act relationships, and role links as shown in Fig. 9.2.

While a useful foundation, the RIM itself cannot fully illustrate each messaging or documentation use case. Thus, following a hierarchical structure, the RIM serves as a modeling approach, which is further subset into specific domain message information models or D-MIMs, which includes classes, attributes, and relationships particular to a domain such as a medical record documenting clinical care or patient administration records documenting insurance and billing. Thus, while the RIM is universal in offering a descriptive model for all domains of healthcare, D-MIMs are a refined subset thereof meaning that any given D-MIM consists of the six classes defined by the RIM but includes a domain-specific set of particular things those classes can represent. One last related concept is that of the refined message information model or R-MIM, which is itself a subset of the D-MIM. Where the D-MIM describes elements and relationships for the data under a whole given domain, such as laboratory values, the R-MIM contains the classes, attributes, and relationships that are required to compose a specific set of messages or to create a specific set of documents. Fig. 9.3 depicts the RIM, D-MIM, and R-MIM relationship.

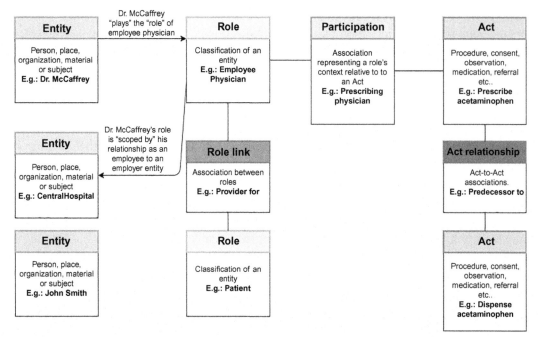

Fig. 9.2

Example relationships between RIM core classes in the context of medication prescription. Note that this example consists of only a subcomponent of a typically larger data model.

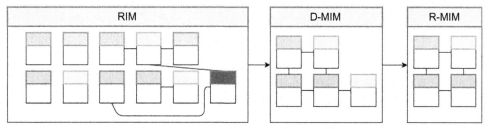

Fig. 9.3

RIM, D-MIM, and R-MIM relationship. Note that a given D-MIM is specified according to the larger RIM and a given R-MIM is specified within the D-MIM.

The most prevalent R-MIM model is the clinical document architecture or CDA, which became popular in large part due to its present among the requirements for meaningful use. It is quite likely that you will encounter the CDA when examining data from health information exchanges, hospital-to-hospital transfers, research studies, personal healthcare applications, and other scenarios so the structure and context are important to know. The CDA defines a broad structure for clinical documents that seeks to embody six core axioms: persistence, stewardship, authentication potential, context, wholeness, and human readability. In short, these requirements define clinical documents as collections of related medical information, which can reliably be obtained from a trusted data source (such as an EMR or HIE) and which serve as a record of medical information through time, existing in an unaltered state. The CDA is a rather sprawling standard, but the general structure consists of a few important anatomical components starting with a header, which includes at least the subject of the document, date of creation, the document author, and the custodian along with several additional optional elements such as the encounter, patient information, and orders. This establishes the context for information within the body of the CDA document. Importantly, if a CDA document contains information that replaces or appends to information contained within another CDA document, such as describing an encounter, which adds a medication to a patient's general medication list, then the header will also include a pointer to that other CDA document to which it refers. The header exists to provide context ultimately to a body, which contains the actual informational payload of the document, including diagnoses, clinical details, medications, and so forth. The information within the body may be presented as free text divided into sections and it may include coded items.

The HL7 standard defines three levels of the CDA, which differ in the extent to which they are constrained to a specific structure.[2] Level 1 is the least structured and often lacks the ability for its contents to be expressed with formal code sets. A patient note, which contains only free text information describing the presenting compliant and medical history, would be an example of a level 1 CDA. Level 2 adds the constraint that the document be broken up into sections, although the sections could themselves contain free text. A patient note with specific sections denoting "presenting compliant" versus "past medical history" would be an example of a level 2 CDA. Finally, level 3 adds entry constraints such that the content with sections is further divided into specific elements. Keeping with the patient note example, if the medical history section were further broken up into a collection of specific medical conditions, which were specifically enumerated within the past medical history section. Because the CDA standard is intentionally broad, the HL7 Group has also produced an implementation guide in the form of consolidated CDA (C-CDA), which describes how to use the CDA standard to generate 12 specific exemplary clinically relevant documents. Thus, the C-CDA puts forth document templates, which themselves are assemblies of smaller sectional templates. As mentioned here, you will likely encounter the CDA while examining data from certain repositories (such as HIEs), but this encounter will often take the form of specific C-CDA templates.

Now that we have covered RIM, D-MIM, R-MIM, CDA, and C-CDA in the abstract, we can discuss how such data are actually represented in practice. This highlights another important change made with the HL7v3 standard and that was the use of a markup language, specifically XML, to represent the information laid out in the RIM. XML stands for "extensible markup language" and its aim is to represent documents—groups of related values much like we discussed in the chapter on nonrelational databases—in a way that is both human- and machine-readable and which can convey both structural data as well as

```
...
<patient>
        <firstName>John</firstName>
        ...
</patient>

<provider>
        <firstName>Peter</firstName>
        ...
</provider>
...
```

Fig. 9.4

XML nesting of firstName tag showing both patient and provider contexts.

metadata. As such, XML describes documents in terms of values called "elements," which are placed between "tags." Tags can have customized names and typically provide dimensions of information to the elements with which they are associated. XML assumes a hierarchical document structure in which tags are nested within other tags providing contextual meaning. For example, in an XML document, I might have a tag called <firstName> (tags are typically denoted by chevron characters), which may rightfully appear in my document both to note the first name of the physician as well as the first name of the patient. The distinction between these two contexts would be encoded by the tags under which the <firstName> tag is nested as shown in Fig. 9.4.

To make this more concrete, let's return to the example of our patient presenting to the emergency department and let's imagine a serum troponin test was ordered. Within the RIM, the troponin test is the procedure, the patient John Smith is a participant who occupies the patient role and the person entity type, and the ED physician Peter McCaffrey is another form of participant in the role of ordering provider (i.e., "assignee"), while the laboratory technician Thomas Technician is yet another participant who is also an assignee in the role of test performer. An HL7v3 message would consider the action in this way and would result in an XML-encoded message as depicted in Fig. 9.5 with a comparable HL7v2 version depicted in Fig. 9.6.

What we see here is, strictly speaking, an HL7v3 message as opposed to a document. Fig. 9.7 depicts an excerpt of what a CDA-compliant clinical document would look like regarding a patient's troponin result.

When compared to HL7v2 messages, one immediately apparent strength of the XML format is its ability to be self-documenting. That is, a person or a computer program can infer the meaning of a value based upon its structural context within the message or document itself (e.g., we know "John" is a first name because it appears between firstName tags) rather than through referencing a separate set of standards. This makes messaging and document creation a far more robust process. An often-confusing aspect of the v3 standard is that it

```
<Message xmlns="urn:hl7-org:v3">
    <creation_time value="2020-01-15T09:30:00"/>
    <version_id>3.0</version_id>
    <ObservationEvent>
        <value xsi:type="dt:PQ" value="0.05" unit="ng/mL"/>
        <interpretation_cd code="H"/>
        <participant>
            <assignee_Person>
                <nm use="L" xsi:type="dt:PN">
                    <dt:family>Technician</dt:family>
                    <dt:given>Thomas</dt:given>
                    <dt:suffix qualifier="AC">MLT</dt:suffix>
                </nm>
            </assignee_Person>
        </participant>
        <patient>
            <patient_Person>
                <dt:family>Smith</dt:family>
                <dt:given>John</dt:given>
            </patient_Person>
        </patient>
        <inFulfillmentOf>
            <priorObservationOrder>
                <cd code="89579-7" codeSystemName="LN" displayName="Troponin-I"/>
                <participant>
                    <assignee_Person>
                        <nm use="L" xsi:type="dt:PN">
                            <dt:family>McCaffrey</dt:family>
                            <dt:given>Peter</dt:given>
                            <dt:given>C</dt:given>
                            <dt:suffix qualifier="AC">MD</dt:suffix>
                        </nm>
                    </assignee_Person>
                </participant>
            </priorObservationOrder>
        </inFulfillmentOf>
        <referenceRange>
            <referenceObservationEventCriterion>
                <value xsi:type="dt:IVL_PQ">
                    <dt:low value="0.0" unit="ng/mL"/>
                    <dt:high value="0.03" unit="ng/mL"/>
                </value>
            </referenceObservationEventCriterion>
        </referenceRange>
    </ObservationEvent>
</Message>
```

Fig. 9.5

HL7v3 XML message representing a serum troponin lab test order. Note that certain elements of the HL7v3 message have been removed for brevity.

```
MSH|^~\&|CH LAB|EDLAB-3|CH OE|BLDG4|202001150930||ORU^R01|CNTRL-3456|P|2.4

PID|||555-44-4444||SMITH^JOHN^^^^^|JONES|196203520|F|||153 FERN DR.^^SOMEWHERE^TX^35292||(206)3345232|(206)752-121||||AC555444444||67-
A4335^OH^20030520

OBR|1|845439^CH ED|1045813^CH LAB|10839-9^TROPONIN-I||202001150730||||||||555-55-5555^MCCAFFREY^PETER^C^^^^MD^^CENTRAL HOSPITAL||||||||F||||||
444-44-4444^TECHNICIAN^THOMAS^^^^MLT

OBX|1|SN|10839-9^TROPONIN-I^LN||0.05|ng/ml|0.0-0.03|H||H|F
```

Fig. 9.6

HL7v2 message representing a serum troponin lab test order.

```
<section>
    <entry>
        <organizer classCode="CLUSTER" moodCode="EVN">
            <templateId root="2.16.840.1.113883.10.20.22.4.1"/>
            <templateId root="2.16.840.1.113883.10.20.22.4.1" extension="2015-08-01"/>
            <id root="a4307cb2-b3b4-4f42-be03-1d9077376f4a"/>
            <code code="89579-7" displayName="Troponin I.Cardiac [Mass/Volume] In Serum Or Plasma" codeSystemName="LOINC">
                <originalText>
                    <reference value="#PanelName3" />
                </originalText>
            </code>
            <statusCode code="completed"/>
            <component>
                <observation classCode="OBS" moodCode="EVN">
                    <statusCode code="completed"/>
                    <effectiveTime value="20200115093000"/>
                    <value xsi:type="PQ" value="0.01" unit="ng/mL" />
                    <interpretationCode code="H" codeSystem="2.16.840.1.113883.5.83"/>
                    <referenceRange>
                        <observationRange>
                            <text>0.0-0.03 ng/mL</text>
                            <value xsi:type="IVL_PQ">
                                <low value="0.0" unit="ng/mL"/>
                                <high value="0.03" unit="ng/mL"/>
                            </value>
                            <interpretationCode code="H" codeSystem="2.16.840.1.113883.5.83"/>
                        </observationRange>
                    </referenceRange>
                </observation>
            </component>
        </organizer>
    </entry>
</section>
```

Fig. 9.7

Excerpt from C-CDA document containing a troponin result.

ambitiously puts forth a way to map healthcare data overall and by domain, adopts a markup format in which to represent that data, and supports the transmission of data adherent to both markup and model-based rules as either a clinical document or as a message. The CDA and corresponding C-CDAs are the most common manifestation of the HL7v3 standard and are appreciated for their wholeness and sense of context but, as we see in Fig. 9.5, it is wholly possible to have message transmissions, which adhere to the HL7v3 standard as well. As with our previous example wherein we are trying to detect in real time the presentation of patients suspected to be having a heart attack, we would have to consider parsing messages over clinical documents as messages serve the role of updating and synchronizing systems in support of an ongoing process. Moreover, the transmission of messages is instigated by trigger events such as the arrival and registration of a patients whether or not those messages are specifically compliant with HL7v2 or HL7v3.

Conversely, though, we may wish to consider all patients had presented to the ED over some timeframe and we may look outside of our own hospital's data warehouse to other facilities or health information exchanges in order to locate information describing those patients. In this situation, we are not interested in message feeds as much as in clinical documents. Moreover, documents, unlike messages, are not tightly coupled to actions but instead represent the state of medical information at the time of document creation rather than the event stream of requests, activities, and acknowledgments that gave rise to the state of medical data represented by the document. As a data engineer or analyst, you will often not be the one deciding how primary healthcare data are stored, but you will have to accommodate whichever format was chosen be it HLv2 or v3 messages, clinical documents, or other formats. You may have the option to transform and move that data into another, more analytically accessible format, which will still require decisions around whether and how to reformat messages as well as an understanding of the mappings necessary to perform those conversions sensibly. If anything, this chapter has thus far illustrated the complex evolution of messaging standards as they have been variably influenced by the computerization of healthcare and the historical obligations currently held by many healthcare record systems.

9.4 FHIR

At this point, you may be tempted to ask whether the problem of messaging is solved and what ultimately became of the HL7v3 standard. As is typical in software engineering, where an initial version of a tool might be lacking in important ways (e.g., HL7v2), the second version of that same tool tends to become overburdened with an attempt to fix everything the first version lacks. When this occurs, that second version can end up being overengineered and unnecessarily—even prohibitively—complex. This is largely the story of HL7v3, which, although it did give rise to certain durable and prevalent contributions such as C-CDA, was difficult to understand and apply by many of the application developers whose cooperation was essential for the standard to have meaning. Thus, in 2011, the HL7 Fresh Look Task Force set to reconsider interoperability standards taking strengths from both HL7v2 and v3. The resulting search for a more modern and resource-oriented way to think about health data and its exchange led to fast healthcare interoperability resources (FHIR), which is formally an HL7 project and in its fourth version at the time of this writing.

To understand FHIR, it is important to understand that the goal of its design was to adhere to what was, at the time, a well-established best-practice for server-client communication and one which was largely absent when HL7v2 and v3 were conceived. This meant communicating via HTTP, taking advantage of OAuth and SSL, and importantly for readers of this book, implementing a RESTful design. Representational state transfer (REST) is a design pattern for server-client communication in which data on the server are structurally divided into resources each of which has a unique location with a corresponding URL. Clients can access and operate upon resources through making requests over HTTP.[3] The ability to act on resources is constrained to a vocabulary of acceptable REST verbs, which are supported by the server. For example, when a client issues a GET request to a server with the URL: http://someserver.com/patients/123/medications, the server would return a list of medications for patient 123 in response, whereas a PUT request accompanied by information describing Tylenol, would add Tylenol to the list of medications for patient 123.

Resources in FHIR are narrower than whole clinical document and consist of lower-level abstraction such a patient, organization, location, or allergy. In practice, an FHIR resource bundles about the same amount of information as a segment in an HL7v2 message. Within a resource, data are broken down into four parts. The first is metadata, which contain data regarding the resource itself, such as its date of creation. Second is the narrative, which contains XHTML in order to support human readability. Third are extensions, which include information not formally defined as part of the resource, analogous to Z-segments in HL7v2, and fourth are the elements, which contain the actual structured data belonging to the resource. Each resource can be accessed in isolation or composed together to create documents if needed.

Here already one strength of FHIR over previous standards has emerged: it is designed with a focus on the server-client relationship and an understanding of the functional way in which users or applications would access and manipulate data. Moreover, REST is an extremely common design approach for such interaction, which means that FHIR gains from being understandable to a broad community of developers. Much as with HL7v3, the structure and interactions that describe a resource are different from the formats in which information about that resource are communicated. For this purpose, FHIR supports XML as well as JSON. JSON, or JavaScript Object Notation, is a very popular way to represent collections of related values as key-value pairs and is self-documenting much in the same way of XML. Fig. 9.8 depicts an FHIR resource as it could be viewed in JSON format.

```
{
  "resourceType": "Practitioner",
  "id": "example",
  ...
  "name": [
    {
      "use": "official",
      "family": "McCaffrey",
      "given": [
        "Peter"
      ]
    },
    {
      "use": "usual",
      "given": [
        "Pete"
      ]
    }
  ]
  ...
}
```

Fig. 9.8

Example JSON representation of a Practitioner FHIR resource.

9.5 DICOM

The subjects of this chapter are interoperability standards as they define the ways in which data should be structured to that senders and receivers can effectively communicate. The focus has been on standards concerning data in the form of text or descriptive numeric values. There is another medium often exchanged in the form of images as ultrasound, X-ray, CT, and MRI images are transmitted from radiology systems to clinical applications. Digital imaging and communications in medicine (DICOM) establishes a standard for image transmission organized into data sets, which bundle metadata tags and image pixel data together to ensure that images are not separated from key descriptions such as identifying information. A DICOM data set is a collection of elements such as patient name and MRN accompanied by one special element containing the pixel data for the transmitted image. Each element itself consist of four fields: an element tag, value representation, value length, and an actual value. Examples of element tags include imaging study date and patient name, which each have unique numeric tags. The value representation is a two-byte character string that describes the data type for a given element such as "PN" for person name and "DA" for date.[4] Value length simply describes the length of the corresponding value in bytes and serves as a sort of check digit to ensure complete transmission of the value field, which includes the actual value for the given element tag, which may include the pixel data for a transmitted image itself. Fig. 9.9 shows an example DICOM message, which includes a patient name and transmitted image pixels.

9.6 Vendor standards

Interoperability standards such as the ones developed by HL7 are ultimately only as real as their implementations, which means that developer, vendor, and hospital choice ultimately drive the structure and format of healthcare data. Realizing that many published standards were challenging for developers to understand and adhere to, several commercial offerings have emerged offering well-documented, stable APIs through which to access health record information. Moreover, these companies typically handle the challenges of mapping their

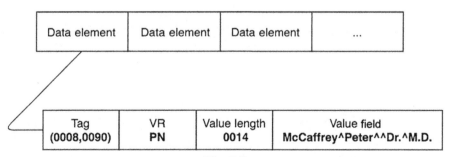

Fig. 9.9
Example DICOM message. Note that the tag (0008,0090) denotes the Referring Physician.

API onto the idiosyncrasies of a given hospital's medical record system, resulting in a more consolidated roll-out process after which subsequent interoperations are expedited through the vendor's own API. Redox and Datica are two such examples each of which have gained traction in healthcare by offering a uniquely understandable and developer-friendly interface in place of either nonuniform HL7v2 formatting or overly complex HL7v3. Importantly, these vendors still maintain FHIR compatibility alongside their own specific API implementations. In addition, many EHR vendors themselves have developed their own APIs with certain vendor-specific peculiarities. It is thus important to acknowledge that EHR APIs are not necessarily equivalent to FHIR and typically EHR APIs diverge in several important ways typically regarding the scope of transmitted data. For example, while FHIR would regard a patient and a patient's appointments as a resource to be served to a requesting client, EHR vendor APIs typically prefer more narrow request-response interactions. This makes sense when one considers the business goals and specific forms of interoperation that drive these APIs. It is beyond the scope of this book to delve into each of these offerings in detail, but it is important to understand that transmitted data may adhere to HL7 standards, vendor standards, or both and that each of these sources may offer documentation through which to understand the meaning of data transmitted through their platforms. While there are myriad ways in which a clinical document or clinical API may actually be implemented, support of modern self-documenting message formats such as XML and JSON makes it possible to investigate a message's internal structure even where documentation is sparse or unclear. Ultimately, however, recognize that this is not an easy task and there may be certain clinical extracts with unresolvable and unclear elements.

9.7 Cloud services

An exciting development, at the time of this writing, cloud vendors such as Google, Amazon, and Microsoft have announced support for both HL7v2 and FHIR as a means to transmit data into their various platforms, making it easier to expose transmitted healthcare data to the many data processing and analysis tools offered by each group. Later in this book, we will discuss some of these in greater detail, including big data tools many of which are offered as a managed service by these same cloud vendors. In approaching the challenges of creating scalable, manageable data ingestion pipelines, these interoperations provide immense value, allowing for reduced time spent on managing infrastructure and more time spent understanding data, which, as the preceding chapter illustrates, are nontrivial.

9.8 Conclusion

This chapter has focused on the complex domain of interoperability standards, healthcare messaging formats, and document architectures. Understanding these concepts is critical for many healthcare data engineering tasks that require analysis of real-time event streams or repositories of healthcare data. Armed with this understanding, there are now a few specific questions to ask when designing a data processing workflow, namely, are the data stored according to a specific HL7 or vendor standard and is there accompanying documentation of that standard, which would allow mapping event or record information to useful and pertinent fields. For example, knowing that a certain repository of information contains consolidated CDA documents such as clinical visit summaries makes it possible to map a large XML document to a specific standard structure and programmatically parse those documents according to the analytical question at hand. Where this chapter focuses on the structure and relationships between values in a message or document, in the next chapter, we will dive deeper into the values themselves and discuss several popular vocabularies, which are used to populate them.

References

1. Quinn J. An HL7 (Health Level Seven) overview. *J AHIMA*. 1999;70(7):32–34 [quiz 35–36].
2. Dolin RH, Alschuler L, Beebe C, et al. The HL7 clinical document architecture. *J Am Med Inform Assoc*. 2001;8 (6):552–569. https://doi.org/10.1136/jamia.2001.0080552.
3. Saripalle R, Runyan C, Russell M. Using HL7 FHIR to achieve interoperability in patient health record. *J Biomed Inform*. 2019;94. https://doi.org/10.1016/j.jbi.2019.103188.
4. DICOM PS3.17 2020b—Explanatory Information. The Association of Electrical Equipment and Medical Imaging Manufacturers (NEMA), 2020. http://dicom.nema.org/medical/dicom/current/output/pdf/part17.pdf.

CHAPTER 10

Ontologies, terminology mappings, and code sets

10.1 Introduction

We spent the last chapter discussing interoperability standards and the various formats in which data are structured for exchange between systems either as a triggered message, a document, or a resource. Now we will discuss the content that typically populates those messages and documents. Certain types of content are self-explanatory with a meaning that is consistently understood the same way such as a first name, last name, or age. Other types of content, such as a diagnoses, are not and could be described in numerous ways by different people using different systems. As healthcare deals with lots of nuanced content with varying interpretation, it relies upon the use of ontologies to standardize the use of certain vocabularies and to give those vocabularies a structure. Ontologies are simply a set of concepts within a subject domain, which captures both the properties of those concepts and the relationships between them. For example, an ontology for diagnoses would note that chronic kidney disease and CKD are equivalent, while acute kidney injury and AKI are equivalent. Moreover a diagnostic ontology would capture the fact that both CKD and AKI are related to one another through their relationship to the kidney but that they are not synonyms and also that proteinuria is a finding, which may occur as a symptom of CKD and AKI but that proteinuria may occur in other contexts as well. Healthcare has many ontologies and they are practically unavoidable in analyzing healthcare data.

10.2 Diagnostic ontologies: ICD and ICD-CM

At its highest level, the International Statistical Classification of Diseases and Related Health Problems (ICD) is an ontology of diagnostic and procedure terms developed by the World Health Organization to provide a globally standardized vocabulary for describing medical concepts for a broad range of purposes ranging from epidemiology to clinical operations.[1] It has gone through multiple revisions since its inception with the 9th (ICD-9) and 10th (ICD-10) revisions being of particular relevance to this book. ICD-9 encompasses approximately 13,000 "codes" service as shorthand for various medical concepts. These codes are grouped hierarchically first into chapters, which encompass broad clinical ideas such as "neoplasms" and further divided into sections such as "benign neoplasms." Within each section are codes

An Introduction to Healthcare Informatics. https://doi.org/10.1016/B978-0-12-814915-7.00010-7

such as "benign neoplasm of lip oral cavity and pharynx," which are finally subdivided to their terminal level of specificity such as, in this case, a specific anatomical site within the oral cavity: "benign neoplasm of the tongue." Fig. 10.1 depicts the ICD-9 code corresponding to this example and its hierarchical structure.

While ICD-9 was created as an international vocabulary, the classification has undergone various national "modifications," which tailor that vocabulary somewhat for particular regional needs. In the United States, the Centers for Medicare and Medicaid Services (CMS) oversees the "Clinical Modification" of ICD-9, known as ICD-9-CM, which was used as the standard and required language for describing and submitting claims for reimbursement by health insurance, and this is often what is meant by reference simply to "ICD-9" in the United States.[2] Since 2015, however, ICD-10 has replaced ICD-9 as the code set in several instances, including for the submission of medical billing claims. ICD-10 substantially expands upon ICD-9, reaching over 70,000 codes broadly divided into formal diagnosis (ICD-10-CM) and procedural (ICD-10-PCS, "Procedure Coding System") code set modifications, both of which are overseen by CMS. Thus, many clinical repositories containing data generated through enterprise medical record systems will contain ICD-10-CM and PCS codes.

It is important to understand that ICD-10 is not simply an update to ICD-9. Instead, ICD-10 introduces several fundamental alterations to the code set's scope and structure. The first is an expansion of the set of chapters it contains. ICD-10-CM contains 21 chapters while ICD-9-CM included 19 with chapters changes, including the expansion of mental disorders to encompass behavioral and neurodevelopmental disorders, the distribution of immune system disorders into several chapters, and the aggregation of disorders of the eye, adnexa, ear, and mastoid process into their own chapters. Second is that, while ICD-9-CM codes were

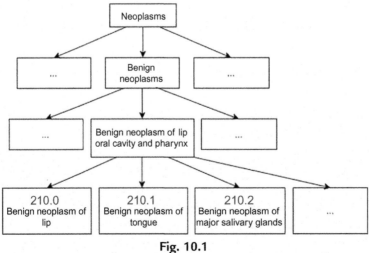

Fig. 10.1

Example ICD-9 code structure with code 210.1.

denoted by a 3-digit category followed by a 1- or 2-digit subcategory, ICD-10-CM codes begin with a 3-digit alphanumeric category identifier followed by up to four digits further specifying the code. The first item of the category identifier is a letter followed by two additional alphanumeric characters, which together encompass both the topical category of the code as well as related conditions. The subcategory code consists of up to three characters the first of which defines the site, manifestation, etiology or stage, and the second or third of which define the location or laterality. Lastly, there is a seventh "extender" character, which changes the overall meaning of the code. An example of a full ICD-10-CM code M1A.3120 describing "chronic gout, due to renal impairment, left shoulder, without tophus" is shown in Fig. 10.2.

In some circumstances, the extender character is needed but the prepending code contains less than six characters. In such situations, the code is padded up to six characters in length using the placeholder character "X" so that the extender code always occupies the seventh character position.

Although there are circumstances where there is a 1-to-1 mapping between an element in ICD-9 and ICD-10, such as the case with Werdnig-Hoffman disease (ICD-9-CM: 335.0, ICD-10-CM: G12.0), there are many more instances where a one-to-many relationship exists between ICD-9 and ICD-10 codes, which would require additional information to specify. For example, ICD-9 code 649.63 "uterine size date discrepancy, antepartum" has three potential matches in ICD-10-CM in the form of O26.841, O26.842, and O26.843 corresponding to "uterine size-date discrepancy" of the first, second, and third trimesters, respectively. Without knowing the particular patient's trimester at the time the ICD-9 code was applied, it would not be possible to "crosswalk" that code over to ICD-10. This can present as a common problem when trying to compare patients in a dataset that bridge the conversion between code sets. In such cases, it is certainly advantageous to have all patient records under consideration share the same ICD revision and to, where a one-to-one equivalence is absent, alternatives include rolling all codes to the most general shared label (e.g., converting the trimester-specific ICD-10 codes to ICD-9) at least for initial data mining or attempting to search elements of the patient records necessary to perform the code crosswalk (e.g., searching for trimester information).

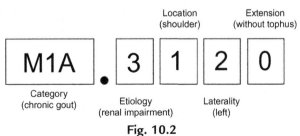

Fig. 10.2

Example ICD-10 code M1A.3120 and code structure.

While the ICD system was created with the goal of being a global reference vocabulary, there are additional domain-specific diagnostic ontologies, which are still commonly used. One important example of this is the Diagnostic and Statistical Manual of Mental Disorders (DSM), which was developed by psychiatric professionals and is published and officially maintained by the American Psychiatric Association (APA). Earlier versions of the DSM had little international participation, which resulted in the DSM and ICD systems differing substantially in their earlier history (e.g., DSM-III and ICD-8 were simply divergent ontologies). Fortunately, recent versions of both ontologies have benefited from collaborative agreements between the WHO and APA and the overall acceptance of a consistent descriptive approach have brought DSM-5 and ICD-10 much closer to one another than their predecessors. Nonetheless, many are still of the view that having two different ontologies for mental disorders is simply not helpful but reconciling these two is made difficult by a few important and resilient differences, including the DSM's focus on specialist clinical users (e.g., psychiatrists) as opposed to the ICD's focus on a more universal and cross disciplinary system. Of course, no discussion of the DSM would be complete without mentioning that it—much like CPT—is a copyrighted by the APA and constitutes a significant revenue stream for the organization. In addition to being the first version of to use an Arabic rather than Roman numeral, the DSM-5 differs from its preceding versions mainly by its introduction of a new framework. Older versions of the DSM considered mental disorders along five axes: primary clinical disorders other than mental retardation or personality disorders (Axis I), personality disorders (Axis II), underlying medical conditions, which could impact a mental disorder (Axis III), psychosocial and environmental factors (Axis IV), and an overall functional score (Axis V). By contrast, DSM-5 has excluded Axis V, replaced Axis IV with psychosocial and contextual features within diagnoses, and discarded Axes I, II, and III by placing all clinical entities within one broad section and has reframed many conditions in light of a more systematic and scientifically official understanding (e.g., "Mental Retardation" under the DSM-IV fell under the class of "Disorders usually first diagnosed in infancy, childhood, or adolescence" while, in the DSM-5 the condition itself was renamed to "Intellectual Disabilities" and placed under the class of "Neurodevelopmental Disorders").

10.3 Procedure ontologies: ICD-PCS, CPT, and HCPCS

Although the ICD-10-CM is used pervasively throughout healthcare, especially in the United States, the ICD-10-PCS is confined more specifically to hospital inpatient stays for the reporting of inpatient procedures as mandated by HIPAA.[3] ICD-10-PCS codes are "built" in a different way than CM codes and they have multiple hierarchical junctions. There are over 78,000 PCS codes consisting of seven alphanumeric characters each with a particular role known as a "character value": section, body system, root operation, body part, approach, device, and qualifier. Root operation is often a challenging aspect of the PCS code set, but it is intended to capture the overall purpose of the procedure such as "bypass," "replacement," or "dilation." Fig. 10.3 depicts a prototypical ICD-10-PCS code 00900ZX, "Central Nervous System Drainage of the brain, open, with no device, for diagnostic purposes" with annotated structure.

PCS codes are compact but highly formulaic making them amenable to expansion into a tabular format to ease analysis. For example, it may be worthwhile to create a table with seven columns, which are populated with the seven character value-encoded terms from a patient's given PCS code and an eighth column with patient's unique identifier. This makes it possible to apply simpler SQL-based selection criteria to identify patients with similar procedure attributes.

The current procedural terminology (CPT) codes were developed by the American Medical Association (AMA) and are used broadly across US healthcare for purposes of documenting reimbursement claims.[4] As a point which has sparked some controversy, the AMA also holds the copyright for the CPT coding system, which is the largest single source of AMA income. CPT codes themselves consist of five characters the first four of which are numeric and the fifth of which is alphanumeric. The code set is divided into three main categories with category I codes being the typical codes used for physician services, category II codes being related to performance tracking and not used for billing purposes, and category III codes, which are temporary and pertain to new technologies awaiting, including into category I. Category I codes are the most common and are out focus here. They are divided into six categories with their own range of codes: evaluation and management, anesthesia, surgery, radiology, pathology, medical services, and procedures. The CPT code set undergoes annual revision one goal of which is to cluster-related codes into adjacent code numbers such as several codes for soft tissue excision, which differ only by excision size. Occasionally, the code namespace is dense enough that new, related codes cannot be clustered adjacent to one another. In such circumstances, these new codes are placed under a different region of the code range, a practice known as "resequencing," and are marked as related. Due to this, it is not

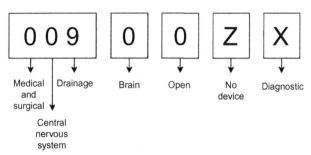

Fig. 10.3

Example ICD-10-PCS code 00900ZX with code structure.

uncommon to see a section of a CPT codebook wherein some codes, which share the same page or section, are not numerically adjacent, these are known as "resequenced codes."

As mentioned previously, CPT codes may exist within the evaluation and management category, which refers to services such as hospital observation, medical consultations, emergency department visits and even rest-at-home, home care, and case management services. The "E&M" codes represent the primary area wherein physicians can capture units of billable service and there is specific attention paid to how these codes are used. In fact, many hospitals have focused billing strategies, which are concerned with which codes are and ought to optimally be used in order to maximize revenue broadly across CPT codes but especially as it concerns E&M codes. Depending upon the historical scope of a patient cohort under consideration, there may be an evolution of CPT use over time even if that use does not strictly reflect a likewise evolution in the services actually performed. Thus, when exploring a new dataset, it is wise to investigate how broad use of certain codes changes as a function of time and it may be wise to fold certain codes into a single label to accommodate this.

The Healthcare Common Procedure Coding System (HCPCS) was developed by CMS to achieve a similar goal as CPT: provide a standardized vocabulary for submission of claims for reimbursement.[5] The breadth of HCPCS is larger than that of CPT, encompassing both goods and services. As a result, the accommodation of CPT within HCPCS is accomplished by dividing HCPCS into three levels with level I being identical to CPT, level II representing an additional set of nonphysician services such as ambulance rides, durable medical goods such as walkers, and level III representing additional "local codes" for use within specific jurisdictions such as state-level Medicaid programs or Medicare contractors. In any case, both HCPCS and CPT codes consist of five characters where, as mentioned, level I HCPCS and CPT codes are equivalent meaning that codes authored as CPT are simply understood as HCPCS level I codes by CMS without any transformation of the code itself.

Level II HCPCS codes all begin with a letter as the first code character and are grouped together by similar services. This gives rise to a colloquialism wherein codes are described by their mutual initial letter such as "J-codes" or "G-codes," which refer to nonorally administered drugs and professional services respectively. For example, J0120 corresponds to "Injection, tetracycline, up to 250 mg" while G0008 corresponds to "Administration of influenza virus vaccine." As J0120 illustrates, the HCPCS Level II codes are specific to the level of medication, route, and dose and can therefore be useful parameters for identifying patient groups and medical conditions from clinical datasets, a practice known as "computational phenotyping," which we discuss in a later chapter. As HCPCS codes are an instrument developed by CMS, their presence in a given dataset will be influenced by the relevant payer. At the time of this writing, HCPCS codes are used by Medicare and Medicaid as well as several third-party payers.

10.4 General ontologies: SNOMED, SNOMED-CT

The Systematized Nomenclature of Medicine (SNOMED) was initially created in the mid-1960s as the Systematized Nomenclature of Pathology (SNOP) and published by the College of American Pathologists (CAP). Since then, however SNOMED has grown well beyond Pathology—officially being rebranded in the mid-1970s—to become a broad conceptual ontology for healthcare processes.[6] Importantly, parallel development in the United Kingdom of an analogous system known as "Read Codes" and the emergence of the Clinical Terms Version 3 (CTV3) from Read Codes lead to a merging of SNOMED and CTV3 ontologies in 2002 as part of a CAP-led harmonization initiative. The resulting SNOMET-Clinical Terms (SNOMED-CT) has since become the most comprehensive healthcare terminology in the world.[7] This is due in part to CAP's decision to provide the National Library of Medicine (NLM) in the United States with a perpetual license for the core SNOMED-CT and its ensuing updates and the resulting addition of SNOMED-CT to the NLM's Unified Medical Language System (UMLS) Metathesaurus.[8] Currently, the intellectual property rights to all versions of SNOMED are held by the International Health Terminology Standards Development Organization (IHTSDO), which supports global development of the standards through the nonprofit organization SNOMED International, headquartered in London. Importantly, as part of Meaningful Use policies in the United States, it was required that EHR systems include SNOMED-CT in order to achieve certification for Stage 2. Our discussion of SNOMED will thus focus on SNOMED-CT as other SNOMED versions will be formally deprecated by IHTSDO. SNOMED-CT is frequently updated, being released twice a year and is accompanied by an online browser to explore concept definitions and relationships.

SNOMED-CT is a broad and very ambitious project consisting of concepts, of which there are over 300,000, relationships of which there are over 1 million, and descriptions of which there are over 750,000. Each concept, description, or relationship is a component identified with a unique SNOMED-CT ID (SCTID) such as "Spontaneous rupture of tympanic membranes of bilateral ears co-occurrent and due to recurrent acute suppurative otitis media" (SCTID: 1083061000119100). While this might seem like a hopelessly large sea of codes and terms, it is important to understand that a key difference between SNOMED and other ontologies. CPT, ICD, and HCPCS are "mono-hierarchies" meaning that they are designed to deliver terminally specific, nonoverlapping labels and their role in billing requires this in order to prevent double counting of diagnoses and procedures. SNOMED's design is very different in that it is a "poly-hierarchy" wherein a given component, such as a concept, can relate to multiple hierarchies depending upon different aspects of its meaning. This is not designed with the goal of producing nonoverlapping labels but, instead, to capture the overlapping and polymorphic nature of clinical concepts.

The SNOMED ontology is structured into top-level hierarchies, of which there are 17, including pharmaceuticals, organisms, and body structures, which are loosely analogous to chapters in the ontologies previously discussed. These hierarchies focus on the concept as the core data type. Concepts are the atomic units of clinical meaning and must represent one clear, unique idea such that no two concepts should share the same meaning. For example, "Appendectomy (procedure)" is a single concept within SNOMED while "Colectomy (procedure)" is another. Concepts are then further characterized through descriptions to give them flexibility to capture a range of possible meanings while not overlapping with other concepts. For example, the appendectomy concept can have multiple descriptions, which localize the concept to specific areas and situations such as "excision of appendix" or "excision de l'appendice." In this way, SNOMED is able to support internationalization by making these specific linguistic manifestations dependent upon a single core item. In addition to having descriptions, concepts have relationships to other concepts and the poly-hierarchy of SNOMED means that a given concept may have parent/child relationships to multiple other concepts. To give a simple example of a parent/child relationship with SNOMED, the concept "laparoscopic appendectomy" is a child of the "appendectomy (procedure)" concept because a laparoscopic appendectomy is a subtype of appendectomy procedures in general. A laparoscopic appendectomy, however, is also a subtype of the concept "endoscopic operation," and thus it actually has two parental concepts which capture different aspects of its meaning. One hierarchy relates to operations on the appendix while the other relates to operative techniques that use endoscopy. Thus, the concept for laparoscopic appendectomy would be retrieved from a search for concepts related to appendectomies and for concepts related to endoscopic procedures. Fig. 10.4 represents both a mono- and poly-hierarchy of SNOMED concepts.

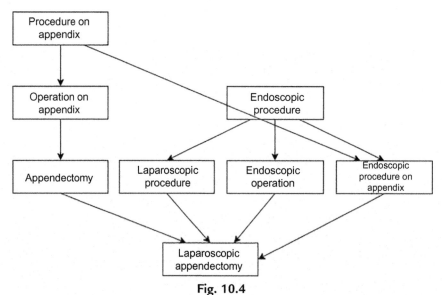

Fig. 10.4

Example SNOMED mono- and poly-hierarchy describing an appendectomy.

As you can appreciate from the figure, SNOMED can flexibly represent an entity as a graph of interrelated concepts reaching across procedural, diagnostic, and pathologic contexts. For example, appendectomy is a type of excision procedure, which is applied to a specific anatomic site, while appendicitis is a condition marked by inflammation which also applies to the same anatomic site.

This is another example of a poly-hierarchy implemented within SNOMED-CT and these poly-hierarchies are a core distinguishing factor between SNOMED and the statistical ontologies introduced thus far. This poly-hierarchy means that SNOMED codes can be queried and composed in different ways depending upon the analytical question at hand and represents unique focus SNOMED has on supporting interrogation and analysis as opposed to reporting and tabulation. This makes sense when one considers that the intended users of ICD, CPT, and HCPCS codes are generally claims processing agents and those interested in epidemiology and aggregate public health statistics, the intended users for SNOMED encompass researchers who may have flexible analytical interests. Let us consider a specific scenario in which considering SNOMED codes has a distinct advantage over considering ICD codes. Imagine we were trying to determine which patients over the prior year had presented to our hospital with some form of bacterial infection. This level of intermediate abstraction would be difficult to achieve with ICD codes because etiology and causative organism are not root categories. Instead, ICD codes are largely broken down by organ system meaning that bacterial infectious will appear in multiple chapters. This is because ICD is not intended to enable this sort of grouping but is instead intended to allow assignment of specific labels to patients. With SNOMED, however, this is quite doable as there is a concept for "bacterial infectious disease," which connects through multiple hierarchies to abscesses, cellulitis, pneumonia, and other bacterial infections. The flexibility of a graph allows for these aggregations in ways that monohierarchies cannot. Though powerful, using SNOMED in this way is not entirely foolproof. For example, let us consider in our above example that we were also interested in patients who had gastrointestinal diseases and we wished for an aggregate count of patients who had either a gastrointestinal disease or some form of bacterial infection. There is a subset of these patients who have a bacterial gastrointestinal disease and so it is quite possible that we would get more matches to our query than there are unique patients because have "double counted" whose patients who relate to both the gastrointestinal disease and bacterial infection concepts. This is easy enough to safeguard against so long as we are vigilant about it. As patients' records have unique identifiers, a good practice for such queries is to take the unique set of matched record identifiers rather than the total list when calculating a count of unique patients fitting these criteria.

It is important to note that SNOMED and ICD are not purely competitive and may actually be used in a complementary fashion. ICD codes can be thought of as encoded clusters of SNOMED concepts and may be specifically useful in circumstances where SNOMED codes are not provided or where a single, specific label is convenient for collecting patients as would be the case when looking for patients who have undergone a particular procedure. The International Edition of SNOMED-CT includes a map from SNOMED to ICD-10 codes and the US National Edition of SNOMED-CT includes a similar map to ICD-10-CM codes, which allow both for compressing groups of SNOMED concepts into ICD-10 codes or in expanding ICD-10 codes into groups of concepts, which can be more easily aggregated than the ICD-10 codes themselves and this map would have been used in our bacterial infections scenario to expand the ICD codes into SNOMED and to be grouped by the bacterial infections concept.

Finally, while ICD is published with an accompanying instruction manual that seeks to standardize the way in which codes are applied, SNOMED is not accompanied by such coding rules or conventions as part of an official release. Instead, SNOMED codes are often "embedded" within EHR applications, which means that clinicians and other members of the healthcare workforce who generate the phenomena encoded by SNOMED concepts do not consciously assign concept codes to their work nor do any dedicated personnel. Instead, the idea of "coding up" a clinical encounter in SNOMED happens largely behind the scenes through system-level mappings established within EHR applications, which can perform concept assignments as notes and orders are created. These mappings typically utilize certain key words within clinical notes and thus are dependent upon the use of accurate clinical terminology when describing patients. The linkages, which tie clinical language to SNOMED concepts, take multiple forms but are typically maintained by the IT teams, which support institutional EHR systems and include direct mappings between diagnoses and procedures to SNOMED as well as, in many cases, automated import of SNOMED vocabularies into EHR products through ingestion tools, which perform SNOMED annotations at scale. Most modern EHR systems support this and are regularly updated with current versions of the SNOMED ontology. Because of this largely automated mapping, SNOMED codes are often a rich way to mine features from patient records as they are consistently populated within institutions.

10.5 Other specific ontologies: LOINC and NDC

Logical Observation Identifiers Names and Codes (LOINC) represents a standard nomenclature focused on health measurements and observations created by the Regenstreif Institute in the mid-1990s.[9] Initially focused on laboratory results, LOINC has since expanded to encompass nursing diagnoses, and outcomes and is thus divided into a laboratory LOINC and a clinical LOINC, but our focus will be on the laboratory LOINC. LOINC codes consist of six parts: the analyte being measured, the method of measurement, when the measurement was performed, the sample measured, the way in which measurements are expressed, and the device type used to make the measurement. Fig. 10.5 shows an example LOINC code for a glucose measurement where Glucose is being measured by Mass Concentration (MCNC)

Fig. 10.5
Example LOINC for urine glucose and code structure.

rapidly at a single point in time (PT) from a Urine sample, and is reported as a quantity (QN), as measured using a Test strip and is reported.

LOINC was identified by the HL7 Group as the preferred ontology for laboratory tests and has since become the predominant representative format for laboratory testing.

National Drug Codes (NDC) are unique drug product identified used in the United States to and assigned to each drug intended for human use.[10] NDCs consist of unique 10- or 11-digit serial numbers divided into three segments. The first segment describes the labeler, which could be the manufacturer or distributer. The second segment describes the product, including its name, strength, dose form, and formulation. The third segment describes the commercial package size, which includes the quantity and package type. NDCs are present on all nonprescription and prescription medication packages. An example NDC for a 100-count bottle of Norco 20 mg tablets from Allergan is shown in Fig. 10.6.

Where 0023 denoted Allergan, 6002 denotes Norco 5 mg hydrocodone/325 mg acetaminophen tablets, and 01 denotes a 100-count package. As we discussed previously, HCPCS includes codes, which describe medications administered. Thus, many NDC codes have corresponding HCPCS codes and can be cross walked from NDC to HCPCS.

10.6 Summative ontologies: DRG

We conclude this tour of ontologies with what we call a "summative" ontology in the form of diagnosis-related groups (DRGs).[11] We call this a "summative" ontology because the goal is to abstract patient encounters away from specific procedures and granular diagnoses and into a category that reflects the difficulty and general care pathway required for managing that patient encounter. As we discussed in Chapter 1, DRGs were born out of an effort to move from

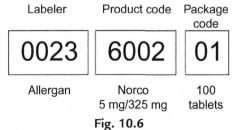

Fig. 10.6
Example NDC code 0023-6002-01 and code structure.

fee-for-service clinical reimbursement toward a "capitated" payment model wherein hospitals payments are given according to how challenging patient care is expected to be. Originating from work at Yale in the 1960s, the hope in doing this was initially to provide an accurate mechanism to monitor quality by facilitating patient grouping into broad, clinically meaningful buckets. The original DRGs consisted of 23 nonoverlapping groups called Major Diagnostic Categories (MDCs) that were partitioned in broad strokes such as major versus minor surgeries, neoplasms, trauma, etc. A logical extension of quality monitoring, the DRG system was first used to guide reimbursement in the late 1970s by the New Jersey State Department of Health and has since grown to be the principal means of abstracting patient care encounters for compensation by payers. The intention of DRGs is to incentivize hospitals to be more cost conscious by establishing a standard price for a given type of patient and patient encounter rather than paying hospitals according to an itemized bill for services rendered. The modern DRG groups patients according to diagnosis, treatment, and the expected length of stay and Groups are assigned based upon both principal and secondary diagnoses as represented by ICD codes and procedures as represented by HCPCS codes. This grouping is typically performed on patient encounters using a specific software application known as a "grouper," which is a critical component of the hospital revenue cycle. There are actually multiple variations of the DRG system each with their own specific tweaks.

There are currently two main systems of DRG assignment, which have slightly different evolutionary origins and concerns. The Medicare Severity DRGs (MS-DRG) encompass approximately 750 groups and seek to capture the medical complexity or severity of a patient by allowing for group modifications in the form of optional "complication/comorbidity" (CC) and "major complication/comorbidity" (MCC) annotations. For example, the MS-DRG ID for "heart failure and shock without CC or MCC" is 293, while the ID for "heart failure and shock with MCC" is 291. Eligibility for CC or MCC designations is based upon certain secondary diagnoses and procedures as defined in the appendices to the MS-DRG tables published by CMS. The focus of MS-DRGs is, unsurprisingly, squarely on the Medicare population to the exclusion of other relevant groups such as children and pregnant women. Thus, an attempt to create a variant of DRGs, which was more broadly encompassing, resulted in the All Patient (AP-DRG) and subsequent All Patient Refined DRGs (APR-DRG) with APR-DRGs serving as an improvement over AP-DRGs through the incorporation of severity of illness subclasses. Thus, APR-DRGs have four basic subclasses for each DRG relating to severity of illness and risk of death: minor, moderate, major, or extreme. As with MS-DRGs these APR-DRGs are assigned first by identifying the principal DRG based upon principal diagnoses and then aggregating secondary diagnoses and their expected severity of illness levels, and modifying severity of illness based on age, primary diagnosis, and additional procedures according to specific APR-DRG grouping logic. For certain analytical questions, DRGs are powerful labels for summarizing patient records because they represent lots of embedded associations between conditions and difficulty of treatment. For example, if we wanted to consider how effective or ineffective our hospital is at managing generally related patient encounters, we would prefer to consider DRGs rather than ICD, HCPCS, or SNOMED systems because DRGs speak to resource expense and length of stay per DRG is a generally useful summary of the efficiency of care. If, however, we noticed that certain DRGs in our institution has widely varying length of stays, we may rather wish to extract patient features in terms of ICD and HCPCS codes in order to identify subgroups accountable for this variation. As with all things, we wish to have the right tool for the right job and the job varies.

10.7 Conclusion

This chapter has been a brisk tour through the predominant ontologies that describe clinical care on various levels. Despite the multiple ontologies covered, this is still not an exhaustive list, but it does represent those systems, which are commonly encountered, useful, and play an important role in healthcare which sustains their prevalence and use. It is challenging to define an analytical scenario that would not encounter at least one of these and, in many cases, multiple of them. Hopefully, this chapter has revealed the intention, structure, and relative contextual strengths of these systems so that they can be utilized effectively to serve analytical interests. This chapter also represents the conclusion of this book's focus on how data are structured and represented and the transition to a subsequent discussion of how data are explored and analyzed and how analytical processes ought to be organized.

References

1. WHO. *International Classification of Diseases*. 11th Revision (ICD-11) https://www.who.int/classifications/icd/en/. (Accessed 11 March 2020).
2. CMS. *2020 ICD-10-CM*. https://www.cms.gov/Medicare/Coding/ICD10/2020-ICD-10-CM. (Accessed 11 March 2020).
3. CMS. *2020 ICD-10-PCS*. https://www.cms.gov/Medicare/Coding/ICD10/2020-ICD-10-PCS. (Accessed 11 March 2020).
4. CPT® (Current Procedural Terminology). https://www.ama-assn.org/amaone/cpt-current-procedural-terminology. (Accessed 11 March 2020).
5. CMS. *HCPCS—General Information*. https://www.cms.gov/Medicare/Coding/MedHCPCSGenInfo. (Accessed 11 March 2020).
6. SNOMED International. *SNOMED—Home*. http://www.snomed.org/. (Accessed 11 March 2020).
7. *SNOMED CT*. https://www.nlm.nih.gov/healthit/snomedct/index.html. (Accessed 11 March 2020).
8. *UMLS—Metathesaurus*. https://www.nlm.nih.gov/research/umls/knowledge_sources/metathesaurus/index.html. (Accessed 11 March 2020).
9. LOINC. *Home*. https://loinc.org/. (Accessed 11 March 2020).
10. FDA. *National Drug Code Directory*. https://www.fda.gov/drugs/drug-approvals-and-databases/national-drug-code-directory. (Accessed 11 March 2020).
11. https://www.cms.gov/icd10m/version37-fullcode-cms/fullcode_cms/Design_and_development_of_the_Diagnosis_Related_Group_(DRGs).pdf. (Accessed 11 March 2020).

Analyzing data

CHAPTER 11

A selective introduction to Python and key concepts

11.1 Python: What and why

Before we go into a discussion of Python, we should first address why we choose to focus on Python in this book. The field of data science and analytics has embraced two primary programming languages in the form of Python and R with some level of perceived competition between them. Moreover, the growth of the Julia language, which reached its milestone version 1.0 near the time of this writing, represents another entrant into an often-contested field of potential choice languages. This leads many to ask the question "which language is best?" to which the proper response is "it depends." For reasons of feasibility, this book focuses on only one of the aforementioned languages and for reasons of broad capability and popularity across many analytical domains, this book centers that focus on Python, which will be the subject of this chapter and several subsequent discussions throughout this text. It should be noted, however, that although it is advised to become comfortable with one language first, it is practically unavoidable that necessity will have you become familiar with at least both Python and R and in all likelihood additional languages beyond those. Thus, the perceived competition is really just that: a perception more than a reality. With that established, let us begin.

In this chapter, we'll take a quick but efficient tour through the Python programming language and establish a foundational understanding of what will be a core competency for informatics. Learning a programming language can seem overwhelming but successfully achieving fluency ultimately depends upon selecting—and sticking to—a focused curriculum. There are many programming books covering the Python language and many of them are quite useful. However, most of these books take readers on a comprehensive tour of the syntax of the Python language. In this chapter, we make a small departure from that approach and focus on key concepts, only introducing syntax in the context of those concepts. Furthermore, we choose only those concepts that are consistently useful when doing data science and informatics rather than covering the full breadth of Python.

Python is the brainchild of Dutch programmer Guido van Rossum who conceived of the language in the 1980s as a hobby project and so named due to his enthusiastic fandom of the television show *Monty Python's Flying Circus*.[1] Python has since grown into one of the most

An Introduction to Healthcare Informatics. https://doi.org/10.1016/B978-0-12-814915-7.00011-9

popular and robust programming languages with a keen focus on readability and expressivity. Python is technically described as an "interpreted," "dynamically typed," "high-level" programming language and each of these features has specific meaning. Interpreted languages are those whose instructions can be written and executed directly and instantly (this ends up being quite important for interactive computing as we'll see in subsequent chapters). This term contrasts with "compiled languages" in which programs have to be entirely written and translated (e.g., "compiled") into machine-readable code prior to being run. Today, it is common for many programming languages to have both interpreted and compiled forms, but the capability to use a language in a directly interpreted fashion makes development and continued reiteration significantly faster. This isn't to say that compiled languages such as Java and C++ are inferior. In fact, the process of compilation in these languages often means that they generate very fast and efficient programs, but speed is not the only concern of data analysis. Instead, analytical work seeks a balance between code that is quick to run and code that is quick to write. "Dynamically typed" and "high level" are related terms that describe the extent to which a language lets us as users abstract away from certain implementation details such as explicitly declaring the type of value each of our variables is intended to represent.

11.2 A note on Python 2 and 3

It is often confusing to newcomers that Python appears to have two prevalent versions, 2.x and 3.x. This is because the release of Python 3 introduced changes, which made its corresponding code uninterpretable to Python 2, which resulted in two parallel development tracks for the language since applications, which consisted largely of Python 2.x code, would otherwise not be able to access new features of the language. At the time of this writing, however, Python 2 is officially being deprecated and so all newcomers to Python should work exclusively with Python 3.

11.3 General structure of the language

We don't cover the particulars of how to install Python or how to compose and execute Python code within both the interactive shell or Python files. We leave this as an exercise for the reader as guidance on installing Python is readily available on the internet with specific instructions for any operating system and set up. Thus, it should not be difficult to get up and running with Python at least the point that one can execute small snippets of code, and so this chapter focuses on the core concepts that will allow you to really understand and use the language. As a general point, code is understood by Python as a collection of related expressions, which are evaluated in different patterns. Something as simple as 1+1 is an expression that evaluates to 2 while more complex, nested expressions such as 1+(1+(1+1)) evaluate to 1+(1+2), which evaluates to 1+3, which evaluates to 4. In this way, complex and expressive statements can be decomposed into nested expressions. When we talk about *how* Python understands code, we're discussing a concept known as "metaprogramming." Although metaprogramming is certainly not the focus of this chapter, it does lend us some useful foundational concepts. When the Python interpreter is told to run code, it proceeds through a workflow, which first involves parsing code into separate pieces called tokens. In the example of 1+1, we have three different tokens: "1," "+," and "1." These tokens are then used to create an *abstract syntax tree*, which is like an expression workflow diagram that establishes the order in which Python is supposed to evaluate certain groups of tokens. Understanding this helps to shed light on why we bother with the vocabulary of values, types of values, operators, and expressions: they each serve an important role in how Python creates that workflow diagram and ultimately dictates how high-level code is translated into specific instructions for the computer to perform.

11.4 Type system

Python, as with all programming languages, has a certain taxonomy of types describing the behavior and functionality of certain values. We will focus on what are called "built-in types" or "primitive types" of which there are four: integers, floats, Booleans, and strings. Values take the form of one of these types. For example, in the basic arithmetic sum 1+1 (which we can run by typing the same into a Python terminal), we are performing the addition operation on two values each of which are of integer type. Types play an important role in Python because they dictate the scope of valid manipulations to which a given value can be subjected. If we consider the addition operator applied to values of the string type, as with "Peter"+"McCaffrey" for example, we would get a very different sort of result: PeterMcCaffrey. So here, addition means something mathematical when we are using integer value types, whereas it means something quite different—to concatenate values—when we're talking about strings. Of course, some operations are only valid for certain types and invalid for others. Take division. Python would evaluate 10/2 as 5 but would give a TypeError when asked to evaluate "Peter"/"McCaffrey".

In addition, we mentioned that Python is "dynamically" typed, which is to say that types apply to values, not variables. This is one of the more obvious syntactical distinctions between Python and languages like Java. As covered in most introductory Python material, Python allows us to define variables, which are named containers for values and it allows us to assign a given value to a variable through use of the equals sign. For example, x=2 assigns the integer value 2 to the variable x, allowing us to use x as a representative for 2 in subsequent code, as with the expression x+1, which would evaluate to 2+1, or 3. Importantly, variables are flexible containers allowing us to reassign new values to the variable x in this case. Dynamic typing further means that we may assign an integer such as 2 to the variable x and then, after that, we may assign a string such as "Peter" without a problem. The variable x in this case is not restricted to a certain type of value that it must hold. Python does offer a built-in function called type() that allows us to check the type of a value or the type of value currently assigned to a variable. If x=2, then type(x) and type(2) both evaluate to int for integer. Similarly, types may be `str` for strings such as "Peter", `bool` for Booleans such as True or False, or `float` for floating point numbers such as 1.23. Floating numbers are so called because there is no set number of digits, which must appear before or after the decimal and, hence, the decimal floats. This is done in order to accommodate the fact that there are a limited number of bits available to represent each number and so a wide range of numbers to varying precision may be captured using floats.

Lastly, as a technical point, the terminology of "primitive" types has its roots in languages such as Java where there was a significant distinction between objects that represented both values and functions and primitives, which were purely values. In Python, `int`, `str`, `float`, and `bool` values are actually all objects as they too have innate functionality they can perform and so the term "built-in type" is actually the correct term. Nonetheless, "primitive type" is a common enough phrase to consider them generally equivalent for our purposes.

11.5 Control flow

Another basic aspect of Python is that of control flow, which allows us to define the circumstances under which certain expressions are evaluated. The most common example of this is a "conditional" taking the form of an "if/else" statement. For example, we may wish to set x to 1 `if` another variable y is greater than or equal to 10 but set x to 0 `if` y is less than 10 and we could succinctly write this like so:

```
If y >= 10:
    x = 1
else:
    x = 0
```

We may compose such conditionals in more complex ways with multiple successive "if" statements intended to capture certain scenarios.

Another important control flow example is that of "for" loops, which allow us to execute a certain set of expressions repeatedly. Importantly, we may have variables reassigned to new values within each successive iteration of a loop. An example of this would be printing the evaluated outcome of x+1 to the screen for a range of possible x values like so:

```
For x in [1,2,3]:
    print(x+1)
```

In this example, we have also introduced our first important data structure in the form of a list as denoted by square brackets. We will discuss this in greater detail later in the chapter. Importantly in the code, for each of the values in the list, x is assigned that value and the expression `print(x+1)` is evaluated causing one to be added to the value assigned to x and the resulting sum to be printed to the screen.

11.6 Functions

Having addressed values, simple operators, and types we can discuss functions. Functions are a similar to variables except instead of acting as container to hold a given value, functions act as container to hold expressions, much like a repeatable recipe. A critical aspect of functions is that they can be defined once and invoked or executed multiple times in multiple circumstances. This is especially powerful because functions can be defined to accept "parameters," which are variables used within the function by its expressions. Then, when a function is actually invoked in a particular circumstance, those parameters are given specific values for that particular execution of the function in which case those values are called "arguments." We tell Python we want to define a function by using the "def" keyword followed by a custom function name and then our desired parameters in parentheses. For example, we can define a function called addThese, which takes a parameter x and a parameter y and return their sum. Then we can invoke this function twice providing different arguments for x and y each time like so:

```
def addThese(x, y):
    return(x + y)

addThese(1,2)

addThese(3,8)
```

Notice how we used the keyword return. This means that the function itself, when executed, acts like an expression that evaluates to what is returned. In the code, the two invocations of addThese evaluate to 3 and 11 and because of that, we could even treat the function invocations as though they were equivalent to the values they return. For example, we could set a variable z to the evaluated expression addThese(2,3) and then print the result like so:

```
z = addThese(2,3)
print(z)
```

This would print 5. Functions may of course contain control flow statements and may themselves invoke other functions.

11.7 Objects

Objects represent entities that contain both attributes and functions. This means that an object is an abstraction that encompasses values and their behavior. As we mentioned, even the "built-in" types in Python are actually objects and this is revealed through their ability to exhibit functionality. A great example of this is the string type. We can convert the letters of a string to uppercase simply by invoking the upper() method on string values. For example, "Peter".upper() evaluates to PETER. We can of course define our own objects and, in so doing, define arbitrary properties and functions and the vast majority of actual Python programming done in data analysis involves interacting with objects defined either within the Python core language itself or within packages authored by others. This brings us to one important distinction and that is the difference between an "instance" of an object and a "class" of an object. When we define objects, we actually define a class representing a category of things. Somewhat like we saw with function definitions, a class is defined to contain variable properties, which are given particular values when specific "instances" of that class are created. We can have multiple instances of any given class. We can define a simple class called "patient" using Python's "class" key word and we can define the patient class to contain a category of things (patients in this case) each of which has a first name, a last name, and the ability to say "Hello, my name is" followed by their first name:

```
Class Patient
    def __init__(self, firstName, lastName):
        Self.firstName = firstName
        Self.lastName = lastName

  def sayHi(self)
    Print(f"Hello, my name is {self.firstName}")
```

We've introduced a few important things here. First and foremost, we have defined two functions inside of our class one of which has a special role. The $\_$init$\_$ function is invoked every time we create a new instance of the patient class, it accepts values specific to that class instance and assigns those values to specific properties of the class instance. As its role is to set up a given instance of the class with initial properties, the $\_$init$\_$ method is known as the "constructor" of the class. Although a class may contain many functions with custom names, it must at least contain the $\_$init$\_$ function. Finally, we use the somewhat odd practice of providing "self" as a parameter to the functions of our class. We do this so that the class instance has a means of self-reference, which is required in order for it to assign and read its own properties and to invoke its own functions. When a function belongs to a class, we conventionally refer to it as a "method" of that class. Note also that we have used a new syntactical convention in the form of self.firstName and self.lastName. We will discuss this later in this chapter when we explore data structures, but we see this convention both when referring to the value attributes belonging to a class as well as when we want to invoke a method from a class. For example, if we want to create a specific instance of the Patient class and invoke the sayHi() method we would could do that like so:

```
peter = Patient("Peter", "McCaffrey")
peter.sayHi()
```

which will print out "Hello, my name is Peter." So, going back to the dot syntax we see in self.firstName or peter.sayHi(), we should consider that the instance of the patient class, peter in this case, is simply a data structure known as a dictionary, which contains values and functions.

The dot syntax, therefore, is just a way of addressing a particular entry in the dictionary data structure. If we want to see this explicitly, we can actually invoke the baked-in "`__dict__`" function of the peter instance, revealing its `firstName` and `lastName` properties:

```
peter.__dict__
```

which returns `{'firstName':'Peter', 'lastName':'McCaffrey'}`. You might wonder why the function `sayHi` is not included in this list and this is because of some internal efficiencies on Python's part. Since the `firstName` and `lastName` attributes take particular values for each instance of the `Patient` class, they are "instance attributes" and are found in an instance dictionary. Alternatively, since the function `sayHi` itself does not take on any values particular to a given class instance, it remains at the class level as a "class attribute" and it may be accessed by inspecting a class dictionary like so:

```
Patient.__dict__
```

As one last point, classes may include other classes among their properties in what is known as "inheritance." While we won't go into detail in this book, there is a rich world of theory and practice known as "object-oriented programming" that focuses on the design of programs as interoperating objects with organized lines of inheritance governing how their functions and properties are defined.

11.8 Basic data structures

Linus Torvalds, the creator and long-time principal developer of the Linux kernel stated in a message to the Git mailing list:

> I will, in fact, claim that the difference between a bad programmer and a good one is whether he considers his code or his data structures more important. Bad programmers worry about the code. Good programmers worry about data structures and their relationships.

Data structures are a critical point in software engineering because they are, at the end of the day, the entire "meat" of programming. Programming languages can be seen as a means of creating and manipulating data structures and the process of effective informatics and data science boils down to a mastery of data structures.

So what are data structures? Simply put, they are collections of values, the relationships between those values and the operations that can be performed upon those values. This will become crystal clear in just a moment when we dive into some examples, but this should sound very familiar as data structures are themselves classes of objects. There are many types of data structures and, as one might imagine, there is an expansive body of theory, research, and practice in computer science around optimizing and defining new data structures to meet various requirements of speed, efficiency, and capability. As we get into deeper discussions around big data tools in subsequent chapters, we'll get to see some of these innovations first hand.

As an informaticist working in Python, you will interact heavily with a set of core data structures and these will come to define the backbone of your analytical approach. With more practice and familiarity, you will become more expressive and efficient in using these data structures to implement analysis. So let's cover the key structures now.

11.8.1 Lists

It is impossible to overstate the importance and ubiquity of lists. Lists in Python are sequences of values with a specific and preserved order. Conventionally, we denote a list by using square brackets ("[]") and we can either declare our list to include initial values or we can declare an empty or partial list and add, remove, or update values as we go. Lists are very flexible data structures and will likely be the most common one that you will use. We create a list and assign it to a variable as we would an integer or float and we can use Python's type checking function to demonstrate that our list is of type "list" like so:

```
myList = [1,2,3]
type(myList)
```

Lists are far more expressive than this, though. We can easily mutate them in various ways such as by adding values to the end of our list using the append() method or by removing them using the pop() method:

```
>>> myList.append(5)
>>> myList
[1,2,3,5]
>>> myList.pop()
>>> myList
[1,2,3]
```

Lists also have a count() method, which accepts a value as an argument and returns the number of times that value appears in the list:

```
[1,2,3,3,3,4].count(3)
>>> 3
```

You may notice that, as with strings, we're invoking methods that belong to the list itself. This is because our list is an instance of the list class, which is defined to have certain built-in methods. We can inspect this class as we did our Patient class by using Python's dir() function: dir(myList).

We can add values of different built-in type to a list as well using the `append()` method or simply by defining a list to include heterogeneous types such as `[1,2,3,5,'banana']`.

We can even add other lists as entries within our list:

```
>>> myList.append([1,5,7])
>>> myList
[1,2,3,5,'banana',[1,5,7]]
```

Unlike some other languages such as Java, Python is very forgiving when it comes to mixing types across variable assignments and within data structures. It's worth noting that this can be a blessing and a curse. Languages like Java have long been favored for enterprise production systems and large open-source projects with many contributors (e.g., Apache Software Foundation projects such as the big data tools we will discuss later) partly because of the strictness of their syntax. When trying to share code between many developers, being forced to be explicit is useful as it makes it easier to track down the root cause of errors. In data science, however, the tradeoff favors quick iteration over almost anything else and so with languages like Python, we can give up some of the explicitness of the code in exchange for a very flexible and rapid coding experience.

The exercises focus on adding values to lists, but this is just the beginning. Lists also offer lots of value in our ability to selectively navigate them, selecting items either by their value or by their position. Each element within a Python list has a corresponding index, which is an ordered, numerical tag corresponding to each of the list's values. Indices are useful because they allow us to selectively grab values out of a list based upon that value's position within the list. Python lists are "zero-indexed" meaning that the first list item is at the 0th position instead of the 1st position (i.e., the first item in a list is as position 0, not 1).

Let's take a look at a few indexing exercises. First, we can select the first element in a list by specifying the appropriate index position in square brackets next to the name of the list:

```
>>> myList[0]
>>> 1
```

Similarly, we can select the third item in the list like so:

```
>>> myList[2]
>>> 3
```

We can also select multiple values from our list, a practice referred to as "slicing" by specifying the start and end index positions of our selection and separating them by a colon:

```
>>> myList[1:3]
>>> [2,3]
```

One thing you should notice here is that, when slicing, the start position is inclusive while the end position is exclusive. This means that when we type something like myList[1:3] as we have, this means that we are selecting all the values from the index position "1" (i.e., the second item in the list) up to but not including the index position "3" (i.e., the fourth item in the list). Take a moment to think on this and try different slicing ranges as it can take a little bit to get the hang of this notation.

Lastly, list slicing can accept an optional third value expressing the "step" of the range. The step simply refers to the frequency with which the slice pulls values from the list. By default, the step is 1, which means that when we type something like myList[1:4], we want all elements from 1 up to—but not including—4. We could, however, set a step of any value like 2, for instance. If we say myList[1:4:2], we're still asking for the range starting from one, up to—but not including—4, but we're now saying that we only want every other element from that selection:

```
>>> myList[1:4:2]
>>> [2,5]
```

11.8.2 Sets

Like lists, sets are collections of values but they differ sharply in that sets do not contain an indexing or slicing functionality which is tied to the fact that lists to not preserve the order of values they contain. Sets are thus like bags of values rather than ordered arrangements of values. Also critical is that sets must contain only unique values so, while a list may contain repeats such as [1,2,2,3,4,4,4], a set equivalent, denoted by curly brackets, would simply look like {1,2,3,4}. While they might seem a bit odd, sets have deep mathematical roots and they are especially useful when trying to compare between two sets for values, which are either shared between them or unique to only one or the other. In fact, sets have their own methods that support this in the form of their intersection() and difference() methods. Complementing these is also the union() method, which merges the unique values between two sets while not duplicating values. We can see an example of each like so:

```
{1,2,3}.intersection({1,2,6})
>>> {1,2}
{1,2,3}.difference({1,2,6})
>>> {3}
{1,2,3}.difference({1,2,3})
>>> {6}
{1,2,3}.union({1,2,6})
>>> {1,2,3,6}
```

11.8.3 Tuples

Like lists, tuples are collections of values and they do have a specific, preserved order as well as indexing, slicing, and count functionality. Unlike lists, however, tuples are "immutable" meaning that they cannot be updated. Thus, tuples do not support append or pop functions. Tuples are denoted by parentheses characters such as (1,2,3). Lists are more common than tuples in most data science and analytical applications, but it is commonly advised to use tuples over lists when immutability is acceptable as tuples are faster than lists to iterate through. This is because the immutability of tuples allows them to exist within one block of memory, whereas lists are not.

11.8.4 Dictionaries

Dictionaries are another very important data structure and can be thought of as a cousin of lists and we often use them to hold collections of values. One key but important difference exists, though since the purpose of lists is to hold values and organize them by their position while dictionaries hold values and organize them by labels, called "keys." Because of this, dictionaries do not maintain a specific ordering of their values as every value has a unique tag. We designate a dictionary in Python by using the curly brackets "{}" but, when we add data to a dictionary, we specify both a key and a value. We can create a dictionary like so:

```
myDictionary = {'firstName: 'Peter', 'lastName': 'McCaffrey}
```

Where we have a comma-separated list of key-value pairs where each pair consist of a key followed by a colon followed by that key's corresponding value. In the example, the dictionary has two such pairs 'firstName':'Peter' and 'lastName':'McCaffrey' wherein 'firstName' and 'lastName' are keys and 'Peter' and 'McCaffrey' are their corresponding values. Of course, we can also add key-value pairs to a dictionary that has already been created by specifying the new key in square brackets next to the dictionary's name and setting that equal to the corresponding value:

```
>>> myDictionary['middleName'] = 'Christian'
>>> myDictionary
{'firstName': 'Peter', 'lastName':'McCaffrey', 'middleName':'Christian'}
```

This might seem a bit confusing at first, but this represents the core purpose of a dictionary and captures its main distinction from a list. Lists are meant to be simple collections of values, whereas dictionaries (as the name implies) are meant to represent associations between sets of values. While we can easily set new key-value pairs in dictionaries, the real power comes in their ability to support "lookups" whereby we can fetch a particular value by referring to its corresponding key:

```
>>> myDictionary['lastName']
```

```
'McCaffrey'
```

We can specify any key in square brackets in order to retrieve the key's corresponding value. The syntax here is not altogether unlike locating items in a list according to their index position.

One last point about dictionaries is that you can easily change the value corresponding to a key just by reassigning a new value to a key like so and thereby overwriting it:

```
>>> myDictionary['firstName'] = 'Chris'
>>> myDictionary
{'firstName': 'Chris', 'lastName': 'McCaffrey', 'age': 31}
```

And we can remove a key/value pair by using the pop operation:

```
>>> myDictionary.pop('firstName', None)
'Chris'
>>> myDictionary
{'lastName': 'McCaffrey', 'age': 31}
```

11.8.5 List and dictionary comprehensions

Finally we conclude with a common stylistic practice in Python known as the "comprehension," which is an efficient way to create lists or dictionaries in a single statement. In the case of the list comprehension, we enclose an expression in square brackets and the expression may contain iterated functionality. For example, if we wanted to step through each item in a list [1,2,3,4] and create a new list wherein each item is multiplied by 4 we could write this:

```
Y = []
for x in [1,2,3,4]:
        y.append(x*4)
```

thereby creating a list y equal to [4,8,12,16]. With a comprehension, however, we could also create this list y with a single expression:

```
y = [ x * 4 for x in [1,2,3,4] ]
```

Dictionary comprehensions operate in a similar way except our expression handles two values corresponding to the key and value of the dictionary entries instead of one value. If we wanted to create a dictionary where each key was a number 1 through 4 and each value was its key multiplied by four, we could create this with a single statement this time wrapped in curly brackets:

```
y = { x:x*4 for x in [1,2,3,4] }
```

where y is equal to {1:4, 2:8, 3:12, 4:16}.

11.9 Conclusion

In this chapter, we discussed the intuitions behind the Python programming language along with its basic use. In subsequent chapters, we will see Python appear in the context of other tools and platforms, illustrating the fundamental role that the language plays in the data science ecosystem. Importantly, this chapter focuses on the core concepts, operators, and data structures that will allow enable you to build your own informatics projects. Moving forward as an informaticist, Python will become an increasingly important skill and one that you should continue to hone throughout your career.

Reference

1. van Rossum G. Computer Programming for Everybody: A Scouting Expedition for the Programmers of Tomorrow. Corporation for National Research Initiatives; 1999. https://www.python.org/doc/essays/cp4e. Accessed 5 February 2020.

CHAPTER 12

Packages, interactive computing, and analytical documents

12.1 Introduction

In the last chapter, we discussed the Python language and introduced important data structures and types as well as functions, objects, and the control flow. These practices all utilize the core Python language meaning that all of the functionality described in the previous chapter is available simply by virtue of installing the Python language. This is a good place to start a discussion of Python, but it is also a woefully incomplete place to finish. In this chapter, therefore, we introduce the concept of packages and their management and we discuss a particular workflow common to analytical projects in Python centered on the Jupyter package.

12.2 Packages and package management

Packages extend the functionality of the core Python language by providing additional functions, classes, types, and data structures. Python has a rich ecosystem encompassing well over 100,000 packages, developed by a diverse collection of community members ranging from professional developers to startups to laboratories and even individual expert and amateur users. Technically, a package is a collection of modules and a module is a related collection of Python code, which can include classes, functions, and variables. Python allows us to bring the contents of a package or module into our current program by use of the `import` statement, which makes the classes, functions, and variables available to the interpreter session running our code. For example, let us say that we designed a function to calculate body mass index (BMI) in either metric or US customary units (recall the formula is weight in kilograms divided by height in meters squared or, alternatively, weight in pounds divided by height in inches squared multiplied by 703):

```
def calculateBMIMetric(weight, height):
    return( weight / height**2 )

def calculateBMIUS(weight, height):
    return( (weight / height**2) * 703 )
```

An Introduction to Healthcare Informatics. https://doi.org/10.1016/B978-0-12-814915-7.00012-0
© 2020 Elsevier Inc. All rights reserved.

This might prove to be a useful pair of formulas for us with relevance to more than one project and perhaps we would like to "modularize" our code by placing these functions into their own separate and reusable element. In order to do this, we would create a file called bmi.py, which includes both of these functions. If we did this, we would be able to import these functions into a Python program like so:

```
import bmi

bmi.calculateBMIMetric(80, 1.5)
```

Notice how we were able to invoke a calculateBMIMetric function without having to define it by using the expression import bmi, which brings the contents of the bmi.py file—which includes the definition of the calculateBMIMetric function—into the current python interpreter session as though we had written the function definitions ourselves. We simply have to invoke the imported function from the module object. This import capability is a powerful feature as it allows Python to be extended for many domain-specific uses. Packages are simply aggregations of modules across separate files. Let us consider that we also want to create a function for calculating the estimated total blood volume and save it to a file called bloodvolume.py:

```
def estimatedBloodVolume(weight, height):
    return( (0.37 * (height**3)) + (0.032 * weight) + 0.60 )
```

while we could import this module specifically with import bloodvolume, we could create a more general package including both of these modules. In order to do this, we place both of the modular python files (.py) in a folder named after our new package, in this case medcalcs and we create a specific file within that medcalcs folder called __init__.py that contains a simple import statement importing each of our modules into the package's init file:

```
import medcalcs.bmi, medcalcs.bloodvolume
```

this will allow us to simply import the medcalcs package using import medcalcs and access all of the modules and their respective functions:

```
import medcalcs

medcalcs.bmi.calculateBMIMetric()
```

This is a simple example but note that packages may be quite large and complex with many constituent modules. Importantly, there are other common alternative import statements, which are suitable in different circumstances. For example, may choose only to import only certain modules or functions from the medcalcs package with the expression from medcalcs import bmi.calculateBMIMetric or we may choose to import the package or a module thereof under a specific alias with the expression `import medcalcs.bmi as bodymass`. We will see more examples of these conventions later in this chapter.

So now that we know what package is, we can discuss how packages are managed. In the medcalcs example, there must be a folder entitled `medcalcs`, which contains the modular python files and that folder must be in a location that the Python interpreter can find. Note that the import statement simply mentions the name of the package to be imported but does not include a fully defined location there the package folder is expected to actually reside. By default, when the Python interpreter comes upon an import statement, it searches for the referenced package from among a list of directories, which include the folder from which the Python interpreter was run, known as the "current directory," or from a list of specific folders enumerated in a configuration parameter known as the `PYTHONPATH`. While the full technical details are not critically important for the focus of this chapter, the existence of the `PYTHONPATH` configuration parameter—set by what is known as an "environment variable"—makes it possible to organize packages and their folders in specific locations, rather than having to copy the relevant package folders to each project-specific location in which Python is being run. Also, this behavior means that you don't spend much time thinking deliberately about where package files actually live as it is a convenient and almost seamless process to install, import, and use the contents of a package. By default, the core Python language comes with its own built-in package manager called `pip` that functions as a command line tool allowing users to search for, install, update, and remove python packages. In order to do this, pip relies upon an index of Python packages known as "pypi" or the Python package index, which is its official third-party software repository. Installing a package from pypi is as simple as issuing a single command to the pip command like tool. For example, if we wished to install the popular numpy package, we could simply write the following command and the package would be downloaded and made available for import in our Python programs:

```
pip install numpy
```

Pip is an extremely common and very well-engineered package manager, but most users in the data science and analysis community use an analogous, although not strictly identical, tool known as Anaconda. Anaconda is a crossplatform tool for managing both packages and entire environments and manages packages using its own Anaconda repository instead of pypi through the command line tool conda and through an optional graphical application. This is advantageous to data science work for a few reasons. First is that pip downloads and installs packages as python source code, which means that this may require the client system to have compatible compilers or other libraries installed in order for package installation to operate. Conda does not share this behavior and instead packages in the Anaconda repository are precompiled binaries, thereby allowing conda to download and install packages without a dependency on the presence or configuration of client compilers. Moreover, conda packages may also contain C or C++ code or other interdependencies such as R packages and are organized into "channels" within the Anaconda repository, which further group packages by field or by other properties. An example of a popular channel is "bioconda," which contains many packages relating to computational biology and genomics. This becomes especially relevant for analytics work because packages for scientific computing, machine learning, parallel computing, etc. sometimes have complex compilation and installation requirements. This relates to the second important difference between pip and conda which is that conda is built to create and manage entirely separate Python environments each of which may have their own installed packages and versions of Python. This allows a single computer to have different and sometimes conflicting Python environments installed and maintained under conda with the ability to switch between environments as needed. This is accomplished by conda's creation and governance over its own PYTHONPATH directories, which include environment-specific portions of the filesystem all typically located within a master anaconda installation folder such as ~/anaconda3, which is the anaconda3 folder in the user home directory. When conda is installed there is only one original "base" environment, but users can easily use the conda command line utility to other environments. For example, we could create a new environment based on python 3.7 called "data-science-1" and install numpy into that environment with one command:

```
conda create -n data-science-1 python=3.7 numpy
```

and another Python 3.5 environment called "data-science-2" with numpy version 1.15:

```
conda create -n data-science-2 python=3.5 numpy==1.15
```

Finally, we could switch into the data-science-1 environment:

```
conda activate data-science-1
```

and we can leave the environment with the statement "conda deactivate." Importantly, if we were to switch into data-science-1 and issue the command "conda list," we would see that the version of numpy is at least 1.17 or higher depending upon when this chapter is being read but that, upon switching out of data-science-1 and into data-science-2 the numpy version is 1.15. Importantly, we can also use conda to print the installed packages, their specific version numbers, and the channels used to find them to a file conventionally called environment.yml by using the command conda env export > environment.yml. This is a key strength of environment management as these environment files are typically packaged with analytical projects such that users trying to recreate the analysis on a different machine can reconstitute an identical conda environment to that originally used by issuing the command conda env create -f environment.yml, which reads the installed packages and their particular versions form the environment file and creates a conda environment based upon them. Note that the.`yml` file extension stands for a YAML or "Yet Another Markup Language," which a common formatting convention for configuration files and is the default conda uses for such files. Conda will natively export environment details to files of this type and will read environment details from files of this type without you, the user, having to manually write files in YAML although it is a pretty straightforward markup standard to understand and work with.

12.3 Key packages

We have seen how conda can be used to install packages, but which packages should we regularly have? This is a common question for newcomers to analysis with Python and the expanse of the package ecosystem can be bewildering. There are far more useful packages than can be covered in a book let alone a chapter section, but there are some basic almost universally essential packages with which you should be acquainted.

NumPy is an essential package for almost all data science and analytical work. NumPy was created to bring numerical computing functionality to Python, an initiative that dates back to the mid-1990s. Those efforts have matured through open source projects with several maintainers and many more contributors, including the creator of Python itself Guido van Rossum. These efforts culminated in NumPy, which formally entered its 1.0 release 2006 led by Travis Oliphant who would later go on to found Anaconda. The core feature within NumPy is a class known as the "ndarray" or "*n*-dimensional array," which is ostensibly similar to a list in core Python, but with a few very important differences. First, ndarrays are homogeneously typed meaning that they cannot contain, for example, integers and strings together but can only contain values of one type. NumPy has its own types, which are similar to core Python but include variably sized signed and unsigned integers, floats, and complex numbers as well as fixed-size Unicode strings. Second, ndarrays are strided views on memory meaning that the elements contained within a numpy array are consistently and often contiguously arranged in memory and that the size of a numpy array is fixed at creation. It is not uncommon that you will encounter a special form of ndarray with a specific data type (`dtype`) known as "object," which means that the elements—typically strings—in the array are not contiguously arranged in memory but that the array instead contains pointers to Python objects stored elsewhere in memory. In other words, the array doesn't actually contain the data in this case but rather serves as an address book for Python objects located elsewhere. This behavior is much like the behavior of a core Python list, but it doesn't have the advantages of memory contiguity enjoyed by more strictly typed ndarrays. While ndarray type and size constraints do add some rigidity when compared to core Python's facilitation of mixed-type and mutable lists, ndarrays are far more efficient data structures. In addition, numpy arrays can behave as vectors, allowing them to represent computations of linear algebra. After installing NumPy through conda, we import it and create two ndarrays each with 5 integers and then add these two vectors together, demonstrating the element-wise behavior of ndarrays under addition:

```
import numpy as np

arr1 = np.array([1,2,3,4,5])
arr2 = np.array([2,2,3,3,4])

arr1 + arr2
>>> [3,4,6,7,9]
```

Of course, more complex linear algebra such as dot products, cross products, eigenvectors, and eigenvalues are available in NumPy along with many more functions defined in the package. Another important strength of numpy is that it allows us to vectorize operations, meaning we can have the CPU perform multiple operations simultaneously rather than one at a time. For example, we can make for loop significantly more efficient by vectorizing it such that all loop elements are computed together. This requires a rewriting and a rethinking of the task at hand but can have significant efficiency payoffs. While this example of element-wise addition is an example of vectorization, NumPy also offers a vectorize function, which allows us to define more customized behavior and then dispatch that behavior against a vector of elements all at once. For example, consider we have two arrays, x and y, and we wish to create a new array z wherein each value is a value from x and y multiplied together with 10 added. Using a basic for loop in core Python, we would do this like so (using the built-in zip function to loop over the two arrays taking one value from each array at each step):

```
x = [1,2,3,4]
y = [2,2,4,4]
z = []
for i, j in zip(x, y):
        z.append( (x*y) + 10)
```

A much faster, vectorized version of this could take one of two forms either directly as a linear algebraic expression:

```
import numpy as np

x = np.array([1,2,3,4])
y = np.array([2,2,4,4])

x = (x * y) + 10
```

or, alternatively, by defining a function and dispatching that function across our vectors:

```
def myFunc(x, y):
        return( (x*y) + z)

vectfunc = np.vectorize(myFunc, dtypes=[np.int], cache=False)
z = list(vectfunc(x, y))
```

In either circumstance, we can achieve very meaningful performance improvements when working with ndarrays rather than core Python lists and, as a result, many of the most popular analytical packages in Python are built atop NumPy and make use of ndarrays as we will see shortly.

Pandas was originally developed by Wes McKinney in 2008 for purposes of facilitating financial data analysis but has since grown to become a ubiquitous tool. Pandas' core value is its DataFrame class, which constitutes a flexible, fast, and powerful data structure. DataFrames are tabular data structures, which store rectangular data in rows and columns. Under the hood, Pandas DataFrames are collections of columnar series, which are a Pandas extension of the ndarray. Series hold a homogeneously typed vector as with ndarrays, but series objects also allow for more flexible indexing of the items they contain. While ndarrays require numerical indexing (as the index is simply a low-level way to indicate how many strides into the ndarray's memory address to read), series allow for customized indices to include string labels, which can be declared by providing a custom index array to the index argument when creating a series. This allows for elements or ranges to be pulled out of the series using either numeric or custom indices as seen in the two expressions:

```
import pandas as pd

series1 = pd.Series(data=[1,2,3,4], index=['a','b','c','d'])

series1[2:4]
>>> c 3
    d 4

series1['c':'d']
>>> c 3
    d 4
```

As you may notice, in both circumstances the result of selecting values from a Series in this way is another series and its formatted in such a way so as to preserve the association between the data and its index. If we wished to extract the raw values back into an ndarray or a core Python list, Pandas Series objects also provide methods for that:

```
series1['c':'d'].values
>>> array([3,4])

series1['c':'d'].values.tolist()
>>> [3,4]
```

As we mentioned previously, the real power of Pandas comes in the form of its DataFrame structure, which is a collection of associated columnar series objects, which share an index. We can create a simple DataFrame and see how, when we set a certain column (which is a

Series itself) as the index of the DataFrame, we're setting that series' values as the index for each of the other columnar series in the DataFrame. Note that we can create a DataFrame using Pandas' DataFrame constructor and providing a dictionary wherein the keys are the column names (series names) and the values for each key are the lists or arrays of the values in the respective columns:

```
myDataFrame = pd.DataFrame(data={'col1':[1,2,3,4],
'col2':[2,2,4,4], 'col3':['a','b','c','d']})

myDataFrame.set_index('col3', inplace=True)

myDataFrame.index
>>> Index(['a', 'b', 'c', 'd'], dtype='object', name='col3')

myDataFrame['col1'].index
>>> Index(['a', 'b', 'c', 'd'], dtype='object', name='col3')

myDataFrame['col2'].index
>>> Index(['a', 'b', 'c', 'd'], dtype='object', name='col3')
```

This might seem somewhat esoteric thus far, but this really comprises the core mechanics of the Pandas DataFrame, which allows us to efficiently select rows, columns, and ranges of both while applying logic such as selecting values in a specific column based upon values in another column:

```
myDataFrame[myDataFrame['col1']>2]['col2']
>>> c 6
    d 8
```

This sort of logical filtering is further enabled by the creation of a Boolean index, which captures the true or false condition of each DataFrame row based upon the filter expression. Thus, in the case of the expression, the statement myDataFrame['col1']>2 create a Boolean series with the same index as the DataFrame:

```
myDataFrame['col1']>2
>>>a False
   b False
   c True
   d True
```

This Boolean index then simply serves as an index on the DataFrame to select certain rows and, finally, the "col2" column of the resulting DataFrame containing filtered rows is returned.

An entire tour of Pandas functionality is beyond the scope of this chapter, but there are many useful books and tutorials, which provide a comprehensive tour of the package. Suffice it to say that in many—most even—analytical workflows you will encounter, data will be pulled into a Pandas DataFrame as one of the first steps of analysis and that Pandas provides powerful indexing capabilities to manipulate rows and columns of DataFrame structures. Importantly, Pandas contains several import functions to create a DataFrame from a file such as a csv, excel, txt or other delimited format or even from an SQL query, and it is most often the case that DataFrames are created via some import function. Since the columns of a Pandas DataFrame are series, which are essentially ndarrays, calculations can be very efficiently performed on DataFrames making them indispensable components of analytical work. Furthermore, DataFrames support groupby and aggregate functions, pivoting, rolling windows on time series, and a host of other transformations. Lastly, Pandas does support plotting functionality allowing users to create various visualizations directly from DataFrames, but it is also very common to extract information from DataFrame for plotting with matplotlib.

Matplotlib is among the most popular Python 2D plotting packages, which supports a wide range of plotting tasks from simple exploratory charts to publication quality figures with highly customized layouts, color schemes, and annotations. Matplotlib introduces a few important plotting objects, which can either be directly manipulated for more customization, using the "object-oriented API," or used at a simpler and more abstract level through the pyplot API. The pyplot API allows for the simple declarative creation of visualizations by providing data and stylistic parameters to one of pyplot's many functions:

```
import matplotlib.pyplot as plt

plt.scatter(x=[1,2,3,4], y=[1,2,2,3])
plt.show()
```

This would create a simple scatter plot with four points the x and y coordinates of which are drawn from the x and y arrays, respectively, as shown in Fig. 12.1.

It is also common—and advisable—to provide pandas DataFrame columns as the numerical arrays corresponding to the x and y coordinate arrays:

```
coords_df = pd.DataFrame(data={'label':['a','a','b','b'],
'x_coords':[1,2,3,4], 'y_coords':[1,2,2,3]})

plt.scatter(x=coords_df['x_coords'], y=coords_df['y_coords'])
plt.show()
```

Pyplot allows for the creation of scatter plots, line plots, histograms, and others with the ability to declare label size, color, and transparency attributes—even using certain DataFrame columns. To do this, we convert a column of labels to a numeric "colormap" that crosswalks each label to an RGB color for plotting as shown here and in Fig. 12.2:

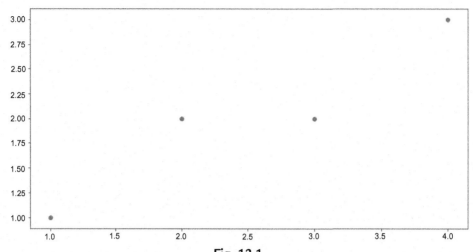

Fig. 12.1
Scatter plot created using matplotlib.

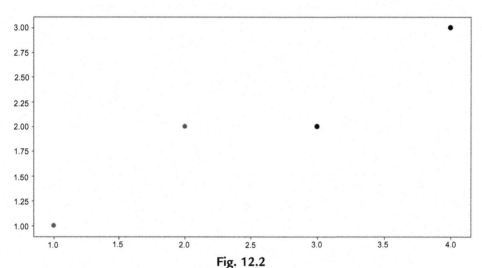

Fig. 12.2
Scatter plot using column labels as color indicators.

```
from matplotlib import cm

viridis_map = cm.get_cmap('viridis', 2)

plt.scatter(x=coords_df['x_coords'], y=coords_df['y_coords'],
c=viridis_map(coords_df['label'].cat.codes))
plt.show()
```

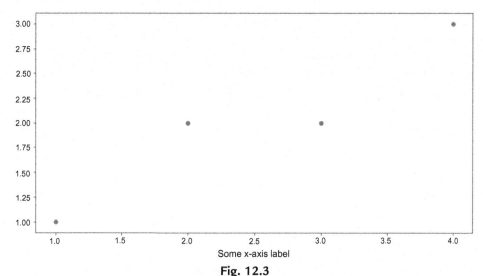

Fig. 12.3
Scatter plot using the Axis API with axis labeling.

The object-oriented API represents a slightly different workflow. Using this API, you create a figure object with axes and then interact with axes objects to control plotted data, x and y axis scaling, tick markings, and annotation. Axes and figure objects can be created using the subplots command as shown here and in Fig. 12.3:

```
import matplotlib.pyplot as plt

fig, ax = plt.subplots()
ax.scatter(x=coords_df['x_coords'], y=coords_df['y_coords' ])
ax.set_xlabel("Some x-axis label", fontsize=24)
plt.show()
```

12.4 Jupyter

We have now covered the core Python language and some of its most important analytical packages. At this point, we can turn our discussion to workflow. In the preceding examples, we have acted as though code was being typed directly into a Python interpreter session. This is acceptable for simple, toy examples such as those shown here, but it offers some serious drawbacks. First is that code typed into a terminal session does not persist beyond termination of the session, and it would be tedious and impermanent to try and compose many lines of code in this way only to have them obliterated when the session closes. In addition, editing code is cumbersome and awkward in a terminal session, especially when that code spans several lines as is the case with function and class definition and a host of other things. If, for example, we wanted to change an aspect of one line of a 5-line function definition, we would have to either rewrite the entire function or use the up arrow to individually access and re-enter each previously typed line. We leave this as an exercise for the reader. A popular alternative to this is the use of an integrated development environment (IDE), which has become the standard way to write code in almost any setting. IDEs vary in their functionality and use but the majority exist to simplify constraints that don't apply as heavily to data science. For example, the IntelliJ IDE for Java offers excellent capabilities to assist with compilation, debugging, and file management as many object-oriented codebases have a complex file structure.

These are virtuous functions indeed, but they aren't quite suited for the specific challenges of data analysis. Analysis is an inherently iterative process, which, although based upon a solid guiding methodology and process, must allow for the generation and investigation of hypotheses. As such, analytical codebases evolve in ways other application codebases typically do not. There are a group of IDEs, however, which do exist to support this methodology and which allow for the asynchronous creation, execution, and editing of lines and block of code within a larger code documents. Thus, instead of writing, compiling, executing, editing, re-compiling, re-executing, and so forth, it is possible to simply alter and re-run pieces of code within a larger persistent session. Wolfram Notebooks and the MatLab Live Editor are popular foundational example of such environments, but they are also tied to their own respective programming languages. A particularly popular incarnation is known as IPython, which was created by Fernando Perez to emulate the behavior of Wolfram Notebooks in Python. Given Python's meteoric rise in popularity, IPython and its successor project Jupyter have become the predominant way to do data analysis in Python. Jupyter does also include the ability to work with other languages, although this not as commonly the case either because certain language interfaces are not as functional or, as with the R language, there is another more commonly used language-specific analytical IDE such as RStudio.

Jupyter may be installed as a conda package just as with numpy, pandas, and matplotlib except Jupyter is not generally imported and used as those packages are. Instead, when installed, Jupyter becomes a shell command, which, when executed, boots up a local server hosting the Jupyter IDE application. This application may then be reached through a web browser as the IP address and port of the host, typically 127.0.0.1 and 8888, respectively. Jupyter also offers a powerful convenience function in that, when the application is launched from the base conda environment, individual notebooks can be created and bound to any of the other installed conda environments (referred to as "kernels"). All that is required to do this is to install the ipykernel package and run the command `python -m ipykernel install -user` within each conda environment. Lastly, at the time of this writing, the Jupyter Project has released a more flexible and functional graphical interface known as Jupyter Lab, which may be installed through the `jupyterlab` conda package and run using the "jupyter lab" terminal command. Fig. 12.4 shows a locally hosted instance of Jupyter Lab accessed through the Google Chrome web browser.

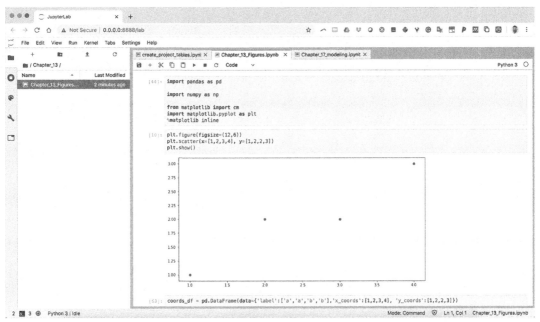

Fig. 12.4
Jupyter notebook accessed through a web browser.

12.5 Analytical documents and interactive computing

The real power of Jupyter comes in its ability to support interactive computing.
The Jupyter application is a launch pad for notebooks each of which is a document divided into separately executable "paragraphs." Importantly, these paragraphs may contain Python code as well as expository documentation written in Markdown. This is an extremely powerful aspect of analytical documents because they are both functional analytical programs and explanatory reports. Markdown is not a programming language as Python is but, rather, it is a simple markup language in which text can be easily formatted to create titles, subtitles, bold and italics, bullets and numbers, embedded images, hyperlinks, and even stylized example code. Fig. 12.5 shows an example Jupyter notebook with a Python paragraph importing packages, a Markdown paragraph explaining the current analysis and denoting the data ingestion step and another Python block, which actually imports data for analysis.

It is helpful to briefly review the architecture of Jupyter as an application as this will help us to understand our subsequent discussion of magic commands. When a paragraph is executed within a Jupyter notebook, the contents of that paragraph are converted to a JSON message and then sent to a message queue via ZeroMQ. This message queue is a first-in-first-out (FIFO) buffer, which further sends its queued messages to a specific Python session for execution. The output of executed statements is then brokered back through ZeroMQ to the notebook

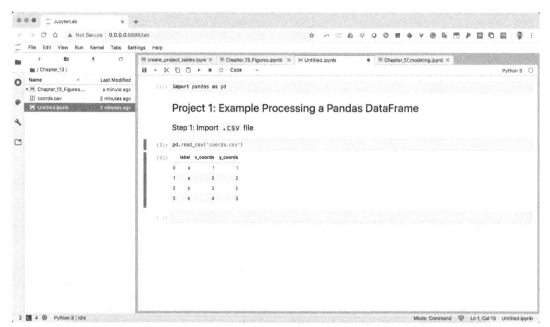

Fig. 12.5
Example Jupyter notebook showing Python and Markdown paragraphs.

frontend and displayed beneath the executed paragraph. This arrangement allows for the notebook application to preprocess messages, attaching certain syntax to functionality (e.g., magic commands) from outside of Python, allowing that functionality to be parsed and triggered before messages are brokered on to the Python session. Fig. 12.6 depicts a

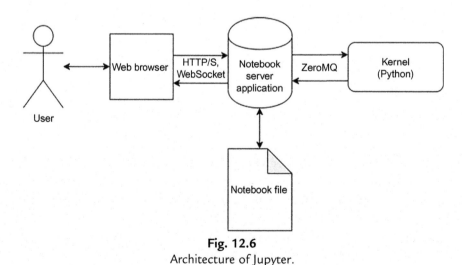

Fig. 12.6
Architecture of Jupyter.

general architectural schematic for Jupyter notebooks as they convey paragraph messages to Python sessions.

Jupyter contains many additional powerful features in the form of specific additional syntactic elements, which bring extended functionality to the notebook. These features take the form of "magic command," which are invoked with either a preceding single or double percent sign within a Python paragraph. Perhaps the most common magic command is `%matplotlib inline`, which, when executed anywhere in the notebook (typically among the import statements in the first paragraph) instructs Jupyter to capture the plots produced by matplotlib and embed them with the notebook document as figures rather than displaying them in a new window. Fig. 12.4 shows a Jupyter notebook with a matplotlib figure embedded inline in this fashion.

Also important are the `%%time`, `%timeit`, and `%%prun` magic commands, which, when included in a Python block, measure the total time taken to run the paragraph once, the average time taken to run the paragraph over several loops, or the time spent on each paragraph's constituent function calls, respectively.

Finally, Jupyter does provide a powerful way to interact with the system shell through the use of the exclamation prefix. When used to prefix a statement, the output will be executed in the host system shell such as Bash or Powershell instead of the Python interpreter. What's more interesting is that Python may be used in a paragraph either to prepare a statement, which is then run within the system shell or to parse the output of a statement after it has been run in the system shell. Fig. 12.7 depicts the creation of a simple shell command to print the statement "Hello, Peter" using Python to prepare the statement's contents before invoking Bash's echo command through Jupyter.

This is far short of a comprehensive tour of Jupyter's functionality, which includes customizable javascript and the ability to embed interactive widgets among other things. Nonetheless, this discussion does cover the most common uses and features, which have made Jupyter such an indispensable tool for analysis. The final point to make is that these analytical documents created within Jupyter may be stored, version-controlled, and shared

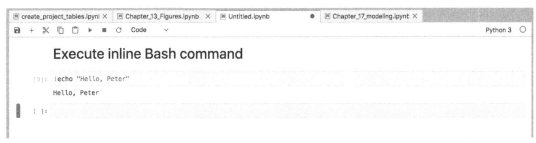

Fig. 12.7

Example Bash command executed inline within a Jupyter notebook.

within and between teams and serve as a critical source of truth and tool for keeping analytical teams and projects synchronized and transparent.

12.6 Conclusion

This chapter has extended upon a preliminary discussion of Python to introduce package management, key packages, and workflow elements, including interactive computing with Jupyter. There are many packages and features, which are not covered in this short introduction, but the hope is that this serves as a "lay of the land" with regard to where these tools fit and how they are used. With this foundational understanding, you will be equipped to learn about, install, and try additional packages through a simple and flexible Jupyter notebook. Moreover, it is almost unavoidable that any specific analytical project you seek to accomplish will require the use of Jupyter, conda, and-at least-the packages discussed here. In the next chapter, we move on to an applied discussion of exploratory analysis using the tools just introduced.

CHAPTER 13

Assessing data quality, attributes, and structure

13.1 Introduction

We have thus far covered database structure interaction whereby data can be extracted from a database into another database or into a file such as a csv, tsv, or even an Excel spreadsheet. We have also discussed the basic tools and workflow elements surrounding data analysis using Python. At this point, you likely have some sort of mental picture of how data could be gathered from a database and loaded through pandas into a DataFrame, but you may be wondering what, then, should you do with those data? This question is the focus of this chapter and is an appropriate topic to discuss at this time as we transition from data storage and representation in the preceding chapters to data modeling and interpretation in the subsequent chapters. We will discuss several key concepts such as data quality and missingness as well as techniques to format data optimally for subsequent analysis. Understand that several volumes would be written on this topic alone, but this chapter will provide a core conceptual foundation for current practice and future learning.

13.2 Importing, cleaning, and assessing data

We begin at the beginning, with data importing and, although we won't dwell here, it is an important topic to introduce. Insofar as the preferred data analysis workflow brings data into Python as a Pandas DataFrame, we can use many functions within Pandas itself to directly import external tabular information as a DataFrame through functions such as `read_csv`, `read_excel`, `read_json`, `read_feather`, and several others, which take a file name and path as an argument and read that file into a DataFrame object. Certain additional options are available such as skipping certain rows or choosing certain imported columns to be the DataFrame index. The Pandas documentation includes full explanations of these functions so, rather than covering them here, just understand that they exist for purposes of importing and you can find more information at pandas.pydata.org/pandas-docs/stable/user-guide/. One additional import function worth explicitly mentioning is `read_sql`, which can take an SQL table or even an SQL query and read the contents into a DataFrame. Pandas' `read_sql` does require some additional setup with regard to database drivers but, once configured, this can be a

An Introduction to Healthcare Informatics. https://doi.org/10.1016/B978-0-12-814915-7.00013-2

seamless interoperation. From here onward, we will assume that data have been incorporated into a DataFrame through one of these methods and, thus, we now turn to exploration of that DataFrame object.

We will be using a data set, which was modified from the University of California Irvine's (UCI) Machine Learning Repository, which is an excellent collection of open tabular datasets. Specifically, we will use a modified version of the "Post-Operative Patient" data set, which describes the vital signs, in terms of blood pressure and temperature, of patients in postoperative care as well as the subsequent destination of those patients when they leave immediate postoperative care: to intensive care, to a general medical floor, or home. We could easily imagine collecting such data in order to develop decision support for patient management or in order to alert other units or services about potential incoming patients. Imagine that we have collected this information from our EMR system's data warehouse after defining the criteria for selected patients and the attributes we wish to select about those patients. This could be expressed as an SQL query, which may require us to join tables together. Perhaps our SQL query even looks something like this:

```
SELECT
      PACU_Patients.Patient_ID,
      Vitals_Flowsheet.InternalTemperature,
      Vitals_Flowsheet.SurfaceTemperature,
      Vitals_Flowsheet.OxygenSat,
      Vitals_Flowsheet.BloodPressure,
      Vitals_Flowsheet.ComfortLevel,
      Vitals_Flowsheet.Vitals_RecordTime,
      PACU_Patients.DischargeLocation
FROM PACU_Patients
JOIN PACU_Patients.Patient_ID = Vitals_Flowsheet.Patient_ID
WHERE PACU_Patients.Encounter_End > To_Date('10-23-2019')
AND PACU_Patients.Encounter_End < To_Date('10-27-2019')
```

Here we have selected the following attributes: internal and surface temperature, oxygen saturation, blood pressure, reported comfort level, and discharge location and we've restricted this to those patients who left the PACU between October 23 and October 27 of 2019. Now, we wish to view the actual contents of our query as a DataFrame. Typically, a good place to start is with Pandas' head() function, which prints, by default, the first five rows of the DataFrame as shown with the output of this function depicted in Fig. 13.1.

```
import pandas as pd
pacu_df = pd.read_csv('pacu_query_results.csv')
pacu_df.head()
```

```
pacu_df.head()
```

	Patient_ID	InternalTemperature	SurfaceTemperature	OxygenSat	BloodPressure	ComfortLevel	Vitals_RecordTime	DischargeLocation
0	O16BWD	37.2	35.5	88.0	118/80	poor	2019-10-11 00:00:00	Floor 5
1	O16BWD	37.4	36.7	93.0	122/74	poor	2019-10-11 01:00:00	Floor 5
2	O16BWD	37.7	35.8	NaN	119/72	poor	2019-10-11 02:00:00	Floor 5
3	O16BWD	38.5	36.7	100.0	118/78	poor	2019-10-11 03:00:00	Floor 5
4	O16BWD	36.0	35.2	NaN	116/76	poor	2019-10-11 04:00:00	Floor 5

Fig. 13.1

Top (a.k.a. "head") of the pacu_df DataFrame.

Here, we can see that at least we have data for each column and our requested columns are at least present—although they may not contain what we expect or assume. Importantly, we can also see that some columns have repeat values. Here, `Patient_ID` appears to repeat several times perhaps due to some issue with the underlying data or perhaps because we have multiple instances of vital signs being collected for PACU patients. We can also invoke `pacu_df.tail()` to view the last five rows of our DataFrame.

While head and tail allow us to view visually formatted snippets of a DataFrame, they can still miss certain important details. One example of this is inconsistencies in column name formatting, which can insidiously cause downstream errors in analysis. For this reason, we can invoke the DataFrame's columns attribute, which will print an array of objects each containing the string name of one of the DataFrame columns. Here you may notice that the `ComfortLevel` column actually has a space at the end. As a matter of best practice, we should remove naming oddities like this. As we will see shortly, we often overwrite columns in DataFrames with modified versions that contain certain updates to their formatting or results of additional calculation. If some columns have spaces at the end while others do not, this creates a risk that we will end up duplicating rather than replacing columns when we do this, which can result in copies of columns which have nearly identical names (e.g., "ComfortLevel" and "ComfortLevel") but different values. This might not seem like a significant issue but consider the common scenario wherein we share this DataFrame with someone else or we save our work and return to it later. In such cases, it is likely that our colleagues and even we ourselves will forget which column was the "correct" one. One of the core goals in analysis is cleanliness and consistency of process without which competing versions of near-identical data can fatally confuse our project and our team. Fortunately, if we can catch such inconsistencies by printing the columns of a DataFrame, we can easily make changes. In this case, we can use the rename function, which takes a "columns" argument consisting of a dictionary in which the current column names we wish to change are keys and the new column names we wish to put in their place are the corresponding values. In order to remove the trailing space from the ComfortLevel column, we would then just do the following:

```
pacu_df.reanme(columns={'ComfortLevel ':'ComfortLevel'}, inplace=True)
```

Pandas DataFrames have a convenient `shape` attribute that will return the number of rows and columns simply by calling, in this case, `pacu_df.shape` which shows us that we have almost 200 rows further implying that these rows likely are on a per-measurement basis.

```
pacu_df.shape
>>> (176,8)
```

Thus far we have merely confirmed that we have rectangular data, so we must move on to assessing the nature of each value in our DataFrame. The head function is useful in that it shows us an excerpt of row contents, but we can use the DataFrame dtypes attribute to report the type of data stored within each column Series. Fig. 13.2 depicts the dtypes for each of our DataFrame columns.

```
pacu_df.dtypes
```

Pandas allows us to explicitly declare the dtype that a certain column should take within a few reasonable constraints. This is useful because often when we import data they may contain unexpected data-type declarations. A common example of this is having integer or float values represented as strings. For example, our `InternalTemperature` looks like it was imported with values such as "37.5" instead of 37.5 hence it has a dtype of `object` and not `float` in Fig. 13.2. We can transform this to a numeric column by using the `astype` function of the column Series: `pacu_df['InternalTemperature'].astype(float)`. Sometimes numerical data are stored as a string because other databases or systems encode missing values with string characters such as a dash: "-" causing the `astype` conversion to fail because the dash cannot be sensibly transformed into a numeric value. In these circumstances, we can use Pandas' `to_numeric` function, which will take a Series as an argument as well as an optional errors argument, which, if specified as "coerce," will convert values that cannot be numerically to null values.

Dtypes show us something else interesting as well: our `BloodPressure` column is of dtype "object," which may be a bit unexpected since we normally think of blood pressure

```
pacu_df.dtypes

Patient_ID              object
InternalTemperature     object
SurfaceTemperature      float64
OxygenSat               float64
BloodPressure           object
ComfortLevel            object
Vitals_RecordTime       object
DischargeLocation       object
dtype: object
```

Fig. 13.2
Dtypes of columns in the pacu_df DataFrame.

across a continuous numerical range. Here, we have a string representing blood pressure that contains a "/" in between systolic and diastolic values. In this circumstance, it would be preferable to split blood pressure into two separate columns, one systolic and one diastolic and we can use Pandas string processing functionality to do this. Recall that since DataFrame columns are really vectors, we can perform these operations efficiently by describing them as operations on the whole column Series rather than looping over each column value explicitly. Thus, in order to split the blood pressure column into separate "Systolic" and "Diastolic" columns, we would use the `split` function. The way we declare this in Pandas is to use the string accessor for a Series and to call the `split` function on that accessor. An "accessor" is a method that governs the way in which we can obtain—or access—the values of a given object. Thus, the pandas Series object representing the values of the BloodPressure column contains properties for each row index and value. The string accessor allows us to use string manipulation methods on the column, while Pandas handles execution of that operation against the values of Series while also returning the collected results as another Series. The `split` operation, then, takes as an argument a "pattern," which is a character or substring by which to split the Series values and a Boolean "expand" argument, which, when `True`, returns a DataFrame wherein each split is a separate column. Thus, a statement as simple as:

```
pacu_df[['SystolicBloodPressure', 'DiastolicBloodPressure']] =
pacu_df['BloodPressure'].str.split(pat="/", expand=True)
```

Will create two new columns containing the corresponding values from the left and right sides of the "/" in the BloodPressure column, respectively, as shown in Fig. 13.3. This sort of initial DataFrame assessment and manipulation is extremely common when viewing a new dataset as we cannot control how information is stored in the EMR or—in many cases—in an enterprise warehouse. The fact that BloodPressure is a string rather than a numeric value could represent either an idiosyncrasy by which our specific EMR stores that information or an idiosyncrasy by which that information is extracted and loaded into a

BloodPressure	ComfortLevel	Vitals_RecordTime	DischargeLocation	SystolicBloodPressure	DiastolicBloodPressure
118/80	poor	2019-10-11 00:00:00	Floor 5	118	80
122/74	poor	2019-10-11 01:00:00	Floor 5	122	74
119/72	poor	2019-10-11 02:00:00	Floor 5	119	72
118/78	poor	2019-10-11 03:00:00	Floor 5	118	78
116/76	poor	2019-10-11 04:00:00	Floor 5	116	76

Fig. 13.3

BloodPressure column split into Diastolic and Systolic columns. Note that these new columns are added at the right side of the DataFrame and not all columns are shown.

warehouse. We would do our best to design ETL workflows, which capture these sorts of oddities but they are nonetheless very common to encounter. As the preceding steps illustrate, it is important to know—for any data set—which columns we have, the types of data they contain, whether they mean what we think they mean, and generally how data are laid out within them. The DataFrame is a powerful tool for this sort of exploration and it has already allowed us to understand certain oddities with the BloodPressure column and to observe that each row likely corresponds to a single measurement with many rows belonging to a single patient.

Next, it is critical to understand how data within each column is distributed and what sort of outlier values there may be. Fortunately, Pandas can help with this as well through a popular function known as `value_counts()` which will take a column name as an argument and, from the column Series, return another Series. This returned series has a special structure in that its indices are the unique values in the original column and its values are the number of times each corresponding value occurred within the original column. Thus, this generates a histogram structure, which proves very useful for detecting outliers. We can inspect the "InternalTemperature" column simply by calling `pacu_df['InternalTemperature'].value_counts()` but by default, this operation sorts the output Series in order of frequency of occurrence with the most frequent values at the top. Often, however, we may wish instead to sort the output Series by value from lowest to highest using the `sort_index()` method, which will make outlier values more obvious. The results of invoking `pacu_df['InternalTemperature'].value_counts().sort_index(ascending=False)` are shown in Fig. 13.4.

```
pacu_df['InternalTemperature'].value_counts().sort_index(ascending=False)

376.0    1
39.0     1
38.8     1
38.7     1
38.6     1
38.5     4
38.3     1
38.2     5
38.1     1
38.0     2
37.9     1
37.8     5
37.7     4
37.6     9
37.5     4
37.4     7
```

Fig. 13.4

Value counts of the InternalTemperature column. Note that not all values are shown.

Right here we can see something unusual, which is that we have one temperature of 376.0. We can hypothesize as to why this may have occurred, perhaps these temperatures are manually entered and the nurse forgot to key in a decimal point, turning 37.6 into 376. In any case, we certainly can't use this value. We may find similar oddities in other columns allowing us to gain insight into how certain data integrity issues may arise and where we need to do some focused cleaning. It is good practice to assess columns for the presence of outliers. Here, we had a particularly obvious outlier, which became apparent simply by using `value_counts()`. However, for numeric columns, there is a more systematic way to go about this by using the describe function. We can invoke describe on individual Series which will return a Series containing the number of nonnull values as well as the mean, standard deviation, minimum, maximum, and quartiles. Alternatively, we can invoke describe on an entire DataFrame, which will return a DataFrame containing the describe information for each numeric column. Fig. 13.5 depicts the output returned by invoking `pacu_df.describe()`. Note that here the temperature of 376 is shown as the maximum value of the InternalTemperature column and its significantly higher than the mean and 75th percentile values.

Pandas interoperates nicely with matplotlib as well, allowing us to visually summarize this same information by providing a column or list of columns as an argument to the boxplot function. Fig. 13.6 shows the result of providing the columns of the `describe` function to the boxplot function like so:

```
pacu_df.boxplot(column=pacu_df.describe().columns.tolist())
```

Recall that a boxplot depicts the median with a line through the middle of the box region, the upper and lower quartile as the top and bottom of the box region, the maximum and minimum as the whiskers extending from the box region. In some cases, as we see in the figure,

	InternalTemperature	SurfaceTemperature	OxygenSat
count	159.000000	176.000000	158.000000
mean	39.083019	36.126705	95.303797
std	26.899982	0.739824	3.746266
min	35.100000	34.000000	85.000000
25%	36.450000	35.600000	92.000000
50%	36.900000	36.100000	95.000000
75%	37.500000	36.700000	99.000000
max	376.000000	38.100000	100.000000

Fig. 13.5
Output of Pandas' describe function.

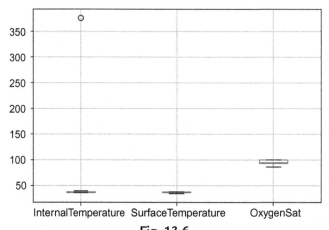

Fig. 13.6
Pacu_df described using matplotlib boxplots.

there are certain values quite far from the median. Conventionally, if these values are above or below the top or bottom of the box region by more than three times the interquartile range (IQR)—that being the distance from the bottom to the top of the box region—then they are formally referred to as "outliers" and are represented by single points floating out from the box and its whiskers.

As mentioned previously, outliers are informative because they can illustrate unexpected properties of the data under consideration or they can highlight problems with data collection. In the latter case, we often want to do something with these values such as block or remove them. Pandas provides a convenient `replace` function, which will take as an argument a list of specific values which we intend to replace and a corresponding value to put in their place. We can invoke replace globally on an entire DataFrame or, more commonly, on a specific Series. In the case of temperature, we know that 376 isn't correct and so we should replace it with a null value. We might be tempted to make a correction instead and replace it with 37.6, but I would stress that often this is not the best move to make. We may think it is likely that 376 represents a missing decimal place, but we often don't really know this sort of thing and making this change would equate to embedding assumptions about data generation into our measurements which we should avoid doing.

To replace 376 with a null value we would simply invoke replace on the "InternalTemperature" column: `pacu_df['InternalTemperature'].replace([376.0], np.nan)`. Notice also that we specifically use `np.nan` to represent "not a number" or a null value. `Nan` is a symbol that, somewhat paradoxically, is intended to represent the absence of anything. Thus, `nan` has some peculiar behaviors such as the fact that `np.nan == np.nan` evaluates to `False`. Although Python does have a special "`None`" value, NumPy's implementation of `nan` in `np.nan` represents none as a float, whereas Python's None is an object. As we discussed previously when talking about numpy arrays, this allows `np.nan` to exist within numerical arrays, which in turn allows Pandas DataFrames to include `np.nan` values while still preserving efficient, vectorized behavior. When it comes to evaluating for the presence of this special Null value, Pandas also has a function called `pd.isna()`, which will return `True` or `False` depending upon whether the argument provided is null. Lastly, the default behavior of the `replace` function is to return a new Series with the replaced values and so, if we wish to replace our original DataFrame column Series with the new modified Series, we can include an additional argument, `inplace = True`.

One very helpful visualization approach for these steps is known as a "missingness" plot, which will highlight certain columns or rows that are devoid of data. Using the `head` operation may not reveal this as it only shows a select few rows and, although using `value_counts()` with the `dropna=False` argument will tally occurrences of missing values, it may not make it obvious when missing values share a row. Thus, a missingness plot provides a graph wherein each box is a value or a cell within our DataFrame and that box is black or white depending upon whether there is a value present. We can easily convert a DataFrame into a matrix of `True/False` values based upon the presence or absence of data by using Pandas `isna()` function and providing the entire DataFrame as an argument. We can then pass that `True/False` matrix directly to a convenient plotting function such as seaborn's heatmap as shown later, resulting in the missingness plot shown in Fig. 13.7. It is often confusing that Pandas supports

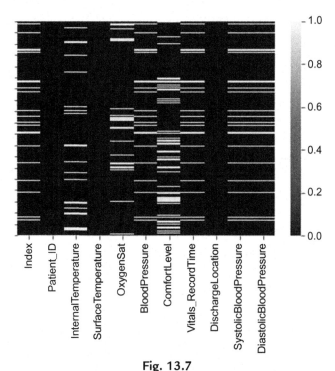

Fig. 13.7
Missingness of values in our DataFrame shown using seaborn's heatmap.

two very similar null-checking functions in the form of `isna()` and `isnull()`, but these are actually identical implementations. The existence of two functions arises due to the historical fact that Pandas is inspired by R DataFrames for which null and na are not identical but instead represent undefined expression evaluations and logical indeterminacy, respectively. By contrast, Pandas' roots in Numpy provide it which a single entity nan instead of either na or null.

```
import seaborn as sns
sns.heatmap( pd.isnull( pacu_df ) )
```

Another very useful package in this regard is "`missingno`," which provides both a missingness matrix and correlation heatmap. The matrix is analogous to the seaborn plot but with the helpful addition of a line plot along the right margin, which depicts the row-wise number of missing values, highlighting that we have three missing values in one of our rows. The correlation heatmap considers each column that has one or more missing values and creates a pairwise matrix where the color of the cells represents the correlation between the missing values in the respective columns. Fig. 13.8 depicts both the matrix and heatmap representations of our PACU data with the heatmap showing another interesting finding, namely, that missing timestamps most often occur with missing BloodPressure measurements. Perhaps this tells us something about the data generation workflow. For example, perhaps oxygen saturation and temperature are measured continuously while blood pressure is measured deliberately at specific times and therefore is the only measure that contributes a timestamp. Being able to visualize missing information and formulate hypotheses about why such missingness patterns occur will inform both subsequent imputation steps as well as upstream interactions with clinical teams providing data.

In addition to missing values, we may also encounter duplicate values. In our DataFrame, we actually have a few of these, which aren't obvious by looking at the head, tail or distributions of column values. Fortunately, Pandas has a `duplicated` method, which, when invoked in a DataFrame, will return a Series with the same number of elements as there are DataFrame rows and the values of which are `True` if the row is a duplicate or `False` if not. Since these Boolean values can behave like integers with `True` being equal to 1 and `False` to 0, we can count the number of duplicates very simply with `pacu_df.duplicated().sum()` and we can remove duplicate rows just as simply with `pacu_df.drop_duplicates(inplace=True)`.

Here we have the first phase of data cleaning, which is understanding the type, format, and presence of the values in our columns and whether these match up with what we expect to find. In some cases, everything is in sync while in others, we may have to read documentation from the EMR or other related applications, from third-party ETL tools, or even from clinical staff in order to understand the nature of the column values. Ultimately, we should have identified and blocked out obviously spurious values and transformed columns into usable data types.

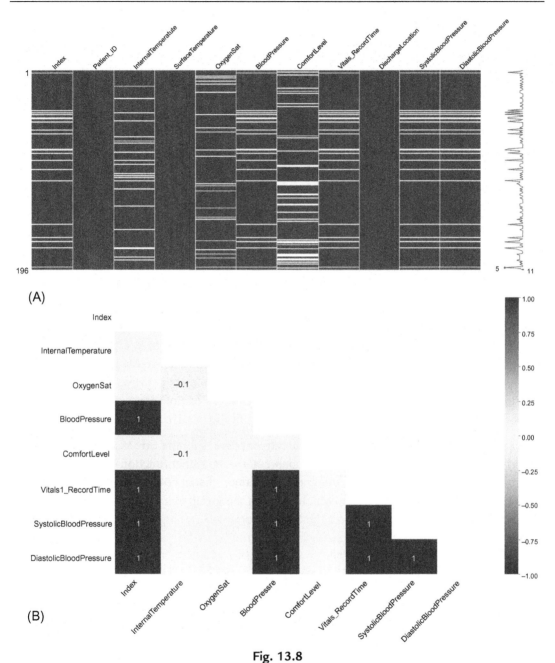

Fig. 13.8

Missing no matrix and heatmap depictions of missing values. Panel A shows the missingness matrix highlighting rows with multiple missing values. Panel B shows the correlation heatmap for which types of values are missing.

13.3 Tidying data

Now that we have evaluated our DataFrame for missingness and the format of its values, we can focus the format of the table itself. This process is referred to as "tidying" data. Tidy is a structural framework for organizing tabular data such that it is well suited for manipulation, visualization, and analysis. This format was described in a paper aptly entitled "Tidy Data" written by Hadley Wickham, who is the author of several widely used R packages, which focus on creating and using tidy data. The basic principles of tidy data are simple: columns should each represent separate variables and rows should each represent single observations. Tidy data may look odd and paradoxically less scrutable to the human eye, but they are far better suited for DataFrame operations. To begin with a simple example, we can imagine a simple DataFrame representing white blood cell counts obtained at three time points throughout chemotherapy for a small group of four patients. As human readers, we may instinctively think the DataFrame should be arranged into five columns: `patient_id`, `wbc_count`, `timepoint_1`, `timepoint_2`, and `timepoint_3` as shown in Fig. 13.9.

This is visually convenient as we can trace the progression of the white blood cell count over time as we scan across a single row and having each row correspond to a patient seems practical. However, this is certainly not tidy as we have neither consolidated the timepoint variable into a single column nor do we have a single measurement per row. To make this tidy, we would instead have a single timepoint column that takes one of three values—1, 2, or 3— and we would have three rows per patient as shown in Fig. 13.10.

We can convert the nontidy version of this treatment table into the tidy version by using a powerful Pandas function `melt()`, which is analogous to the gather function in provided by R's tidyr package. Melt's arguments are an input DataFrame, a list of columns to combine, and one or more columns known as `id_vars`, which serve as the group identifier for the melted rows. Thus, if our original DataFrame is assigned to the variable `non_tidy`, then we can transform it into the tidy version like so: `pd.melt(frame=non_tidy, id_vars='patient', value_vars= ['timepoint_1','timepoint_2','timepoint_3'])`.

	patient_id	timepoint_1	timepoint_2	timepoint_3
0	patient1	6.5	6.0	7.1
1	patient2	7.2	7.5	8.0
2	patient3	5.8	5.5	4.9
3	patient4	4.9	4.0	5.0

Fig. 13.9
Nontidy table structure.

	patient_id	timepoint	value
0	patient1	timepoint_1	6.5
1	patient2	timepoint_1	7.2
2	patient3	timepoint_1	5.8
3	patient4	timepoint_1	4.9
4	patient1	timepoint_2	6.0
5	patient2	timepoint_2	7.5
6	patient3	timepoint_2	5.5
7	patient4	timepoint_2	4.0
8	patient1	timepoint_3	7.1
9	patient2	timepoint_3	8.0
10	patient3	timepoint_3	4.9
11	patient4	timepoint_3	5.0

Fig. 13.10
Tidy table structure.

There is an opposite transformation to melt known as `pivot`, which is analogous to the spread function in tidyr. Pivot will take a column and unpack its unique values into separate columns. You might wonder why we would want to do this given what we just discussed about tidy DataFrames. The answer is that sometimes tidiness is violated by having separate variables rather than variable values in a column. For example, in our DataFrame, imagine we had one column called `vital_sign` that indicates whether a given row records a temperature, or a blood pressure and a corresponding column called "value" that records the measured value for that vital sign as shown in Fig. 13.11.

This structure certainly is not tidy because we have entirely different variables sharing the VitalSign column. Thus, we can pivot these into their own columns by invoking the pivot method of the DataFrame (referring to the DataFrame from Fig. 13.11 as `unpivoted_df`):

	patient_id	vital_sign	value
0	patient1	BloodPressure	128/80
1	patient2	BloodPressure	130/82
2	patient1	Temperature	37
3	patient2	Temperature	37.9

Fig. 13.11
Unpivoted DataFrame.

vital_sign	BloodPressure	Temperature
patient_id		
patient1	128/80	37
patient2	130/82	37.9

Fig. 13.12
Pivoted DataFrame.

`unpivoted_df.pivot(index='patient_id,' columns='vital_sign,' values='value')` resulting in the DataFrame shown in Fig. 13.12.

13.4 Handling missing values

We discussed earlier how we would go about evaluating missing data in a given DataFrame and we presented a scenario with a temperature of 376 wherein we may want to remove a value and replace is with a Null placeholder as though it were missing. Once we have missing values, there are a few potential ways we can decide to go about handling them. One simple option is that we can leave them as-is, preserving the nan values in our DataFrame throughout subsequent steps of analysis. As we discussed earlier, it is possible to represent null values in two ways within Pandas, as the Python None value (which is an object) and as nan from Numpy (which is a float) and the two are not equivalent. Since nan is a float, then having numeric arrays, which contain nans means that those arrays will still work with arithmetic operations like sum and mean whereas having None in in arrays transforms the to the object dtype. Thus, if we decide to leave null values in place, we should be careful that our numeric columns remain numeric. Fortunately, Pandas does attempt to be smart about this, often converting None to nan but inspecting dtypes in our DataFrame will signal whether such a conversion was successful.

Alternative to leaving null values in place, we can remove or "drop" them through the dropna() function. When invoked without an argument, dropna() will remove all rows for which any of the values are nan. That is, a row with a nan only for ComfortLevel will get removed just as will a row with nans for PatientID, RecordTime, and BloodPressure. Unsurprisingly, this approach often removes more data than we would want if there are certain columns with high missingness. We can modify `dropna`'s behavior by specifying a subset of columns within which nans cause a row to be excluded but outside of which nans are not penalized. Additionally, we can also specify a threshold of a minimum number of non-nan values per row above which a row is dropped, resulting in less of an all-or-nothing behavior.

Finally, we can fill missing values with something else using the `fillna()` method which, as with `dropna()`, can be invoked on a column Series, collection of column Series, or an entire

DataFrame. Fillna expects, as an argument, a value which it will use to replace nan values and this value can also be the result of an expression. Thus, we could replace all of the missing values in the ComfortLevel column with the mean of all values in the ComfortLevel column like so: `pacu_df['ComfortLevel'].replace(value=pacu_df['ComfortLevel'].mean(), inplace=True)`. We could choose different summary calculations as well such as the median, which would be preferable in circumstances where we have outliers in our column. Lastly, we would apply a single fillna value to an entire DataFrame or, alternatively, we could provide a dictionary as the argument to fillna where the keys correspond to DataFrame column names and the values to fill values for the corresponding column, thereby allowing us to perform these null value substitutions on a more specific per-column basis.

Finally, once we have assessed the quality of a DataFrame and remedied issues of missingness, formatting, structure, and dtypes, we would programmatically assess for the completeness and validity of these changes. DataFrames are often too large to directly inspect each row; however, Python's built-in assert function will allow us to define assumptions about a DataFrame, which, if false, will produce an error. One obvious example of doing this may be to demonstrate that we have removed all nan values from a given column or DataFrame. We could accomplish this through a statement such as: `assert pacu_df['ComfortLevel'].notnull().all()`, which evaluates whether all values in the ComfortLevel column are not null, returning `True` if we have removed all null values and asserting the result. If assert is asserting either a value or an expression that evaluates to `True`, then it will return nothing but if it is asserting a value or expression which is `False`, then it will generate an `AssertionError`. Assertions constitute potent validity-checking rules, which will explicitly generate errors from Python when violated and they are very useful to confirm the intended behavior of data cleaning and validation operations.

13.5 Conclusion

In this chapter, we discussed the processes by which we can evaluate a DataFrame upon import. This is a crucial competency for data analysis and is especially important in healthcare as we have very complicated and domain-specific data models and imported data often contains unforeseen peculiarities. If there is an overall rule to go by, it is simply that we should expect the unexpected and we now have a process by which to identify and address unexpected issues with the integrity if imported data. Pandas contains many more capabilities than those discussed here, but these constitute a core toolbox for Pandas-based data evaluation. In the next chapters, we will discuss various applied topics of machine learning, computational phenotyping, and deep learning all of which require that data be evaluated and rectified where issues arise. As you proceed through these subsequent chapters, imagine how you might use Pandas in order to make such remedies and how this might be important to downstream analysis.

CHAPTER 14

Introduction to machine learning: Regression, classification, and important concepts

14.1 The aim of machine learning

Much of this book has focused on data models, data storage technologies, and healthcare-specific considerations around how data are generated, transacted, and used. These are weighty and important things to understand as data engineering often consumes the most time and effort of any phase of data application development. That being said, data brokerage is not the reason why we develop data-driven applications. Instead, we invest time and effort into organizing, cleaning, and collecting information so that we can do something with it that enhances our work or broadens our understanding. This is where machine learning takes center stage as its techniques allow us to use data into derive predictions or highlight relationships that would not otherwise be apparent to us.

Formally stated, machine learning describes a group of computational techniques, which can generate and iteratively refine predictions or relationships based upon exposure to data and which can do so without explicit instructions regarding the performance of their objective task. This is considered a subset of artificial intelligence and a superset of deep learning, which we discuss in a subsequent chapter. In many machine learning texts, the learning algorithm is termed the "learner," while the data with which it presented is termed "experience" and, more specifically, a particular organized subset of that experience is termed "training data" and serves the critical purpose of allowing the learner to make attempts at the objective task, assess correct versus incorrect outcomes, and use that to modify future attempts. Importantly, machine learning algorithms must have a specific goal to which they are deployed (e.g., accurately predicting which patient will respond to chemotherapy) and they achieve that goal through a process known as "optimization," in which attributes of the machine learning model are repeatedly modified in an attempt to minimize either the number or the egregiousness of incorrect attempts. We will dive into these concepts throughout this chapter and we will use them to understand two key machine learning approaches: regression and classification. By the end of this chapter, you will hopefully understand how these particular approaches work, when

An Introduction to Healthcare Informatics. https://doi.org/10.1016/B978-0-12-814915-7.00014-4

to use them, and hopefully how to think about many other ideas in machine learning, now armed with a solid foundation. The history of machine learning is rich indeed but knowing that history is not intrinsically necessary to enhance your present understanding of these points and so we will dive right into the technical content and elaborate on core concepts as they arise.

14.2 Regression

The goal of regression is to predict, as correctly as possible, certain real-valued properties of items based upon other properties of those same items. Consider we wish to develop a model that can examine a census of clinic appointments, review the chart of each patient, and tell us how many minutes that patient's visit will take. Such a tool could be very useful for staffing a clinic or informing patient scheduling. Ultimately, this model will consider each patient as a distinct entity with potentially many known attributes (e.g., age, diagnoses, prescriptions, lab results) and will seek to predict the presently unknown value for the specific attribute in which we are interested: the number of minutes spent during that patient's next clinic visit.

This is a classic regression task with a more formal definition as follows:

We have a matrix of features X organized as rows representing patients and their attributes with each row denoted as x. Our model aims to learn a function $f(x)$ that maps each vector x in X to a value $y\hat{}$ (where x is a vector containing an individual patient's age and number of diagnoses for example. Here, $y\hat{}$ (called "y hat") is the model's prediction of the number of minutes spent during that patient's visit. In order to do this, the model must be provided the true labels for patient records in its training data set (these would be previous patient visits for which the patient's age, number of diagnoses and, importantly, the number of minutes spent in her visit are fully known, which we denote y). The model evaluates its performance by applying the function $f(x)$ to input vectors of X and applying a loss function to measure the difference between the prediction outputs $y\hat{}$ and their correct labels y. The learning happens because the outputs of that loss function directly inform changes to be made to the function $f(x)$, thereby bringing the model outputs $y\hat{}$ closer and closer to the true labels y and reducing the error of the regression. The anatomy of this matrix X, its vectors x, true labels y, and predicted outputs $y\hat{}$ is shown in Fig. 14.1.

At this point, this description might seem daunting, but we will walk through it and demystify many of its intimidating aspects. The first thing to bear in mind is that machine learning is inherently geometrical and so explanations often discuss points, spaces, vectors, lines and so forth. In fact, it is easiest to consider that, from the perspective of the machine learning model, each record or observation (in this case each patient) is a point in some space where each dimension is an attribute of that patient. This could be a two-dimensional, three-dimensional, or 100-dimensional space and often machine learning models work with spaces of over 100 dimensions. Unfortunately, the human brain can scarcely conceptualize in more than three

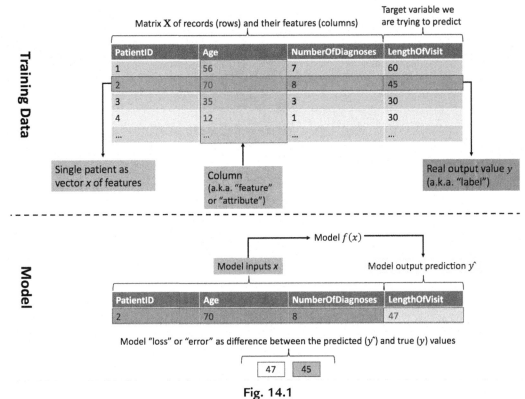

Fig. 14.1
Structure of feature vectors, labels, and the matrix containing them.

dimensions and so we will start there. Imagine that, for each patient record, we know two attributes, the patient's age, and the number of diagnoses she has, and we are aiming to predict the third (length of the next visit). Each patient, therefore, can be considered a point which we can plot in a space of three dimensions x, y, and z, where x might be the age of the patient, y might be the number of diagnoses the patient has, and z might be the number of minutes for which that patient's visit lasted. We could plot these patients as shown in Fig. 14.2.

Note that, in this case, z is the variable we're trying to predict and so we would call our prediction $\hat{z}$. As we mentioned earlier, such an example would have to consist of visits that have already happened (otherwise we wouldn't know the number of minutes for these patients' visits) and we might gather those historical visits into a dataset for the purpose of establishing our regression model. This is a classic, perhaps *the* classic example of a "supervised" machine learning task. Supervision in this case, refers to the fact that we have a dataset for which we do already know the "answer" and we're simply trying to create a model that can see those examples, train on them, and only then be confronted with new example lacking such an answer and fill in the blank. In the next chapter we will cover some additional circumstances where

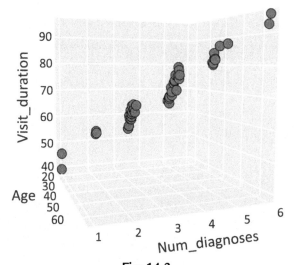

Fig. 14.2

3D scatter plot showing age, number of diagnoses, and duration of visit. Note that the graph is oriented such that the dependent variable (the *z* axis or the visit duration) is vertical.

such an answer is not known (this being the "unsupervised" case), but it will be easier to understand such a case once we have completed a discussion of supervised learning.

14.3 Functions as hypotheses

So how might our model approach the task of "predicting" the visit time? For starters, it would have to formulate some hypothesis from the training data whereby it could relate certain properties to other properties. More concretely, this hypothesis would take the form of a function whose inputs are a patient's age and number of diagnoses and whose output is a number representing the visit duration in minutes. This function is simply a mathematical operation that expresses how *x*, *y*, and *z* are related to each other over many different specific values. We could imagine such a function and plot that amid our points as shown in Fig. 14.3.

Notice now that our points exist in relationship to a line in this space and that the positioning of our points follows fairly closely—although not exactly—the shape of this line. If we could peer into the "mind" of a machine learning algorithm, this function represents what that system "knows" about our patients, it represents a relationship that it could have derived from observing a dataset we provided.

In this initial case, we simply placed this line in the space based upon *our* geometrical understanding of the points here (hence we said that the algorithm "could have" arrived at such a relationship). In actuality, such an approach wouldn't qualify as machine learning. Instead, the real magic that creates intelligent behavior is that the computer process can create this

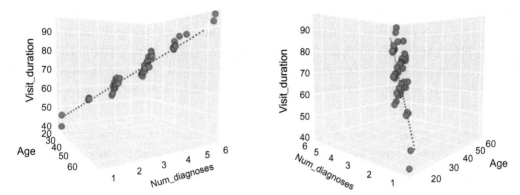

Fig. 14.3

Patient visit points with our hypotheses represented as a linear function in *red* (*gray dotted line* in print version). Note that the graph is shown in two perspectives.

function, arriving at this relationship using only the data points provided to it. This approach is actually quite simple, the algorithm first attempts a function, however incorrect, sometimes even randomly defining one, and places it within the space as shown in Fig. 14.4.

Then something critical happens. The algorithm needs to assess how far its current function is from the points in the space, often described as the "error" of the function, and then use that error to make modifications to the function, repeating this process until error can no longer be reduced. Recall that a linear function such as what we have here consists of values and coefficients, which are added together to produce an output. In this case, the object we have in this space represents a formula that looks like this:

$$z = ax + by + c$$

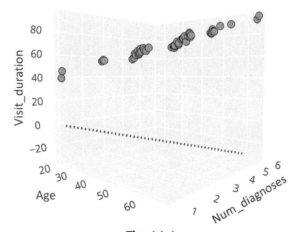

Fig. 14.4

Initial placement of hypothesis function. Note that this initial placement does not adequately capture the relationship between our points.

where z is the visit minutes while x and y are the age and number of diagnoses. Since x, y, and z are known for each patient in our training set, these values don't change. Thus, in order to move this object around in our space, we can modify the coefficients, a and b, and the constant c. These coefficients are also commonly referred to as "weights" because they represent how much emphasis the model puts on a given feature. Let's see this in practice over a few graphics.

If we regard the age and number of diagnoses equally, then a and b would both be 1 and if we don't include any bias term, then c would be zero giving us the function in Fig. 14.5.

We could shift this whole relationship up or down by adjusting our bias term c. For example, we could set $c = 15$, giving us Fig. 14.6.

We could also consider age to be much more influential on the number of visit minutes and increase the weight of a to 3, for example, while keeping the weight at 1 for b, the number of diagnoses as shown in Fig. 14.7.

This is also how our regression model would define different potential hypotheses, by iteratively modifying the weights a and b or the bias term c and assessing the consequential error. In more technical parlance, the collection of possible functions that our model could consider is called our "hypothesis space" and although this could consist of infinitely many possible functions, we typically "constrain" this space in some way. In this circumstance, we have constrained the list of functions our algorithm could use to consist only of those taking the form:

$$z = ax + by + c$$

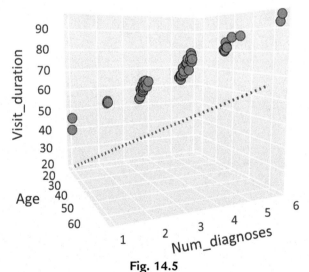

Fig. 14.5

Example hypothesis function where $a = 1$, $b = 1$, $c = 0$.

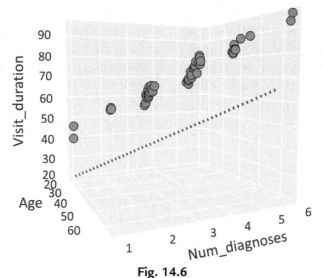

Fig. 14.6

Example hypothesis function with $a = 1$, $b = 1$, $c = 15$.

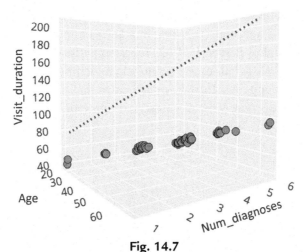

Fig. 14.7

Example hypothesis function with $a = 3$, $b = 1$, $c = 15$.

This could include any real-valued numbers for a, b, and c, including any fractions, but it would exclude exponential terms, for example, so our model wouldn't be allowed to consider something of the form

$$z = ax^2 + by + c$$

or

$$z = ax^3 + by^2 + c$$

In doing this, we have restricted our model to only *linear* functions and, thus, we know we will be performing strictly linear regression. A common source of confusion for many who are new to machine learning is that "linear" does not mean 2-dimensional although linear regression is often taught with 2-dimensional examples. In fact, we've been using a 3-dimensional linear function as an example this whole time. We could also have a 100- or 1000-dimesional linear function. Linearity refers to the form our function takes. It allows any number of "terms" (those being combinations of coefficients and variables such as ax or by or even c (whose coefficient is just 1) but requires that the coefficients (a, b, and c) have exponents no larger than 1. In other words, a linear equation is a polynomial of degree 1.

14.4 Error and cost

Having covered how our model represents a hypothesis and how it may implement a change to that hypothesis, we can finally address the important question of *why* it would alter the hypothesis. As we mentioned previously, for any given function, there is a corresponding error and it is the goal of machine learning to reduce that error. Consider Fig. 14.8 with our function plotted amid our points.

Here we have represented our hypothesis function as a plane instead of just a line. This is more accurate as the hypothesis function captures how x, y, and z relate to one another across a range of values in each dimension. Note that this is still a linear function since, as we discussed, it's a polynomial of degree 1. If our function perfectly captured the relationship between all three dimensions for all of our points, then the plane created by this function would pass through all of our points. In practice this never really happens and, instead, we want to arrive at a hypothesis function, which is mostly accurate or, more concretely, which is

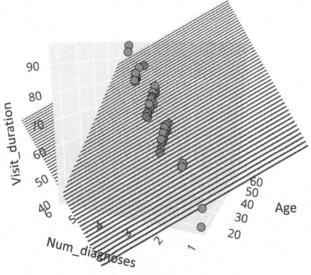

Fig. 14.8
Example hypothesis function as a plane.

generally closest to the most points possible. This is often referred to as "empirical risk minimization" because we tune our model by simply trying out several functions on the training data we have in front of us until we arrive at the one which results in the least error (or "risk" of being wrong).

Consider each of our points in the plot. Since each of these represents a true set of values *x*, *y*, and *z*, we consider these as representative of actual values of *z* given some input *x* and *y*. To estimate what our model would have predicted for this point if we hadn't known the value of *z*, we can simply take the *x* and *y* values (our input values patient age and number of diagnoses) and select the point on the plane where a line from that *x* and that *y* value would have intersected the plane. The value of *z* at that point is what the model would have assumed *z* to be based upon its hypothesis as shown in Fig. 14.9.

We can easily imagine that this patient—as perhaps a bit of an outlier—has a real visit duration that isn't quite a match for this prediction as shown in Fig. 14.10.

The greater this distance, the greater the error in our prediction because our predicted *z* was farther off from the truth. Perhaps as a more minor point, if it is our goal simply to predict the value of *z*, then we consider this distance only along the *z* axis or, in other words, we consider the error only in terms of how wrong we were about the duration of the patient visit. Importantly, we have some quantity of error for each point in our training data set. There are different approaches for representing the error across a whole dataset, but one common such method is known as Mean Squared Error and simply means that we add up the square

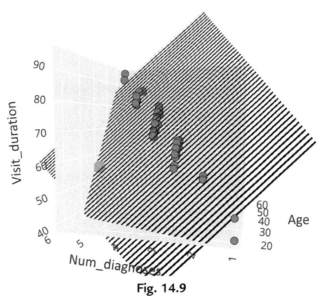

Fig. 14.9

Example hypothesis plane with predicted *z* value given new *x* and *y* values shown in *yellow* (*light gray* in print version).

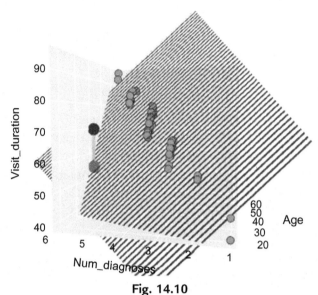

Fig. 14.10

Example hypothesis plane with actual z value given new x and y values shown in *green* (*gray* in print version).

of these distances for each point in the training data set. Squaring these distances is helpful because it makes everything positive and most often we don't specifically care whether the model over or underestimates its target values (although here are certainly some cases in which this may matter to us). We can represent this mathematically as follows.

If we call the hypothesis function h and show that it represents a relationship whereby z depends upon x and y like so:

$$z = h(x, y) = ax + by + c$$

Then we can refer to our error as the "cost" of our model like so:

$$\text{Cost} = \frac{1}{n} \sum_{i=1}^{n} \left(h(x, y)^i - z^i \right)^2$$

where the cost is the average, over all of our data points (assuming we have n number of data points), of the square of the distance between the predicted and the actual value of our target z. Put plainly, the equation says that the cost is equal to the sum, for each of our data points, of the squared distance between the actual value of z for that data point and the predicted value of z according to our function, divided by the number of points we have. Referring back to Fig. 14.10, we imagine a *pink line* (*dark gray line* in print version) for each point marking its distance to the plane and the cost is the sum of the squares of all of the *pink lines* (*dark gray* lines in print version).

There are many different potential cost functions one could choose, but this is a common selection and appropriate for many different problems. Perhaps more important than the particular cost equation is the notion of a cost function itself as it is core to many machine learning techniques as generally almost all such approaches and related training schemes take the form of an optimization problem seeking to minimize cost according to some target output.

14.5 Optimization

So how does optimization actually occur? After all, this is represents the "learning" part of machine learning. We'll turn now to a pervasive algorithm in optimization known as "gradient descent," which is the missing link between quantifying the error of a given hypothesis function and adjusting the weights of that function by however much and in what direction—positive or negative.

To start, let's imagine a different space in which our function lives in Fig. 14.11. Our hypothesis function $h(x, y)$ has two weights a and b (for simplicity sake, we will assume there is no bias and c is equal to zero), which we wish to tweak and which determine the output z for any given x and y. Earlier, we imagined a three-dimensional space consisting of x, y, and z and a function dictated by a, and b. In this second space, we imagine a new three-dimensional space consisting of the weights that describe a particular hypothesis function, a and b, and the cost over all training data points n when that particular function *parameterized* by a and b runs over all these points.

Ponder this for a minute. What would a surface in this space represent and how much information is revealed about this space when we run a given single hypothesis function over our data?

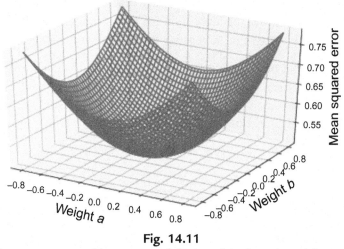

Fig. 14.11

New error space with axes as weight a, weight b, and model error.

As it turns out, a surface in this space would represent many potential weights a and b and thus it would represent an entire family of hypothesis functions. Along those same lines, when we run a given hypothesis function one time—even if we have thousands of data points in our train and test set—we end up with a single point summarizing the overall error that function has over all of our data points. Nonetheless, that point is situated on some surface in that space.

Thinking a bit more about that surface, we can make some important general assumptions about its shape. First is that we would expect there to be either a single best choice of a and b, which, even if it doesn't eliminate error, reduces error the lowest value possible or a close group of mutually best choices whose values for a and b are similar to one another. In other words, we wouldn't expect there to be two very different options for a and b each of which are tied for the lowest cost. This isn't always the case as we'll discuss at greater length in the chapter on Deep Learning, but we can say this is a reasonable assumption here because the goal is to describe a single plane in the x, y, and z space that cuts closest to the most points and significant differences between a and b would lead to planes in very different locations and at very different angles, which would have fundamentally different proximities to points in the z dimension.

Thus, if each point described in this new space is the error when some function is parameterized by a given a and b, and we would expect that there is some best choice for a and b and that being farther from that choice of a and b would increase cost, then the shape of our surface comes to resemble that of a bowl as we see above.

This condition of having a "convex" error surface is quite important as it means that gradient descent can, after enough loops, arrive at the values of a and b for which the cost is lowest or, in other words, it can arrive at the bottom of the bowl: the global minimum of the cost. As the name implies, gradient descent accomplishes this by taking the error for a given a and b and determining the slope of the underlying function (the bowl-shaped surface) at that point. With the slope known, the algorithm can then "walk downhill" by decreasing weights when the slope is positive or increasing weights when the slope is negative.

One point of confusion that may arise here is exactly how this "slope" is determined so we'll walk through that. Since we know the form of the Cost equation and we consider it a function of the choice we make for a and b, we can write it like so, summarizing the difference between predicted and actual z values as simply as "error":

$$error = (h(x, y) - z)$$

$$Cost_{a,b} = 1/n \sum \left(error_n{}^2 \right)$$

Then we take the partial derivative of this error with respect to a and b, respectively:

$$\frac{\partial Cost}{\partial a} = 2(Error) * \frac{\partial}{\partial a}(Error)$$

$$\text{where } \frac{\partial}{\partial a}(Error) = \frac{\partial}{\partial a}(ax + by - z') = x$$

$$\text{thus } \frac{\partial Cost}{\partial a} = 2(Error) * x$$

$$\frac{\partial Cost}{\partial b} = 2(Error) * \frac{\partial}{\partial b}(Error)$$

$$\text{where } \frac{\partial}{\partial b}(Error) = \frac{\partial}{\partial b}(ax + by - z') = y$$

$$\text{thus } \frac{\partial Cost}{\partial b} = 2(Error) * y$$

With these equations, we've shown something important, which is that from a single point in our *a*, *b*, cost space and from knowledge that this is a first-order polynomial hypothesis function, we can derive the slope of the error surface with respect to each of our weights individually. Lastly, since we know the specific values of *a* and *b* that we used to generate the error for a given iteration of algorithm, we have all the ingredients necessary to determine the direction and magnitude by which to shift *a* and *b*. In the following equation, a^i and b^i are the weights used for the current iteration, while a^{i+1} and b^{i+1} are updated weights to be used on the next iteration. We also introduce one more term known as the "learning rate," which is a tunable parameter that can be any real number and which adjusts the extent to which these weight changes are actually applied. If the learning rate is small, then we only make small updates to our weights and if it's large, we make large updates:

$$a^{i+1} = a^i - Error * x * Learning\, Rate$$

$$\text{and } b^{i+1} = b^i - Error * y * Learning\, Rate$$

This relationship is quite sensible. In essence we're saying that if, for example, our predicted *z* for a given point was way BELOW the actual value (the error would be negative in this case because we undershot the target), then our update for weight *a* will be positive and proportional to the magnitude by which we were off, the learning rate we've set and, importantly, the value of *x* used for that prediction. If we undershot the target *z* by a large margin we'll increase the weight we assign to the input *x*, but we also take into consideration that, if the value of *x* being used to make that prediction was small, then this reduces *x*'s contribution to that error a bit and, in turn, reduces the magnitude by which we might want to increase the weight of *x*. Importantly, we can do this for our weights *a* and *b* independent of each other and according to how much the inputs to which those weights apply were responsible for the error of the prediction.

The goal of all this is to nudge weights up or down proportional to how much those weights contributed to an overshot or undershot prediction and eventually to *converge* on the weights that give us the lowest overall cost. Note that we'll never visit all of the points that exist on this error surface. In fact, we only visit a few of them as we progress along a single path from a random starting point dictated by random initial values for a and b toward the bottom of the bowl. As a general statement, the assumption of convexity doesn't always hold depending on the model and sometimes that bowl has a wavier appearance perhaps even with multiple valleys, which we will discuss in subsequent chapters. Since we don't t-test every possible value for a and b, we don't measure the empirical risk incurred by every possible combination of weights (it would be too computationally expensive to do so) and we don't really know that the error surface looks like at points we haven't visited. The best we can do in most cases is walk downhill until we get to a point where everything immediately around us is uphill. In other words, we walk downhill until we can't walk downhill anymore. This process of shown in Fig. 14.12.

Because the error surface for linear models such as linear and logistic regression is convex, this is sufficient but we will discuss neural networks later on as a prime example wherein this is not the case.

Strictly speaking, if we refer back to our equation:

$$a^{i+1} = a^i - Error * x * Learning\,Rate$$

We need to draw attention to a subtlety. In practice, the traditional form of implementing gradient descent is known as "batch gradient descent" so named because the protocol calls for calculating error $* x$ for all points in the entire training dataset, averaging the results and then multiplying by the learning rate and then subtracting that from a^i. Formally, that looks like this:

$$a^{i+1} = a^i - \left(Learning\,Rate * \left[1/n \sum_{i=1}^{n} ((h(x_i, y_i) - z_i) * x_i) \right] \right)$$

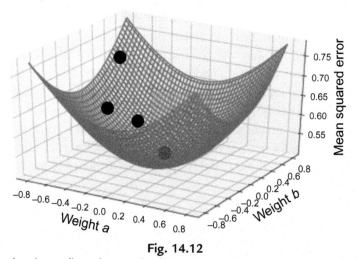

Fig. 14.12
Stochastic gradient descent "walking downhill" over the error surface.

And the same goes for weight *b*. As mentioned previously, this is not typically done in practice as it is quite computationally expensive since the algorithm ends up processing every training data point on every iteration. More interesting is that, while this approach generally requires fewer overall iterations to reach the error minimum (although keep in mind that each iteration is computationally very expensive) it relies more heavily on the assumption of convexity and struggles more in scenarios where the error surface isn't truly bowl-shaped.

Instead, the common technique used is called "stochastic gradient descent" so named because, on each iteration, the algorithm only considers a single, randomly sampled training example—or, in the case of "mini-batch gradient descent" a few randomly selected examples—and uses that to represent the general error over the whole training set. This is much faster if a bit sloppier and, quite interestingly, it's this sloppiness that makes SGD more adept at handling nonconvex error surfaces as it is prone to take uphill steps on occasion, which, in some cases, just might end up causing it walk over a ridge and into a lower valley.

14.6 Classification

We have used the discussion of regression to outline many important concepts in machine learning: hypotheses, error functions, cost, and optimization. Fortunately, we can carry those concepts forward into a discussion around classification as it shares many of the same conceptual pillars. We can even maintain our same example save one minor modification. Where previously, we had set about the task of predicting the number of minutes in a patient visit, here we set about the task of predicting whether a patient's visit will be "long" or "short" defined as over or under 30 min. Understanding how classification problems look in machine learning is, then, all about understanding how a hypothesis function outputs labels instead of numbers on a continuum and how we assign cost to those predictions.

Typically, classification tasks consider labels numerically and in a form known as one-hot encoding. In the case of a two-class prediction such as we have here, a one-hot encoded representation would typically be a 0 to represent short visits (less than 30 min) and a 1 to represent long visits or alternatively a vector [0,1] for short visits and a vector [1,0] for long visits. Keeping with the first approach, when we consider our training dataset, we have the same values for *x* and *y* but now we want all values for *z* to be either a 0 or a 1 as shown in Fig. 14.13.

There are several existing strategies for classification some important examples of which we will discuss in the subsequent chapters. In this section, however, we will focus on a modification of the linear regression approach known as logistic regression as it very widely used. If you examine the figure, one important difference may immediately become apparent. Where our linear regression task aimed to create a hypothesis function that got as close as possible to as many points as possible, here the aim is to create a hypothesis function that passes between the 0's and 1's on the *z* axis and divides as many of them as possible into homogeneously labeled groups.

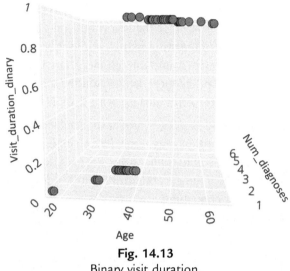

Fig. 14.13
Binary visit duration.

How would this actually work? The trick is in the use of a logistic function, hence the name, which has a sigmoidal shape. Where linear hypothesis functions take the form $z = ax + by + c$ as we discussed previously, logistic hypothesis functions build upon that linear equation by passing its output to an exponential function. Thus, to consider weights a and b with features x and y, and constant c, our hypothesis function would look like this:

$$h(x, y) = \frac{1}{1 + e^{-(ax + by + c)}}$$

The effect of such a transformation is to "squash" the large range of outputs that $z = ax + by + c$ can emit into a range from 0 to 1. In doing this, typically 0.5 is established as the tipping point between whether $ax + by + c$ assigns a label 0 or a label 1 and, by design, the function is the most sensitive to change at and around 0.5 where decisions are "on the fence" but becomes precipitously less sensitive to change at the extremes where decisions are of high confidence as shown in Fig. 14.14.

Of course, the question remains as to how cost is assigned to a function like this. This is actually accomplished typically by the use of two nonlinear functions, one for when the correct class label is 0 and another for when the correct label if 1:

$$Cost(h(x, y), z) = \begin{cases} -\log(h(x, y)) \: if \: z = 1 \\ -\log(1 - h(x, y)) \: if \: z = 0 \end{cases}$$

Doing this cleverly creates a cost behavior that considers a very confident assignment of an incorrect label worse than only an intermediately confident one and this is important for optimization because such methods still use stochastic gradient descent and its related

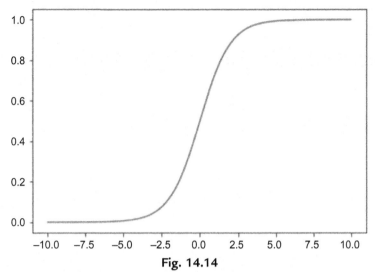

Fig. 14.14

Example logistic function, which compresses an infinite range of values on the *x* axis to the 0 to 1 range on the *y* axis.

techniques, which require there to be a continuous error surface. Recall that these cost functions exist in the *a*, *b*, cost space rather than the *x*, *y*, *z* space and, because they are continuous, we can take a derivative for error and adjust weights accordingly.

As you can see, the majority of classification by logistic regression adheres to the same internal mechanics as predicting a continuous value by linear regression including the critical task of iterative optimization. The implementation details relevant to logistic regression are in the use of the logistic function to map outputs of hypothesis functions to a range from 0 to 1 while still preserving the fact that the core hypothesis is still linear and emits values across a range and each of those values have a cost and gradient which can be used for gradient descent.

One last point to make here regards a subtlety about how exactly a model such as a linear regression actually determines how far a given data point is from the decision boundary. We say that the underlying linear equation traces a decision boundary in the *x*, *y*, *z* space that divides short from long appointments. We can visualize this as a curved line representing the function that turns *x* and *y* input values into a predicted *z* value on the range from 0 to 1. Since these conveniently represent probabilities where 1 is certainly a long appointment and 0 is certainly not a long appointment, we commonly establish 0.5 as the cutoff to pick between long and short. Thus, we can also imagine this space as cut in half by a plane located at $z = 0.5$ as shown in Fig. 14.15.

In this case the learned weights *a*, *b* are used to multiply the features *x*, *y* for a given data point and it's this number that we're squashing with the sigmoidal logistic function. Importantly, when we use training data to locate the right decision boundary, we're really selecting the

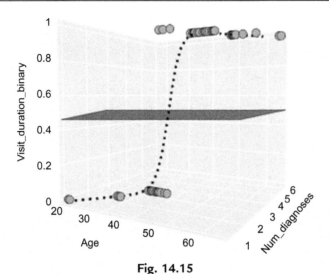

Fig. 14.15
Logistic decision function as a *curved line*.

correct weight vector [*a*, *b*]. Once trained, executing the model to perform classification is as simple as calculating the dot product between the weight vector [*a*, *b*] and a point's feature vector [*x*, *y*] and transforming the output through the logistic function. To bring this full circle, Fig. 14.16 shows where this logistic function would predict *z* to be (in *yellow* (*light gray* in print version)) compared to where it actually is (in *green* (*gray* in print version)). Since the *yellow* (*light gray* in print version)) and *green* (*gray* in print version) points are on the opposite sides of the decision boundary, this error would result in a misclassification there the model would predict a short visit when in actuality it was long.

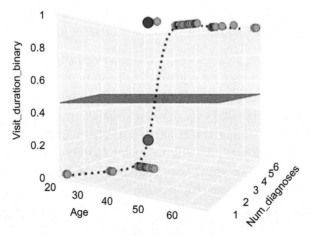

Fig. 14.16
Example prediction (*yellow* (*light gray* in print version)) compared to actual data point (*green* (*dark gray* in print version)) resulting in misclassification.

14.7 Additional considerations: Normalization, regularization, and generalizability

As a final conclusion to this discussion of regression, there are a few additional concepts that are essential to building and implementing machine learning models.

Normalization typically refers to the process of ensuring that different collections of values share the same range. For example, we might normalize the x and y features for our training data points because they initially have quite different specific values and distributions with x ranging from 25 to 75 and y ranging from 1 to 4. There are many different methods for normalization, which usually depend upon how the input data are distributed. One common method is called min-max normalization where, for each value n, we subtract from n the minimum value for n in our dataset and divide that by the range of values n takes:

$$n_{minmax} = \frac{n - n_{min}}{n_{max} - n_{min}}$$

Rather than cover the myriad techniques, it's more useful to think about why we would want to do this. Recall that gradient descent relies on the magnitude of the features x and y in order to adjust their relevant weights. If these features occupy two very different ranges, then one will bear more influence than the other and will be tweaked more aggressively by gradient descent than the other. Imagine that we also had height in cm as a feature. The cost of our function will be much more heavily influenced by height values like 150 and 175 than by problem numbers like 2 and 3. This results in an error surface that becomes more elongated in some directions than others.

Regularization and generalizability are inter-related concepts. Regularization strictly refers to limiting the complexity of our hypothesis function the point of which is to ensure that it does not come to rely too heavily in particular features or observations in the training data. Doing this is important because the real test of our model will be whether it can make accurate prediction on new, never-before-seen data in the form of new patients. This ability to learn a hypothesis function on training data and effectively apply it to new datapoints outside of the training dataset is known as model generalizability. By choosing a linear hypothesis function, we implemented a form of regularization by ensuring that we can only consider first-order polynomials. Other common approaches include L1 and L2 regularization both of which limit the amount of weight a model can assign to any given feature. L1, also known as "LASSO" regression, penalizes the absolute value of the weights over all feature in a model. This has the effect of driving some weights toward zero in effect ignoring certain features, resulting in sparse models. L2, also known as "Ridge" regression instead penalizes the square of the weights over all the features in a model.

14.8 Conclusion

This chapter has aimed to introduce the core concepts and approaches to machine learning and to lay the conceptual foundations for both the subsequent chapters on machine learning and deep learning and for additional study beyond this book. Machine learning is an incredibly broad topic with many different approaches and domain-specific considerations. The models discussed here comprise some of the most common tools used for analysis and are readily available to implement in Python using the scikit-learn or TensorFlow libraries.

Introduction to machine learning: Support vector machines, tree-based models, clustering, and explainability

15.1 Introduction

The previous chapter was an ambitious introduction to machine learning and its foundational concepts. Using the example of predicting the length of future patient visits, we explored how hypothesis functions are created, constrained, and modified to reduce error. The techniques of linear and logistic regression are foundational and popular, but they are by no means comprehensive. As with the preceding chapter, this is a quick tour through technical ideas and it should be assumed that this content may require multiple read-throughs. So, onward we go bearing in mind that we are covering quite a lot of ground.

15.2 Support vector machines

Picking up where we left off, let us return to the task of predicting the duration of patient visits, focusing on the scenario of classification where we're not trying to predict the number of minutes but rather we are trying to categorize a visit as "long" or "short." Previously, we had discussed logistic regression as a technique for doing this and we focused on the fact that, in logistic regression, we have a cost function that not only penalizes the model when it assigns the wrong classification label but it scales that penalty in accordance with how confident the model was in making the wrong assignment. That is to say, if the model would predict that a visit would be in the "short" category with a probability of 0.99 and the visit ends up being long, then this prediction gets assigned a much higher penalty than if the model was only slightly in favor of saying that the visit would be short, say with a probability of 0.55. The goal of model scoring, cost counting, and optimization is ultimately to identify the "best" plane, which divides our data points into short and long categories. Recall that we still have to make a decision in the design of our model about what we mean by "short" versus "long" and we have to establish some length cutoff and we had said that a short visit is less than 30 min in duration. But what do we mean by the "best" dividing plane? The mechanics of logistic regression entail a presumed answer to this question. To see how that works, let's consider again how a particular hypothesis function is scored: as the average error over all of the data points. Since this is true, strongly misclassified outliers contributing more influence on this score than other points. Thus, logistic regression will try to move all of the points onto their correct respective sides of the dividing plane and, where that fails, it will at least try to move the dividing plane closest to misclassified points so at least they not placed too far into the wrong class territory.

We assume we're constraining such a logistic regression so that we can only have linear hypothesis functions and we assume we're simply trying to optimize the mean error although we could to something fancier if we wished. With all of that in mind, we're going to make one simplification, which will help make the following graphics more understandable: we're going to drop down into two plotting dimensions instead of three. We focused on 3-D examples in the previous chapter because it enhances the explanation of gradient descent allowing us to discuss error slopes with respect to only certain features. However, this discussion will require us to eyeball dividing planes between points and this is pictorially not as clear in the 3-D case. Thus, we will modify our problem slightly to only plot the age and number of diagnoses as axes and to use color-coding to represent whether the visit was long or short. You can think of this as looking straight down on a 3-D plot from above. Understand that everything we discuss here could work in 2-D, 3-D, 1000-D, and so on but human-to-human explanation works best in low-dimensional spaces. Consider now Fig. 15.1, which shows our data points with the age on the x-axis and number of diagnoses on the y-axis with color representing the visit duration is "short" or "long" in a 3D and 2D representations.

With these color-coded points, it looks as though we can draw a dividing plane that actually splits all of them correctly—even though things don't often work out this well in reality. Moreover, observe that we could draw several potential such dividing lines each at different angles all of which still successfully split all of the data points correctly as shown in Fig. 15.2.

The difference between logistic regression and support vector machines (SVM) can really be summed up as the approach each model takes to picking the best line from within this "wiggle room," but we discuss it here because it also illustrates a more important general point in machine learning, which is that we train models on observed data in the hope that they will generalize to unobserved data and so we have to examine model behavior with that fact in mind. Whatever training data we do get our hands on—even if we do a great job of finding and collecting patient cases—we will always only have some sample from all of the possible data points our model will encounter. Fig. 15.3 shows a dividing line the type of which logistic regression would select as the best. What do we think about this selection? We've added one extra *blue* (dark gray in print version) data point, which looks like an outlier separated from the rest of its class. Notice how the decision boundary tries to accommodate this, what do we think about this behavior?

Within our sample of training data, this point represents an unusually short visit for a patient whose age and number of diagnoses are more similar to people with long visits; it's really in our data but is it really representative? Let's imagine the ways in which this could

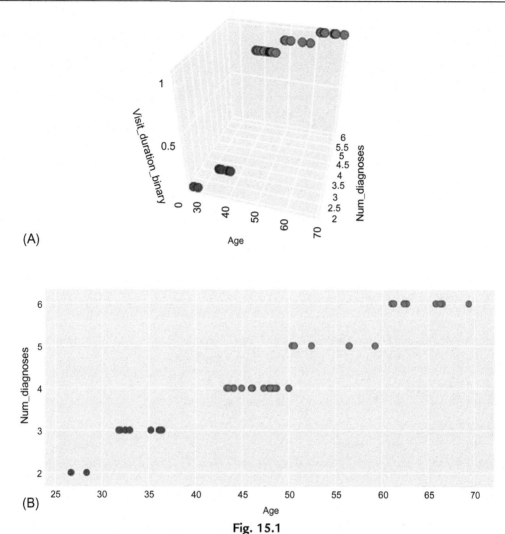

Fig. 15.1

(A) 3D Plot of visit duration, age, and number of diagnoses. (B) 2-D plot of visit duration and patient age achieved by looking top-down at the plot in panel A. Long visits are in *red* (*gray* in print version), short visits are in *blue* (dark gray in print version).

occur that may not be representative. Imagine that this patient had already had a comprehensive physical examination the week before and so he's just presenting this time for a blood draw or maybe a prescription. In the data we have, we don't have a way to determine whether a visit was a repeat or if the same patient had multiple adjacent visits. We can imagine getting the data from a warehouse or registry where this kind of detail is simply not there. Hearkening back to earlier chapters, we might want to adjust our patient selection to remove these sorts of issues but we haven't done that here. Bear in mind, we don't always know why a point is an outlier but we still know when it sits in an unusual position and we can assume that there are reasons at play some of which we may know about and some of which we

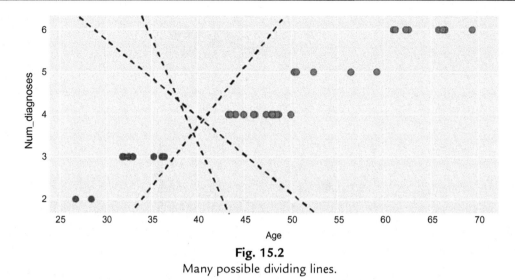

Fig. 15.2
Many possible dividing lines.

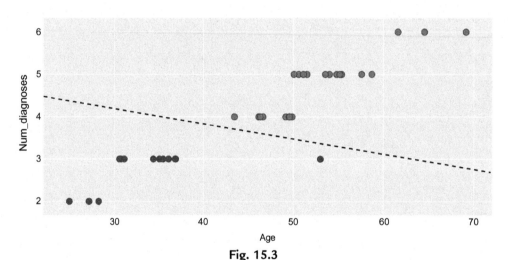

Fig. 15.3
Logistic regression decision boundary with outlier.

do not. What we can do is consider such points cautiously. With all that said, we may therefore not actually want the dividing line to be influenced by this point as it is in the case of logistic regression.

Enter SVM. Simply put, the goal of SVMs in this context is to identify a dividing line but with a unique constraint: it also aims to maximize a "margin," which is a distance between the dividing line and its closest points on either side. Fig. 15.4 depicts our data as it might be divided by an SVM as opposed to a logistic regression model.

Since the margin represents the territory closest to the dividing line, it represents the area of least certainty about classification decisions. Thus maximizing and protecting this margin

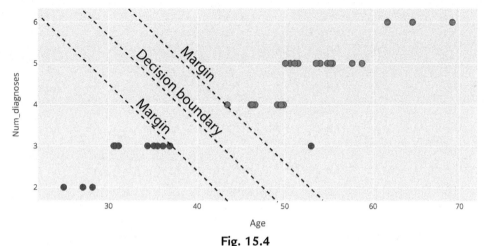

Fig. 15.4

Example dividing line chosen by a support vector machine.

is a tactic for picking the least uncertain dividing line by making sure that, at least for the data we do have, it divides the classes with as much certainty as possible. Note that in Fig. 15.4, the margins are each denoted by a dotted line that runs parallel to the solid dividing line on either side. These *dotted lines* also pass through at least one point on their respective sides, it could be more points but at least one will lie on the margin. This is because the margin is defined by the presence of the data points, which are closest to being misclassified within their respective groups. Each data point is also a vector containing the values for each dimension of the plot—number of diagnosis codes and minutes of visit in this case—and therefore these specific data points, which define the margin are called the "support vectors" and the dividing line is situated equally between them. Thus we have a "Support Vector Machine." Note here that this model does not consider the other points, which are not support vectors and thus only a subset of the data points actually influence placement of the dividing line.

As with the logistic regression and even linear regression examples, this is still an optimization problem. The dividing line represents a hypothesis function, which can be adjusted by assigning different weights to out inputs. More specifically, the diving line, or "decision boundary" between long and short visits will take the familiar form:

$$y = ax + by + c$$

where y corresponds to either the "long" or "short" label, a is the patient age, y is the number of diagnosis codes and we get to adjust a, b, and c to shift and rotate the dividing line. We might initially just pick random values for a, b, and c start out plotting our first attempt at the dividing line, measuring our error and then optimizing to reduce that error. However, the specific way in which we calculate the error for each data point differs from the logistic regression example. Here, we consider predictions on the wrong side of the dividing line to be more wrong in proportion to how far over on the wrong side they are—probably not a surprise. When it comes to correct classifications, though, we consider anything on the right side of

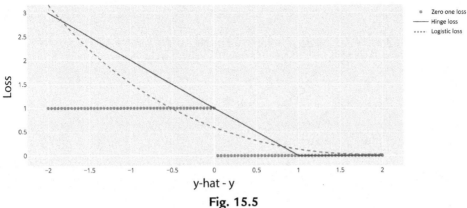

Fig. 15.5

Hinge loss and logistic loss.

the dividing line—but within the margin—to have some small error, which decreases as the farther points get from the diving line on the correct side. However, we consider everything beyond the margin on the correct side equally correct with no error. Fig. 15.5 depicts this type of error formula, known as the "hinge loss," as a function of how far points are from the dividing line on either side. Also depicted is the "logistic loss" function used by logistic regression as well as the "zero–one loss," which simply assigns a loss of 1 if the classification is correct and a 0 otherwise.

This comparison illustrates this different behavior between SVM and logistic regression when it comes to outliers. Notice that, as we get farther from the dividing line on the wrong side, our logistic loss grows much quicker than the hinge loss which is linear the farther we get in the wrong direction. Thus, the SVM is more tolerant to extreme wrong answers because they don't generate as much cost. Graphically, this means that misclassified outliers will tend to "pull" on the diving line more so with logistic regression than with in the case of SVM during optimization. So SVMs have certain advantages. In seeking a wide margin from the nearest points and being less volatile to outliers, they can leads to more generalizable hypothesis functions. This does not mean that we would toss out logistic regression in favor of SVM across the board. As we mentioned, logistic regression models output probabilities on a continuous range from 0 to 1 while SVMs typically output discrete labels as either 0 or 1. This probabilistic interpretation for the outputs of logistic regression can actually be quite useful since it can be interpreted directly as a measure of classification confidence. Interestingly enough, it is possible to estimate probability scores from SVM outputs using a technique known as Platt scaling. We won't go into detail about Platt scaling here, but it highlights that logistic regression and SVMs are essentially the same on the inside save for a different loss function, which is what accounts for their different strengths and weaknesses.

SVMs are, however, often discussed for another reason, which provides a nice segue into next Chapter's discussion of Deep Learning which is that of constructing "nonlinear" classifiers.

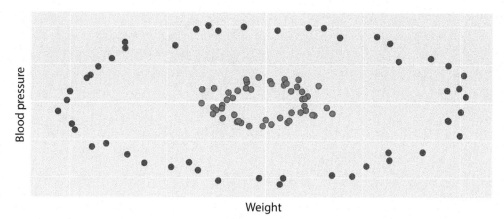

Fig. 15.6
Circular distribution of points that is not linearly separable.

In order to explore this, let's consider a modification to the visit minutes example and instead let's consider that we are trying to learn a hypothesis function that can distinguish normal healthy from abnormal patients on the basis of weight and blood pressure. Taking a bit of artistic license we could imagine ending up with something like Fig. 15.6, which has an inner core of one class—those with normal variation in weight and blood pressure—and an outer rim of another class. Hopefully it is obvious that we cannot establish a dividing line which separates these two groups.

One clever way to approach this problem is to actually create a new feature for each point in the hope that this new dimension offers better separation. In some cases, this could be a literal exercise of measure more information from our patients and adding to the training dataset but much more often that isn't possible and so we do this as a mathematical transformation within the dataset itself. To see how this might work, let's suppose we select 4 points from within the dataset to serve as landmarks and we then calculate a similarity score between each of our data points and these landmarks. We would pick really any function for such a score but one popular example might be what's known as a "radial basis function" (RBF), for reasons which will become clear in a moment, which looks like this:

$$\exp\left(-\frac{\|x - l\|^2}{2\sigma^2}\right)$$

To unpack that a bit, x would be one of our data points and l is a datapoint which has been chosen as a landmark. Thus, thus equation measures the distance between x and l and the sensitivity to that distance can be adjusted by adjusting the parameter sigma. Lastly, this result is used as the exponent for e. Don't bother trying to step through all of that on the first try just understand that, when we do this, we get convenient similarity score which is one when the data point x is identical to the landmark and goes toward zero as x gets infinitely far away from the

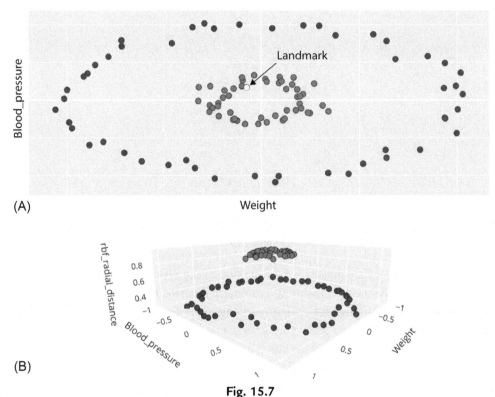

Fig. 15.7

(A) Points with landmark highlighted. (B) Results of RBF kernel calculated using the landmark in Panel A.

landmark. Fig. 15.7 shows the landmark point highlighted in 2-D space alongside the result of adding a third dimension which is the RBF distance between each point and that landmark.

The powerful thing about this transformation is that it pushes the datapoints into this third dimension in such a way that now the two classes are linearly separable in this new 3-D space by using a plane which clips off the tip of this cone shape. RBF is just one kind of kernel and there are many that can be used (Gaussian, polynomial just to name two popular examples). In general, this is a common technique for SVMs which enhances the separability of data by transforming it into new dimensions. Strictly speaking, kernels could be used with other models as well such as with kernel logistic regression wherein kernels are used to add new dimensions to the dataset after which logistic regression is used to find a dividing line. Also, just to round out this discussion, it is still possible that we could try to separate the data from Fig. 15.6 without a kernel by defining a nonlinear decision boundary such as an ellipse, a circle, or a more complex sort of shape. It turns out, this is less commonly done because the more convoluted our decision boundary, the more we run the risk of overfitting our training data. Thus, kernels allow us to keep the decision boundary linear, which is not required but often preferred because of its simplicity and—hopefully—its generalizability.

15.3 Decision trees

Continuing on the topic of data, which is not linearly separable, let us consider another example. Suppose we look back to the weight and blood pressure dataset, but we relabel our healthy vs unhealthy patients into quadrants as shown in Fig. 15.8.

Decision trees are a popular largely because their internals are familiar and mirror human intuition by representing features of the training dataset as a flowchart where each branch point represents some criteria placed on a feature with alternative considerations for each outcome. When decision trees are used to solve classification or regression prediction problems, they are called "classification and regression trees" (CART). These trees consist of root nodes each of which represents an input dimension and terminate in leaf nodes, which represent the ultimate labels we would assign to our data points after following a series of decisions depicted by the tree. With the dataset we have here, we can actually imagine what a functional decision tree would look like, shown in Fig. 15.9.

But how might an algorithm go about creatine something like this? First, by examining the depiction, we can understand that each node, insofar as it represents some decision to made about data points based upon a certain feature, effectively splits the data into smaller bins. For example, if I have a node, which represents a rule such as weight $>=115$ lbs., then the application of the rule represented by this node splits the weight dimension into two smaller bins: <115 lbs. and $>=115$ lbs. The process of deciding how nodes should be arranged and what rules they should represent is termed "tree growing" and it begins with considering each predictor and determining the best "split" for that predictor. More specifically, this process starts with considering weight and blood pressure separately and, for each of these features, exploring several different potential split points and picking the best one. In the case of weight, this would involve sorting the dataset from lowest to highest weight and then testing each

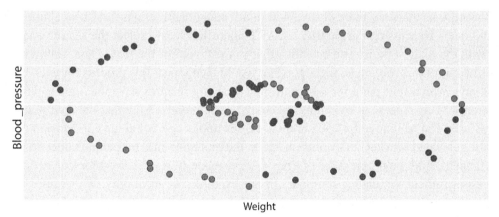

Fig. 15.8
Example dataset in quadrants.

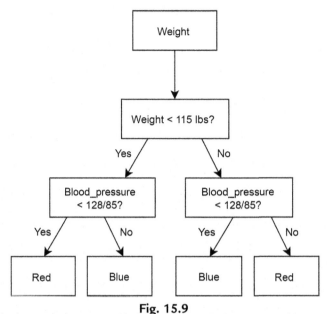

Fig. 15.9

Decision tree for data points with roots and leaves labeled.

weight as a potential break point for splitting the samples. Which split it "best" is typically determined using a metric known as "Ginian purity," which captures how homogeneous the groups created by a given splitting rule are. Ginian purity is represented by the Gini index, which is the sum of the squared probabilities of each class:

$$\text{Gini} = \sum\nolimits_{i=1}^{n} \left(P_i^{2.} \right)$$

where n is the number of different classes (2 in the case of our example). Walking through this formula, we can see that for a group of only one class the Gini index would be 1 while the index goes toward 0 as there are more classes with more equal distributions (and hence more equal probabilities). Thus, using this metric, a CART algorithm would select the feature and split point with the highest purity and establish that as the "root" of the tree. Then, following establishment of that root node, the algorithm would then repeat this process for each branch, determining which split point for which of the remaining features have the highest purity for each branch. This process is known as "recursive partitioning." Note that the split points and features used can be unique for each branch. For example, one could have a decision tree for predictive elevated beta hcG that splits on age as the root node and, for people under 50 (which is one branch), splits on the presence of a positive pregnancy test while for people over 50, splits on levels of follicle stimulating hormone. In our example, we have only two features for simplicity's sake so after picking one as the root node, there is only one more feature to try. That being said the branches of a decision tree don't all need to be of the same length. If, for example, splitting on weight resulted in one of the branches already being entirely pure for one class, then recursive partitioning would designate that branch as a leaf meaning that the decision pathway ends for that branch and there should be no more splits and branches. To restate this more quantitatively, recursive partitioning requires that splits result in groups with a greater Gini index than if no splitting occurred. Thus, if any split created by the decision tree ends up being completely homogeneous for one class, there could be no increase in the Gini index and that branch will become a leaf.

It should come as no surprise that decision trees have the potential to become very complex with numerous branches. This can become a form of overfitting where, in the more extreme case, each training data point has a separate series of decisions precisely leading to it. In those cases, such a decision tree would be unlikely to generalize and so there needs to be a way to regularize decision trees. One common way to do this is called "pruning" where branches are removed, which contribute little or none to the purification of class labels. Regularization is also commonly done by limiting the maximum depth that a tree is allowed to have and by setting increasingly strict "stopping criteria," which are thresholds for when recursive partitioning should stop. For example, establishing that each leaf must have at least five data points or that a branch can become a leaf with a Gini index of 0.85 as opposed to 1.0 will tend to make trees smaller and simpler and hence regularized.

Finally, an especially powerful approach to creating regularized decision tree models involved creating multiple decision trees from the training data set and then, for future samples, running that sample through each decision tree and picking the class label selected by most of the decision trees. Creation of these separate trees involves a technique known as "bagging," which can take one of two forms. In the case of sample bagging, a random subset of the training data points are selected with replacement and a tree is built separately from each sample. In the case of feature bagging, a random subset of the features are selected—also with replacement—at each split within each tree. Overall, the creation of these multiple trees is naturally called a "random forest." We have been considering classification examples in this discussion but, as the CART name implies, decision trees can be used for regression as well, outputting real-valued numbers instead of just class labels.

15.4 Clustering

We will conclude our discussion of machine learning models by discussing clustering. While there are many specific variants of this approach, we will focus on a particular use case known as "unsupervised clustering" wherein we assume there are meaningful relationships in our data but we don't have formal labels. We can modify our earlier example to accommodate this use case by assuming our task isn't to predict the duration of a patient visit but rather to drill into why such differences in visit duration might exist. Imagine also that we have no pre-existing assumptions about what underlying relationships there might be thus we collected the visit duration, age, and number of diagnosis codes for a population of patients and we wish to see whether those data points fall into any sort of grouping according to these properties.

We will turn to a very popular approach to unsupervised clustering known as k-means clustering. This algorithm may be given an arbitrary number of potential underlying clusters, denoted by the variable k and often provided as a parameter to the algorithm. Upon initialization, the algorithm positions these k points, called "centroids," at random initial locations among the set of training data points and then iterates over each data point, assigning it to the cluster belonging to its closest centroid as shown in Fig. 15.10 showing this approach on the visit duration data from earlier in this chapter. Note that our centroids are marked by *yellow (light gray* in print version) *points* at that these don't need to correspond to any points present in our dataset. Also note that the *blue* (dark gray in print version) outlier is now *red (gray* in print version) because it's closer to the *red (gray* in print version) group's centroid. In this example, our data weren't already labeled, hence the use of clustering to determine that there are two natural groupings within the data, which we would then label *blue* (dark gray in print version) and *red* (gray in print version), respectively.

Following this, the algorithm will then iterate over each of the k centroid points, calculating the average of the distance from that centroid point to all data points assigned to that centroid's cluster. In its typical form, the algorithm will then relocate each of the k centroids to the centers of their respective clusters and then reassign the data points to new clusters using these newly relocated centroids. The centroid placements, which result in the lowest cost, are chosen as the ultimate centroid locations and final cluster assignments are based upon those centroid locations. In this way, the k-means algorithm can arrive at grouping of similar data points,

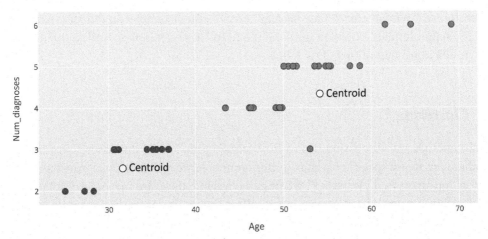

Fig. 15.10
Centroids and points assigned to cluster centroids.

which is helpful in such an unsupervised task when the goal is to surface underlying structure that can be further investigated. Importantly, the k-means clustering algorithm is not guaranteed to converge meaning that, if the algorithm is run multiple times each with different centroid starting locations, it may result in different final clusters. Thus, it is typical to repeat execution of the algorithm multiple times using different initial centroid locations.

With these clustering results, for example, we may come to the conclusion that there are particular groups of younger patients with fewer problems and older patients with more problems to discuss with their physicians and we may wish to delve into these further.

15.5 Model explainability

Now having discussed several popular and important machine learning models, we can address another important concept: model explainability. In most real-world scenarios the simple fact that a model seems to perform well is not enough to completely trust that a model is correct or robust. This is especially true in healthcare where the risk of incorrect prediction and classification can be dire. Thus, it is imperative that users can explain "why" a model arrives at a given prediction or classification, even if that model is trained and highly performant. Importantly, model explainability requires that the behavior of a model be understandable in "human terms." Decision trees are a popular class of models in large part because they are inherently explainable, offering a series of explicit rules successively applied to input data points. However, as we mentioned, techniques such as bagging and aggregation of trees into random forests obscure this direct relationship a bit since the overall most commonly voted upon class does not reveal how exactly underlying votes were distributed and since trees created on bagged samples may have different behaviors on un-bagged samples. Thus, even in the case of decision trees, there is a need to understand how a trained model functions and how it uses input data in order to make predictions and classifications.

The field of model explainability is broad and growing, but there are some established approaches that are important to understand. The first is known as "permutation importance," which is an approach to experimentally testing which input features a trained model relies upon more than others. In the case of our visit duration prediction model, we might have several features is variable importance such as age, diagnosis codes, hair color, and height. We may expect that hair color and height would be less relevant to predicting the duration of a visit than age and diagnosis codes but that wouldn't prevent a model from potentially learning coincidental associations (or "covariances") between those features and the duration of a patient visit. Thus, we want to understand which features the model depends on as a way to assess for such behavior. Permutation importance involves taking our trained model reiteratively testing its performance using a separate subset of data points. The trick here is that, for each of these iterations, we take a single feature of that subset and scramble the values, measuring how detrimental such scrambling is to model performance. More specifically, this would involve taking a subset of input data and randomly shuffling the height value while keeping all of the other values in place. If this sort of mix up catastrophically impacts model performance, then we know that the model was heavily dependent upon that feature in order to make predictions. Otherwise, if the model is resilient to scrambling a feature, we know that feature is not very important to the model. In this example, we would hope that scrambling hair color would have no impact on the model's performance but—if it did—we would reconsider whether our model is really trustworthy and generalizable or whether it may have overfit to a meaningless association that just so happened to be present in the training data we collected. Although permutation importance may not provide as nuanced of an assessment of feature use as other approaches we will discuss next, it is appealing and quite popular because it is simple to understand and simple to use.

A more in-depth method of assessing model behavior is known as "partial dependence," which is similar to permutation importance above with a few key differences. In assessing partial dependence, we still take our trained model and reiteratively test it on a held-out sample of data except we don't scramble the values of a given column. Instead, we test the trained model repeatedly on individual data points, incrementally shifting the values of individual features each time. For example, we would take our trained visit duration model and test it using a new patient example except we would iteratively shift the height of that patient and retest the model's prediction. In essence, this approach is testing how much variance in a feature is tolerable by the trained model before its performance breaks down. If a feature could be totally variable—even random—then it is unimportant to the model but if even slight alterations destroy the model's performance, we know it is tightly dependent upon that feature. If, for example, moving the height of a patient down by 1 in destroyed model performance, we would be concerned about some sort of overfitting to that feature whereas if moving the height down by 3 ft destroyed performance we may consider this acceptable as it might relate to a pediatric versus adult visit. Partial dependence will provide us with a functional assessment of how models behave over a variation—not just scrambling—of their features and we can plot the results of partial dependence assessment, nicely summarizing certain model behaviors. An example partial dependence plot showing a tight dependence of a visit length model on patient height is shown in Fig. 15.11. Consider this graph for a moment. What we see here is that our model is pretty much unaffected by the number of diagnoses a patient has but appears to base its prediction of a long visit almost entirely on whether the patient is short or tall. In some cases this might be ok but perhaps this would cause us to question a model that "thinks" in this way when it comes to predicting visit duration. This sort of rich evaluation is why explainability is so crucial.

There are many more advanced techniques and tools in the domain of model explainability, which are worth exploration for the interested reader. One particular example are Shapley Additive Explanations, which provide a measurement of how a model would perform if given features were at the dataset baseline values rather than the particular value observed for any

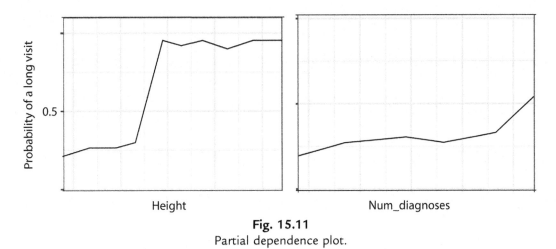

Fig. 15.11
Partial dependence plot.

given data point. Others include feature interaction, accumulated local effects, and both local and global surrogate methods. The two methods covered here are useful and easily understandable, providing a great place to start attempting model explanation.

15.6 Conclusion

In this chapter, we built upon the introductory machine learning models and concept of the last chapter to explore kernels, support vectors, decision trees, and even unsupervised clustering. Throughout this discussion, we have also developed an understanding of models as functions which perform regression or establish decision boundaries and we have built up an intuition about feature importance and behavior in our discussion of explainability. This is by no means a comprehensive treatment of machine learning but you will find that these core models and concepts are foundation and come up time and time again. In the next chapter, we will solidify many of these concepts in this book's second example project where we will walk through selecting, designing, and building a model. Lastly, these discussions have laid the foundation for this section's final chapter on deep learning where we will round out our discussion of models.

CHAPTER 16

Computational phenotyping and clinical natural language processing

16.1 Introduction

Unlike the preceding chapters, here we will discuss both computational and noncomputational constraints around the process of selecting relevant patients and understanding information about those patients. This will prove to be a critical cross-sectional discussion as medical informatics is dually concerned with both the discrete challenges of optimization and calculation as well as the more ambiguous ones of specificity, knowledge, and labeling. We will start with an ostensibly simple question: "How many patients in our medical record system have sepsis?" and we will discuss different strategies for answering such a question. At its core, the task at hand is one of "phenotyping" or determining what are the real-world attributes of our individual patients, but we must determine this through the secondary impressions that those attributes make in documentation *about* those patients. As we will see, this is nontrivial but nonetheless sufficiently solvable as a challenge.

16.2 Manual review and general review considerations

Before diving into purely computational approaches to identifying patient populations, it's worth discussing the process of manual record review and the general considerations surrounding this process. As we will see, manual review—while traditionally the only means of identifying patients—is still a critical arm even of computational approaches as it establishes the source of truth in the form of accurately labeled patients and their medical records and we judge the performance of computational approaches through their ability to approximate the labeling of this source of truth collection of patients.

The first step, therefore, in performing the phenotyping task is to determine what level of evidence is necessary to substantiate the phenotype of interest. In the case of sepsis, this does not automatically yield a single answer, rather, it requires us to specify from among a surprisingly large space of potential options. For example, do we define sepsis linguistically as the presence of the term "sepsis" in the clinical note, or do we require the presence of SIRS criteria (elevated white blood cell count, heart rate, respiratory rate, and temperature)? Do we absolutely require the presence of positive blood culture results or do we make

An Introduction to Healthcare Informatics. https://doi.org/10.1016/B978-0-12-814915-7.00016-8

allowances for potentially undiagnosed cases of sepsis? Do we consider septic shock a different phenotype? As we can see, we have to make several initial decisions about the question we intend to propose and codify those as the level of evidence required to demonstrate our target phenotype. Though somewhat onerous, this is a critical initial step in any analysis. Certain tradeoffs also become apparent here, namely, that the stringency of our phenotype will result in more numerous rules, a higher level of evidence and, consequentially, fewer phenotypically matched patients.

Manual review relies, of course, on the work of reviewers—of which there are typically more than one and, in some circumstances, many. These reviewers each interpret a patient's medical record to determine whether the level of evidence is sufficiently fulfilled. Typically, this can be accomplished with reviewers who have limited medial knowledge but, in circumstances where a latent diagnosis must be made (such as if we were specifically interested in those patients who might represent undiagnosed sepsis) then this would require a physician reviewer. It is almost always advisable to employ multiple reviewers even if the workload is feasible for a single reviewer and it is common practice to have two reviewers assess each patient chart as a "paired review" and compare their respective assessments. This is because we are often blind to our own biases and idiosyncrasies and, just as with a machine learning model, we may interpret charts in a way that is less generalizable than we would assume. Having multiple reviewers overlap with one another makes these personal variations in medical record interpretation explicit. In practice, quantifying this disagreement can be done using the kappa statistic which represents a ratio between the observed interreviewer agreement versus the probability of agreement. Fig. 16.1 depicts the formula for calculating the kappa statistic as well as a worked example using a confusion matrix of reviewer assessments. When disagreements do arise—as they almost certainly would in the case of sepsis—we can resolve such disputes in a number of ways. One obvious but effective way is to have reviewers discuss with one another and mutually work out a consensus label for the patient. Alternatively, we could have a third reviewer provide a tie-breaking vote to determine the patient label or we could assign more weight to the reviewer with the most expertise, such as an attending physician. In many cases, the consensus option is favorable because it brings interpretive differences out into discussion and makes everyone more acutely aware of sources of bias and variation.

The performance of manual record review should be formalized into a review instrument, which captures and structures the determined patient labels (e.g. "sepsis") and the pieces of evidence that support them. This can take the form of something as simple as an Excel spreadsheet or even paper medical record review forms and is best honed through iteration. Typically, this is done by deciding on an initial set of patient attributes assumed to be useful in determining the phenotype, using those variables to review a small collection of patient records, and then reviewing how difficult and accurate it was to use those variables for patient phenotyping. Following this, new variables can be introduced, or existing ones may be removed

Kappa statistic formula

$$k = \frac{P_{Observed} - P_{Expected}}{1 - P_{Expected}}$$

Confusion matrix

	Reviewer 1 sepsis	Reviewer 1 no sepsis
Reviewer 2 sepsis	10	1
Reviewer 2 no sepsis	2	8

Full calculation

$$P_{Observed} = \frac{\text{Observed agreement}}{\text{All results}} = \frac{10 + 8}{10 + 8 + 1 + 2} = 0.86$$

$$P_{Expected} = P_{Yes\ at\ random} * P_{Not\ at\ random}$$

$$P_{Yes\ at\ random} = \frac{10 + 1}{10 + 8 + 1 + 2} * \frac{10 + 2}{10 + 8 + 1 + 2} = 0.30$$

$$P_{No\ at\ random} = \frac{1 + 8}{10 + 8 + 1 + 2} * \frac{2 + 8}{10 + 8 + 1 + 2} = 0.20$$

$$P_{Expected} = 0.30 * 0.20 = 0.06$$

$$k = \frac{0.86 - 0.06}{1 - 0.06} = 0.89$$

Fig. 16.1

Walkthrough calculation of the kappa statistic.

from the scope of review. For example, we might initially think that it would be useful to record the antibiotic protocol used for each patient but we may find that this information is typically missing or recorded in a different system and that searching for and documenting these values for each medical record is not feasible. If this is the case, quick iterative testing of the review instrument can identify this, allowing us to tweak the instrument to be both useful in the phenotyping process but also efficient to implement. Eventually, this process should converge onto a performant review instrument after which point the process of manual review can be scaled to more reviewers accompanied by the creation of a review protocol which outlines the features to be extracted from a patient chart as well as the rules by which these are interpreted and documents in the review instrument. At this time, it is typically worthwhile to consider using a tool that will formalize the process of completing the review instrument. An example of this is REDCap, which is commonly used for this purpose and which merges a secure database of review information with a graphical form-like completion interface that forces the reviewer to complete all fields and abide by certain field-specific constraints, such as choosing from a dropdown of acceptable options. While something like this could be done in

Excel, using a spreadsheet opens the review process up to insidious form of error such as users accidentally filling out information from one patient in the row that actually belongs to another patient.

It's important to reiterate that although manual review is used as a primary means of patient phenotyping and record identification, it is still critical for computational approaches as it establishes the ground truth, labeled dataset against which computational approaches would be benchmarked. As we proceed through discussion of computational approaches, assume that this manual portion would have to be done in order to identify the reference set of patients and their records.

16.3 Computational phenotyping: General considerations

To continue with our sepsis example, we could incorporate computational phenotyping in one of two ways: we could place it entirely after manual review in which case we use the manual process to fully describe our target patients and their relevant variables prior to formalizing that process (e.g., the review instrument and protocol) into a computational workflow or we could take a more integrated approach whereby we take our initial draft of relevant patient variables, perform queries based upon these variables and then subject a subset of the returned results to manual review, tweaking this process as we evaluate both the performance of the variables and the underlying queries used to obtain them. This latter approach is often preferable because it lets us use the power of computational tools like SQL to search for patients while still making results subject to manual oversight and it allows us to iteratively build out the computational algorithm in parallel with manual review. In any case, what we will see with almost any variable in healthcare is that their ideal and actual performance diverge in many ways due to inconsistencies in documentation or diagnostic workflow. As we have discussed before, healthcare is full of organized terminology (e.g., LOINC, ICD, CPT, SNOMED etc.), which serve a very useful and real purpose, but which cannot be assumed to automatically allow for high-fidelity patient identification. As a result, we have to quantify and track the performance of each variable and each query using that variable with regard to how effectively it aligns with manual labeling of the patient.

Let us consider a specific example, the International Classification of Disease and Related Health Problems, 10th Edition (ICD-10), is a naming system created by the World Health Organization to describe a list of universal terms for symptoms, diagnoses, findings, complaints, causes of disease, and even contexts such as social circumstances. In the case of sepsis, numerous possible codes could apply to a target patient, including A41.9 ("Sepsis, unspecified Organism") or R65.20 ("Severe sepsis without septic shock"). Moreover, there will be cases where a septic patient lacks any ICD-10 code for sepsis at all and, for many queries, cases where older encounters were coded according to ICD-9. How do we deal with this? One useful systematic approach is to include both ICD-9 and ICD-10 codes in our initial scope of variables and begin with a reasonable set of relevant filters (such as stipulating that the ICD-10 code is equal to A41.9 or R65.20). When we actually gather patient charts, we then create specific confusion matrices describing the performance of these variables and filters in terms of sensitivity, specificity, and predictive value along with specific drill-downs into the false positives (cases where these codes were present but manual review determined that the patient did not have sepsis) and false negatives (cases where these codes were absent but manual review determined that these patients did have sepsis). This allows us to gather useful quantitative information about the performance of these variables in identifying target patients and we will use this information later as we finalize search queries and search logic. For example, we may ultimately write our search query to assign different weights to different variables according to their predictive value. Fig. 16.2 depicts such a confusion matrix in the case of sepsis along with the false-positive and false-negative drilldowns.

ICD codes and CPT codes are a common hook for computational phenotyping because they are structured and more consistently documented than many other attributes. This is largely due to their role in billing as both ICD and CPT codes are key parts of the process wherein medical encounters are submitted for reimbursement from insurance companies. That being said, their variable performance highlights the pervasive and critical issue in medical informatics of reality vs descriptions of reality. On a slightly philosophical note, what we are actually interested in is the pathophysiology and health of real people out in the world, but what we actually have are documented descriptions of those people in the form of notes, lab values, images, etc. While some of those descriptions, such as chemistry results from a blood test, are more straightforward, many others are heavily influences by the documenting

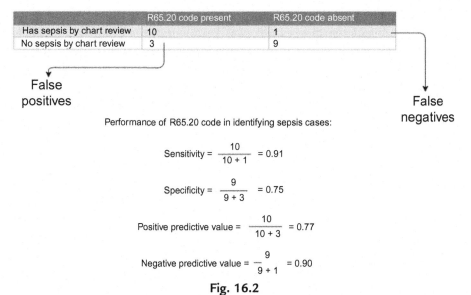

	R65.20 code present	R65.20 code absent
Has sepsis by chart review	10	1
No sepsis by chart review	3	9

False positives

False negatives

Performance of R65.20 code in identifying sepsis cases:

$$\text{Sensitivity} = \frac{10}{10 + 1} = 0.91$$

$$\text{Specificity} = \frac{9}{9 + 3} = 0.75$$

$$\text{Positive predictive value} = \frac{10}{10 + 3} = 0.77$$

$$\text{Negative predictive value} = \frac{9}{9 + 1} = 0.90$$

Fig. 16.2

Example confusion matrix and performance calculations for ICD code R65.20 in identifying sepsis.

physician's differential diagnosis at the time, or with the workflows around billing, or with technical idiosyncrasies that impact the electronic record. Thus, while computation favors consistent, straightforward labels, the process of applying and interpreting these is often neither consistent nor straightforward. As a consequence, we find that the performance of ICD and CPT codes are widely variable across the code set and that, in some diseases, applicable codes actually change over time as the diagnosis evolves. Finally, since these codes fulfill a primary operational purpose related to billing rather than analytics, there are circumstances where a diagnosis code which perhaps imperfectly describes a given patient may be deliberately chosen so as to ensure that related procedures and medications required for patient care are successfully reimbursed by insurance. Medical care is complex, and patients do fall into certain gray areas where the nearest diagnostic label and the best course of management don't completely align. Conversely, false-negative situations arise on many cases due to technical details around coding practice. For example, outpatient healthcare visits are typically limited to include only four ICD codes. As a result, for patients with complex medical histories who may reasonably have several codes apply, we may not find our target code simply because the patient encounter reached its limit of applicable codes. Imagine we were trying to assess for outpatients with a history of alcohol consumption. Even if true—and perhaps documented somewhere in the free text portion of the outpatient visit note—the relevant ICD code may very well be absent from the encounter if that patient had other more pertinent diagnoses. CPT codes offer a useful complement in that they can be very specific for certain conditions (e.g., J9271 "Injection, pembrolizumab" is very unlikely to identify anyone without cancer) but provide little context in isolation. Fortunately, if we have a framework for assessing the performance of different variables for capturing target patients, we can evaluate and make rational decisions about what variables to use.

Laboratory values are an interesting case because, while they are discreet numerical measurements, they are often impossible to incorporate without context. Many patient queries will capture patients going back years or even decades and, over such timeframes, changes in test methodology may alter the reportable range for a test or the units of measurement. For example, ALT is a commonly measured liver enzyme that is typically considered in the evaluation of hepatitis. However, newer testing approaches such as ALTV are more precise but report activity slightly differently resulting in a shift to the normal range. In many cases, testing such as ALTV may be deployed to replace ALT and may be ordered under the same test name and, although a memo to the medical staff was likely distributed at the time of the transition, this would not be clearly apparent simply by querying for ALT result values. Moreover, medicine differs strongly from other fields such as finance or meteorology, which have regular monitoring of stock prices and temperatures, in that key measurements such as lab testing are typically only pursued when a sufficient prior probability of some disease state is met. This means that we always must consider variables from a patient chart jointly as they exert considerable influence upon one another.

Clinical observations and medications, although very common, also have important considerations. For example, observations such as blood pressure are typically called many different things (e.g., noninvasive blood pressure, NIBP, arterial blood pressure, blood pressure systolic, etc.) as the name used varies across record systems and system versions. Additionally, data warehouses may contain observations in each of these recorded forms and may not have a unified column where they can all be found. Medications, on the other hand, are relevant but typically nonspecific identifiers of specific phenotypes due to the prevalence of off-label use of medication and the subtle relationships between diagnosis and medication dose or route of administration. Although tedious in many ways, exploring and testing these variables highlights these issues of data cleaning and gives us a systematic approach to confronting these many sources of error. Taking all of this into account, any performant computational phenotyping algorithm will take into account several variables across different types. For each potential algorithm, we will want to abstract a summary performance metric that describes the whole algorithm's capability to identify target patients. Often, this is best done by calculating a receiver operating characteristic (ROC) curve, which captures the relationship between sensitivity and specificity over a range of possible cutoffs. For example, say that after evaluating the specific performance of several variables, we create three different sepsis identification algorithms each of which outputs some overall probability of having sepsis (a number between 0 and 1) and we wish to compare how these tests perform as we shift the cutoff for what we consider positive. In doing this, we can create three different ROC curves, one for each algorithm, and a corresponding AUC as shown in Fig. 16.3.

Finally, it's important to note that while the AUC is a useful summary metric of algorithm performance it is a context-dependent metric that is driven by our goals for the algorithm. If we were trying to identify a cohort from a large database with tens of thousands of patients, we may want a balance between sensitivity and specificity (a high AUC) but if our goal was to drill down into a very specific clinical category, we may instead favor specificity more than sensitivity. Now that we've discussed how we approach the design and evaluation of a computational phenotyping algorithm, the remainder of this chapter will focus on specific methods we can use to actually create these algorithms.

16.4 Supervised methods

Computational phenotyping is a broad and active field of research a comprehensive review of which is beyond the scope of this book. Nonetheless, efforts can be roughly divided into supervised and unsupervised domains, the former of which represents the more traditional case where we have a labeled set of phenotyped patients and the goal of the algorithm is to find similar patients. In the simplest case, we can take our collection of manually reviewed records and create explicit Boolean rules using the most performant variables.

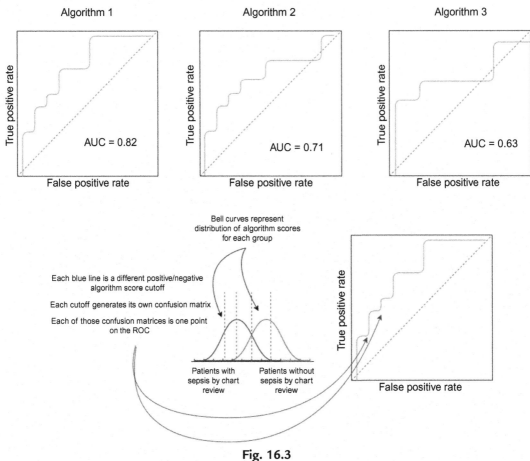

Fig. 16.3
Example ROC curves and AUCs for three sepsis algorithms.

More interesting, we can add an inference component to this and draw upon the machine learning chapters. In order to do this, we would take our manually reviewed ground truth set, divide it into test, train, and validation subsets and build a model based upon the training set. One potential approach might be to create a logistic regression model that assigns various weights to each clinical variable and adjusts those weights in accordance with how the model performs against the known labels for the test cases. We iteratively measure the model's error against the training dataset for the purposes of adjusting feature weights and its error against the validation set for purposes of estimating overfitting and then finally test the trained model against a held-out test set as depicted in Fig. 16.4.

If we decide to do this, however, we must be mindful of which modeling approach is preferable. For example, logistic regression works best in scenarios where our features can be thought of as absolute attributes of the patient (e.g., the final diagnosis or the average blood pressure). Moreover, logistic regression may encounter challenges when we have different combinations of features that are separately meaningful for qualifying a phenotype (e.g., elevated white blood

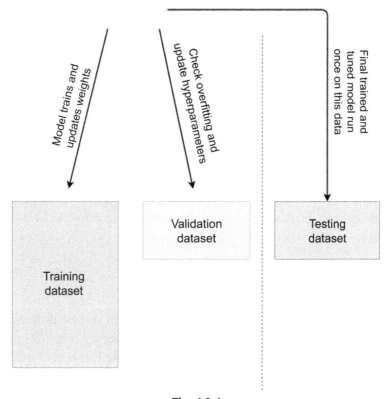

Fig. 16.4
Model training schematic.

cell count coupled with positive blood culture or a decrease in white blood cell count coupled with a high fever). In such circumstances, we are dealing with nonlinear classification boundaries and we may consider something else like a multilayer perceptron or decision tree. As with anything, model choice should be heavily influenced by project goals. In practice, it is common to use combinations of explicit rules because this efficiently supports the common case of extracting a population dataset for subsequent refinement and analysis. However, there are instances wherein we may want to deploy a learning algorithm that can adaptively identify patients prospectively or even predict undiagnosed patients. In such cases, we will likely still use manual review and rules-based phenotyping algorithms to gather our cohort of labeled patients and this represents an almost universal framework for approaching these efforts.

16.5 Unsupervised methods

Before concluding our discussion of computational phenotyping, it is important to mention the growing and uniquely exciting domain of unsupervised approaches. As we discuss in the chapter on machine learning, these approaches look for inherent structure in the data based upon comparisons between features as opposed to a truth set of official labels. More specifically, these approaches examine patients in terms of how similar or different their various attributes really are and, in so doing, often surface both expected and unexpected similarities and differences between patients and their medical records. This is an exciting area in particular because it does not require validation by manual review and, therefore, does not have to abide by any particular system of diagnostic classification. In healthcare, this introduces both present opportunities to identify new patients which may fit a diagnosis as well as future opportunities for new diagnostic categories to emerge as a result of similarities identified by unsupervised approaches. Various particular methods are used including spatial clustering and compression using autoencoder networks. A treatment of these approaches is beyond the scope of this book, but the emergence of this field speaks to the growing influence for statistical inference to emulate and inform medical understanding in surprisingly fundamental ways.

16.6 Natural language processing

Natural language processing is an expansive topic that can fill several dedicated volumes. Nonetheless, we can—and should—understand the core concepts behind this practice as they will be necessary to work with textual information such as clinical notes, order and result comments, messages, medication instructions and more. Despite the use of electronic documentation systems, much of the valuable information contained within the medical record exists in an unstructured, free-text form. The goal of natural language processing, therefore, is to make language understandable for machine algorithms. In order to do this, text must be formatted in such a way that its patterns are numerically evident and so that statistical patterns such as the repeated use of key words are not overwhelmed by unrelated elements of the same text. The practice of systematically understanding language in this way is broadly called "computational linguistics" and work in this field has surfaced some important best practice points when it comes to preprocessing and modeling text.

First and foremost is standardization. Computational systems presently lack the sort of abstract reasoning that humans regularly practice and this manifests itself as a difficulty for computational systems to recognize trivial versus important differences between measurements. Because of this, text should be sanitized for variation in letter case and in the presence of punctuating symbols and it should be "tokenized" by breaking long strings of text into specific linguistic units such as words. More practically, this typically means converting all text to lowercase, breaking sentences up into individual words, removing periods, commas and other punctuation, and removing dates, numbers and other special tokens which don't have a general linguistic meaning. Typically, this tokenized sentence is then "stemmed" or "lemmatized" both of which are linguistic forms of normalization intended to remove specific inflectional versions of words and replace them with a common token. Stemming is a simpler case in which words are truncated to a common root such as converting "patient," "patients," and "patient's" simply to "patient," whereas lemmatization replaces words with more general equivalents based upon morphological characteristics such as converting the words "am," "are" and "is" to the word "be." Finally, this intermediately processed text is then cleaned of "stop words," which are highly recurrent words that have little topical meaning such as the definite and indefinite articles "the", "an," and "a." Fortunately, there are many effective software packages, which can perform these operations, including Python's Natural Language Tool Kit (NLTK), `scikit-learn`, and `gensim` packages. Fig. 16.5 depicts what this process might look like.

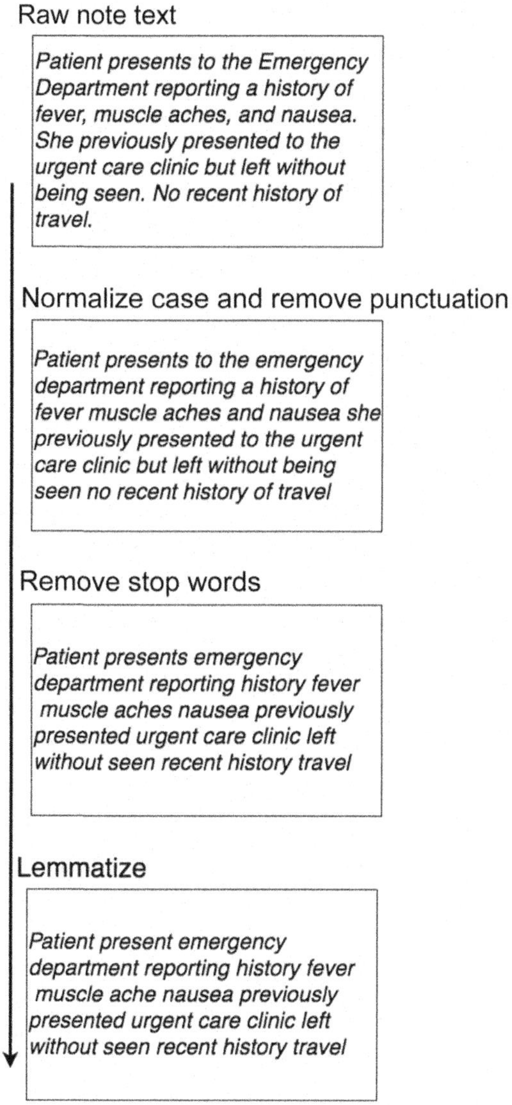

Raw note text

> Patient presents to the Emergency Department reporting a history of fever, muscle aches, and nausea. She previously presented to the urgent care clinic but left without being seen. No recent history of travel.

Normalize case and remove punctuation

> Patient presents to the emergency department reporting a history of fever muscle aches and nausea she previously presented to the urgent care clinic but left without being seen no recent history of travel

Remove stop words

> Patient presents emergency department reporting history fever muscle aches nausea previously presented urgent care clinic left without seen recent history travel

Lemmatize

> Patient present emergency department reporting history fever muscle ache nausea previously presented urgent care clinic left without seen recent history travel

Fig. 16.5
Example NLP text preprocessing steps.

Now with preprocessed text, we have a more uniform vocabulary representing free-text documents. We could apply simple declarative keyword rules such as the presence of the word "sepsis" or the absence of the word "fever" or we could do something a bit more elaborate such as converting each document into a "bag-of-words," which is simply a list of unique words in a target vocabulary along with the count of each time each of the words occurred in the target document. Typically, we don't consider all words for inclusion in the bag although we certainly could do that if we wanted. Instead, we may examine a few exemplary notes or even a whole set and determine which words appear in those documents, restricting the set of unique words to that list. This prevents new documents from adding to the scope of the bag. Finally, with each document as a set of words and word counts, we can use these counts as features in a model such as a logistic regression, we may cluster them to uncover related note types or we may simply place retrieval rules around notes with certain word abundances and we may enhance this somewhat using flexible word matching logic in our rules via regular expressions. Alternatively, we could employ a technique known as Term Frequency-Inverse Document Frequency (TF-IDF), which measures the relevance of certain words as they occur within certain documents, extracting groups of marker words which implicitly represent topics with which the words containing documents are concerned.

Of note, both the bag-of-words and TF-IDF approach are a particularly fast and loose form of NLP, which still performs well in many cases. However, it doesn't preserve the order of words and throws away much of the linguistic structure of the parsed text in order to produce a compressed representation. In some cases, we may wish to preserve some of the word order sequence and a common approach to do this is to convert text into n-grams, where n is an adjustable number that establishes a window of consecutive words. A common example is the 2-g or "bigram," which breaks a sentence up into overlapping pairs of adjacent words. Fig. 16.6 depicts a sentence as it would be transformed into a bag-of-words versus n-gram representation.

Many modern natural language processing tools take advantage of a technique, which extends these concepts known as "word embeddings." These are representations of both words and their context, which allow for meaningful comparisons of words and documents according to topic and meaning. The creation of word embeddings starts with one of two slightly different forms of text representation known as the "continuous bag of words" and "skip-gram." In the continuous bag of words, text is converted to a subset of adjacent words called a "context window" on either side of a target word. The skip-gram generates a very similar type of bag except it considers the target word as a predictive label for its surrounding words as opposed to considering the surrounding words as predictors of the target word. Fig. 16.7 compares the continuous bag of words and skip-gram representations of a text string.

As a final step, we create a dictionary of unique words representing our vocabulary and we substitute word strings for their numerical identifier within that dictionary. Doing this places all

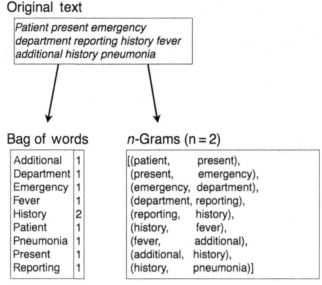

Fig. 16.6

Example preprocessed sentence converted into a bag-of-words vs an *n*-gram for *n* = 2.

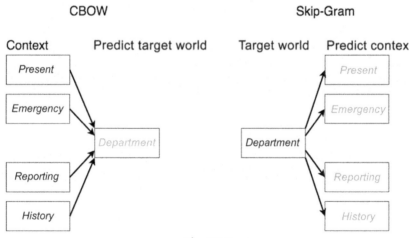

Fig. 16.7

Example CBOW vs skip-gram representations with context windows of size 2.

words in an *n*-dimensional space where each dimension represents a certain word in the vocabulary. Ultimately, these representations are fed into a neural network with two layers the output of which are vectors in an embedding space that represents the associations the network has learned between target words and surrounding words. The embedding space refers to a space of fewer dimensions in which our higher-dimensional input may be more compactly represented and, importantly, it is within this embedding space that similar data points come closer together based upon latent similarities they shared in the higher-dimensional input space but which were not explicitly obvious. This is a very geometrical representation of learning itself as a collection of many separate initial measurements, such as a vocabulary of different words in documents, collapses into a smaller set of attributes dictated by underlying similarities, which places similar things close to one another and dissimilar things far from one another. This has proven to be surprisingly robust as demonstrated by the associations between words and meaning that are apparent when representations of certain words are compared within the embedding space as shown in Fig. 16.8.

One subtle challenge of word2vec is that, when creating word embeddings from a corpus of text, it does not consider the overall cooccurrence of words within the training corpus. In order to address this, a group at Stanford NLP created global vectors (GloVe), which differs from word2vec in a few important ways. First, word2vec is a predictive algorithm and generates embeddings by gradient descent and optimization against the task of accurately predicting nearby words in text subsequences using other text subsequences as examples. GloVe is a dimensionality reduction technique, which considers the corpus en masse and generates a cooccurrence matrix representing important overall statistics about words, which appear together. In the end, the competitive performance between these two approaches is task-specific with word2vec and GloVe outperforming one another in particular scenarios. Both of these approaches, however, suffer from an inability to accommodate unknown words and so a language model is tied to a specific vocabulary. This problem was the target challenge behind Facebook's creation of FastText, which considers characters instead of whole words and which constrains FastText to an alphabet rather than a vocabulary thereby giving the resulting model the ability to generalize to new text corpora.

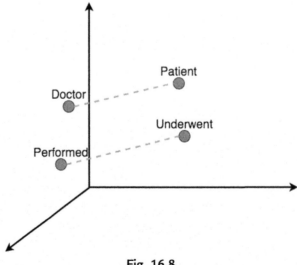

Fig. 16.8
Example embeddings of related words.

The aforementioned techniques just described are common curricula for introductory NLP and are important to grasp; however, recent developments over the past several years and a particularly interesting collection of advancements occurring at the time of this writing mean that word2vec and its related methods are a far departure from state of the art. Instead, NLP has advanced in light of a few critical technical achievements and, while this book will not deeply explore these approaches, we can provide some overarching context. Many of the aforementioned approaches are based upon either global statistical distributions of words (e.g., bag-of-words and TFIDF) or nonetheless generalized vectors representing words or characters (e.g., word2vec, GloVe, and FastText). Each of these cases are still challenged by a) context, since a given sequence of letters, a word, or a given sequence of words can mean very different things in different contexts and/or b) fragility to new words and text corpora and recent work has contributed a few key innovations to address these challenges. The first takes the form of byte-pair encodings, which present a capable tokenization technique which can recursively decompose text into meaningful semantic parts based upon letter-wise cooccurrences within provided text. The second is a sentence-wise modeling approach developed by OpenAI known as a "transformer," which leverages a concept known as attention to detect both short- and long-range patterns between words in the context of larger sentences and text fragments efficiently. Third is the advent of transfer learning, pretraining and finetuning as described with ULMFit, which means that language models are first trained on a broad corpus of text before being trained in a shorter episode on a smaller domain-specific corpus. Fourth, the current state-of-the-art approaches for many widely accepted NLP tasks use bidirectional networks, as in the case of Allen Institute for AI's ELMo, Google AI's BERT and its lighter and more efficient incarnation, ALBERT which leverages several tricks around model parameter sharing and sentence order prediction to achieve state-of-the-art while being simpler to train and deploy.

Pretraining and finetuning may be applied broadly including to the models discussed and this is a particularly relevant advancement for healthcare as the size of any data set, including note text corpora are limited and this approach is strategically appealing because models would first learn general structural rules of English, for example, before trying to learn specific linguistic attributes of clinical notes, being more efficient to train and more performant. This is indeed an evolving area especially as it relates to text analysis in healthcare but current trends suggest that winning strategies will involve general training (e.g., Google News or Wikipedia) before specific training (e.g., clinic notes) with additional training devoted to elements of the vocabulary, which may be encountered only in the healthcare domain corpora (e.g., "hypogammaglobulinemia"). Recent trained versions of BERT in the form of SCIBERT and BioBERT exemplify this by focusing on corpora of scientific text. Importantly, these models may be used in different ways depending upon the task but are amenable to clustering documents such as patient notes into related topical groups.

16.7 Conclusion

In this chapter, we have focused both on considerations around patient phenotyping as well as techniques to define and improve upon phenotyping approaches. Certainly, the goal of this chapter and this book as a whole is to educate the reader on how data is structured, located, aggregated, and processed with comparatively less attention paid to how data is modeled and analyzed. Nonetheless, there are key concepts extending from the machine and deep learning chapters through the discussion of NLP here that are essential to guide how one understands and approaches the process of analysis. The scope of particular tools grows by leaps and bounds each day, it is still constrained by general axioms which are pragmatically based. With these in mind, you will be well equipped to confront the idiosyncrasies of real patient charts, assess the performance of variables, refine and establish phenotyping methods, and even apply text processing to those tasks.

CHAPTER 17

Example project 2: Assessing and modeling data

17.1 Introduction and project background

Back in Chapter 4, we imagined that we were interested in capital planning for outpatient clinics and we wanted to understand which clinics have comparatively more visit volume so that we could add personnel, capacity, or equipment to those locations. In the pursuit of information relevant to that initiative, we used SQL to query information regarding clinic and provider visit traffic, patient composition, and diagnostic properties. In this chapter, we will imagine that upon completion of this initial project, we were able to create additional positions within our physician group practice with a particular focus on central city clinic given its increased traffic relative to other sites. Unfortunately, our cost-benefit analysis for this decision precludes us from hiring as many extra physicians as we had intended to deploy to each clinic location and so instead we're allowed only a few additional positions and we have to make up the rest by increasing the efficiency of our existing clinical workforce.

In order to do this, we want to understand whether visits at our clinics will likely run long or short. Knowing this, we may be able to predict which clinics will have scheduling backups based upon the visits scheduled for that day and that information would allow us to dispatch additional clinical workforce from other sites where we predict that we won't have a backup. This could lead to a powerful gain in efficiency, but it does require that we can effectively predict visit length based upon other visit attributes. In this chapter, we will try to build a model that can do this from the data we extracted from our data warehouse in Chapter 4.

17.2 Data collection

In Chapter 4, we discussed various SQL queries and operations we could use to report information from our database and this proved very helpful in getting the answers we need. Here, we're going to take a step back and consider the scope of our information requirements. Then, we will extract these from the database into a .csv file that we can bring into Python for additional modeling work. As a departure from the SQL Chapter, we can't say exactly what

An Introduction to Healthcare Informatics. https://doi.org/10.1016/B978-0-12-814915-7.00017-X

information is necessary of sufficient to predict the duration of a patient visit—after all, this is what we're trying to get the model to do—but we can generally outline attribute we would expect to be helpful some of which we can locate in our database and others which we may not be able to locate. We're also going to make another simplifying assumption in this case which is that the scope of available attributes is rather limited. This will result in a more simplified data extract and it will allow us to explore the model mechanics more in depth.

If we're going to predict patient visits, we know that we at least want to have visits, the duration of visits, demographic information about patients, and probably some information about their diagnosis codes and we're fortunate that all of this information lives somewhere within our database. In order to ease this a bit, we're going to assume that we only get the number of different diagnosis codes per visit, the patient age, and the duration of a patient visit based upon the time difference between some check-in and check-out appointment event and we're also going to assume that these timestamps are accurate and useful. With that in hand, we can then formulate a SQL query that would give us this information:

```
SELECT
 MAX(patients.age) as "age",
 COUNT(diagnoses.icd_10_code) as "num_dx",
 (MAX(visit_times.end_time) - MIN(visit_times.start_time)) as "visit_minutes"
FROM visit_times
JOIN visits
ON visit_times.visit_id = visits.visit_id
JOIN patients
ON patients.patient_id = visits.patient_id
JOIN diagnoses
ON diagnoses.patient_id = patients.patient_id
GROUP BY visits.visit_id, patients.patient_id;
```

age	num_dx	visit_minutes
56	2	38
48	3	27
48	1	26
...	...	...

We can then export this to a .csv file that we'll be using for the remainder of this chapter.

17.3 Data assessment and preparation

Now we can transition to Python and make use of Pandas to import and manipulate this table. There are many ways one could interact with Python, but it is highly recommended to use an interactive notebook like Jupyter. First things first, we can import our .csv file into a table we will call `visit_times` and we can explore the top rows and datatypes of this table:

```python
import pandas as pd

visit_times = pd.read_csv("sql_report_df.csv")

print(visit_times.dtypes)
print(visit_times.head(3))
```

Which will return the following:

```
age              int64
num_dx           int64
visit_minutes    int64
dtype: object

     age     num_dx     visit_minutes
0    49      4              27
1    51      5              27
2    47      5              30
```

Here we can see already that we have our three columns, each of which is numeric. We can also appreciate that we successfully extracted the duration of patient visits in minutes. This is certainly helpful but we're wanting to predict simply whether or not a patient visit will run long, and so we want to convert these minute numbers to a simpler binary label such as "long" or "short." In speaking with our clinicians, we come to understand that the meaningful breakpoint for this distinction is at 30 min since that's roughly how clinic sites consider partitioning the schedule where a "fully packed" schedule has each 30-min slot occupied and of any visit goes beyond 30 min for that day, it will definitely collide with and back up other visits. We may also come to realize that going longer than 30 min does not generate additional reimbursement and so those extra minutes are uncompensated. Thus, we can imagine that—due to reasons such as these—our optimum visit time is less than 30 min and we want to know when we'll go beyond that so we can preemptively deploy staff.

With that information in hand, we can then create a simple categorical column called `visit_class` which is either "short" or "long" based upon the `visit_minutes` column:

```python
visit_times['visit_class'] = visit_times.apply(lambda row: "long" if row
["visit_minutes"]> 30 else "short", axis=1)
```

And we can create a numeric version of this label column where we encode "long" with a 1 and "short" with a 0 as this will be required for our modeling steps:

```
visit_times['visit_class_num'] = (visit_times['visit_class']=='long').astype(int)
print(visit_times.head(3))
     age   num_dx   visit_minutes      visit_class      visit_class_num
0    49    4        27                 short            0
1    51    5        27                 short            0
2    47    5        30                 short            0
```

And here we can see that we have added a new column, which contains "short" or "long" labels based upon whether the minutes of the visit are greater than 30 as well as the corresponding numerical label column. This is the outcome label that we will build a classification model to predict. Again, as part of our simplifying assumptions, we have only two features: age and num_dx, the latter of which is the count of unique diagnosis codes pertaining to the patient during a given visit. In reality we would want to capture more input features but these will suit our purposes for this chapter. It is still quite important to apply some common sense assessment when collecting model features. Although there can be powerful predictive models capable of learning their own hypothesis functions, if all they have are obviously confounded or unrelated features then they will either be unable to formulate a hypothesis or they will formulate a meaningless and nongeneralizable one. In either case, that would not be a successful outcome of our efforts. Fortunately for us, we would reasonably expect that a patient's age and number of diagnoses should be useful to inform the likely duration of her clinic visit.

As a last step, we would want to check out the missingness of our table with the output in Fig. 17.1:

```
msno.matrix(visit_times)
```

We can see that we have 500 rows across 5 columns and no missing information. We can imagine what we might do if we did have missing information however. Rows where both of our features were missing—both the patient age and the visit minutes—would be impossible to use as we couldn't even label them short or long much less have any predictive features. However, what if we had rows where visit minutes were intact but we were only missing age? We could certainly remove these too but we could also attempt some imputation to fill them in.

17.4 Model creation

Now that we have a complete table of output labels and input features, we're ready to work on some models. In this section, we will make heavy use of the scikit-learn and matplotlib packages to experiment with different models as they provide several convenience functions to

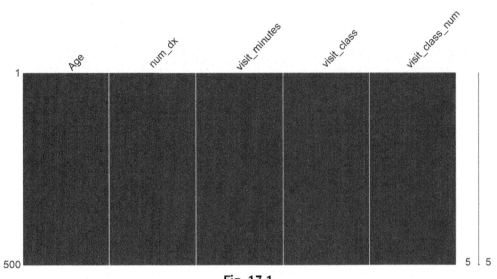

Fig. 17.1
Missingness plot.

parameterize, train, and profile what we're building. Of course, it is still up to us to determine what sorts of models we wish to build and knowing that we wish to perform classification will help us in this regard. We should start with something fairly simple and see how it goes and we can successively experiment with different models as we move forward.

17.4.1 Logistic regression

Hearkening back to our recent chapters on machine learning, it would be reasonable to start with a logistic regression. As a reminder, this will take our input values and emit a score in the range from 0 to 1 which will then be summarized as 1 for predicting a long appointment and 0 otherwise.

One of the first things we will want to do is take our DataFrame and separate the labels from the features where the labels (the 0's and 1's corresponding to short and long appointments) constitute the vector y and the features (the age and num diagnoses columns) constitute a matrix X:

```
X = visit_times[['age', 'num_dx']].values
y = visit_times['visit_class_num'].values
```

Now we need to split our data into test and train sets, designating that 20% of the rows go to testing while the remaining 80% go to training. Scikit-learn's `train_test_split` function will take our input feature matrix X and label vector y, shuffle and then divide the rows according to our `test_size`:

```
X_train, X_test, y_train, y_test = train_test_split(X, y, test_size = 0.20,
random_state = 42)
```

Then we use scikit-learn's `LogisticRegression` to simply create a logistic regression model fit to our training features and training label:

```
clf = LogisticRegression(random_state = 42).fit(X_train, y_train)
```

Finally, we can see how well this model performs by scoring the model against our test features and comparing the predicted outcomes to our test labels using the classifier's `score` function, in this case returning an overall model score of 0.9:

```
clf.score(X_test, y_test)
0.9
```

Exactly how the `score` function is implemented differs based upon the model being used but for the `LogisticRegression`, it's the mean accuracy for the test data and its labels.

This seems alright but we shouldn't stop there. We want to go further and understand some things about model behavior such as whether this 90% mean accuracy score is consistent across all visit types or if perhaps our model is oversimplifying some things. We can turn to the ROC curve to help us understand this and, importantly, we can create several of these curves using different subsets of the data in what is known as cross-fold validation. Again scikit-learn will help us here as it also has powerful convenience functions to make this process simple and efficient. We'll break our data into six sections—or "folds"—and create an ROC curve for each fold. We would expect that the performance of the model would be consistent across folds and, if this is not the case, it might tip us off to a subset of our data that our model isn't adequately representing. Doing this in scikit-learn is simple enough:

```
cv = StratifiedKFold(n_splits = 6)
clf = LogisticRegressionCV(cv = 5, random_state = 42)
print(clf.fit(X, y).score(X, y))
```

Which outputs the mean accuracy across all folds:

```
0.888
```

We can make this more visually informative by using the StratifiedKFold object we created to divide our data into folds, fit our model to each fold, and generate an ROC curve for that model on that fold before adding all of these curves to one plot. What follows is a longer sample of Python code that steps through this process. Note that we incorporate the matplotlib package in order to create the actual ROC curve figure. Using matplotlib, we create both figure and axis objects and successively add fold-specific ROC lines to the figure:

```
tprs = []
aucs = []

mean_fpr = np.linspace(0, 1, 100)
fig, ax = plt.subplots(figsize =(12,9))

for i, (train, test) in enumerate(cv.split(X, y)):
    clf.fit(X[train], y[train])
    viz = plot_roc_curve(clf, X[test], y[test],
        name ='ROC fold {}'.format(i),
        alpha = 0.3, lw = 1, ax = ax)
    interp_tpr = interp(mean_fpr, viz.fpr, viz.tpr)
    interp_tpr[0] = 0.0
    tprs.append(interp_tpr)
    aucs.append(viz.roc_auc)

ax.plot([0, 1], [0, 1], linestyle ='--', lw = 2, color ='r',
    label ='Chance', alpha =.8)

mean_tpr = np.mean(tprs, axis = 0)
mean_tpr[-1] = 1.0
mean_auc = auc(mean_fpr, mean_tpr)
std_auc = np.std(aucs)

ax.plot(mean_fpr, mean_tpr, color='b',
    label = r'Mean ROC (AUC = %0.2f $\pm$ %0.2f)' % (mean_auc, std_auc),
    lw = 2, alpha =.8)

std_tpr = np.std(tprs, axis=0)
tprs_upper = np.minimum(mean_tpr + std_tpr, 1)
tprs_lower = np.maximum(mean_tpr - std_tpr, 0)

ax.fill_between(mean_fpr, tprs_lower, tprs_upper, color ='grey', alpha =.2,
    label = r'$\pm$ 1 std. dev.')

ax.set(xlim =[-0.05, 1.05], ylim =[-0.05, 1.05])

ax.legend(loc ="lower right")

plt.title("Receiver operating characteristic example", fontsize = 18)

plt.show()
```

And the output is shown in Fig. 17.2.

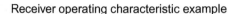

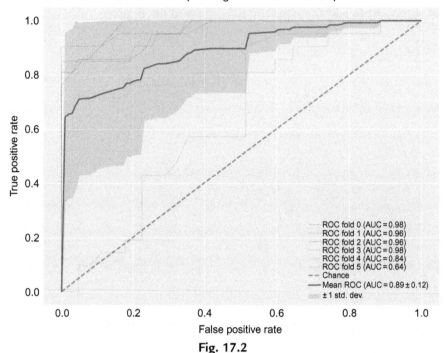

Fig. 17.2

Example ROC curves for each of six folds using a logistic regression.

This now tells us something very useful about our model, which is that, although the mean accuracy is pretty high, we have some folds (such as Fold 5 in Fig. 17.2) that perform quite poorly. This tips us off that there is perhaps some subset or visits that the model is not adequately accommodating. Since we have only two input features, identifying this subset shouldn't be too hard and we can investigate this with a simple scatter plot of age versus num_dx, color-coded by our numeric visit label, where red (gray in print version) corresponds to a long appointment and blue (light gray in print version) to a short appointment. This is shown in Fig. 17.3.

```
visit_times.plot.scatter(x ='age',
                         y ='num_dx',
                         c ='visit_class_num',
                         colormap = cm.coolwarm,
                         figsize =(10,8))
```

Already we can begin to understand why our model is struggling on a subset as the relationship between num_dx and visit duration is different for younger patients than for older patients, as evidenced by the fact that the red (gray in print version) and blue (light gray in print version) points split vertically for younger patients but horizontally for older patients.

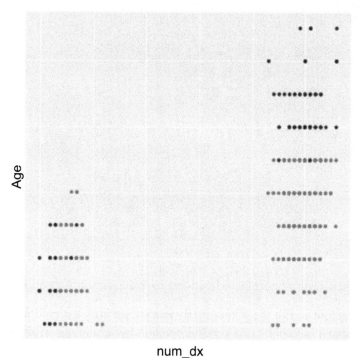

Fig. 17.3
Scatter plot of visits by age, num_dx, and duration.

We can go a step further and overlay the decision boundary of out model on top of the scatter plot:

```
xx, yy = np.mgrid [0:70:1, 0:10:1]

grid = np.c_[xx.ravel(), yy.ravel()]

probs = clf.predict_proba(grid)[:, 1].reshape(xx.shape)

f, ax = plt.subplots(figsize =(10, 8))

contour = ax.contourf(xx, yy, probs, 50,
        cmap ="coolwarm", vmin = 0, vmax = 1)

ax.scatter(visit_times['age'].values,
    visit_times['num_dx'].values,
    c = visit_times['visit_class_num'].values,
    s = 50, cmap ="coolwarm", vmin = 0, vmax = 1,
      edgecolor ="white", linewidth = 1)

ax.set(xlabel ="age", ylabel ="num_dx")

plt.show()
```

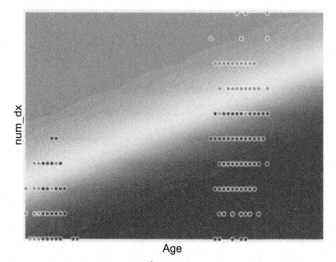

Fig. 17.4

Logistic regression decision boundary overlaid on top of data points.

As we see in the output in Fig. 17.4, this really lets us see how the model attempts to compromise between a horizontal and vertical division by setting one at an angle, but this still ends up working out much better for older than younger patients.

We can also make this clear by investigating a partial dependence plot as shown in Fig. 17.5.

Here we can see that our model is generally much more likely to predict that younger patients will have longer appointments especially when those patients have fewer diagnoses. Otherwise,

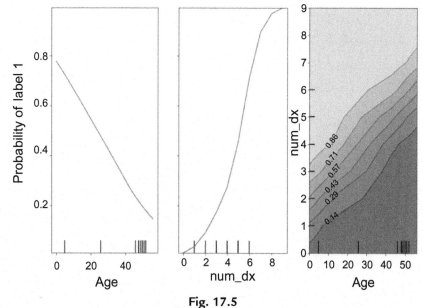

Fig. 17.5

Partial dependence plot of logistic regression model.

the model relies very heavily on the number of diagnoses to make this prediction but these visits with more diagnoses are much more present among older patients. This is, therefore, a great example of the model just not being able to represent data with this sort of complexity as it tried to reconcile these points under one linear model. One last illustration of this behavior comes about when we simply plot a bar chart of the weights that the model assigns to age and num_dx, respectively, but to make this more interesting, we're going to split the dataset up by younger and older patients, train separate logistic regressions, and see what their respective weights look like.

We can select our older and younger populations (pop1 and pop2, respectively) simply by filtering our visit_times DataFrame:

```
X_pop1 = visit_times[visit_times['age']> 30][['age', 'num_dx']].values
y_pop1 = visit_times[visit_times['age']> 30]['visit_class_num'].values

X_train_pop1, X_test_pop1, y_train_pop1, y_test_pop1 = train_test_split(X_pop1,
                                                                        y_pop1,
                                                                        test_size = 0.20,
                                                                        random_state = 42)
X_pop2 = df_raw[df_raw['age']< 30][['age', 'num_dx']].values
y_pop2 = df_raw[df_raw['age']< 30]['visit_class_num'].values

X_train_pop2, X_test_pop2, y_train_pop2, y_test_pop2 = train_test_split(X_pop2,
                                                                        y_pop2,
                                                                        test_size = 0.20,
                                                                        random_state = 42)
```

And then we can train two separate classifiers, one for each population:

```
clf_pop1 = LogisticRegression(random_state = 0).fit(X_train_pop1, y_train_pop1)
clf_pop2 = LogisticRegression(random_state = 0).fit(X_train_pop2, y_train_pop2)
```

With these two classifiers trained, we can separately compare their scores, noting that now each of them scores very highly when the data set is broken apart like this:

```
clf_pop1.score(X_test_pop1, y_test_pop1)
0.9875

clf_pop2.score(X_test_pop2, y_test_pop2)
0.9
```

And if we plot the relative weights each model applies to age and num_dx, respectively, we can see that this performance increase is because the models behave differently as shown in Fig. 17.6.

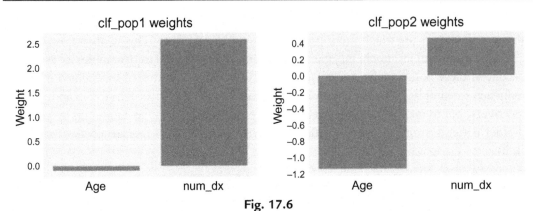

Fig. 17.6

Differential weights between clf_pop1 and clf_pop2 models.

The model trained exclusively on older patients considers num_dx to vastly more important than age while the model trained on younger patients considers age to be much more important than num_dx. Note that weights can be positive or negative but "importance" here just refers to how high the value is in either the positive or negative direction.

What it looks like we need is to try a different model that can handle a more nonlinear decision boundary.

17.4.2 Decision tree

As we discussed in previous chapters, decision trees can be useful nonlinear models especially when we want to make "boxy" decision boundaries. Given that our dataset has two groups, one of which divides according to number of diagnoses and the other according to age at least give us a reason to expect that a decision tree may be helpful. We won't need to repeat all of the code shown, especially those elements that focus on plotting but we will go over specific parts that do change. Using scikit-learn, we can create a crossvalidation decision tree very easily:

```
cv = StratifiedKFold(n_splits = 6)
clf = DecisionTreeClassifier(random_state = 42)
```

And we can plot the fold-wise ROC curves, producing the output shown in Fig. 17.7.

Interestingly now we see that we have much more consistency between our folds as well as a higher mean AUC. This indicates that now our model is more capable of accommodating the idiosyncrasies of each visit group. As mentioned, tree models result in boxy decision boundaries and we can actually visualize this by again plotting the decision boundary overlaid upon the original data points as shown in Fig. 17.8.

Notice that, in Fig. 17.4, the logistic regression model had an ambiguous area between the red (gray in print version) and blue (light gray in print version) decision territories because it allows for intermediate values between 0 and 1. The continuous nature of its outputs is useful in this

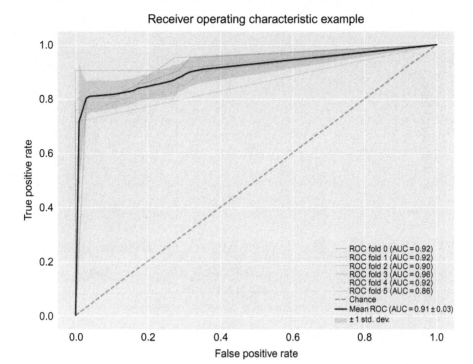

Fig. 17.7

Example ROC curves for each of six folds using a decision tree.

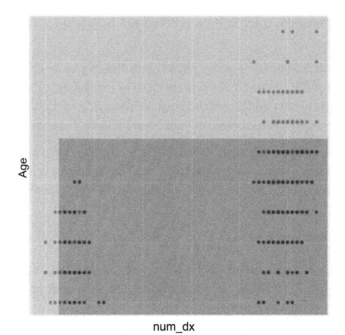

Fig. 17.8

Decision tree decision boundary overlaid on top of data points.

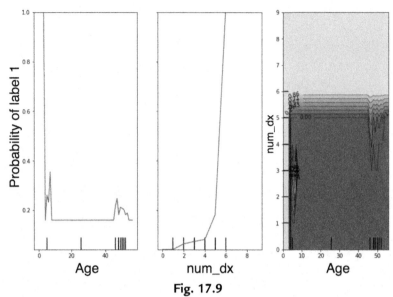

Fig. 17.9

Partial dependence plot of decision tree model.

way because it allows them to be interpreted as probabilities. Recall from our previous chapters that the decision boundary takes a sigmoidal shape and so this plot can be thought of as looking down at a wave-shaped surface from a bird's-eye view up above where the gray ridge is the vertical part of this wave surface. By contrast, the decision tree does not allow this sort of nuance and instead makes strict, discontinuous cutoffs between outputs as evidenced by the sharp transitions between red (gray in print version) and blue (light gray in print version) territories.

We can also see this boxy behavior in the partial dependence plot as shown in Fig. 17.9. For example, there are specific age wherein the probability of predicting a long visit jumps up and specific ages where it is lower and the model does not have a problem having age ranges with both high and low predictive value being very near one another or even potentially interleaved.

At this point, our decision tree seems to perform a lot better than our logistic regression. We could decide to stop here but we may consider a support vector machine as it is a smoother form of nonlinear classifier that may create more authentic hypotheses which might even perform better.

17.4.3 Support vector machine

Without further ado, we can use scikit-learn again to create our SVM. Note that we're using a radial basis function (RBF) kernel as we had discussed previously and we can do this simply by providing scikit-learn with a kernel = "rbf":

```
cv = StratifiedKFold(n_splits = 6)
clf = SVC(gamma = 1, C = 5, kernel ="rbf")
```

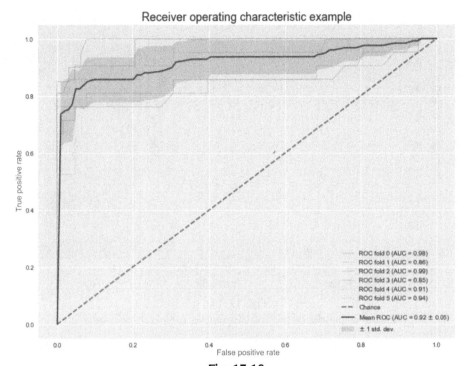

Fig. 17.10

Example ROC curves for each of six folds using a support vector machine.

And create our fold-wise ROC as shown in Fig. 17.10 showing that we have a higher mean AUC than either of our previous models and still with good consistency.

We can also get the overall mean accuracy when one model is trained on all training samples and tested on the test samples:

```
clf.fit(X_train, y_train).score(X_test, y_test)
```

And the results of this are also pretty good at 0.93. We can also take a look at the partial dependence plot in Fig. 17.11.

We can see that the behavior of this model is certainly much smoother with regard to features than the decision tree, something that's also readily apparent when we plot the decision boundary in Fig. 17.12.

17.5 Exporting and persisting models

We will decide to go with the SVM model in this case to predict patient visit duration. As we discussed in our chapters on machine learning, a trained model differs from a naïve one primarily with regard to the feature weights that were determined through training. Therefore,

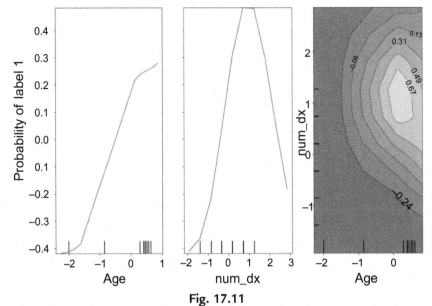

Fig. 17.11
Partial dependence plot of support vector machine model.

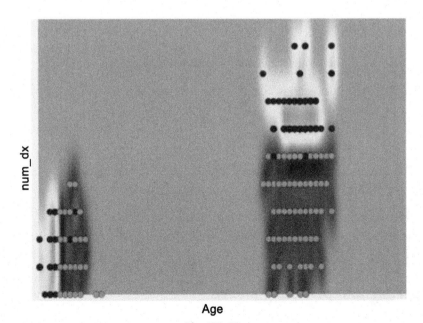

Fig. 17.12
Support vector machine decision boundary overlaid on top of data points.

when we deploy our model, we need to preserve the weights and package them with the model code so that it performs the same in different environments. We can take advantage of a Python package called `pickle` that can take objects in Python and preserve them to a file. We could do this in a number of ways, of course, but using pickle is convenient in this case because we don't have to think about specific import and export transformations to move between our model in the Python runtime and the model saved to a file. Using pickle, exporting our model is as simple as:

```
import pickle
with open('clf.pickle', 'wb') as outfile:
    pickle.dump(clf, outfile)
```

And loading that model back into Python is as simple as:

```
with open('clf.pickle', 'rb') as infile:
    pickle.load(clf, infile)
```

In the case of more complex scikit-learn models with many parameters, there is a more performant—although very analogous—way to do this using the `joblib` package:

```
from joblib import dump, load

dump(clf, 'clf.joblib')
clf = load('clf.joblib')
```

Finally, when persisting trained models that are going to be copied, transferred, and run elsewhere, it's good practice to include some critical elements of metadata, including the actual source code used to create, train, and tune the model, the training data themselves—or, if this is too big at least a link to it somewhere—the versions of scikit-learn, Python, and all other packages used to develop the model and the cross validation scores obtained using the training data.

17.6 Conclusion

At this point, we may conclude that we're ready to use this model in a pilot project and see how it goes. We would very likely not just deploy even this trained model directly to use but would instead allow it to run prospectively for a period of time wherein we can determine how accurate or inaccurate it is and how overall useful it would be in a realistic setting. As for the model development steps, this is something that is truly an ongoing process as businesses and populations evolve and models require retraining and tweaking over time. If anything, this chapter has hopefully demonstrated how powerful the combination of SQL and Python are to extracting data and iterating over potential modeling approaches. It has hopefully also demonstrated code recipes and techniques for profiling and interpreting model behavior. There are many more models than those discussed here and we could decide we wanted to use one. For example, we may decide that a neural network would serve as a good nonlinear classifier. Scikit-learn can help us with this as can other Python packages such as TensorFlow and PyTorch. In the next chapter, we will introduce neural networks and deep learning to round of our survey of data preparation and modeling.

CHAPTER 18

Introduction to deep learning and artificial intelligence

18.1 Introduction

As the final chapter of this section on analysis, deep learning is an exciting and thoroughly appropriate topic to explore. Before diving in, we should understand that deep learning describes a general class of models and therefore is a subset of artificial intelligence. In fact, the models we have discussed previously are all methods of constructing AI. In their seminal text "Artificial Intelligence: A Modern Approach," Russel and Norvig define AI as the construction of intelligent agents that both receive percepts from the environment and take actions that influence that environment.[1] In other words, AI is defined by how a model behaves insofar as it ingests information from a given environment provide a consequential output. While classical examples of this include things like autonomous systems, which have a very obvious presence and interaction with their surrounding, this can make equally legitimate—if more subtle—forms such as ingesting patient data and notifying scheduling personnel about days which are overbooked based upon predicted visit duration (as has been our running example). There may be some debate as to what strictly qualifies as AI, but the definition is typically relaxed enough in healthcare to include systems that ingest information and provide notifications, opinions, labels, which may not have a direct physical consequence but which impact physician or nurse behavior, workflow, and patient care. This is the viewpoint we will take regarding AI in this chapter and more broadly in this book, which includes decision support and related tools alongside the more obvious examples of fully autonomous diagnostics. With that context in place, we can see that AI is a broad umbrella under. Machine learning, therefore, is a field focused on methods of applying AI and sits beneath that broader umbrella with deep learning existing as a specific category of machine learning, as shown in Fig. 18.1.

18.2 What exactly is deep learning

This chapter will focus on a collection of modeling techniques known as "neural networks," which, as the name suggests, comprise interconnected and repeating units. Generally speaking, these units perform some transformation between the input they receive and the output they emit and the exact nature of this transformation can be controlled by parameters that

An Introduction to Healthcare Informatics. https://doi.org/10.1016/B978-0-12-814915-7.00018-1
261

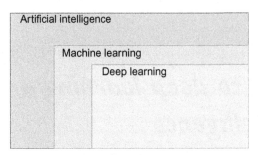

Fig. 18.1
AI, ML, and DL hierarchy.

the units—and the model as a whole—can learn. The exact nature and function of these units along with how they are connected to one another is what defines the "architecture" of a neural network and it is what constitutes the difference between the different types of networks we will cover in this chapter. There are also broad dimensions of a network such as how many units there are and whether and how these units are organized into "layers," which we will also cover. Thus, one could have a simpler model with few units in fewer layers—a "shallow" form of a network—or one could create increasingly more complex models with more units and more layers, which would therefore be "deep" compared to shallow versions. Thus, "deep learning" is somewhat of an imprecise term that generally describes more architecturally complex designs with multiple layers. The relevance of having a concept of deep learning at all is that many of the complex and seemingly intelligent behaviors accessible to neural networks arise when they surpass some minimal threshold of complexity becoming capable of learning very nuanced hypothesis functions but also requiring significantly more computational resource in order to do so. In the end, were just discussing various ways to configure and scale neural network models.

18.3 Feed forward networks

We will start by spending some time on what are known as "feed forward" networks using the specific example of a "multilayer perceptron" and building upon many of the intuitions from the previous machine learning chapters. To begin, let's hearken back to the goal of a support vector machine (SVM), which, in a simple case, is to identify some linear function, which serves as a dividing line—a "decision boundary"—between data points belonging to different classes. These data points have certain properties which we call "features" each of which describes a dimension of a "feature space" in which they are located. Going back to our example of visit duration, we have a 2D feature space consisting of age and number of diagnosis codes as the respective dimensions. We also discussed the case that real-world datasets commonly have nonlinear dividing lines meaning that there is simply no straight line we could draw that would adequately discriminate between points of each class. Fig. 18.2 depicts patients as points in our 2D space, color coded according to whether the visit was short ($< 30\,min$) or long in duration.

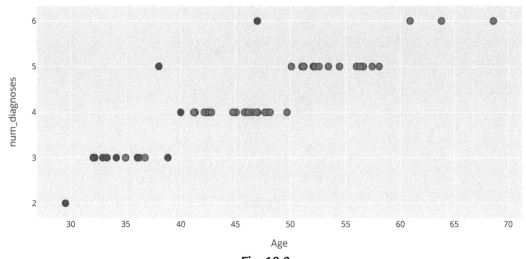

Fig. 18.2
Labeled points not linearly separable.

In our discussion of SVMs, we talked about ways in which those models can deal with data such as this that is not linearly separable through the use of additional transformations known as "kernels," which provide additional dimensions according to the transformed output. The radial basis function (RBF) kernel, for example, added a third dimension corresponding to the radial distance between a point in the original 2D space and a given landmark point that we designate. In the case of the RBF kernel, this third dimension provided an axis along which the data was linearly separable, allowing the SVM to define a plane that sliced this 3D space analogous to "snipping" off the top of the cone created by the kernel, as shown in Fig. 18.3.

As you might have suspected, this technique is powerful but insufficient to solve the problem of learning nonlinear hypothesis functions for many real tasks and the multilayer perceptron provides additional behavior which at a high level is analogous to a decision tree composed of SVM or logistic regression units to learn these more complex hypothesis functions. So we return to our problem of separating the points in Fig. 18.2 using a model that can learn the parameters necessary to locate an appropriate decision boundary. We begin with the simple case of a logistic regression where we have—in the 2D case—a function of the following form where the model will learn the parameters a, b, and c in order to rotate and shift the decision boundary places in the x, y coordinate space:

$$\hat{y} = ax + by + c$$

This simple linear transformation corresponds to the behavior of a single unit in the multilayer perceptron network. More specifically each unit takes a vector of features for some data point—a specific age and number of diagnosis codes in this case—applies vector of weights corresponding to each of the features—the weights being a and b in this case—and adds

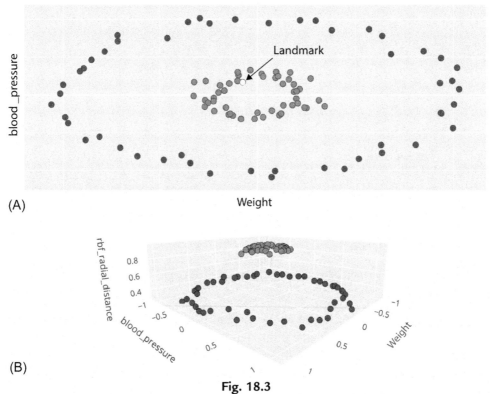

Fig. 18.3

Recap of SVM RBF kernel space. Panel A shows our dataset in two dimensions with a point near the center selected as a landmark. Panel B shows the effect of using an RBF kernel in three dimensions, allowing our datasets to be more easily separated.

a bias term. This is quite familiar to us at this point, but critical "network" aspect of the multilayer perceptron arises through connecting these units to one another. If we imagine a very simple, two-layer perceptron where each layer has one unit (as shown in Fig. 18.4), the first unit consumes features and applies weights and biases to those features while the second unit consumes the outputs of the first unit, not the original input features.

In other words, while the first unit learns a decision boundary in the 2D space of age and diagnosis codes, the second layer learns a decision boundary in the 1D space of outputs from the first node. This is an oversimplified example but it illustrates the idea that feedforward networks consist of linear models, which learn in the input feature space at the first layer followed by subsequent models that learn decision boundaries in the space of the preceding layer's outputs. Let's extend this to the case of a perceptron now with three layers where the first and second layers each have two nodes as shown in Fig. 18.5.

Now we get to some more powerful behavior. In the first layer, we have two separate but parallel linear models learning transformations of the input feature space. Each of these Layer 1 nodes gets the full feature vector for each input—that is, they both get the age and

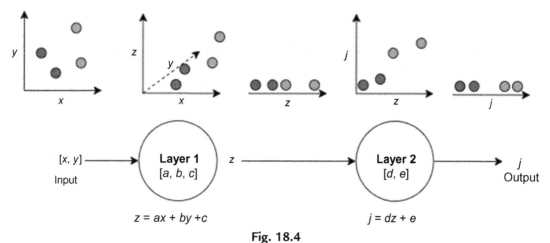

Fig. 18.4

A simple multilayer perceptron with two layers of one node each.

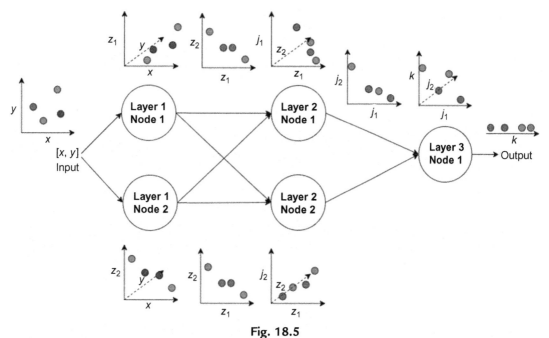

Fig. 18.5

A more realistic multilayer perceptron with three layers.

diagnosis codes—but they can learn and apply their own separate weights and biases and, therefore, their own transformations. These Layer 1 units then each output a scalar value and provides this to each of the Layer 2 nodes. Thus, nodes at Layer 2 also receive a 2D vector of inputs but these are Layer 1 outputs, not raw input features. Moreover, they themselves learn a transformation in this new 2D space and, as with Layer 1, they each receive the same inputs but get to learn and apply their own weights and biases. Finally, in Layer 3, there is

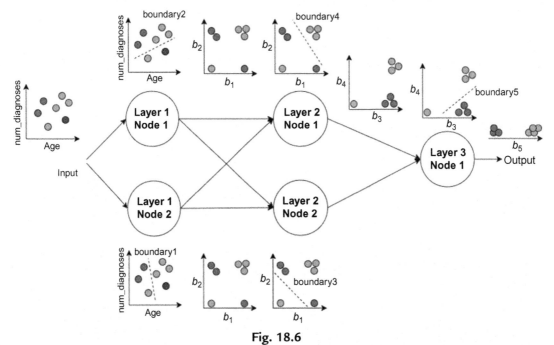

Fig. 18.6
Visit duration data as modeled by an example multilayer perceptron.

a single node, which consumes both Layer 2 node outputs as a 2D input, applies its own learned transformation, and outputs a scalar value. This layered approach means that each layer defines a new "subspace" the dimensions of which are the outputs of that layer's units. To clarify further, Fig. 18.6 depicts our visit duration dataset as it might be understood by the perceptron from Fig. 18.5 and we can see that Layers 2 and 3 do not have axes corresponding to age and diagnosis codes but instead their axes correspond to the outputs from each of the preceding units to which they are connected. In order to make this a bit more readable, we're going to represent the transformations performed at each layer as a decision boundary that crates a new dimension ranging from 0 to 1 corresponding to which side of the decision boundary a given point falls.

Finally, there is another important point to discuss about how these neural network units are constructed. After consuming a feature vector and applying weight and bias vectors, these units then apply a nonlinear function to the result of that linear transformation passing along the nonlinear output to their connected nodes. This additional "nonlinearity" is known as an "activation function." It's worth taking a bit to ponder why this nonlinearity is useful at all. Recall back to Chapter 15 in our discussion of logistic regression that the way classification operates in the case of the simple logistic regression model is by taking a vector of weights and a vector of features, and calculating the dot product between two vectors. This dot product's inner workings are not critical at this point but suffice it to say it captures the perpendicular distance between the data point and the decision boundary.

If we take a step back we can also consider this as relocating or transforming input data from a 2D x, y feature space to a 1D distance space, essentially a number line corresponding to the distance between a data point and the decision boundary. Keeping this perspective, each unit of the perceptron performs this transformation, outputting a value representing this distance determined by the dot product relative to that unit's own decision boundary like we saw in Fig. 18.6. Moreover, several units then propagate these values to the units to which they are connected, defining new dimensions within which those units create decision boundaries and determine distances between those boundaries and points in those new subspaces passing those distances on to their connected nodes and so forth. In the absence of any nonlinear activation function, this elaborate tiering of neural units actually simplifies into just a single large linear operation. Let us consider the simple case of a perceptron with only two nodes from earlier. If we consider the first node to be node 0 and the second to be node 1, we can assign them each their own weights. Node 0 has a 2D weight vector $[a_0, b_0]$ and node 1 has a 1D weight vector $[a_1]$ we will call w_1. If node 0 just directly passed its outputs along to node 1, then we get the following equation describing the whole perceptron:

$$yhat = (a_0 x + b_0 y + c_0)a_1 + c_1$$

Which actually just simplifies to:

$$yhat = (a_1 a_0 x) + (a_1 b_0 y) + (a_1 c_0) + c_1$$

Which is just a linear function of our original x and y. Thus, despite all of our interconnected nodes, we would actually just end up with a linear decision boundary reducible to the linear decision boundary in a simple linear regression. In fact, if we had no nonlinear activation functions and only placed one nonlinearity in the whole network and that nonlinearity was the sigmoidal function, we would have a perceptron that performs just like a logistic regression model from Chapter 15. To expand on this just a bit more, if we think about this from the perspective of network units transforming their input points to a new output space (this would be the application of weights a and b and bias c to inputs x and y), then a network without any nonlinear activation functions would only be able to perform linear transformations such as rotating, shearing, and stretching the point space. Fig. 18.7 depicts these operations as they

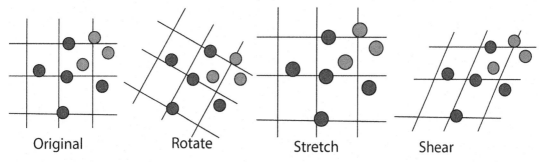

| Original | Rotate | Stretch | Shear |

Fig. 18.7

Linear transformations on nonlinearly separable data providing no helpful separation.

could be performed on an input space with nonlinearly separable data, showing that these transformations do not provide a very useful way to transform the data that makes it linearly separable.

The importance of nonlinear activation functions is to deepen the sort of transformations each unit is capable of. At the time of this writing, the most commonly used activation function is known as the "rectified linear unit" (ReLU) which is shown in Fig. 18.8. The ReLU simply converts all negative numbers to zero and keeps all positive numbers the same.

Let us now consider what happens when the ReLU activation function is included in our network. Fig. 18.9 depicts a piece of our perceptron. In this example, features x and y are provided to a unit and transformed using a decision boundary that this unit has learned. In this new transformed space, let us now allow the axes to range broadly across positive and negative numbers corresponding to how far the point is above or below the decision boundary. This layer applies its weights and bias to the input features, producing points in a new output subspace as we have seen previously. Now we can consider the different impact of using

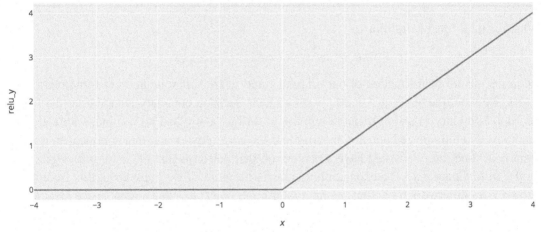

Fig. 18.8
ReLU activation function.

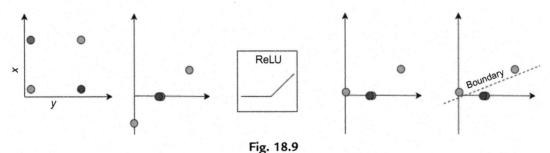

Fig. 18.9
Impact of using a nonlinear activation function.

versus not using a nonlinear activation function on these transformed points. In Fig. 18.9, panel A shows the result without a ReLU activation and panel B shows the result with a ReLU activation.

Importantly, we can now see that the ReLU activation converted one of the Layer 1 outputs, which was negative to zero in effect "folding" a data point over. This sort of transformation is not possible without nonlinear activation functions and, with the ReLU activations, we have Layer 2 units, which can create useful decision boundaries in their transformed space.

Ultimately, this process of taking input features, applying weights, biases, and activation functions and successively passing that output along to other connected units is known as "forward propagation" because the transformations move from input through units to a final output value. It is also important to mention at this point that the "neural" aspect of neural networks is simply the expression of the fact that these units are biologically inspired, operating in a fashion with we abstractly believe to be similar to that of neurons in the brain where upstream signals are received, potentially from many connected neurons and those signals are propagated forth at varying intensity to potentially many downstream neurons.

18.4 Training and backpropagation

Understanding the terminology of forward propagation is useful especially because it mirrors another critical aspect of neural networks known as "backpropagation," which is the means by which the error between a true label and that predicted by forward propagation is used to tweak weights in all of the interconnected units throughout the network. In essence, much of this is similar to the discussion of loss and optimization from Chapter 15: we have a correct label z for a given data point and the network uses that data point's features x and y to predict z and we create some way to measure whether this prediction is right or wrong and by how much. The "backpropagation" part comes into play when we have a number for that error and we want to use that to perform optimization. We had discussed the idea of gradient descent in Chapter 15, and this is still the approach used for neural networks. The trick is that, just as we consider the perceptron as a network of interconnected units with their own point space in which to place decision boundaries, we also consider it a network of interconnected point spaces in which to plot their respective errors. As such, the error of a given prediction is first passed along to the last unit in the network, the one most responsible for "making" that prediction and that unit is able to consider that error as a function of its weights just like we discussed in Chapter 15.

The cleverness of backpropagation, however, is that the prediction made by that last unit in the network is actually a weight being applied not to a direct input feature but to another function, which describes the application of weights, bias, and nonlinear activation in the preceding unit and that preceding unit applies its weights and bias to a function representing its preceding unit and so forth. Thus, it's appropriate to say that the final output of the network and the error of that output is, in our case, a function of a weight, bias, and nonlinear activation applied to the output of a weight, bias and nonlinear activation applied to an input feature vector. We can use $g(x,y)$ to denote the operation of applying weights and biases to x and y inputs and we consider each unit to correspond to its own function g. Labeling each specific such function by its layer and unit (e.g., the first unit of layer 0 has $g_{0,1}$), we can therefore describe the output of a two-layer, three-unit perceptron like so:

$$z = g_1(g_{0,1}(x, y), g_{0,2}(x, y))$$

where

$$g_{0,1} = a_0 x + b_0 y + c_0$$

$$g_{0,2} = a_1 x + b_1 y + c_1$$

With this established, the chain rule of calculus states that the derivative of the error of our function of functions z (which we will call E_z) is:

$$\frac{\partial E_z}{\partial x} = \frac{dz}{dg_1} * \frac{dg_1}{dg_{0,1}} * \frac{\partial g_{0,1}}{\partial x}$$

And the equation is almost identical for the partial derivative of E_z with respect to y. What this all amounts to is a connected series of error surfaces relevant to each unit as shown in Fig. 18.10 with the ability to assign each unit proportional responsibility for the error between the final unit's predictions and the target label. By allowing networks to push error back across their connected units, this backpropagation algorithm therefore allows a network to update the weights and decision boundaries at all of its interconnected units during training.

In practice, there are some numerical issues with this approach that have motivated the use of ReLU over other candidate nonlinearities such as the sigmoid or tanh functions. In these cases, these problems can be summarized as that of "vanishing gradients" where a very high weight in either the positive or negative direction will result in output that is at the extreme plateau of a squashing function and, therefore, at a position with very little slope and hence a very small derivative making those unit weights essentially resistant to updates. This is why the ReLU unit preserves a simple linear relationship between pre- and posttransformed values as long as they are positive.

18.5 Local versus global minima

In our earlier introduction to gradient descent in Chapter 15, we talked about the notion of convexity as a critical property of guaranteeing the success of these optimization algorithms. Convexity is a familiar concept and means that the error surface—a 2D one in the a, b space in our case—is bowl shaped and that there is a single lowest point in the bowl which all other points consistently see as "downhill." In the case of neural networks, the presence of multiple nonlinearities creates a nonconvex error surface, which we can think of almost

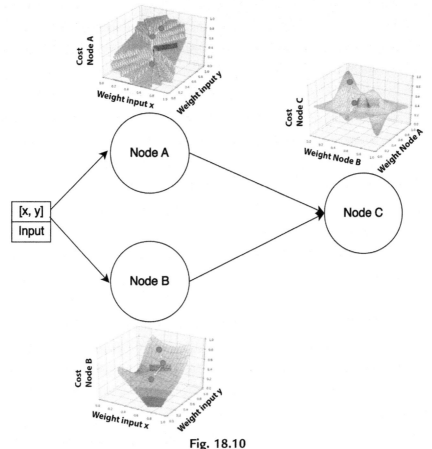

Fig. 18.10
Neural network with error surfaces at each unit.

as a rippling fabric in the *a*, *b* space. This has some important consequences for training. First is that there may be more than one globally lowest point—that is more than one "global optimum" representing more than one combination of weights *a* and *b* which both result in the lowest achievable error. Second—and more relevant—is that there are many "local minima," which are not the lowest achievable point but which are the lowest in their neighborhood of points. These represent combinations of weights *a* and *b*, which perform best among some neighborhood or constrained range of values. Since gradient descent explores the error surface empirically by testing points, measuring slopes, and "walking downhill" by adjusting weights in the direction opposite the slope, these local minima are like valleys, ravines, and potholes in which this walking journey can get "stuck" seeing everything immediately around it as uphill while not being aware that there may be a much deeper valley in another location.

We also discussed in Chapter 15 the idea that the learning rate is a parameter used to define the size of weight adjustment—or steps downhill—allowable at one time. More advanced optimization algorithms adjust this learning rate depending upon how steep the error surface is—represented by what is known as Jacobian matrix whose values are slopes in each dimension—or even how quickly the error surface's slope is changing—represented by the Hessian matrix containing the rates of changes of the slopes—so as not so run too fast downhill and overshoot the lowest point or to redirect the walking path—the way in which weights are updated—so that the path downhill is more direct (as is seen in the popular case of Nesterov momentum). Whichever technique is used, the core mission remains the same, to identify the lowest point on an error surface through exploration using gradient descent and many of the popular deep learning libraries will allow you to select from numerous pluggable optimization algorithms. Finally, the same concept of stochastic gradient descent and minibatch stochastic gradient descent apply in this case the way they do in the simple linear regression case we discussed in Chapter 15.

18.6 Convolutional networks

The perceptron has served as a useful introductory example of neural networks, but there are several architectural variants with their own ways of interconnecting units and their own ways of designing units themselves. Enumerating each variant is both impractical and unhelpful, but there are some general categories, which are important to know. First among these are the convolutional neural networks (CNNs), which have gained considerable popularity in the domain of image analysis but which have examples reaching beyond that use case into areas such as natural language processing (NLP) and genomics. As the name suggests, the key distinction of a CNN is the use of network units, which perform convolution. More strictly speaking, this is a "convolutional kernel" meaning that it is an operation performed on input data—a matrix of pixel values representing an image for example—which creates a new feature dimension containing transformed values. In other words, convolutional kernels are a way to "featurize" an input by creating new values describing it, much in the same way that we saw with the radial basis function kernel from Chapter 16.

Why then the convolutional kernel in particular? Convolutions are a special kind of operation that captures how the shape of one function of modified by another. More specifically, in image processing convolutional kernels commonly consist of matrices often much smaller than the input image to which they are applied, with a special method for combining the two. For example, if we consider a kernel like so:

$$
\begin{matrix}
1 & 0 & 0 \\
1 & 1 & 0 \\
0 & 0 & 1
\end{matrix}
$$

Then, in order to convolve this kernel with a 3-by-3 section of an image, we would line up the two matrices, perform pairwise multiplication, and then return the sum of all values, producing this result:

$$\begin{bmatrix} 1 & 0 & 0 \\ 1 & 1 & 0 \\ 0 & 0 & 1 \end{bmatrix} \circledast \begin{bmatrix} 1 & 2 & 2 \\ 0 & 2 & 1 \\ 0 & 0 & 1 \end{bmatrix} = [4]$$

These convolutional kernels are typically "slid" over a larger image in a serpentine pattern, resulting in a matrix of convolution values each representing the result of the convolution operation between the kernel and the section of the image over which it was places. Importantly, convolutional kernels can take several different specific forms each of which has the effect of highlighting certain attributes of the source image to which they are applied. For example, a kernel with a central column of 1's but 0's elsewhere has the effect of highlighting vertical edges. Fig. 18.11 shows such a kernel being slid over an input image of a square, and the output matrix that this produces.

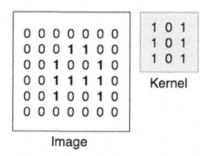

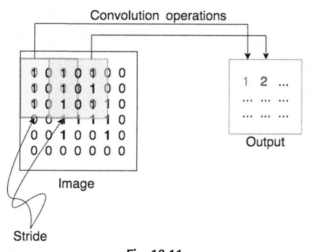

Fig. 18.11

Example of a kernel detecting vertical edges slid over image of square, serpentine pattern with output matrix.

This highlights the real power of convolutional units which is that they serve to featurize images in useful ways. In CNNs, different units at different layers can use different kernels, extracting many important features from an input image (e.g., vertical edges, horizontal edges, diagonal edges, etc.). Of course, since the convolutional unit outputs a matrix, this too may be the input to another convolutional unit which applies its kernel, resulting in a successively more abstract featurization where the edges detected by earlier layers become corners and parallel lines extracted by later layers, which become whole shapes extracted by later layers and collections of shapes extracted by even later layers. Typically, these convolutional layers are interspersed with other units which serve the purpose of aggregating and summarizing values by "max pooling" or "average pooling," which take the maximum or average respectively over several adjacent values in a convolutional output matrix. This is helpful to constrain the size of the matrices and the computational cost that the convolutional layers must handle. Ultimately, though the convolutional layer features are passed onto a more conventional neural network as discussed previously, which performs a task such as classification but which can now learn a nonlinear hypothesis function using the features extracted by the convolutional layers rather than raw pixel values directly from an input image; this proves to me much more powerful and nothing short of a revolutionary breakthrough in model design. Fig. 18.12 depicts an example convolutional network, demarcating the featurization and classification sections.

18.7 Adversarial examples and local minima

We had discussed previously that the error surface for neural networks is nonconvex and, thus, optimization may conclude at local—rather than global—optima. This sort of behavior is poignantly illustrated by convolutional networks' fragility to "adversarial examples." Convolutional layers are certainly powerful at capturing geometric features and their classification layers are certainly able to formulate impressively useful decision boundaries using them,

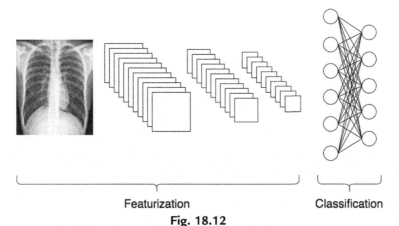

Featurization   Classification

Fig. 18.12

Example convolutional network with featurization and classification components.

but this process is certainly not as clean as one might think. Adversarial examples are specific images, which highlight unexpected model behavior and sometimes profound classification failure often due to model overfitting on an image attribute that is either imperceptible or obviously irrelevant to humans. Thus, when developing such a model, it is important to scrutinize the selection of images used for training. Furthermore, this sort of fragility highlights the need for further development in model explainability especially in domains as critical as healthcare.

18.8 Recurrent networks

We have thus far talked about purely "feed forward" networks, which follow a linear path from input to successive nodes to output. There are, however, many more ways to interconnect nodes a very powerful example of which is the "recurrent" network whose units exhibit "memory" by capturing state across different inputs where those inputs typically represent successive timepoints. Popular examples of recurrent networks include long short-term memory (LSTM) networks popular in many timeseries tasks such as speech and handwriting recognition.

18.9 Autoencoders and generative adversarial networks

We have also discussed applications of networks for purposes of prediction and classification but there are other powerful applications. In the case of autoencoders, networks are designed such that the layer size diminishes from the input toward the middle of the "stack" and then expands again to generate output often of the same dimension as the input, as depicted in Fig. 18.13. An example might be to reconstruct an input image as output with

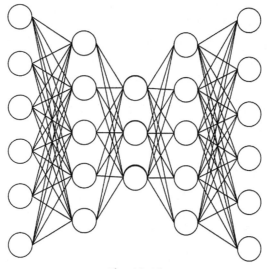

Fig. 18.13
Example structure of autoencoder net.

cost measured as the difference between the input and reconstructed output image. As a bit of a departure from the classification examples previously, the goal of optimizing such a network is actually the units in the middle since, in order for such a network to succeed, they must have learned an efficient, low-dimensional way to represent the input such that the output could be reconstructed from it. This "latent representation" has many applications in compression, denoising, and summarization.

Generative adversarial networks (GANs) are a particularly interesting case whose design consists of a "generator" and a "discriminator" model whose respective goals are to create a target—such as an image of a face—from random noise and to tell whether that target is authentic or synthetic. The clever trick behind GANs is one familiar to game theory, which is that if both networks operated perfectly, the generator would become a perfect forger of facial images while the discriminator would fail to distinguish real from fake images. Stated another way, an optimal discriminator is not expected to tell that an image is a fake if there is legitimately no obvious symptom that it is so. Thus, the adversarial counterposition of training a generator against a discriminator results in powerful generative models, which can create surprisingly realistic artifacts. At present, GANs are the subject of intense research and clever application spanning from synthetic data generation—potentially allowing for the creation of fake, nonconfidential medical images, for example—to molecule design.

18.10 Conclusion

This chapter concludes the section on data analysis with an introduction to neural networks and deep learning. This is a rapidly evolving and expansive field, which continually gives rise to new model designs and techniques. These innovations nonetheless build upon a common core, which this chapter has hopefully introduced. For the interested reader, there are many excellent resources providing deeper explorations of these topics but even if the goal is not to code and develop models directly, the concepts are increasingly necessary to understand and communicate with artificial intelligence and machine learning fields both outside and within healthcare.

Reference

1. Russell SJ, Norvig P. *Artificial Intelligence: A Modern Approach*, Prentice-Hall, Englewood Cliffs, NJ, 1995.

Designing data applications

CHAPTER 19

Analysis best practices

19.1 Introduction

Thus far, this book has contained a wide-ranging discussion of data models, analytical techniques, and organizational considerations. As we enter this last section, we will introduce several important topics relating to how data engineering and analysis can be performed using large and heterogeneous data sources, how machine learning can be developed and implemented on such data, and how the cloud can further enhance the scalability and cost effectiveness of these endeavors. Key to that discussion is a symmetrical introduction to how data analysis should generally be organized to ensure consistency and repeatability of results as well as to cultivate a meaningful and shared understanding of the project work among the analytical team. Big data and cloud technologies are transformative catalysts, but they will not compensate for poorly organized analytical process. This concept of "analytical hygiene" relates to how a general problem is understood and translated into a cleanly organized project. The importance of such hygiene is often inadequately emphasized but is impossible to overstate as a poorly organized analytical workflow will belie even the best analytical resources and infrastructure. This chapter will thus cover organization across three key aspects of data engineering and analysis: workflow, documentation, and data governance.

19.2 Workflow

We begin with a useful abstraction, which will come up again in the subsequent chapter on big data. This abstraction is the "graph," and more specifically the "directed" graph, and has several meaningful applications both technical and nontechnical. To review, a graph is a data structure consisting of nodes (also called "vertices") and edges, which connect those nodes. Fig. 19.1 depicts a general directed graph containing five nodes A, B, C, D, and E and which represents that the same end product E is derived from two upstream products C and D and that C is itself derived from two upstream products A and B.

Graphs can be used to represent many things and are very well suited to represent computational workflow. This is an important formalism because it allows us to organize the steps in collecting and transforming data in a rational way. To explain, let us consider the following example: we are asked by health system management to report on test utilization by providers in different units. Among the particular metrics of interest, there are monthly order

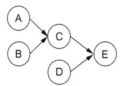

Fig. 19.1
Example of a simple directed graph.

volumes by test, assessment of normal versus abnormal results, and clustering of test order patterns by provider, location, and patient diagnosis. One immediate "real-world" problem, which presents itself in such a project, is that the requisite data elements are often not all contained within one place and are accessible at varying levels of granularity from different sources. In the name of expediency, it may be tempting to immediately seek out each precomputed metric independently from several different sources. That is to say, that it may be tempting to ask one team on the laboratory to provide how many of each test are ordered per month, while asking another lab team to provide a report on which tests are normal versus abnormal and perhaps we even go outside of the lab and ask a team in finance or revenue cycle which diagnoses were assigned to which patient encounters.

Although convenient, this approach presents many critical and insidious problems. The first is that we have asked separate teams for reports and not measurements. By asking for a laboratory team to provide us with a report outlining how much of each test was ordered each month, we have not asked them to convey measurement data—which would be the direct and atomic order events themselves—but rather their own product of analysis. Unfortunately, even if the quality of their analytical work is impeccable, we do not know how such analysis was performed. Were there edge cases where certain orders "didn't count"? What happens to canceled orders? What happens to orders, which are ordered at the end of 1 month and resulted 48 h later at the beginning of a new month? Because these decisions were not made by the analytical team and because they are not captured in the formal pipeline of this analytical project, we are unable to estimate either the nature or the impact of such decisions on our present analysis. This is a very common scenario in the healthcare enterprise where it is quite common to delegate analytical work in this way. Equally problematic is that these incoming data resources are provided by an external team such as the lab team who prepares and send us a spreadsheet or csv file in many cases. Thus, we do not have the ability to update this information in a dependable way as new months come around. Instead, we have to rely on the responsiveness of an external team and, more importantly, since we again do not have access to how test orders were assigned to specific months, we are also unable to evaluate important considerations such as whether orders are duplicated. For example, what if an order was pending as the end of last month when the lab team sent their report but has since been canceled, are we removing that order or is it being counted still in last month's tally? If so many considerations arise from a scenario as simple as counting test orders by month, imagine how many more arise in other, more complex analyses. Understand that it is not realistic to imagine that there is a clean answer to all such consideration around data. Instead, analysis entails a series of decisions each of which frame the final result. What is realistic and important, however, is that the nature of such decisions should be transparent across the analytical process.

So where do graphs come into this discussion? Continuing with the project, we could reconsider the steps in data collection and processing as a directed graph wherein each node represents a data artifact—such as a table, which either goes into an analytical function or which is produced by such a function—and each edge is an analytical operation that transforms one or more input artifacts into one or more output artifacts. This is useful for two reasons. The first and most pragmatic is that this exercise forces us to articulate at the outset which data assets are necessary for the report in question and from what sources they may be obtained. Importantly, it is often the case that a single measurement-level data asset is useful for multiple downstream metrics, and this is made explicit when workflow is organized as a directed graph. The second is that the graph workflow also capture and makes explicit all of our analytical transformations and additionally include the structure of each data asset at each node. Thus, when we need to update analyses, we can think of this simply as re-executing the ordered steps of the directed graph simply with additional rows added. Fig. 19.2 depicts our example analytical workflow for calculating order volume per test per month and the ratio of normal versus abnormal results by test as a directed graph. Note that in this case—as in many real-world settings—multiple initial measurement sources are needed such as orders, test results, and specimen cancelations or refusals.

An additional virtue of organizing analytical work in this way is that is does much to prevent unnecessary duplicate labor downstream. Analytical projects are naturally evolving as one question often leads to several subsequent interrogations or as an effective strategy for achieving one analytical answer is equally valuable for answering a new analytical question either in whole or in part. Perhaps at some later point, we wish to know if there is a correlation between the monthly use of Procalcitonin testing and whether certain providers are on service. This would again require us to know order volumes per test per month as a

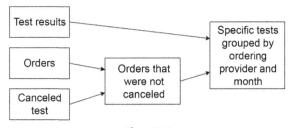

Fig. 19.2

Example directed graph in the context of an analytical project.

requisite data asset in order to answer this question. That piece of information would not be sufficient to answer the question as we would still have to add information about which providers are on service, but that information is certainly necessary to do so. Fortunately, the directed graph articulates a series of steps to get from source data to this necessary data asset and we can borrow this piece of our earlier workflow graph—a subgraph—as a component of the graph describing this new project's process. A powerful advantage here is that if we were to update something substantial about how we calculate orders per test per month, we have a single reference implementation for how to execute this calculation and thus a change to that implementation can efficiently update all the graphs to which that subgraph has membership. Fig. 19.3 depicts a directed graph for this new question and highlights the subgraph, which could be borrowed from the previous graph.

In the beginning of this book, we spoke loosely about data warehouses in our discussion of relational and nonrelational systems. In subsequent chapters, we will talk about big data tools, which allow for increasingly larger and more heterogeneous data sources to become available for analyses. However, the reason for such tools may not be immediately obvious if we did not first discuss the concept of a "data lake." Traditionally, the general anatomy of analytical processes involved the complex transformation of "raw" source data into a relational, tabular format, which can be queried with SQL. This is certainly useful to do, but this complex transformation process is in a sense analogous to the issues in our previous example whereby the lab team bundled raw orders data into counts data. More precisely, the efficiency and cleanliness of data marts is achieved through data summarization and abstraction, which can have both obvious and insidious impacts upon analysis and understanding. In the end, a performant data mart may not be so much an efficient catalog of phenomena as it is a specific representation and framing of that data the biases and details of which are tucked away into the complex transformation processes we mentioned. As a result of this, many enterprises

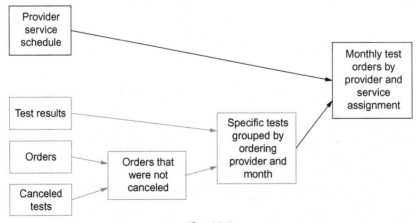

Fig. 19.3

Example of a new graph with highlighted shared subgraph highlighted in *blue* (*gray* in print version).

have seen data marts lead to furthered "information siloing" as topical, departmental, or project-based data marts each adhere to their own local structures, formatting rules, and presentation goals.

The concept of a "data lake" is therefore a large, often enterprise-wide collection of data in its raw format. That is to say that a healthcare data lake may very well contain transactional information from a medical record system such as test order and test result events as well as whole radiology images and individual claims data. Unsurprisingly, the heterogeneity and size of most data lakes precludes them from fitting into a relational database system as a data warehouse might. As a result, there has been a likewise proliferation of technologies focused on making the broad data lake a feasible target for analysis—Hadoop MapReduce and Spark, which we will discuss in the next chapter are perhaps the most prominent examples thereof. Commonly, data warehouses will still be created and serve a purpose, but they can be better contextualized as abstractions atop the information contained within an underlying data lake. An important theme motivating such designs is that it is always better to retain data throughout its analytical lifecycle as is exists in raw format and in various transformations. Data generation is significantly more costly that storage as data cannot be regenerated efficiently or at all in many cases. Thus, as we see a continual decline in storage cost—further driven by cloud technologies, which we will discuss in the final chapter—data retention will be a more and more a universal assumption.

Finally, a discussion of workflow would not be complete without addressing the notion of the "spreadmart," which is a colloquial and often pejorative term an analytics system wherein numerous disparate spreadsheets reside among different individuals and teams each of whom performs their own last-mile analyses. We have already discussed the major drawbacks of such a system as they are the same prime evils of disorganization, duplication, lack of transparency, and conflict between analyses, which are performed without a systematic process or means of interconnection. This is not to universally shame spreadsheets as Excel remains a popular and useful tool. Instead, the notion of spreadmarts is a more general phenomenon and, where apparent, should be taken as a diagnostic sign that many user needs are inadequately met by existing analytical resources either because those systems cannot perform the specific analytical operations users need or, more likely, because users either do not have access to such systems or because users do not know how to use those systems for analyses. For these reasons, workforce education for core technologies such as SQL and Python is a critical step in bringing deeper analytical hygiene to reality in organizations as is selecting technical architectures, which make it possible to perform analyses on data contained within data marts without having to repeatedly export snapshots of information and sever the causal link between nodes of the analytical workflow graph.

Lastly, it is a common practice to see organizations wherein reports—even those with tabular data—are shared in PDF format. Although this is not inherently bad when presenting summary results, this decidedly should not be used as a means of transporting data between systems as converting tabular, structured data to a pdf upon export, impedes rather than assists further analysis on that data. Nonetheless, this practice is seen wherein data lakes contain pdf extracts from some upstream system. Frankly put, this not ideal and should be avoided.

19.3 Documentation

Despite the obvious mathematical and computational nature of data engineering and analysis, these efforts are inescapably subservient to the greater reality that all analysis is a process of constructing some sort of shared human understanding. Thus, while it is entirely possible to normalize, join, aggregate, and classify data from millions or even billions of observations, this alone does not equate to such understanding. Instead, analytical work inherits its underlying validity from that of its underlying and preceding assumptions. If we compute a result from a column with unclear meaning, then we get an equally unclear outcome. This argues the case for both for data dictionaries and analytical source code version control, each of which we will discuss presently.

Strictly defined, a data dictionary is a central collection of metadata or data about data contained with some database, data mart, or data lake. This metadata includes information suchas column or attribute names and their interpretive meaning. It may also include information about source systems from which such attributes were obtained. Consider the earlier example with laboratory test orders. Even in such a simple case, we could enumerate multiple questions in need of clarification. What exactly constitutes an order? What happens if the same test is ordered twice but only performed once or what happens if an order is canceled? From where exactly in the electronic record system did this order information originate, was it directly from some table within a Laboratory Information System (LIS)? The goal of a data dictionary is to provide a shared source from which to answer these questions. Entailed in this concept is also the need to maintain consistent naming attribute and column practices such that each attribute can be found as a corresponding entry in the data dictionary and that relationships between such attributes (e.g., the "test_order_counts" column is created by aggregating values in the "lis_test_orders" column) are also made known.

Data dictionaries can take many forms. Ideally, they should be available broadly by all users involved in the analytical process to read and they should likewise be available for technical and IT staff, governance, and subject matter experts to write. This latter point is less commonly seen than the former, but its impact can be profound. Considering again the exemplary analytical project described previously, it may very well be the case that determining what exactly should happen when an ordered test is canceled is a decision best left to a clinician. Allowing such experts to document and maintain these details improves the richness of the data dictionary while also improving its accuracy. Commonly, this expertise is the subject of several meetings with clinical or other expert teams but the compilation of those discussions is performed by nonsubject matter experts which introduces an opportunity for miscommunication to intercede at the documentation level and to undermine the intent of such expert involvement in the first place. Thus, a "documentation culture" is needed wherein a diverse collection of users take responsibility for ensuring that their expertise is accurately represented in the data dictionary.

Although even a simple word document can deliver significant value as a data dictionary, specialized technologies for this purpose substantially reduce the burden around its access and maintenance. Moreover, dedicated data dictionary tools maintain a functional rather than simply coincidental relationship to the data they describe. Thus, while all naming conventions and changes made to actual data sources must be intentionally updated in a Word document, dedicated tools for this purpose are able to extract column and table names, data sources, file names and related content directly from associated data sources, making the relationship between the actual data infrastructure and its documentation far more substantial. This highlights a very common theme in data engineering and analysis which is that there is a constant and tenuous balance between robustness and utter chaos as complex systems, while powerful, are also more prone to entropy. The ironic realization that this brings is that a separate data catalog such as a Word document, although intended to explain the state of the underlying data infrastructure, can actually work to obfuscate it if it is not a current and accurate representation thereof. Thus, planning around technology selection, the prioritization of data documentation as a practice, and the establishment of a dedicated and functionally interconnected data dictionary tool—not a Word document—as a *sine qua non* of data warehouse and data lake development is imperative.

At the time of this writing, we are also seeing a growth in discussions around "augmented data dictionary" or "augmented data catalog" tools with a special focus on machine learning augmentation of such tools. These augmented tools use machine learning to provide more interactive nuanced features such as semantic search whereby users can find relevant attributes or columns by name but also by description as though using an internet search engine. Such technologies also scan connected data sources to ascertain information related to data quality such as the prevalence of missing information. Moreover, such tools are aware of how commonly data sources are accessed and by whom and are thus able to report common recourses which are used together and even to suggest such resources to users searching for related information. Machine learning augmentation also allows for meta analyses upon the underlying data landscape. We had discussed clustering previously as a common approach to identifying unlabeled structure in datasets. Thus, such clustering can identify data sources, which are not only commonly use together but also those which contain similar and potentially redundant information which may be targets for consolidation. These data cataloging tools are also increasingly able to interoperate with SQL query interfaces, allowing users to search for data sources and attributes, understand their relative quality and relevance, and access relevant documentation provided by subject matter experts all within the same tool and user experience as query formation itself.

Source code version control can be thought of as analogous to documentation where it is the functional activities of data access, extraction, and transformation that are being preserved and assigned a specific version. This concept reaches far beyond analytics as such version control is essential to manage large engineering projects of any type. One of the most popular tools for this purpose is known as git, which happens to share the same creator as the Linux kernel. Git is an open source command line tool that captures the full state of a collection of files as part of a project and captures changes to that state as the content of files area altered. Importantly, when multiple collaborators are working together, git will track the updates each collaborator makes to the project down to each specific addition, deletion, and modification made to all project files. Git further organizes code into branches wherein each user records their modifications to the project's code as a "commit" thereby creating a new version, which is available to all other collaborators. Moreover, git and related tools often integrate with more full-featured platforms that host project code and present the various branches and commits it contains for simplified navigation. The importance of mentioning git here is less to explain how exactly to use the tool and more to explain the fact that use of such tools is a valuable way to record the abstract directed workflow graph as a complete repository of executable code, which can be copied between systems and executed in totality. As git is a version control tool, users may obtain the content of both current and previous commits, allowing for analytical transformations to be run in repeatable fashion to include recent updates or to "roll back" to earlier commits, which contained previous functional content. This is incredibly powerful for making the process of change management tenable as both the impermanence of personal memory and the complexity of team communication and collaboration are quick to scramble what may have initially been clear and well-understood analytical decisions.

Another very useful practice around version control systems—and popularly used with git—is the activity of "merging." More specifically, while git allows users to fork project code into different versioned subprojects called in the form of branches, these branches—many of which are developed by individual analysts or for specific purposes such a particular complex transformation—can be merged into the other, shared branches, thereby more broadly incorporating the code being tracked in a smaller specific branch into more central elements of the project. For example, consider we are developing an ETL process a part of which consumes from both a computerized provider order entry (CPOE) system as well as a pharmacy information system (PIS) and we wish to transform granular records of medication orders and order fulfillment into a table, which contains each order, when and whether it was fulfilled, and what medication was dispensed. Already, many questions may arise surrounding canceled orders or orders where the intended medication was changed upon fulfillment either by a pharmacy stewardship team or other clinicians on the care team. These decisions manifest as elements of our respective SQL queries and potentially also as additional code, which may further format normalize, or type cast our data, which may introduce additional elements of Python code.

In the basic git workflow, we may consider the development of the overarching ETL process the domain of our project while the specific considerations around creating a pharmacy order fulfillment table are a subproject thereof. As such, we would create a specific branch dedicated to the development of the pharmacy order fulfillment table, which contains and tracks our SQL code, Python code, and other resources as we develop this particular component. All the while, we would have other analysts on the team working on other parts of the whole ETL project perhaps working within their own specific branches particular to their relative assignments. The powerful benefit of the branching, versioning, and merging workflow is that we can quickly and iteratively make changes and commit them to our own task-specific branch without impacting the overall state of the project from which other participants have created their branches. However, once we have reached completion of our task merging will allow us to insert the code within our branch into the main project codebase, thus updating the state of the main project code for all participants. Importantly, when branches are merged, it is generally best practice to do so through a "pull request," which is not automatic but instead notifies other project participants of which branch is intended to be merged and highlights all of the code changes that merging such a branch would introduce to the main codebase. This should be accompanied by a symmetrical process within the team whereby those changes and their impact are reviewed prior to approval of such a request. This both reduces the likelihood of unexpected changes taking effect upon merging new code as well as ensures a deeper understanding of the project state and its impending changes across team members. Finally, when a pull request is approved, code in the recipient branch is updated for all members.

19.4 Data governance

As the name suggests, data governance concerns the management of data within an organization. More specifically, data governance focuses on defining accountability for data within an organization's complex topology. Accountability itself encompasses several themes such as usability, security, quality, and availability of data. In short, defining accountability is the basis upon which these additional themes can be assured and by providing a system through which to assign that accountability, data governance organizes and ensures the accomplishment of these objectives. Considering our running example of the laboratory test order volumes, what might we do if the information comes from both an LIS as well as a CPOE system? In many organizations, these systems are managed by different teams in different departments. If it remains unclear who is actually responsible for the test-per-month data, then it will be presumed that nobody is responsible and who then would be in charge of that information, whether it can be accessed, whether it is accurate, how the process is updated? Data governance therefore is a framework for preventing this sort of ambiguity.

Foundational to a data governance framework is the appointment of data stewards who are individuals—or teams comprising individuals—tasked with the responsibility for specific data assets. It may seem redundant to restate that teams are comprised of individuals, but this actually speaks to a common avenue by which data governance initiatives degenerate. Data stewardship must ultimately be the inescapable responsibility of specific people and, if teams are set as stewards, membership on those teams must be equally concrete otherwise the stewardship role becomes ephemeral and ineffective. Establishment of stewards and stewardship teams should therefore include enumeration of all assigned individuals and there should be a minimum duration of the stewardship commitment where, for example, roles are only altered on an annual basis.

Once data stewards have been identified, good data governance would then suggest that those groups establish and agree to specific data standards and procedures. These decisions encompass everything from whether data are stored in a relational system to how tables are structured, how ETL processes work, and how the accuracy of imported and transformed data is tested. Importantly, while data stewardship teams are specifically tasked with making these decisions regarding the data over which they are directly responsible, this should not be a task done in isolation across stewardship teams. Instead, stewards and stewardship teams should report to an institutional data governance committee and teams should have regular interaction both with that committee and with each other as they determine the details of these standards and procedures. The preceding discussion on workflow organization as a directed graph, for example, is exponentially more powerful when that graph reaches across teams. Regular horizontal interaction, planning, and discussion of comparative standards and procedures will both prevent duplication and will also prevent one team's decisions from adversely impacting those of another. Lastly, the process of establishing these standards should not be an afterthought but should be considered a critical part of designing analytical workflows and creating an environment suitable for meaningful analysis to occur; they should be given adequate and dedicated time as a deliberate planning phase of such endeavors and intersteward interaction should be expected to continue regularly in perpetuity. This regular interaction should also be considered among the responsibilities assigned to each steward and stewardship team. Of course, key to defining standards and assigning responsibility is the implementation of those standards and the formal assignment of that implementation as an additional stewardship responsibility. This is often more involved than it initially seems as implementation necessarily encompasses several crosscutting decisions such as which technology would be used, and whether something must be procured in order to achieve implementation. This phase also requires that some level of consensus has been reached regarding standards and procedures without which it would be unwise to proceed with implementing a unnecessarily heterogeneous set of processes, which may only further complicate workflow and entrench deficiencies.

Data governance is as much a political and personal process as it is a technical one and, as such, it is vulnerable to hindrances of both organizational and technical forms. For this reason, it is critical to assist the establishment of governance procedures with some measure of progress, which can be displayed to involved parties and act as an orienting guide for the effort. Specific metrics are goal dependent, but they can be classified into four fundamental types: data quality scores, counts of adverse events, rates of adoption, and the cost of data asset rectification. Quality scores include such usual suspects as missingness, duplication, contradiction (e.g., the number of measurements, which oppose one another such as seeing the same ordered test as both canceled and resulted), and compliance with subject matter expertise. Adverse events, on the other hand, concern things such as data loss, the number of repeat analyses performed, and the number of reports and dashboards, which are dependent upon inaccurate data. Rate of adoption is perhaps the most oblique of such metrics but can be assessed in terms of how many users regularly receive report information and the level of consolidation of those places. For example, if only 30% of ICU nurses received data relating to their rate of hemolyzed specimen draws, this should be improved or if 60% of those nurses receive that information from one dashboard while the remaining 40% receive it from a spreadsheet, this is should also be improved. Lastly, the costs of data rectification should be calculated both in terms the person-hours and infrastructure costs required to bring external data sources into compliance with the governance standards and procedures and in terms of the person-hours and infrastructure costs that present consolidation efforts avoid by being compliant.

19.5 Conclusion

This chapter is far from an exhaustive treatment of analysis best practices and design patterns, but it has focused on those key to maintaining organized processed as analytical endeavors grow to involve more people, more organizational units, more technology, and more data. The importance of prioritizing these considerations cannot be overstated as all projects suffer from a strong inherent tendency to devolve into unclear, chaotic, and overcomplicated processed. These considerations should thus be an initial and formal focus of institutional analyses and compliance with them should be vigilantly assessed with regularity. In the next chapters, we will discuss several big data and cloud technologies, which, if not deployed within an overarching framework, may just as easily impede as enhance data engineering and analysis.

CHAPTER 20

Overview of big data tools: Hadoop, Spark, and Kafka

20.1 Introduction

For much of this book, we have focused on the collection and modeling of data. These are indeed critical aspects of any project without which there could be no rational informatics to speak of. As a matter of convenience and simplicity, we have kept our discussion within a fairly local context wherein data could be queried from some warehouse and imported into Python either directly via an SQL query or perhaps after being imported from a delimited intermediary format such as csv or even Excel. This is a fair assumption and likely holds true for many analyses. However, there are many analytical questions the nature and scope of which preclude this local simplicity. For example, consider a bioinformatic analysis, which involves assessment of millions of genomic variants across thousands of samples in pursuit of variants with significant correlation to therapeutic response in cancer. In such a case, we cannot expect to load all relevant data into a local machine nor can we expect to run such interrogations in a reasonable timeframe on a local machine. Alternatively, consider that we are assessing laboratory test order data aggregated across several hospitals in our system or GPS coordinates for couriers or patient transportation for which we want to make incoming data immediately available to analysis. The simple, local example does not apply in this case as we have entered into the fabled domain of "big data."

The formal definition of big data considers three core values: volume, velocity, and variety, which are commonly referred to as the "three Vs." Volume typically means that data requires enough storage that outfitting a single server for the task would be cost prohibitive or at least costly enough to motivate a search for alternative solutions. Velocity means that data need to be incorporated into analyses as soon as possible to the moment it is created, while variety means that incoming data may exist in multiple formats both structured and unstructured. There is an additional fourth V of big data, which is that of veracity, which means that the calculations created from big data must be accurate and trustworthy. More specifically, veracity encompasses the bias, duplication, and inconsistency of big data aggregations and requires that these considerations be addressed in the design of ingestion and analysis workflows using big data tools. A fifth V, which is not typically discussed but worth including, is that of volatility or how often data elements are subject to change. For example, the age

An Introduction to Healthcare Informatics. https://doi.org/10.1016/B978-0-12-814915-7.00020-X

of a patient is more volatile than the name of a patient as it changes once a year. For this reason, we would not store age as a value but would instead store birth date as age can be calculated at the time of analysis from that nonvolatile value. I would offer my own more colloquial definition of big data, which are data that are large and complex enough that you have to specifically think and plan around how to handle it. Once you begin to ask questions such as "where can I put this information," "how will I calculate a value using pieces of information from these different systems," or "how will I calculate the real time value of some measurement," then you have likely entered into the realm of big data.

In this chapter, we will not cover all of the tools in the big data ecosystem as it is both expansive and rapidly evolving but we will discuss three of its core technologies each of which plays an important role in big data platforms and each of which are key services on popular cloud platforms. Understand that, while many large institutions and Fortune 500 companies initially developed their own on-premises big data platforms or deployed popular vendor platforms such as Cloudera, Hortonworks, or MapR, these technologies are increasingly well integrated into the major cloud platforms and are typically used and managed there. Nonetheless, understanding the tools themselves is necessary to understand when and how to use them regardless of whether they are used directly, through an on-premises platform or as part of a cloud offering.

20.2 Hadoop

Hadoop is, at its core, a technology for storing large quantities of data across many separate computers as well as a technology for processing that distributed data. Hadoop's roots date back to work on the Google File System in the early 2000s and its main development occurred at Yahoo! where the goal was to support the storage of very large indexes of internet content and search among them in an efficient manner. As such, Hadoop's goals were both to support speedy analysis and to allow for the aggregation of several computers (with the largest cluster containing 4500 smaller servers or "nodes") while making that platform resilient to the inevitable failure of any single computer within the cluster. A concept associated with this motivation is that of "scale up" versus "scale out" approaches to computing power. The scale-up approach is both costly and risky, requiring successive upgrades to increasingly expensive and large servers eventually reaching an insurmountable asymptote beyond which no single server can be augmented. By contrast, the scale-out approach seeks to distribute work across many smaller servers each of which is relatively inexpensive. These comparative performance-to-hardware functions are depicted in Fig. 20.1.

More formally speaking, Hadoop is an open source framework whose development is supported by the Apache Software Foundation, which consists of four core modules: Hadoop Common, the Hadoop Distributed Filesystem (HDFS), Hadoop YARN, and Hadoop MapReduce. Hadoop Common will not be a focus of our discussion as it primarily contains

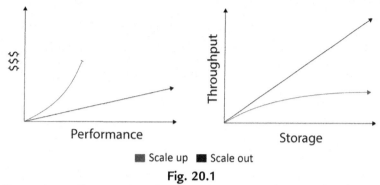

Fig. 20.1
Comparison of cost and performance between scale-up and scale-out.

libraries used by other modules. We will discuss YARN and MapReduce as complementary parts of the data processing technology in a moment, but we will begin with a focus on HDFS as the key enabling technology behind Hadoop's parallelism. As Hadoop was designed to operate as a cluster of interconnected servers, it assumed a certain topology where specific servers have specific roles. Moreover, HDFS is a master/worker architecture, which means that these roles are tiered into a server process which coordinates work and many worker processes which perform that work. An HDFS cluster, consists of a single NameNode, which is a master server responsible for storing filesystem metadata such as file names, file permissions, and directory locations where files are stored. Importantly, the NameNode is only responsible for storing and maintaining this filesystem metadata and it not tasked with storing any of the actual data belonging to any file.

This is very much by design as the topology of a Hadoop cluster seeks as much as possible to separate responsibilities between filesystem organization and filesystem content. Maintenance of the state of the filesystem, including which files exist, where they are stored, whether they are currently being written to, and who has access to them require consistency, meaning that the data structure capturing that information needs to be as complete and current as possible at all times in order to coordinate filesystem operations between many clients who are interacting with the cluster. As such, this is difficult to duplicate without creating an untenable risk that different clients are presented with different and conflicting states of the filesystem. In many cluster configurations, there are one or more NameNode failovers, which maintain near real-time copies of the NameNode information in the case of a hardware failure on the NameNode itself, but only one instance of the NameNode is actually active and occupying the NameNode role at any one time. This is in contrast to the DataNodes, which purposefully exist in multitudes containing tens, hundreds, or even thousands of instances. This is possible because each DataNode is simply a repository of file data and each DataNode continuously updates the NameNode with a BlockReport including an inventory of which blocks of data the DataNode currently contains. Thus, the topology of a Hadoop cluster naturally meets these constraints with one active NameNode,

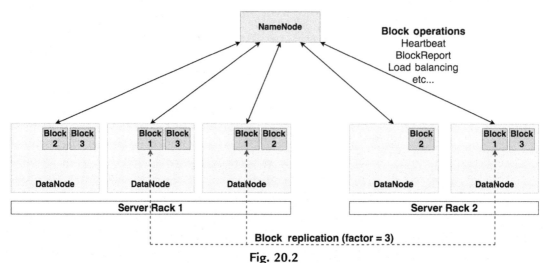

Fig. 20.2
Hadoop cluster NameNode and DataNode topology.

potentially additional nonactive failover NameNodes, and numerous active DataNodes. Fig. 20.2 depicts this general topology.

The NameNode performs an additional and especially critical role of data replication in addition to distribution. It is one thing for a large collection of files to benefit from a similarly large collection of hard drives across many DataNodes but that alone fails to solve some important problems. First is that of fault tolerance meaning that in the inevitable case that one of the DataNodes fails (e.g., due to an electrical surge, faulty cable, spilled water, kernel dump, etc.) the data contained within that DataNode must be immediately available from another DataNode elsewhere in the cluster such that the data are not lost and the workflows requiring use of that data can still operate. Second is that of bottlenecking such that if all relevant data for a given analysis are stored on a single DataNode then computation upon that data will be constrained by access to that Node's data and would not benefit from the parallelism afforded by being in a cluster. Fortunately, replication offers a measure of resolution to both of these problems and is a key aspect of HDFS. Every file stored within a Hadoop cluster is first parceled into blocks the size of which is a configurable parameter but is 128 MB by default in current versions of Hadoop. Each block contains a segment of the bits that comprise the whole file and, importantly, it need not be the case that a file be evenly divisible by the block size. For example, an 80 MB file would be allocated one 80 MB block while a 260 MB file would be allocated three blocks of sizes 128, 128, and 4 MB. The second important concept of that of the replication factor, which determined how many copies of each block should be created. This is also a configurable parameter, although its default value is three meaning that, by default, each file placed within HDFS is broken up into 128 MB blocks and three copies of each block are created. It is the NameNode that determines which DataNodes have which blocks and which DataNodes should receive blocks when a new file is added, DataNodes simply know what blocks they contain, and they report this to the NameNode periodically.

Importantly, block placement is "rack aware" meaning that the NameNode knows not just the individual identify of each DataNode but also within which physical server rack the DataNode resides. This allows the NameNode to coordinate the placement of blocks according to risk management or efficiency-based policies. For example, it is common that, for three replicate blocks, one will be placed on a DataNode within the rack local to the NameNode while the remaining two blocks would be placed on separate DataNodes both of which are in a different physical rack. This way the data have been spread between two racks to mitigate against lost of a physical rack but not three racks, which would incur additional and perhaps unwanted network latency for related operations. Understand that HDFS has many configurable parameters and there are different organizations better suited for different circumstances depending upon whether the goal is purely loss aversion, efficiency, or a mixture of the two.

Finally, it is important to mention that communication with a Hadoop cluster occurs through use of a Hadoop client, which is a smaller program installed on the local machine of a user and through which that user reads, writes, or inspects the contents of HDFS. When a user places a file within HDFS, for example, an ostensibly simple command such as "hdfs dfs -put / Hadoop/myfile.csv ~/myfile.csv" performs a fairly complex interaction with the cluster. First, the NameNode is contacted and the metadata regarding myfile.csv is sent to the NameNode. Second, the NameNode then adds the destination path to its index and locks that path such that nobody else could read or write to that location during the file placement process. Third, the NameNode will inspect the DataNodes and, if the replication factor is three, it will identify three DataNodes who should receive the file data, providing the IP addresses of those DataNode instances back to the client. The client then divides myfile.csv into its 128 MB blocks and then sends the first block to a single DataNode at which point the recipient DataNode directly sends a copy of the block to two other DataNodes. More specifically, the DataNode receives the 128 MB block as a stream of smaller, 4 KB pieces and will immediately copy each piece to a replicant DataNode once copies. Thus, while a block is being sent to a target DataNode, that node is also actively propagating replicate block data to the other replicate DataNodes in a process known as "replication pipelining." Once complete, the DataNode informs the client that it is ready for the second block and so on until the file is fully transferred into HDFS. Note that, while DataNodes can directly transfer replicate blocks to each other, they only do so within a set of DataNodes initially selected by the NameNode for this file placement operation.

Shifting focus now to data processing, the initial version of Hadoop had MapReduce performing both the function of resource management and that of data processing but in current versions, these roles have been broken out such that MapReduce is exclusively a data processing technology while YARN serves the role of resource management. YARN or, "Yet Another Resource Negotiator," is a technology consisting of both resource management and job scheduling functionality and, as with HDFS, it consists of a cluster of separate processes split into a master/worker hierarchy. At the top of this hierarchy is the ResourceManager, which comprises two components: the Scheduler and the ApplicationsManager. Also as with HDFS, there are numerous computation nodes each of which runs a NodeManager, which continuously updates the ResourceManager with that node's available resources. When a client submits an application to be run, this request is communicated directly to the ResourceManager, which has visibility over each worker node and its available resources. Much as with block sizing, work on a Hadoop cluster is parceled into abstract units known as resource containers, which contain associated volumes of CPU, memory, disk, and network resources. The ApplicationsManager reaches out to a single available NodeManager with adequate resources with which to initiate an ApplicationMaster and initiates that process on that manager's node. Following this, the ApplicationMaster will query the ResourceManager for which other nodes have available resources to support resource containers apportioned to its application's tasks. This decision of node and resource availability is then made by the scheduler within the ResourceManager. In response, the ResourceManager provides the ApplicationMaster with a list of nodes eligible for the necessary tasks and the ApplicationMaster directly contacts those NodeManagers and initiates resource containers necessary to complete the application's tasks. Upon completion, the application quits and the resource containers are eliminated, liberating their resources to be used for other applications. The architecture of YARN is depicted in Fig. 20.3.

Importantly, just as any given task may take place across many worker nodes, any given worker node may host multiple resource containers performing work for several different applications.

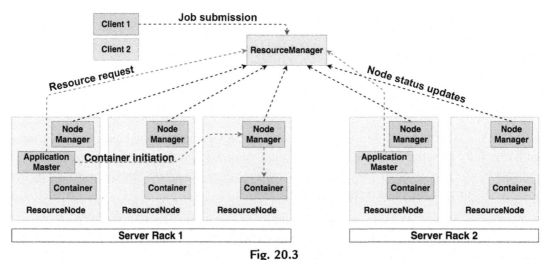

Fig. 20.3
YARN architecture.

Each application is really a temporary allocation of cluster resources to the completion of a particular job and consists of one ApplicationMaster with potentially numerous associated resource containers. Hadoop may, of course, support "long-running" jobs such that applications and their related containers are requisitioned and allocated for long or indefinite periods of time but we still refer to this as "temporary" because it starts and ends within the overall uptime of the cluster and is subject to cluster scheduling.

MapReduce was first popularized by Jeff Dean and Sanjay Ghemawat at Google for the purposes of inverting links to build and update Google's search index using webpage data distributed across many clustered nodes. MapReduce is formally a way of conceiving and designing parallel operations but is often taken to be synonymous with the specific implementation packaged with Hadoop, known properly as "Hadoop MapReduce." As with SQL, this interchangeability between a theoretical approach and an implementation is rarely valid but as the Hadoop implementation has gained majority use and uptake, this equivalence is commonly assumed. In the MapReduce framework, there are three critical operations into which a job should be decomposed: map, shuffle, and reduce. Consider the following task: we have a Hadoop cluster of 250 DataNodes containing laboratory test results from a large reference lab and we wish to calculate the how many of each test have been performed. The MapReduce approach to solving this problem mirrors the fact that these test result tables are broken up and distributed across thousands of blocks throughout our cluster. First, to map this task, we have many workers responsible for performing smaller local count-by-test operations on the data directly available to them, this results in perhaps hundreds of smaller tables residing with each worker, which reflect the number of tests ordered based upon only the blocks available to that worker. Second, we shuffle this worker data such that each worker contains all the separate counts for a given test. Third, we reduce this task by having each worker calculate the sum of its separate test counts and report the results to a single master node, producing a final table, which contains the total counts of each test which in our case would then be written back to HDFS. This approach affords increased efficiency by allowing both map and reduce tasks to be performed in parallel across several workers. Fig. 20.4 depicts this example lab test MapReduce job as it propagates from DataNode blocks to final summary results.

In the earlier days of Hadoop, MapReduce Jobs were written directly in Java, compiled into jar files, and added to the cluster whereupon they could be invoked using YARN. More recently, the advent of Hadoop Streaming has made it possible to write mapper and reducer functions with any executable script including Python since the mapper and reducer operations read from and write to the common denominator of STDIN and STDOUT. MapReduce is a critical concept to understand but, for the purposes of this book, using Hadoop MapReduce is less of a consideration as we will focus on Spark as a preferred technology for parallel processing.

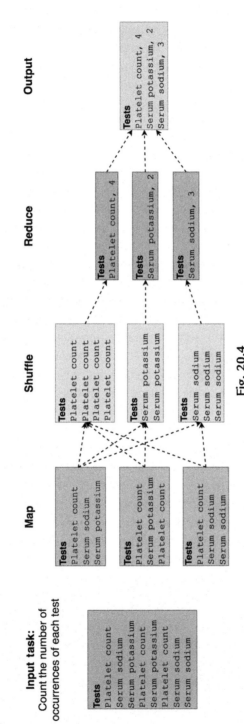

Fig. 20.4

Example MapReduce workflow for test count.

20.3 Spark

It is difficult to overstate the importance of Spark, having grown to become the most popular open source project on Earth at the time of this writing. Born out of the AMPLab at The University of California, Berkeley, the original creator Matei Zaharia and his AMPLab advisors Ali Ghodsi and Ion Stoica would later go on to found Databricks, which offers one of the leading commercial distributions of Spark. Spark is purely a parallel processing framework and, as such, does not directly compete with the Hadoop ecosystem as a whole. Instead Spark can be thought of more as an alternative to MapReduce. As Spark has no persistence layer like HDFS, it is common to run Spark within a Hadoop cluster such that Spark reads and writes distributed data from and to HDFS. Spark does have the ability to run in "standalone" mode, allowing it to directly provision and manage its own worker nodes within a cluster but, alternatively, Spark may work through an external cluster resource manager such as YARN or Mesos and so it is also common to see Spark deployed "on YARN" meaning that it operates through Hadoop YARN within a Hadoop cluster to access and manipulate data in HDFS using resource containers allocated and coordinated by YARN as previously described. Understand that Spark is highly configurable in this way and even supports execution through very elastic container-based resource managers such as Kubernetes (which we will discuss in the next chapter) and variable persistence layers outside of HDFS such as cloud object storage or other databases such as Cassandra and HBase. As Spark is increasingly integrated within managed cloud services, these configuration decisions become more flexible and, in some cases, less of a deliberate concern for interaction and analysis. Thus, this section will focus on Spark itself as a relatively isolated tool, building upon many of the cluster-centric architectural patterns introduced in the preceding discussion of Hadoop.

Spark currently consists of four main components each of which sit atop Spark Core, which is responsible for the scheduling, dispatching, and execution of tasks within Spark. The key innovation behind Spark is its decomposition of processing tasks into a directed acyclic graph (DAG) of more atomic transformations. By definition, this DAG describes a unidirectional sequence of transformational steps such that each edge described a transformation and each node described a stable position between transformational steps in the workflow, thereby representing a checkpoint whereupon the workflow could be stopped and restarted. By design, the nodes represent immutable versions of the data being process such that each transformation creates a new, posttransformation data structure separate from the pretransformation data structure. The pretransformation data structure may be optionally persisted but, more important, is the fact that any such data structure can be defined as a linear sequence of transformations from the origin and thus it may be arbitrarily regenerated by replaying those necessary transformations. Together, these aspects provide a robust means of fault tolerance and, equally important, the design of the DAG allows for subdivision of tasks into increasingly atomic and parallel functions. Fig. 20.5 depicts an example structure of such a

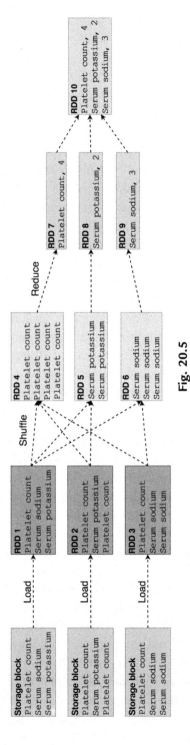

Fig. 20.5

Example DAG workflow structure in Spark.

DAG highlighting how this elegantly captures both computational workflow and interstep checkpoints. Another general strength of Spark is that it operates upon data in-memory, which is much faster to access than data stored to disk, providing Spark with an oft-cited performance increase of "up to $100\times$" compared to Hadoop (on particular workflows of course). Overall, Spark still enjoys a comprehensively superior performance to that of Hadoop MapReduce, which is a large driver for its popularity and success.

As this DAG defines operations upon and transformations between various data structures, it's important to note that Spark also does what is known as "lazy evaluation," which means that the constructed DAG isn't actually executed until an output is actually called for at which point all of the DAG's data structure transformations are executed along the path between inputs and the requested output. Now we can delve a bit into what exactly those data structures are. The core data structure in Spark is the resilient distributed dataset (RDD), which is a collection of elements that can be partitioned into smaller subcollections while still retaining overall lineage that they are part of a larger original collection. RDDs are objects in memory which are aware both of their dependencies—that is, the parent RDDs from which they are derived via transformation—as well as the locality of their partitions— that is, the node upon which a particular partition resides, which makes it possible to preferentially dispatch-related job tasks using resource containers on the same node as their requisite data partition. Finally, each RDD has a compute function, which encapsulates a specific operation to perform on a partition. This is flexible indeed and RDDs were the top-level Spark data type throughout its early versions but RDDs nonetheless suffered from a few drawbacks owing to the fact that this level of flexibility precluded Spark from making intelligent optimizations of various transformations or from compressing RDDs because Spark was not aware of specific RDD data types and had no insight into their functions. Subsequent Spark versions brought incrementally more structure by offering a collection of optimized high-level operations such as filtering, selecting, and counting with which DAGs could be composed. A critical advancement in Spark was the creation of DataFrames, which are structured collections that maintain a tabular row and column relationship with the further ability to declare DataFrame schemas including specific names and data types for DataFrame columns. Importantly, DataFrames are build atop RDDs through these additional constraints. There is an additional RDD abstraction known as the dataset, which is a collection of objects like the RDD but with the additional provision that these objects are strongly typed. As Spark has evolved, the APIs for interacting with datasets and DataFrames have merged such that, a DataFrame can be thought of as a dataset organized into multiple named columns. That is to say that a DataFrame is a dataset of rows. These distinctions are meaningful and one may choose to interact with data in Spark as a DataFrame, a dataset, or directly as an RDD depending upon the situation. For example, when processing unstructured free text, it may be necessary to manipulate data as an RDD, generating a DataFrame after initial steps of a Spark job have preprocessed the textual information.

The architecture of Spark is not entirely different from that of Hadoop MapReduce in the sense that there is a MasterNode, which hosts a "driver program" responsible for analyzing, distributing, and scheduling work across several "executors," which are responsible for actually carrying out the functions of the job in question. Executors thus have a simple responsibility: they execute specific steps assigned them by the driver program and report those results back to the driver program. Spark organizes these executors and the plan they execute into a Spark application, which is controlled through a component of the driver process known as the Spark session, which provides a channel to declare and dispatch user-defined data manipulations across the cluster as a DAG of operations performed by Executors. Fig. 20.6 depicts this architecture.

As mentioned previously, Spark comprises four components, which rest atop Spark Core. These are Spark SQL, Spark Streaming, MLlib, and GraphX, all of which interoperate with RDDs, datasets, and DataFrames to provide increasingly higher level functionality. Spark SQL is a particularly exciting and impressive achievement because it allows for the execution of SQL queries upon Spark DataFrames, enabling users to query large data distributed across potentially hundreds of cluster nodes using the expressive and very familiar syntax of SQL selections, aggregations, and joins and without explicit concern for the distributed nature of the underlying data. I say "explicit" because, while it is functional to perform flexible SQL queries upon large DataFrames partitioned throughout the cluster, there are certain types of queries, which have decidedly suboptimal performance the classic examples of which involve joining DataFrames where join keys are very unevenly present in the corresponding tables or there are only a few join keys in the relevant tables, which prevents adequate parallelism. Spark SQL

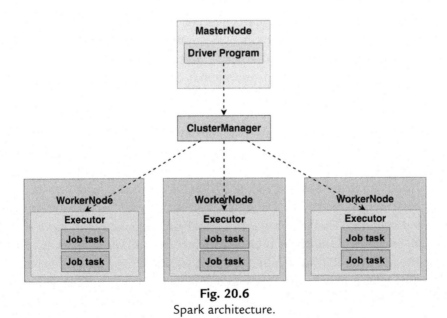

Fig. 20.6
Spark architecture.

queries may be executed through JDBC or ODBC as though connecting to a relational database or they may be formulated and dispatched through one of Spark's many language-specific APIs a popular example of which is PySpark for Python.

Spark streaming allows Spark to ingest and operate upon real-time data such as that coming from Kafka. The key to Spark streaming is the discretized stream (DStream), which encapsulates an unbounded stream of data and breaks it up into small batches known as "micro batches" for incremental operation. As with DataFrames, DStreams are built atop RDDs. Because Spark streaming is discretized to small batches, it allows Spark to maintain a single data processing engine for both batch and streaming workflows by simply approximating stream processing through the use of very small batches. Following the advent of Spark streaming, Spark structured streaming offered an additional way to handle incoming stream data based upon Spark SQL by considering the stream as an unbounded DataFrame by mapping stream input data to a tabular format. In structured streaming, records of an input stream are mapped such that Spark can parse out and operate on atomic data records contained within the stream. An example of this might be consuming a stream of records from Kafka where each record represents the information from a single lab test order. Within Spark structured streaming, the query defines how to unpack and transform the contents of this record and write those transformed contents to a "sink," which is a collective destination such as a file in HDFS. These transformations can be expressive, even including the creation of a defined Spark DataFrame and execution of a Spark SQL query on each microbatch collection. Each streaming query has an associated trigger, which defines how often that query should be executed. Cleverly, Spark is able to handle aggregations such as the SQL window function, which change with additional batches by preserving the state of the aggregation at each batch and updating that state with each subsequent batch, capturing these state updates in a write-ahead log.

We won't go into detail regarding MLlib or GraphX except to say that these provide APIs to support the construction of machine learning and graph-based analysis, respectively, while leveraging Spark's parallelism and fault tolerance. What we have covered, the DAG, RDDs, DataFrames, and streaming are essential to understand in order to effectively use these the MLlib and GraphX APIs, each of which is well documented elsewhere, including the official Apache Spark documentation. At the time of this writing, several important advancements are afoot in the Spark community, including the Koalas Python package, which enhances Spark's PySpark API such that it is compatible with Pandas and makes Spark more seamless for Python-based users and the growth of Delta Lake, which sits atop Spark, wrapping interactions with Spark DataFrames so as to provide ACID transactions, narrowing the gap between DataFrames in a Spark cluster and tables in a more traditional RDBMS.

We can conclude this section with an example of using PySpark in order to count the occurrences of each word from a text document, creating the "bag of words" we discussed earlier. Thanks to Spark's power, we could execute this on arbitrarily large collections of text such as one, 10, or even millions of clinic notes or claims reports. If we just collect all note text into a single large text file, we can get our counts as easily as:

```
text_file = sc.textFile("hdfs://all_note_text.txt")
counts = text_file.flatMap(lambda line: line.split(" ")) \
            .map(lambda word: (word, 1)) \
            .reduceByKey(lambda a, b: a + b)
counts.saveAsTextFile("hdfs://word_counts.txt")
```

And Spark handles all of the internals, reading in a large text file called `all_note_text.txt` from Hadoop's file system, performing the MapReduce workflow to count words, and then saving the output back to Hadoop's filesystem as `word_counts.txt`.

20.4 Kafka

We wrap up this chapter with a discussion of Kafka, which is technology for organizing real-time streams of data. A single Kafka instance can handle hundreds of megabytes of reads and writes per second from thousands of clients and Kafka trivially allows for partitioning of data streams across multiple instances without any downtime. Kafka organized incoming feeds of messages into categories called "topics" and considers processes that provide data to Kafka streams as "producers" and those who read data from Kafka streams as "consumers." Consumers access stream data by subscribing to specific topics. Moreover, each Kafka instance hosts a process known as the Kafka "broker" many of which comprise a Kafka cluster, as depicted in Fig. 20.7.

Kafka topics are categories into which published messages are organized and they provide a useful abstraction for creating organizational channels between producers and consumers. More specifically, each topic is an ordered but immutable sequence of records to which producers continually append additional records. Topics are partitioned such that each topic contains multiple separate but associated queues while each record within a queue is assigned an ID number known as the "offset," which denotes its ordinal place in the list of records.

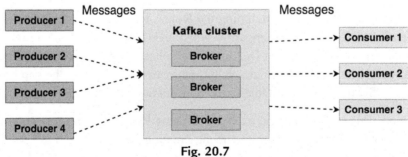

Fig. 20.7
Example Kafka architecture.

Kafka has a configurable parameter known as the "retention period," which determines how long published records should remain in a topic before being deleted. As each record can be uniquely identified by the topic, partition, and offset associated with it, Kafka stores and continuously updates the offset of each consumer as a way of tracking what records they have and have not yet read.

Although ostensibly simple, Kafka is very powerful in its ability to handle and route numerous streams of data essentially without regard for the volume of data being brokered. Importantly, Kafka can also be incorporated among other big data tools flexibly and in many different configurations. For example, Spark streaming can optionally consume data as a subscriber to a Kafka topic or it can produce data as a publisher to a Kafka topic. Note that, while a message broker at its core, Kafka also supports its own Streams API, which allows for stream processing of messages between producers and consumers. A technical treatment of Kafka streams is beyond the scope of this chapter, but one theme, which hopefully is becoming apparent, is that the Big Data ecosystem is quite large with many tools that perform ostensibly similar functions but that have different contextual strengths. In many cases, stream processing in Spark—at least for more complex functions—is desirable for the fact that Spark's breadth and functionality allow for a single development framework, which offers other benefits to team efficiency and code maintenance.

20.5 Conclusion

In this chapter we by no means covered the entirety of the big data ecosystem, but we did address three highly relevant and important components each of which represents a set of essential concepts inherent to many big data tools. Understand that this ecosystem is rapidly evolving and currently being increasingly integrated into managed cloud services. Moreover, we are seeing a trend of consolidation among these tools perhaps most exemplified by the growth of Spark, which encompasses increasingly more comprehensive functionality such as SQL on distributed data that formerly was the focus of many dedicated technologies such as Hive, and Impala, which plugged into complex Hadoop clusters. If this trend continues, we will likely see many of the big data tools fall increasingly out of use as key central technologies such as Spark come to fulfill more numerous and diverse roles. Thus, the selection of technologies in this chapter was motivated as much by their present and future relevance as by their historical worth. Going into the next chapter, we will apply many of these concepts to understanding the landscape of popular cloud platforms, which utilize these same technologies.

CHAPTER 21

Cloud technologies

21.1 Introduction

The idea of centrally aggregating computing resources for client use is not new and the abstraction of considering such aggregate resources as a "cloud" dates back to at least the 1970s. That being said, the current understanding of "cloud computing" has taken a more specific definition, referring to a collection of computing resources (disk storage, CPUs, memory, network bandwidth, etc.), which are available for use on-demand and purchasable as abstract packages of said resources. This conception was mainly popularized by Amazon's release of its Elastic Compute Cloud in 2006, although since then Amazon and several other cloud platform vendors have swelled in popularity. The impact of this business model has been broad and substantial, relegating what were previously formidable technical and financial burdens such as purchasing, setting up, securing, and maintaining a server to little more than line items in many project budgets which have substantially lower cost and administrative burden. Healthcare is certainly not among the early adopting industries for cloud computing, yet even still cloud computing is growing quickly throughout healthcare as it becomes generally recognized by many that the total cost of operation (TCO) is often lower both in terms of the direct cost of computing resource and the indirect cost of additional personnel, facilities, disaster recovery and so forth. One oft-cited concern many enterprises voice regarding cloud computing—especially in healthcare—is that of security.

While a deep treatment of cloud security is beyond the scope of this book it is worth mentioning that the cloud and on-premises data platforms each have their own strengths and weaknesses but increasingly more enterprises are migrating secure workflows to cloud platforms. At the very least, it should be said that the cloud deployments are not constitutively less secure than an on-premises deployments and that, in either case, security is an element of platform design and should be a genuine consideration from the initial planning phases. In most enterprises, there is—or at least there should be—an information security department who should be engaged early and often in the planning of any data processing pipeline. Perhaps surprisingly, it is also likely that this department is not averse to using the cloud, provided that there is a plan to achieve appropriate security compliance.

An Introduction to Healthcare Informatics. https://doi.org/10.1016/B978-0-12-814915-7.00021-1

21.2 Data storage

We spent much of the last chapter discussing Hadoop and understanding HDFS as a means to store large volumes of data across many separate machines. In that discussion, it hopefully became apparent that setting up and managing a cluster that could efficiently support HDFS is nontrivial. Indeed, managing large-volume data storage in a fault-tolerant way is both a technical and logistical challenge as one must consider data replication, machine location, physical security, fire and water damage, and host of other things. Unsurprisingly, one of the first areas in which cloud platforms demonstrate obvious is in data storage. Typically, this storage takes a few different forms supporting both what is known as "object storage" and what is known as "block storage."

Object storage is what many think of when discussing "cloud storage," but it is technically different than file storage as it would work on a local machine. Object storage lumps together the data and metadata for individual files into an abstraction referred to as an "object." This means that, although object storage may appear to have familiar organizational conventions such as hierarchical folders, this not actually how object data is organized. Instead, since objects have names among their associated metadata, these names simply look like folder paths and objects may share common elements of their names as though they were organized into folders. For example, "cloud_drive/project1/file1.csv" and "cloud_drive/project1/file2.csv" appear as though they are located within the same project1 folder in some filesystem when, in reality, they are just two separate data objects which share a common element in their name. Thus, objects within a cloud object store exist in a flat structure known as a "storage pool" rather than as members within a hierarchical file tree. This distinction might sound unnecessarily academic, but it does have real implications. Because object storage is not POSIX-compliant, certain conventional filesystem operations and behaviors may not work as expected. A classic example of this is that object storage does not support incremental changes to a file in place. Thus, to update a file in object storage is simply to replace it with a new copy of the entire file. Second, renaming directories is not atomic as there really is no specific folder to rename but, rather a collection of object names some part of which must be renamed. Third is that directory permissions are ephemeral and do not work as they would on a normal filesystem, which can create issues with cluster tools which depend upon such permissions metadata (e.g., Apache Ranger).

That all being said, the advantage of cloud object storage is that it offers essentially infinite capacity for placing and persisting data assets while abstracting away granular management of the data and the drives on which it resides. As a result, formerly daunting considerations such as redundancy across drives, computer, and even physical or regional datacenters are either automatically entailed or configurable with a single option. As a result, cloud platforms allow users to create drives or buckets into which they may load, store, encrypt, backup, and audit all forms of data. Certain domains such as bioinformatics or digital pathology for which it is not uncommon to reach hundred-terabyte or even petabyte storage requirements are revolutionized by the ease and availability of cloud object storage.

As an additional point, because cloud object storage abstracts significantly from direct interaction with disks, there are some additional considerations when trying to process data directly from such storage locations. For example, it is quite possible that cloud storage may increase the variance of input-output operations as a result of requests for data having more intermediary relay points than if data was stored on directly available drives through HDFS. Fortunately, these are by no means insurmountable issues. In fact, development among both cloud providers and big data projects are increasingly making it such that data may be either directly loaded from such object storage into tools such as MapReduce and Spark or into other, highly scalable databases. In both cases, users are not burdened with the direct management of underlying resources but instead may quickly provision even entire clusters or database systems with failover and back up in an impressively expeditious manner through simple initial configuration and almost one-click deployment. To be more specific, in the case of interoperating Hadoop MapReduce or Spark with a large collections of data stored in object storage, this has now become an essentially seamless process with files in object storage being addressable directly by Hadoop or Spark jobs as though they resided within HDFS simply by using the object name as though it was a file path and the appropriate cloud prefix (e.g., "gs://project1/file1.csv" in the case of Google Cloud or "s3a://project1/file1.csv" in the case of Amazon Web Services). This sort of integration is a significant leap forward in making big data tools accessible to small teams or those wishing to prototype data pipelines and solutions as they no longer require the overhead of managing their own deployment or data storage.

Alternatively, many cloud platforms also offer managed databases of both relational (e.g., Amazon Aurora, Google Cloud Databases, or Azure Databases), column-store (e.g., Amazon Redshift, Google Cloud BigTable), document store (e.g., Google Cloud Firestore, or Azure Cosmos DB), and even graph varieties (e.g., Amazon Neptune) as well as a host of other services. In such cases, new databases can be crated and made fault-tolerant entirely through the cloud vendor interface or formerly on-premises databases can be transported to cloud services to reduce the burden associated with managing them. Moreover, many cloud providers support standard database breeds such as PostgreSQL, MySQL, and others further easing the migration process.

Another strength of object storage is the ability to establish lifecycle policies, which determine where and how data are stored, based upon conditions such as time elapsed since upload or frequency with which data has been access by users. This is a particularly powerful feature for controlling costs. For example, many cloud providers offer separate "storage tiers" with different corresponding costs. These storage tiers adjust pricing based upon either how redundantly the data is stored, that is how many copies of the object are made and spread out, and how quickly data from cloud storage may be accessed with the most expensive option providing the lowest risk of data loss and the quickest data retrieval. Generally the most archival form of storage among these tiers is some form of magnetic tape storage which is very cheap to use when storing large volumes of data but has a significant delay to retrieve data from storage with can range from seconds up to days with applicable retrieval costs. One might ask why such a high-latency retrieval tier would be desirable but there are several compelling examples, one prominently cited member of which is archival of medical record data to include emails which may contain patient information. It may rarely-if ever-be necessary to access these records directly but they may not be legal to delete them due to regulatory requirements. In such circumstances, the lowest cost mode of archival storage is optimal while retrieval latency is not much of a concern.

We had mentioned block storage in the beginning of this section as an alternative mode of cloud data storage. Block storage devices are fixed-size raw storage containers, which organize bits of recorded data into blocks. They may be directly mounted by operating systems and support formatting of several filesystems such as FAT32 or EXT4. Block storage devices are most familiar as hard disks and may be created and attached to various cloud servers as though attaching an additional storage disk to an individual server. When using cloud-managed Hadoop services such as Amazon EMR (which we will discuss a bit more later on), data may be read from object storage or from block storage with the latter generally having more stable and shorter I/O latency with the drawback that data is stored in HDFS across many separate cloud disks which, in addition to being size-limited, fragmented, and somewhat less convenient, are ephemeral in when such virtual disks are created as part of a generated cluster, meaning that data stored within those devices is persisted only as long as the cluster is running and the disks and their data are deleted upon cluster termination. Thus, it is most common that processed data is persisted in object storage with more temporary copies transiently existing within cluster block storage during the execution of jobs while job endpoints are still recorded back into persistent block storage.

There are cases where block storage is not ephemeral, however, and use of which is convenient. The best example of this perhaps is the simple case of provisioning individual virtual servers on the cloud within which to host applications—perhaps web applications, specific database applications not otherwise available as cloud services, or as work areas to test and prepare data—which often require an available block storage device. It is also worth mentioning that cloud block storage volumes are used by many managed services for backups, failovers, and also as part of their standard functionality. Block devices may be created in a variety of flavors which vary not only in capacity but also in the frequency and volume of allowable read and write operations.

21.3 Compute

As mentioned previously, the first popularization of modern cloud computing took the form of an elastic compute cloud. This service allows users to define and create servers using virtualized resources, not unlike what occurs when on-premises IT departments create virtual machines (VMs). The novelty here was that this service was directly available to consumers who could then parse a seemingly infinite pool of compute and storage into servers with customizable CPU, RAM, and disk resources. In the simplest case, this allows users to create and boot up such virtual servers with their preferred operating system and connect to them directly using a secure shell as though the server had been physically assembled and installed within a data center. Moreover, users could simply terminate these virtual servers or "virtual machines" when the job was done. This gained almost immediate traction for many use cases such as hosting web servers or creating larger, enhances workstations for analytical computing. In such cases, block storage devices act as separate, persistent, attachable and detachable storage which may be attached to a VM with one resource configuration (e.g., a small, low-CPU instance, low-memory instance, which downloads data into the attached block device) and then re-attached to a different VM with an alternate configuration (e.g., a multi-CPU, high-memory instance for purposes of data analysis). This level of abstraction made is significantly easier and more affordable to access high-performance computing infrastructure.

Through the continued growth and popularization of cloud platforms, this use case—while still handy—is comparatively quaint with additional services existing that allow for more automated and strategic methods by which to create and delete such compute infrastructure. Key to understanding such innovations are the ideas of autoscaling and instance demand. Autoscaling allows for the definition of policies, which establish resource-based thresholds such as CPU utilization and responsiveness, which trigger the further creation of new instances to support additional demand and their decommissioning when demand drops below those stated thresholds. Instance demand is a contextual parameter, which allows users to decide whether the desired VM should be created immediately upon request or whether it is acceptable to wait until resource availability on the overall platform is high enough such that the instance may be created for a reduced price. This may seem like an odd mechanism, but it achieved a mutual optimization between user demand for instance resources and provider desire to maximize overall resource utilization—and billing—across the platform at all times. As much of the demand for cloud resources follows daily, weekly, and seasonal cycles with surges during conventional "working hours" and lulls during "off hours" there is a secondary approach to pricing these virtual resources which is based upon the ratio of currently unused compute. This is attractive for certain workloads as provisioning resources off hours is cheaper than doing so during peak hours, but the tradeoff is one of volatility wherein those provisioned resources will be suddenly extinguished once demand rises enough that the calculated immediate price of resources is higher than what it was when those resources were previsioned. Thus, the general use is that work, which need to be completed immediately or which needs to be guaranteed to complete in a time-sensitive manner—such as running a daily report—would benefit from the regularity and consistency of on-demand virtual resources while those which have more flexible timetables, which would allow both that they be run off hours and that they be restarted if the resources are destroyed intercurrently—such as a quarterly report a data processing task, which is not accountable to an immediate deadline—are amenable to cost optimization through "spot" pricing. As a last point on this topic, virtual instances may also be reserved for long terms even spanning multiple years, which confers another cost advantage provided that the relevant workloads are at least approximately continuous.

In the previous chapter, we mentioned a technology known as Kubernetes, which we will discuss at some greater length now along with a collection of related topics such as containerization and Docker. Understand that this is the tip of yet another large and evolving iceberg with broad and significant impact in distributed systems. Nonetheless, in keeping with this chapter's intended function as a survey, the following is a concise overview. To begin at the beginning, containers are an analogous concept to those of VMs except that they have less stringent isolation properties and are thus more "lightweight." Although virtualized themselves, VMs are created to support a full operating system within each VM, providing those VMs with direct access to hardware resources—as though they were physically dedicated to those VMs—or, in some alternate cases, with access to an intermediately abstracted form of hardware resources in the case of para-virtualization. In either case, the packaging of a complete operating system within the VM adds overhead even if it also adds isolation between different instances. By contrast, containers require an underlying VM responsible for providing basic services to all containerized applications while still allowing containers to have their own filesystem, CPU, memory, and process space as though they were independent machines. While this may seem like yet another layer of unnecessary packaging, consider that a single VM can—and almost always does—host several containers at any one time and that initiating and destroying a container is comparatively a lower latency and lower impact process than doing so with a VM. Docker is a widely popular example of a container technology although additional tools such as LXC exist and are actively developed. We will focus mainly on Docker given its widespread use.

Containers gained much popularity for their ability to conveniently package applications and their installation dependencies, such as python packages and system configurations, and to support running those applications on a variety of host machines. While this portability is critical, their composability, that is the ability to create, interconnect, and destroy containers as singletons or as entire fleets makes them powerful tools for distributed systems. Kubernetes is an example of a container orchestration tool the function of which is to compose containers. More specifically, Kubernetes allows for declaration of policies that govern the behavior of entire systems of containers. Such operations may include creating multiple containers simultaneously all of which are aware of one another and establishing particular networking rules whereby those containers communicate or having certain containers balance traffic between a collection of other containers as well as a host of other complex functions. While it is unlikely—although not impossible—that you would directly author such policies in the name of data engineering and analysis, container orchestration is a core component of many cloud services including those which allow users to define and bundle computational tasks into Docker containers and trigger their execution against large tasks queues without particular concern for job scheduling. This apparent magic which operates in services such as Amazon Web Services Batch, Azure Batch, or Google Cloud Pipelines fundamentally works because the functional resources necessary to accomplish a task are packaged with the container and so, given a general pool of CPU and memory resources, these services can create one or more VMs upon which to create numerous task containers each of which executes the desired task upon a specific input file from the batch queue. This is a very powerful service for many things not least of which of data transformation or ingestion and is a very common pattern for genomic or image processing workflows where certain initial transformations often need to be done before data are imported into a big data environment such as Spark. To continue with the bioinformatics example, it is common to take input raw sequencing files in FASTQ format, map their reads to a target reference genome, and identify sample-specific variants using a batch service and load data structures representing those variants, such as.vcf files, into a big data computing environment. Importantly, it is also possible to add additional dimensions to the policies governing jobs such as that compute resources should only be provided to containers on off-hours according to "spot" pricing as previously discussed.

Having discussed VMs, clusters thereof, and the further abstraction of containers, it is worth mentioning yet a further abstraction in the form of "serverless" architectures, which, of course, are not actually serverless but which allow for the definition and execution of computation work at the level of atomic functions with equally granular pricing. These are commonly used for smaller computational tasks which are triggered by events such as new files appearing in object storage. The asynchronous nature of such triggered tasks and—for certain things such as image resizing—the simplicity of such tasks makes it preferable to pay for task executions rather than to create and pay for longer running infrastructure. Note that there are limitations to such services, namely, that they do have relatively low upper limits on resource allocation and function duration. In other words, they have their place alongside but not instead of the other aforementioned data processing tools.

There are many more compute services than could be covered in a single section or chapter, but those discussed here are not only popular and relevant to data processing but also illustrate a breadth of important cloud concepts. Important to also mention is that streaming services such as Kafka or analogs thereof are also available as cloud services with the standard benefit of being easier to deploy and maintain. It is common, therefore, that streaming ingestion, asynchronous processing, persistent object storage, and distributed computation are mutually accomplished through a composition across several cloud services and the deployment of such composites is further simplified by the fact that many cloud big data services instantiate more than one specific component of such a cluster. For example, Microsoft Azure's HDInsight is a managed service for Hadoop, Spark, and Kafka, allowing users to create clusters of all three technologies as a matter of configurable orchestration rather than having to create individual VMs and configure their communication and processes. What might formerly have taken an entire department can be accomplished by only a few people or even a single dedicated individual.

21.4 Machine learning and analysis services

Also an ever-expanding field, cloud machine learning is growing by leaps and bounds and doing so across multiple dimensions. Given what we have covered thus far, it should come as no surprise that many cloud platforms provide services allowing users to create Jupyter or Zeppelin notebooks and use them to work with other data and compute resources. Using these interactive computing interfaces, it is possible to author and execute business intelligence queries or machine learning models as these notebooks can directly communicate with a Spark session on the underlying cloud cluster and, importantly, configuration of this interconnection is almost entirely automated.

Previously we had mentioned elastic compute and the creation of VMs—especially as workspaces for resource-intense or highly iterative analyses, which are not easily amenable to utter parallelization. Cloud machine learning services extend into this use-case as well. In addition to the obvious provision of increasingly powerful packages of virtual resources, such as increased CPU count and Memory, VMs may also be configured to contain graphics processing units (GPUs) for purposes of training neural network algorithms or running other GPU-optimized analyses. GPUs are notoriously expensive components compared to CPU, memory, and disk and GPU utilization also typically assumes a peak-and-trough pattern with intense periods of utilization during model training followed by near idleness in between. As a result, an important optimization is also available on major cloud platforms, which allows for the recruitment of GPUs as an elastic resource. Amazon Elastic Inference, Google Cloud GPUs and TPUs (with TPUs referring to a more specialized neural network-focused variant of GPUs known as Tensor Processing Units), and Azure Machine Learning all support this functionality. As a side note, at the time of this writing, we are witnessing several specialized chip-level processing architectures emerge. While Google's TPU is perhaps the most popular example at present, Amazon's Inferentia—which is also currently available for use—and both Microsoft's Brainwave and Graphcore AI chips are examples of thematically related emerging technologies with their own specific foci. This book does not focus on the evaluation of hardware elements such as GPUs, TPUs, Inferentia, and so forth, but such components are fast becoming a ubiquitous ingredient in analytical computation. Importantly, these resources may be provisioned with elasticity both in terms of capacity—from the equivalent of a single GPU up to an entire fleet of GPUs—and commitment—with the ability to retain such resources and pay for them only for as long as they are actively being used.

There is also a growing collection of more abstracted, managed services for the purpose of supporting analytical work, including machine learning. For example, Amazon SageMaker is a service that allows users to deploy a scalable Jupyter environment, which comes packaged with an expanding collection of prebuilt models and which benefit from various optimizations and enhanced interoperation with other cloud services. For example, users may train models from Spark DataFrames retrieved from a Spark cluster and may deploy GPU resources necessary for training through elastic inference. Importantly, services like SageMaker further allow model developers to deploy trained models by managing their hosting and execution. That is to say that, once a model is trained, it can be transferred as an artifact to object storage and made accessible through an API, making the trained model highly available and distributed through use of other core cloud services. This is a powerful capability since machine learning and analytics-related content focuses on model development often at the expense of discussing how one makes trained models available and manages their use, which is an equally—if not more—important component of the process. This hits upon another topic, which is that of machine learning operations (MLOps) which concerns the key logistical and practical considerations around models such as deploying, versioning, and monitoring use. Azure machine learning, for example, provides several helpful services to ease these concerns such as the ability to create machine learning pipelines, which contain reproducible and orderly steps necessary for data ingestion, preparation, model training, and model scoring. This significantly eases the process of iteratively extending models to train upon new data without falling into the all-too-common trap of disorganization and nonrepeatable idiosyncrasies in model development, thereby making model results inconsistent or, worse, impossible to reproduce. Additional MLOps concerns include the ability to assign specific versions to models and establish policy-driven model lifecycles, which govern when models are made available and when they are to be replaced.

Also among the ecosystem of abstracted machine learning services are those which simplify model design and assessment in addition to the management of underlying infrastructure and compute resources. That is, instead of providing a Jupyter environment with Python with which users may build models using code, these services such as Google Cloud Platform AutoML, allow users to configure both prepackaged models, organized into broad domains such as vision and language, as well as to build custom models using a simplified graphical user interface. This increasingly extends machine learning capability to those with limited expertise and is representative of a general democratization of such tools. This is not to say that machine learning is relegated to a design-free endeavor, but it is to say that the value in machine learning expertise will likely shift from such a sharp focus on those with pure technical expertise in model development and tuning to a focus on those with additional domain knowledge of applicable opportunities and uses cases where machine learning can prove useful. This future course further highlights the value of healthcare informatics and its practitioners as possessing a unique blend of both technical understanding and domain understanding. These services will hopefully make machine learning more available but they will not magically make it more valuable to the enterprise. After all, no model can be performant if applied to an ill-suited task and no model can be useful if applied to a task that is not relevant to some core mission or need.

21.5 Conclusion

In this chapter, we have covered a whirlwind tour of cloud platforms using some of the core concepts of distributed systems, which were introduced in the last chapter. Understand that cloud technology is a rapidly evolving space that encompasses several transformational technologies in the domains of big data, artificial intelligence, serverless computation, and containerization just to name a few. As such, it should not be the goal to learn the entire scope and operation of cloud platform tools from this or any other book. Instead, this chapter focuses on specific technologies within the relevant domains of storage, compute, and machine learning services. Moreover, these technologies were chosen both because they are effective vehicles through which to introduce many important technical concepts but also because their unique strengths give them longevity and an integral—and therefore more lasting—place in this rapidly growing domain. Each cloud provider, including the main three discussed in this chapter, have extensive documentation and even formal certification pathways designed to provide focused and practical education regarding their use. I highly recommend completing such certifications in the process of planning and initiating a cloud-based analysis project. What this chapter is intended to do, though, is to provide some orientation to that learning endeavor and a rough structure to the categorical technologies that exist within these platforms and what they do, as a useful initiation for more detailed, platform- and project-specific investigation.

Index

Note: Page numbers followed by *f* indicate figures and *t* indicate tables.

A

Abstract syntax tree, 146–147
Accession number, 106–107
Accessor, 178–179
Accountability, 287
Accountable Care Organization (ACO) run, 45
"Add-on" tests, 107–108
addThese function, 149
Admit discharge transfer (ADT) message, 114, 114*f*
ADT A04 message, 114
Aggregate functions, 36–37, 37*f*
All Patient DRG (AP-DRG), 140–141
All Patient Refined DRGs (APR-DRG), 140–141
ALT, 232
ALTV, 232
Amazon Redshift, 69
American Medical Association (AMA), 133–134
American Psychiatric Association (APA), 132
Anaconda, 161–162
Analytical documents, 171–174
Analytical hygiene, 279
ANSI SQL, 32
Appendectomy, 135, 136*f*
Application level, 7–8, 8*f*
ApplicationsManager, 295–296
Arguments, 149
Arrays
  dimensionality of, 79
  multidimensional, 80–81
  and MUMPS, 78–79, 81–85

B

Artificial intelligence (AI), 261, 262*f*
AssertionError, 189
Assessment, data, 175–185
Atomicity, 24–25
AUC, 233, 234*f*
Augmented data dictionary/ augmented data catalog tools, 285
Autoencoders, 275–276, 275*f*
Auto indexing, 69
Availability, 64
Axis API, 169, 169*f*

B

Backpropagation, 269–270
Bagging, 221, 223
Bash, 173, 173*f*
Batch gradient descent, 204
Benign neoplasms, 129–130
Bias, 96
Big data
  definition of, 291–292
  tools
    Hadoop, 292–298
    Kafka, 304–305
    Spark, 299–304
Billing, 111–112
  and coding, 7
Binary tree (btree) index, 49–50
Bioconda, 161–162
Bioinformatic analysis, 291
Biological CASs, 92
Block storage, 308, 310
BloodPressure column, 179–180, 179*f*

Board of Directors, 11
Body mass index (BMI), 159–160
Boolean index, 166
Built-in types, Python, 147
Byte-pair encodings, 241

C

Cache, 65–66, 75–76
CAP Theorem, 64–65
CART. *See* Classification and regression trees (CART)
Cellular automaton, 92, 93*f*
Centers for Medicare and Medicaid Services (CMS), 4–5, 130
Character value, 132–133
Chief Data Officer (CDO), 12
Chief Information Officer (CIO), 11
Chief Medical Informatics Officer (CMIO), 11
Chief Security Officer (CSO), 11
Chief Technology Officer (CTO), 11
Chronicles, 85–86
Clarity, 85–86
Classification and regression trees (CART), 219–221
Classifiers, 253
Cleaning, data, 184
Clinical decision support (CDS), 7, 10
Clinical document architecture (CDA), 118–119
  levels of, 119
Clinical documentation, 7
"Clinical Modification" of ICD-9, 130

Clinical notes, 109–110
ClinicIDs, 27–28
Cloud computing, 126, 310–314
Cloud storage, 308
Cloud technologies
  compute, 307, 310–314
  data storage
    block storage, 308, 310
    cloud-managed Hadoop
      services, 310
    object storage, 308–310
    machine learning and analysis
      services, 314–315
Cluster centroids, 222, 222*f*
Clustering, 221–223
CNNs. *See* Convolutional neural
  networks (CNNs)
Colectomy, 135
Column stores, 68–71
ComfortLevel column, 177–178
Communication level, 9
Complete case analysis, 97
Complex adaptive system
  (CAS), 91
  components of, 92
  healthcare as, 91–95
Comprehension, in Python, 156
Computational linguistics, 236
Computational phenotyping, 134
  general considerations,
    230–233
  manual review and general
    review considerations,
    227–230
  natural language processing,
    236–241
  supervised methods, 233–235
  unsupervised methods, 235–236
Computerized provider order entry
  (CPOE), 7, 8*f*, 106
Conda packages, 161–162
Conference/Committee on Data
  Systems Languages
  (CODASYL), 61–62
Consistency, 25, 64
Consolidated CDA (C-CDA), 119,
  122*f*
Consolidated Framework for
  Implementation Research
  (CFIR), 99–100

domains, 100
Contact serial number (CSN), 104,
  104*f*, 108–109
Continuous bag of words (CBOW)
  vs. skip-gram, 238, 239*f*
Convexity, 270–271
Convolutional neural networks
  (CNNs), 272–274, 274*f*
Copy forwarding, 110
Cost equation, 202
COUNT key, 35
Current directory, 161
Current procedural terminology
  (CPT) codes, 111–112,
  133–134, 231–232

D

DAG. *See* Directed acyclic graph
  (DAG)
Data and trust, 100–101
Data assessment and preparation,
  245–246
Data Base Task Group (DBTG),
  61–62
Data collection, 243–244
Data dictionary, 284–285
Data engineering and analysis, 279
  data governance, 287–289
  documentation, 284–287
  workflow, 279–284
DataFrames, 165–166, 175–176,
  301
  BloodPressure column, 179–180,
    179*f*
  missingness plot, 183–184, 183*f*
  pivoted, 187–188, 188*f*
  quality assessment, 175–185
  unpivoted, 187–188, 187*f*
Data-generating processes, 103
Data governance, 287–289
Data importing, 175–176
Data lake, 10, 282–283
DataNodes, 293–295
Data qualiy, 175
Data-science-1, 161–162
Data-science-2, 162
Data stewardship, 100–101
Data structures, 151–156
Data warehouses, 10
Datica, 125–126

DBViz, 31
Decision trees, 219–221, 223,
  254–256
Deep learning, 191–192, 202,
  216–217, 261–262, 262*f*
Describe function, Pandas, 181,
  181*f*
Device level, 7–8
Diagnoses table, 51–52
Diagnosis-related groups (DRGs),
  111–112, 139–141
Diagnostic and Statistical Manual
  of Mental Disorders (DSM),
  132
Diagnostic ontologies, 129–132
"__dict__" function, 150
Dictionary, in Python, 65, 150,
  155–156
Digital imaging and
  communications in
  medicine (DICOM), 125,
  125*f*
Directed acyclic graph (DAG),
  299–301, 300*f*
Directed graph, 279, 280*f*
DISTINCT key, 35
Docker, 312–313
Documentation culture, 284–285
Document stores, 66–68, 67*f*
Domain message information
  models (D-MIMs),
  117, 118*f*
Dropna() function, 188
Dtypes, 178–179, 178*f*
Duplicated method, Pandas, 184
Durability, 25
Dynamic typing, 147–148

E

Edges, 71
EHR APIs, 125–126
"80/20" rule. *See* Pareto principle
Electronic data interchange (EDI),
  114–115
Electronic medical record (EMR), 7,
  8*f*
Electronic Medical Record systems,
  66–67
Electronic medication
  administration, 7

Electronic prescribing
(e-prescribing), 7
Elements, 119–120
"E&M" codes, 134
Empirical risk minimization,
198–199
EMR system's data, 175–176
Encounter ID, 21–22
Encounters, 103–105
Enterprise Master Patient ID
(EMPI), 104, 104*f*
Entity relationship diagram, 23, 24*f*,
53, 53*f*
Environment variable, 161
Epic, 85–86
Epic Chronicles, 85–86
Episode of care, 105
ETL process, 286–287
EVN segment, 115

F

Fallacy, drivers of, 95–96
False discovery rate, 95–96
Fast healthcare interoperability
resources (FHIR),
123–124
JSON format, 124, 124*f*
resources in, 124
strength of, 124
FastText, 240
Feed forward networks, 262–269,
275
FHIR. *See* Fast healthcare
interoperability resources
(FHIR)
Fields, 114–115
Fillna() method, 188–189
Foreign keys (FK), 21–23, 24*f*
"For" loops, 148
Forward propagation, 269
FROM key, 33
Full table scan, 41–42
Functions, 149

G

GAN. *See* Generative adversarial
networks (GAN)
G-codes, 134
Generalizability, machine learning,
209

General ontologies, 135–138
Generative adversarial networks
(GAN), 276
Ginian purity, 219–221
Gini index, 219–221
Git, 286
Global arrays, 78–81, 83
Global vectors (GloVe), 240
Google File System, 292
Governance, data, 287–289
GPUs. *See* Graphics processing
units (GPUs)
Gradient descent, 201.
See also Batch gradient
descent
Graph data model, 71–72, 71*f*
Graphics processing units
(GPUs), 314
GROUP BY statement, 36–37,
37*f*
Grouper, 139–140

H

Hadoop, 292–298
cluster, 293–296, 294*f*
core modules, 292–293
goals, 292
MapReduce, 292–293, 295–297,
298*f*, 309
streaming, 297
Yet Another Resource Negotiator
(YARN), 292–293,
295–297, 296*f*
Hadoop Distributed Filesystem
(HDFS), 292–295, 299
Hadoop distributed filesystem
(HDFS), 308–310
HBase, 70
Header, 18
Healthcare Common Procedure
Coding System (HCPCS),
134, 137
Healthcare IT
architectures, 6
challenges and opportunities,
13–14
communication level, 9
device and application levels,
7–8
growth of, 3–5

organization roles, 11–12
physician and nurse
informaticists, 12–13
process level, 9–10
regulations, 13
Health Information Exchanges
(HIEs), 9–10
Health Information Technology
for Economic and Clinical
Health (HITECH) Act, 4–5
Health Insurance Portability &
Accountability Act
(HIPAA), 13, 132–133
Hessian matrix, 272
Hewlett-Packard's Vertica, 69
Hinge loss, 215–216, 216*f*
"History and physical" (H&P) note,
109–110
HL7 (health level 7 standard),
113–116
HL7 message, 113–114
HL7v2, 9, 113–116
HL7v2 messages, 113–114, 122*f*
HL7v3, 116–123
HL7v3 XML message, 120, 121*f*
Horizontal partitioning, 69
Hypothesis space, 196

I

ICD codes, 111–112, 231–232
ICD-9 code, 129–130
hierarchical structure, 130*f*
ICD-9-CM, 133*f*
ICD-10 code, 96, 129–130
M1A.3120, 130–131, 131*f*
ICD-10-CM, 133*f*
ICD code R65.20, 230–231, 231*f*
ICD-10-PCS, 133*f*
00900ZX, 132–133, 133*f*
Id_vars, 186
Implementation process, 100
Implementation science, 99–100
Importing, data, 175–176
Indexes, in SQL, 41–42
Informatics, role of, 5–6
Information bias, 96
Information Management System
(IMS), 63
Information_schema.tables, 46–47
Information siloing, 282–283

Inheritance, 151
The__init__ function, 150–151
INNER JOIN, 39–40
Inner setting, CFIR, 100
IN1 segment, 115
Institutional billing, 111
Integrated Database Management
    System (IDMS), 61–62
Integrated Data Store (IDS/2),
    61–62
Integrated development
    environment (IDE),
    169–170
Intellectual Disabilities, 132
IntelliJ IDE, 169–170
Interactive computing, 171–174
"InternalTemperature" column,
    180, 180*f*, 182–183
International Health Terminology
    Standards Development
    Organization (IHTSDO),
    135
International Statistical
    Classification of Diseases
    and Related Health
    Problems (ICD), 111–112,
    129–130, 231–232
  ICD-9, 129–130
  ICD-10, 96, 129–130, 230–231
Interpreted languages, 145–146
Interquartile range (IQR),
    181–182
InterSystems, 75–76
InterSystems Cache, 75–76,
    81, 85
Intervention, CFIR, 99–100
IPython, 170
Isolation, 25

J

Jacobian matrix, 272
Java, 153
J-codes, 134
Joining tables, 19–20
JOIN statement, 38–40, 40*f*
JSON format, 124, 124*f*
Jupyter, 169–170, 171*f*
  architecture of, 171–173, 172*f*
  Bash command, 173, 173*f*
  features, 173

with Python paragraph importing
    packages, 171, 172*f*
Jupyter IDE application, 170
Jupyter Lab, 170

K

Kafka, 303–305
Kappa statistic, 228, 229*f*
Katacoda, 45
KB_SQL, 85–86
Kernels, 170
Keys, 155
Keyspace, 69
Key-value stores, 65–66
Kubernetes, 312–313

L

Laboratory information system
    (LIS), 7, 8*f*, 106–107
Laboratory testing, 106–109
Laparoscopic appendectomy, 135,
    136*f*
LASSO regression, 209
Learner, 191–192
Learning rate, 203
LEFT JOIN, 39–40
LengthOfStay, 28
Linear function, 195–196, 195*f*
Linear transformations, 267–268,
    267*f*
Linux kernel, 286
Lists, in Python, 152–154
List slicing, 153
Local minima
  adversarial examples and,
    274–275
  vs. global minima, 270–272
Logical Observation Identifiers
    Names and Codes (LOINC),
    96–97, 138–139, 139*f*
Logistic decision function, 207,
    208*f*
Logistic loss, 215–216, 216*f*
Logistic regression, 205, 207*f*,
    211–212, 234–235,
    247–254, 252*f*
  partial dependence plot of, 252,
    252*f*
  vs. support vector machines
    (SVM), 212

LOINC. *See* Logical Observation
    Identifiers Names and Codes
    (LOINC)
Long short-term memory (LSTM)
    networks, 275

M

Machine learning (ML), 191–192,
    211, 247, 257–259, 261,
    262*f*
  and analysis services, 314–315
  augmentation, 285
  classification, 205–208
  clustering, 221–223
  decision trees, 219–221
  error and cost, 198–201,
    199–200*f*
  generalizability, 209
  hypothesis function, 194–198,
    195–197*f*
  model explainability, 223–225
  normalization, 209
  optimization, 191–192, 201–205,
    201*f*
  regression, 192–194,
    193–194*f*
  regularization, 209
  support vector machines,
    211–218
Machine learning operations
    (MLOps), 314–315
Machine Learning Repository,
    175–176
Major Diagnostic Categories
    (MDCs), 139–140
MapReduce, 292–293, 295–297,
    298*f*, 299, 309
Markdown, 171, 172*f*
Master Patient Indexes (MPIs), 9
MatLab Live Editor, 170
Matplotlib, 167
  pacu_df, 181, 182*f*
  scatter plot, 168*f*
MAX() aggregate function, 37
Mean squared error, 199–200
Medical notes. *See* Clinical notes
Medical record number (MRN),
    104, 104*f*
Medicare Severity DRGs
    (MS-DRG), 140–141

Medication administration record (MAR), 109
MEDITECH, 75–76
Meditech Interpretive Information System (MIIS), 75–76
Metadata, 284
Metaprogramming, 146–147
Microsoft's Azure Cosmos DB, 65–66
Microsoft SQL Server, 17
Microsoft's Windows Registry, 63
MIN() aggregate function, 37
Mini-batch gradient descent, 205
Min-max normalization, 209
Missing at random, 96–97
Missingness, 96–99, 98f
Missingness plot, 183–184, 183f
Missing no matrix, 184, 185f
Missing "not at random", 96–97
Missing values, 188–189
MLOps. *See* Machine learning operations (MLOps)
M/MUMPS, 63–64, 72, 75–78
    arrays and, 78–85
    data infrastructure, 85–87
    definition, 77
    goal of, 75
    history, 75–76
    SQL statement, 86–87
Model generalizability, 209
Module, 159–160
MSH segment, 114–115
Multidimensional arrays, 80–81
Multilayer perceptron network, 263–264, 265f
Multiple imputation, 97–98
myArray, 82
MySQL, 17, 21
myValue, 82

N

NameNode, 292–295
National Drug Codes (NDC), 139, 139f
National Library of Medicine (NLM), 135
Natural language processing, 236–241
Natural Language Tool Kit (NLTK), 236–237

ndarray (*n*-dimensional array), 163–165
Neoplasms, 129–130
Network data model, 62, 62f
Neural networks, 261–262
    with error surfaces, 270, 271f
NodeManager, 295–296
Nonlinear activation function, 266, 268f
Nonlinear functions, 206
Nonrelational databases, 61
    column stores, 68
        traditional, 68–69
        wide, 69–71, 70f
    document stores, 66–68, 67f
    graph data model, 71–72, 71f
    hierarchical model, 63
    key-value stores, 65–66
    M/MUMPS models, 63–64
"Nonstandard" standard, 115–116
Nontidy table structure, 186, 186f
Normalization, 26–28, 209
"No-SQL" databases, 65
NULL values, 20–21
NumPy, 163–164

O

Object, 149–151, 163–164
Object-oriented API, 167, 169
Object-oriented programming, 151
ObjectScript, 81, 85
Object storage, cloud, 308–310
One-dimensional arrays, 79
One-hot encoding, 205
Ontologies, 129
    diagnosis-related groups (DRGs), 139–141
    diagnostic, 129–132
    general, 135–138
    LOINC and NDC, 138–139, 139f
    procedure, 132–134
Optimization, machine learning, 191–192, 201–205, 201f
Oracle, 17
ORDER BY statement, 35
"Orders-only" encounter, 103
ORM message, 115
ORU message, 115

OUTER/FULL JOIN, 39–40
Outer setting, CFIR, 100
Outliers, 181–182

P

Packages, 159–163
Pacu_df DataFrame, 176–177, 177f
    dtypes, 178, 178f
Pandas, 165–167, 175–176, 245
    describe function, 181, 181f
    duplicated method, 184
    pd.isna() function, 182–183
    replace function, 182
Pandas DataFrames, 178
Parameters, 149
Pareto principle, 13–14, 94
Partial dependence, 224, 225f
Partition Tolerance, 64
Patient ID, 22–23
Patient identification (PID), 115
Patients array, 83
Pd.isna() function, 182–183
Permutation importance, 223–224
Pg_indexes table, 49
Pharmacy information system, 7
PhoneNumberID, 26–27
Physician and nurse informaticists, 12–13
Picture archive and communication system (PACS), 7, 12
PID segment, 115
$piece, 84
Pip, 161–162
Pipe and hat, 114–115
Pivot, 187
Pivoted DataFrame, 187–188, 188f
PM&R's assessment, 105
PostgreSQL, 17, 43, 47
Predicate variables, 18
Primary keys (PK), 21–23, 24f
"Primitive" types, Python, 148
Procedure Coding System (PCS), 130, 132–133
Procedure ontologies, 132–134
Process level, 9–10
Professional billing, 111
Programming languages, 151
Providers table, 50–51
Pruning, 221
Public schema, 46–47

P-values, 95–96
PV1 segment, 115
Pypi (Python package index), 161
Pyplot, 167–169
PySpark, 303–304
Python, 37, 43, 145–146, 245,
    257–260
  built-in types, 147
  control flow, 148
  data structures, 151–156
    comprehension, 156
    dictionaries, 155–156
    lists, 152–154
    sets, 154
    tuples, 155
  functions, 149
  interpreted languages, 145–146
  objects, 149–151
  primitive types, 148
  structure of, 146–147
  2 and 3, 146
Python array, 82–83
Python None value, 188
PYTHONPATH, 161

Q

Query planner, 31

R

Radial basis function (RBF),
    217–218, 263
Radiology information system
    (RIS), 7, 108–109
R DataFrames, 183–184
RDD. *See* Resilient distributed
    dataset (RDD)
Read Codes, 135
Receiver operating characteristic
    (ROC), 233, 234*f*, 248–249,
    250*f*, 254, 255*f*, 257, 257*f*
Rectified linear unit (ReLU), 268
  activation function, 268–269,
    268*f*
  use of, 270
Recurrent networks, 275
Recursive partitioning, 219–221
Redis, 65–66
Redox, 125–126
Reference information model
    (RIM), 116–123

classes of, 117, 118*f*
Referential integrity, 23
Refined message information model
    (R-MIM), 117, 118*f*
Regression, 192–194, 193–194*f*
Regularization, 209
Relational database, 45
Relational Database Management
    Systems (RDBMS), 21, 31,
    32*f*, 46–47
Relational databases
  ACID components, 24–25
  normalization, 26–28
  primary and foreign keys, 21–23
  SQL and, 17
Relational model
  overview of, 18–20, 19*f*
  vs. SQL, 20–21
ReLU. *See* Rectified linear unit
    (ReLU)
Replication pipelining, 295
Representational state transfer
    (REST), 123–124
Resequenced codes, 133–134
Resequencing, 133–134
Resilient distributed dataset (RDD),
    301
ResourceManager, 295–296
Result comments, 106–107
Revenue cycle management, 111
Ridge regression, 209
RIGHT JOIN, 39–40
RIM. *See* Reference information
    model (RIM)
Routines, 84–85
R packages, 161–162
RStudio, 170

S

SageMaker, 314–315
Scale-out approach, 292, 293*f*
Scale-up approach, 292, 293*f*
Scatter plot, 250–252, 251*f*
  axis API with axis labeling, 169*f*
  3D, 194*f*
  using column labels as color
    indicators, 168*f*
  using matplotlib, 168*f*
Schemas
  definition, 46–47

in SQL, 42
Scikit-learn, 246–248, 254
Selection bias, 96
SELECT statement, 33, 34*f*
Sensitivity analysis, 97
Sentence-wise modeling approach,
    241
Sepsis, 227–228, 230
Sets, in Python, 154
Single imputation, 97
SNOMED-CT ID (SCTID), 135
SNOMET-Clinical Terms
    (SNOMED-CT), 135, 137
SOAP format, 110
Sort_index() method, 180
Source code version control, 286
Spark tool, 299–304
  architecture, 302, 302*f*
  components of, 299–301
  directed acyclic graph (DAG),
    300*f*, 301
  resilient distributed dataset
    (RDD), 301
  SQL, 302
  streaming, 303, 305
  Yet Another Resource Negotiator
    (YARN), 299
Spreadmart, 283
SQL (structured query language),
    17, 230, 243, 259–260
  comparison operators, 33, 34*t*
  Count() function, 47
  GROUP BY statement, 36–37,
    37*f*
  indexes, 41–42
  JOIN statement, 38–40, 40*f*
  FROM key, 33
  MUMPS and, 86–87
  ORDER BY statement, 35
  querying data with, 45–59
  schemas, 42
  SELECT statement, 33, 34*f*
  structure of, 31–32
  subqueries, 42–43
  vs. relational model, 20–21
  WHERE key, 33
  WINDOW functions, 40–41
SQL query, 244
"Standard" SQL, 32
State-of-the-art approaches, 241

Stewardship, 100–101
Stochastic gradient descent, 204*f*, 205–207
Stochastic imputation, 97, 99*f*
Storage pool, 308
Storage tiers, 309–310
Structured English Query Language (SEQUEL), 17
Subqueries, in SQL, 42–43
Summative ontologies, 139–141
SunQuest Information Systems' Laboratory, 85
Supervised machine learning, 193–194
Support vector machine (SVM), 211–218, 262–263
SVM RBF kernel space, 263, 264*f*
Systematized Nomenclature of Medicine (SNOMED), 135–138
  mono- and poly-hierarchy, 135–136, 136*f*
  ontology, 135–136

T

Tables
  entity relationship diagram, 53, 53*f*
  querying, 53–54
    average number of patient visits per provider, 57
    average number of visits per day per location, 54–55
    average patient age and patient sex per location, 56–57

diagnosis codes and average age per clinic location, 58–59
  viewing, 46–53
Table scan, 68
Tags, 119–120
Tensor Processing Units (TPUs), 314
Term Frequency-Inverse Document Frequency (TF-IDF), 238
Tidying data, 186–188, 187*f*
Tokens, 146–147
TPUs. *See* Tensor Processing Units (TPUs)
Traditional column stores, 68–69
Training data, 191–192
Transactions, 24
Transact SQL, 43
Traversals, 72
t-test, 203–204
Tuples, 18, 155

U

Unified Medical Language System (UMLS) Metathesaurus, 135
Unpivoted DataFrame, 187–188, 187*f*
Unstructured data, 64–65

V

Value, 65, 187, 187*f*
Value_counts(), 180–181, 180*f*
Vendor standards, 125–126
Vertical partitioning, 68

Vertices/nodes, 71
Virtual machines (VMs), 310–312, 314
VisitLocation, 27
Visits table, 50, 54
Vital_sign, 187, 187*f*

W

Weights, 195–196
WHERE key, 33
Wide column stores, 69–71, 70*f*
WINDOW functions, 37, 40–41
Wolfram Notebooks, 170
Word2vec, 240
Write-ahead log, 25

X

XHTML, 124
XML (extensible markup language), 119–120
XML nesting, 119–120, 120*f*

Y

Yahoo!, 292
YAML (Yet Another Markup Language), 163
Yet Another Resource Negotiator (YARN), 292–293, 295–297, 296*f*, 299

Z

ZeroMQ, 171–173
Z-segment, 115–116

Printed in the United States
By Bookmasters